FUNDAMENTALS OF
MOTOR VEHICLE TECHNOLOGY

FUNDAMENTALS OF MOTOR VEHICLE TECHNOLOGY

V. A. W. HILLIER T. Eng (CEI) FIMI AMIRTE
*Senior Lecturer in Automobile Engineering
at Croydon Technical College*

F. W. PITTUCK AMIMI AMIRTE FRSA
*Late Lecturer in Automobile Engineering
at Kingston Technical College*

HUTCHINSON EDUCATIONAL
LONDON

HUTCHINSON EDUCATIONAL LTD
3 Fitzroy Square, London W1

London Melbourne Sydney Auckland
Wellington Johannesburg Cape Town
and agencies throughout the world

First published May 1966
Reprinted February 1967
Reprinted December 1967
Reprinted December 1968
Reprinted September 1969
Reprinted July 1970
Second Edition June 1972
Reprinted August 1973

This book has been set in Times type, printed in Great Britain
on smooth wove paper by Anchor Press, and
bound by Wm. Brendon, both of Tiptree, Essex

ISBN 0 09 110710 5 (cased)
0 09 110711 3 (paper)

ACKNOWLEDGEMENTS

We should like to thank the following firms for permission to make use of copyright material: Borg and Beck Ltd., C.A.V. Ltd., Girling Ltd., Hardy Spicer Ltd., Laycock Engineering Co. Ltd., Lockheed Brake Co. Ltd., Schrader Ltd., S.K.F. Ltd., S.U. Carburetter Co. Ltd., Jensen Motors Ltd., Dunlop Co. Ltd., Joseph Lucas Ltd.

Though many of the drawings are based on commercial components, they are mainly intended to illustrate principles of motor vehicle technology. For this reason, and because details of design change so rapidly, no drawing is claimed to be up to date. Students should read manufacturers' leaflets for the latest information.

CONTENTS

INTRODUCTORY NOTES

FIRST EDITION

For this book we have drawn upon our experience of some twenty years as teachers and external examiners in automobile engineering. We believe that what is needed is a textbook covering the construction of motor vehicles and their components in a manner simple enough to be understood by young apprentices beginning their training as mechanics, and detailed enough to serve as a solid foundation for later work.

Even the brightest student will not find this book sufficient on its own. He will require the help and guidance of a competent teacher who has had no little experience of practical work on motor vehicles, and the student should himself be working in a motor vehicle repair shop, handling the actual components. He needs also to develop the habit of examining the components in order to become familiar with the details of their design and construction, so that he can, if called upon to do so, describe and sketch these details from memory with reasonable accuracy.

The book is divided into sections, each of which covers a major topic or component. Each section is divided into chapters which deal with a particular aspect of the topic. This enables the teacher to select appropriate chapters from various sections to suit his own scheme of work. We must emphasise that we expect the teacher to amplify the content of the book wherever necessary. The widest possible range of examples of each component, assembly, unit and layout should be handled and discussed by the student.

Most of the drawings have been kept simple but, bearing in mind that usually a teacher has little time for more than a simple sketch on the blackboard, many of them are deliberately pictorial. Drawings have been preferred to photographs on account of their greater clarity of detail.

The book is intended particularly for students preparing for examinations such as the City and Guilds of London Institute's examinations in Motor Vehicle Mechanics' and Technicians' Work.

but is flexible enough to be suitable for any course of a similar level.

We should like to thank many friends for their help and also manufacturers who have co-operated in the preparation of the book. Where drawings have been redrawn from a manufacturer's publication, acknowledgements have been made.

Finally, we should welcome comments and suggestions from teachers, which we shall bear in mind when preparing future editions.

V.A.W.H.
F.W.P.

SECOND EDITION

The necessity for reprinting has given us the opportunity to make minor corrections and up-date the various topics presented in the first edition. Attention has also been given to the system of units used—in this edition S.I. values are stated as well as Imperial units; in each case the value is 'rounded-off' to give sufficient accuracy for the application.

Since the book was originally written, many external examination authorities have amended their syllabuses to complement the practical training recommended by the Road Transport Industry Training Board. To comprehend fully this practical training the apprentice should understand the basic principles underlying each topic and his attendance at a local technical college is intended to cover this aspect.

We intend this book to assist the student by supplementing and complementing the theoretical work presented by a college lecturer. Also we hope that the ample presentation of each topic will be of help to any student of Automobile Engineering, whether he is studying for a certificate or reading for general interest in the subject.

Because of the various changes outlined, we have enlarged the book to include topics such as Wankel engines, gas turbines, superchargers, automatic gearboxes, power-assisted steering layouts, alternators and many other items.

1972
V.A.W.H.
F.W.P.

Vehicle Development and Layout

1.1

VEHICLE DEVELOPMENT

(Please read the Introductory Note if you have not already done so.)

At a very early stage in his descent from the apes, man must have realised that the means of transport with which nature had provided him left much to be desired. He was severely limited in the loads he could carry, the distances he could carry them and the speed at which he could travel, even without a load. Furthermore, it is a safe guess that the physical exertion involved was no more to his liking then than it is today.

The taming and training of suitable animals enabled heavier loads to be carried greater distances, often at greater speeds than man was capable of attaining, and there was the added advantage that most of the effort was provided by the animal, while the man could travel at his ease.

Heavy loads were dragged upon sledges until an early and unknown engineer invented the wheel. This made it possible to construct crude carts upon which even heavier loads could be carried more easily. The one drawback to the use of wheeled vehicles was —and still is—the necessity of providing a reasonably smooth and hard surface upon which the wheels could run. The development of wheeled vehicles is closely related to the development of roads.

As new materials and manufacturing methods were developed, it became possible to make improvements in vehicles, but so long as animals were the only form of motive power it was not possible to increase loads and speeds very much. The development of the steam engine during the eighteenth and nineteenth centuries led to its application to the driving of vehicles, and though some of the early attempts were crude and not very successful, several extremely promising carriages were produced which might have been developed into very practical vehicles had not restrictive legislation forced them off the roads.

The steam engine proved less suited to road vehicles than it did to the railway. It was the successful development of the light high-speed internal-combustion engine towards the end of the nineteenth century which really opened up the way to the power-driven road vehicle, and which made possible the development of the modern motor-car, lorry, bus and coach.

Motor vehicles were developed from horse-drawn carriages—they were, in fact, called 'horseless carriages'—and naturally owed something of their general form to those carriages. For instance, the system of four wheels arranged one at each end of two transverse axles so that their points of contact with the ground are at the corners of a rectangle, as shown in Fig. 1.1.1(a), has been used on carts and waggons from time immemorial and is still by far the commonest arrangement. Whilst three wheels are sufficient to give

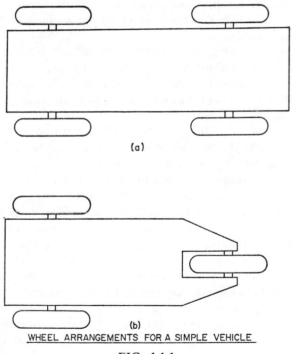

(a)

(b)

WHEEL ARRANGEMENTS FOR A SIMPLE VEHICLE

FIG. 1.1.1

stability, they do not provide so much 'useful space' for a given amount of road space taken up (compare Fig. 1.1.1(b) with Fig. 1.1.1(a)).

The horse was invariably put in front of the cart where he could see where he was going and where the driver could keep an eye on him. He steered the vehicle through shafts attached to a front axle which could pivot about its centre, and when it came to replacing the horse by an engine, it was natural that front-wheel steering should be retained at least for a while. It was not long, however, before vehicles with rear-wheel steering were tried, and it was soon found that rear-wheel steering had disadvantages which ruled it out for general use. For example, a vehicle steered by its rear wheels would steer to the *right* by deflecting its rear end to the *left,* making it impossible to drive away *forwards* from a position close to a wall or kerb, as illustrated in Fig. 1.1.2. A car moving

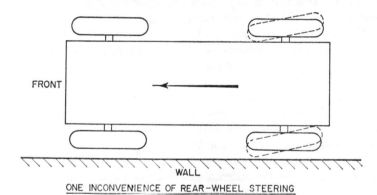

FRONT

WALL

ONE INCONVENIENCE OF REAR-WHEEL STEERING

FIG. 1.1.2

at any speed and coming alongside a wall, kerb, ditch or another vehicle could very easily find itself in a situation in which a collision could not be avoided.

The swivelling axle arrangement is not very satisfactory for powered vehicles, partly because a good deal of space must be left for the axle and wheels to swivel, and also because if one wheel strikes an obstruction, such as a large stone, it is extremely difficult, without the leverage of the long shafts, to prevent the axle swivelling about its pivot, causing the vehicle to swerve off the road. An alternative arrangement in which the wheels were carried on *stub axles* free to pivot at the ends of a fixed axle had already been used on some horse carriages, and this was soon adopted for motor vehicles.

When it came to using mechanical power to drive vehicles, it was natural that the power should be applied to the non-steerable wheels, since the problem of driving these is simpler than when the driving wheels have also to be swivelled for steering purposes. This explains the almost universal adoption of rear-wheel drive, which has the added advantage that the weight carried on the driving wheels is automatically increased when climbing hills or accelerating, thus increasing the grip of the driving wheels on the road when it is most necessary. The weight on the front wheels is decreased under these conditions, and if the surface of the road is slippery, the driving wheels of a front-wheel drive vehicle tend to lose their grip and spin. In spite of this, front-wheel drive does have several advantages which will be discussed later, but it is principally the greater simplicity of driving the rear wheels, combined with their better grip of the road, that has made this the more usual arrangement.

The most convenient source of power so far developed for driving road vehicles is the internal-combustion engine, which derives its power from the burning of fuel *inside the engine itself.* Alternative power units are the steam engine and the electric motor. The former requires a boiler to generate the steam, in addition to the engine itself, making the complete installation rather bulky. Also, there are heat losses in the boiler as well as in the engine, so that it is less efficient than the internal-combustion engine. During temporary halts, it continues to consume fuel in order to maintain steam pressure, whereas the internal-combustion engine consumes fuel only when it is actually running.

An electric motor needs a supply of electrical energy to operate it: if this is to be carried on the vehicle, it must be in the form of *batteries* or *accumulators* which are both heavy and bulky in relation to the amount of energy they can store, limiting the range, speed and load-carrying capacity of the vehicle. If an external supply of electrical energy is to be used, the vehicle must be connected to a distant power station by some means such as a system of wires, suspended at a safe height above the road, with which contact is made by suitable arms mounted on top of the vehicle and provided with some form of sliding connection to the wires. Such a system has obvious limitations.

Although both steam and electric vehicles have been used, the internal-combustion engine is now almost universal.

If you look at Fig. 1.1.3 you will see that the width between the

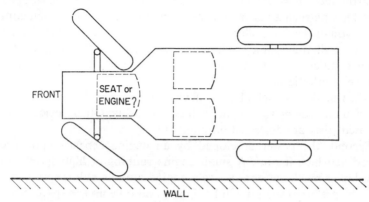

ONE REASON FOR PLACING THE ENGINE AT THE FRONT

FIG. 1.1.3

front wheels is restricted by the necessity for the wheels to swivel for steering purposes, but there is a space which might provide room for one seat. However, people seem to prefer to sit side by side, and, though there may be much to be said in favour of placing the driver by himself in the extreme front of the vehicle, this arrangement is not popular. The engine can be made to fit into this space very conveniently, and although the earliest vehicles had their engines elsewhere, this position was adopted by almost all manufacturers from a very early stage.

The internal-combustion engine has two characteristics which necessitate certain arrangements in the mechanism connecting the engine to the driving wheels. First, the engine cannot produce any driving effort when it is not running. When a steam engine is at rest, it is necessary merely to admit steam under pressure from the boiler, by opening a valve, and the engine will at once start to work. An electric motor needs only to be switched on. An internal-combustion engine, on the other hand, must be driven by some external means before it will begin to run under its own power. Once it is running, it has to be connected to the driving wheels of the vehicle by some arrangement which permits the running engine to be coupled smoothly and without shock to the initially stationary wheels. For instance, most early motor-cycles had their engines connected directly to the rear wheels by a belt: the engine was started by pushing the whole machine, and, once it started, the rider had to leap smartly aboard. To stop the machine, the engine had to be stopped too. Driving such a machine in modern city traffic would soon convince you of the desirability of a more convenient arrangement, even for so small and light a machine as a motor-cycle: the necessity for similar antics to start a motor-car would be enough to damp most people's enthusiasm.

Most modern vehicles have a device called a *clutch* which enables the running engine to start the vehicle smoothly. Other devices may be used: they are described on page 313.

Second, the power developed by an engine depends upon the speed at which it runs. A small engine running at high speed can develop as much power as a larger engine running at low speed, and is to be preferred since it will be lighter and take up less space. Such small high-speed engines generally run at a speed some four or five times greater than the road wheels, so a speed-reducing gear has to be included in the driving mechanism connecting the engine to the driving wheels.

There is, moreover, a minimum speed below which the engine will not run. Most modern engines have a speed range from about 400 revolutions per minute (rev/min) to about 4000 rev/min or more, so that if the maximum speed of a car is, say, 80 mile/h, its minimum speed will be about 8 mile/h, unless the clutch is partly disconnected or *slipped*. In starting off from rest, the clutch cannot be fully engaged until the road speed has reached at least 8 mile/h, during which time a great deal of heat will have been generated in the slipping clutch, which will damage it. This difficulty is overcome by providing additional gearing in the driving arrangements which can be brought into use—either by the driver or automatically—to enable the car to move slowly with the clutch fully engaged and the engine running faster than its minimum speed. Several such *speeds* or *gears* are usually provided in a mechanism called the *gearbox*.

Another function of these gears is to allow the engine to run at high speeds when the car is moving slowly, so making its maximum power available for climbing steep hills or accelerating rapidly from low speeds.

We now have an idea of the *main* components of modern motor vehicles, and may next consider how they are arranged in some of the chief classes of vehicle.

VEHICLE LAYOUT

These are designed to carry from one to eight persons, the usual number being four, one of whom will be the driver. The layout of a typical four-seater is shown in Fig. 1.2.1.

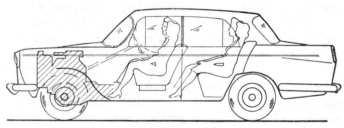

TYPICAL 4-SEATER CAR

FIG. 1.2.1

Wheels

Most private cars run on four wheels which are fitted with hollow rubber tyres filled with air under sufficient pressure to support the loads they have to carry. These absorb shocks caused by small road irregularities: greater unevenness of road surface is taken care of by fitting springs between the wheels and the vehicles which allow some vertical movement of the wheels in relation to the vehicle.

Front Axle

This is used for steering: the wheels are carried on *stub axles* which swivel upon *king pins* at the extremities of the axle. The two stub axles are linked together by *steering arms* and a *track rod*; and they are swivelled about the king pins by a *steering wheel* operated by the driver, which is linked to one of the stub axles by a shaft, a gearbox and a suitable linkage. The axle used to be a one-piece beam upon which the vehicle was supported by springs, but this has been superseded on modern cars by an arrangement in which the wheels are free to rise and fall vertically, independently of each other, under the control of springs. This arrangement is known as *independent front suspension* (see page 458).

Rear Axle

This is usually a tube enclosing driving shafts to which the rear wheels are fixed, with suitable bearings upon which the wheels rotate. The tube is enlarged at the centre to enclose the *final-drive gears,* which provide the main speed reduction between the engine and the driving wheels, as well as changing the direction of the drive from the fore-and-aft line of the propeller shaft to the transverse line of the axle shafts.

If the two rear wheels were connected by a shaft, they would both rotate at the same speed. It is obvious that, when going round a corner, the outer wheel has a greater distance to travel than the inner one, and if both wheels rotate at the same speed, one or both will be forced to slip on the road surface, causing excessive tyre wear and severe twisting loads on the shaft. Even on straight roads, the two wheels can only turn at the same speed without slip if they are of *exactly* the same diameter, which is not necessarily so. For instance, tyres of different states of wear may be fitted on opposite sides: tyres of the same nominal size made by different manufacturers may differ in their actual dimensions, and even those made by one manufacturer will not be exactly the same. (Try taking a few measurements for yourself.) Different inflation pressures, too, will alter the effective size of a tyre by altering its rolling radius (the distance from the wheel centre to the ground).

To solve this problem, each wheel has its own separate *half-shaft*; these meet at about the centre of the axle and are connected by a *differential gear*. This device allows the drive to be applied to both wheels equally while leaving them free to rotate at different speeds (see page 399).

The vehicle is supported on the axle by springs, to prevent the transmission of shocks from uneven road surfaces to the vehicle.

An alternative arrangement which is increasingly used involves mounting the final-drive gears and the differential gear in a casing attached to the frame, and connecting them to independently sprung wheels by means of shafts which incorporate what are called *universal joints*. These allow the parts of the shaft which they connect to operate at an angle to one another, and are necessary to allow for the vertical movements of the wheels relative to the frame (see page 381).

Power Unit

The engine is an *internal-combustion engine* and is mounted at the front end of the car, with the clutch and gearbox immediately behind it: engine, clutch and gearbox are assembled into a single unit.

Propeller Shaft

The output shaft of the gearbox is connected to the rear axle by a long shaft called the *propeller shaft*. In a few cases, this is enclosed in a tubular casing, but much more commonly it is exposed or *open*, and has a universal joint at each end to permit changes in shaft alignment as the rear axle rises and falls over road bumps. Even when the final-drive gears are fixed to the frame and the wheels sprung independently, universal joints are still used, because precise alignment of the shafts cannot be ensured; also, misalignment would result from the flexing of the vehicle structure over bumpy roads.

Frame

The component parts of the vehicle need a frame of some kind to which they can be attached and by which they can be supported. At one time it was the usual practice to construct an approximately rectangular frame of steel pressings riveted together, to which all the components, including the body, were attached. The assembled vehicle without the body was called a *chassis,* and the frame alone the *chassis frame*. It was once common practice for vehicle manufacturers to supply the chassis only, the bodywork being built by a *coachbuilder*, but as the production of cars increased, more manufacturers made their own bodywork. It is now rare for a coachbuilder to build a special body. With the development of large *presses*, and sheet steel which could be pressed into complicated shapes without splitting, it became usual to design the body of the vehicle as the main structure capable of carrying the loads which were previously borne by the chassis frame. The separate frame has now been abandoned on all but a few cars; the present method of construction, called *chassisless* or *unitary* construction, is lighter and stiffer than the older arrangement consisting of a chassis onto which a separate body was built.

Jacking Point

It is sometimes necessary to raise the wheels of a vehicle clear of the ground: this is usually done by a *jack*, of which there are several types. In *jacking up* a vehicle great care must be taken to see that the jack is applied to a part which is sufficiently substantial to take the load. Modern cars generally have special *jacking points* to which the jack can be attached.

Brakes

Vehicles are required by law to be fitted with an efficient braking system, and this usually takes the form of brakes attached to each of the four wheels. There are two types of brake used: the older type consists of a pair of shoes, carried on a stationary plate, which can be expanded into contact with a rotating drum mounted on the wheel. The newer type consists of one or more pairs of pads carried in a caliper attached to the axle or wheel-supporting linkage, which can be made to grip the sides of a disc mounted on the wheel. The brakes are applied by pressure on a pedal, but those on the rear wheels can also be applied by a hand lever, acting through a separate linkage and locked in the 'on' position.

Electrical Equipment

Vehicles are required by law to show certain lights at front and rear during the hours of darkness, and these are invariably electric. Besides these lights, others are used such as *fog lamps* to provide the best possible lighting in fog.

An electric motor is used to start the engine, and the fuel is ignited inside the engine by electric sparks generated by an *ignition system.*

Various other items are also operated electrically, such as windscreen wipers, horns (means for giving audible warning of approach), direction indicators, heaters, radio receivers and, in some cases, the mechanism for raising and lowering windows.

The electrical power to operate all this equipment comes from a *generator* which is driven by the vehicle's engine. Since certain items may be needed when the engine is not running, a *battery* or *accumu-*

lator is also fitted, which is kept charged by the generator (when it is running), and stores up energy to be used when the generator is not running.

OTHER ARRANGEMENTS

The layout of the main components so far described is the one most commonly used, but there are others which offer certain advantages and at the same time have certain drawbacks. One of the chief criticisms of the usual arrangement is the way in which the mechanism intrudes upon the space required for the passengers. To give stability and decrease wind-resistance, cars should be reasonably low-built, and the floor is usually within about 18 inches of the ground. Thus the propeller shaft is at about floor height, and it is necessary to make a bulge or tunnel in the floor to clear this shaft, which reduces the space for passengers' feet. The gearbox intrudes to quite an extent into the front end of the body space, making it difficult or even impossible for the driver to use the nearside door (it may sometimes be dangerous to get out through the offside door).

If *all* the mechanism could be placed at one end of the car the long propeller shaft could be eliminated, providing a flat floor and saving both weight and space. There are, therefore, two alternative arrangements in fairly common use.

Rear Engine

By placing the engine at the rear of the vehicle it can be made as a unit incorporating the clutch, gearbox and final-drive gears. With such an arrangement it is necessary that some form of independent suspension of the rear wheels be used.

So far the rear-engine layout has been most successfully applied to fairly small cars; a large and heavy engine at the rear has been found to have an adverse effect on the 'handling' of the car by making it 'tail-heavy'. It also takes up a good deal of space which on a front-engined car would be used for carrying luggage. Most of the space vacated by the engine at the front end can be used for luggage but this space is usually less than that available at the rear of a front-engined car. Although vertical engines of conventional form are sometimes used in rear-engined cars, a 'flat' engine, such as a conventional engine placed on its side, offers the advantage of leaving some space for luggage above the engine.

One advantage attributed to the rear-engined layout is that it increases the load on the rear driving wheels, giving them better grip of the road, but, as already pointed out, it may also make the car tail-heavy.

Fig. 1.2.2 shows a small rear-engined car. Notice that the front seats are nearer the front wheels than in the case of the front-engined car, and the floor is quite flat.

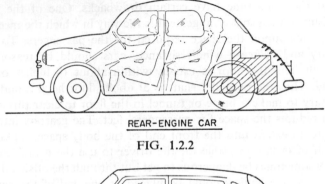

REAR-ENGINE CAR

FIG. 1.2.2

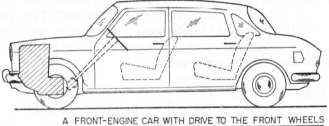

A FRONT-ENGINE CAR WITH DRIVE TO THE FRONT WHEELS

FIG. 1.2.3

Front-wheel Drive

Fig. 1.2.3 shows a popular arrangement consisting of an engine mounted transversely at the front of the vehicle, driving the front wheels through a clutch, gearbox and final-drive gears, the latter being placed behind the engine. From the final-drive gears power is transmitted to the driving wheels through shafts having universal joints at both ends. The joints at the outer end are usually of a special type capable of operating through quite large angles: this is necessary to enable the front wheels to be used for steering as well as driving.

A criticism of this arrangement is that the driving wheels have less grip of the road when accelerating and hill-climbing, and although this can be compensated for by placing the engine well forward so that as much weight as possible is carried on the front wheels, the car is then liable to become nose-heavy. However, very many cars of this type have been made and are claimed to handle very well indeed.

Central Engine

One other possible arrangement may be worth mentioning at this stage, and that is the central engine as used in present-day racing cars. This arrangement has two advantages: it concentrates the weight near the centre of the car, and it allows the driver to be seated low down. These advantages, whilst of great importance for racing cars, are outweighed in the case of everyday cars by the fact that the engine takes up the space which would normally be occupied by passengers.

BODYWORK

The main purpose of the bodywork is to provide accommodation for the driver and passengers, with suitable protection against wind and weather. The degree of comfort provided will naturally depend upon the type of car and its cost, ranging from the bare minimum to luxury of a standard beyond that found in many homes.

Bodies may be *open*, in which case a hood is usually provided and can be erected to give some protection in bad weather. Most, nowadays, are of the permanently *closed* type, having a fixed roof. There are also those with a substantial hood which, when lowered, gives all the advantages of an open body, but which can be raised to give a degree of protection hardly less effective than that of a closed car; these are called *drop-head* or *convertible* bodies.

Yet another arrangement is the *sunshine roof*, consisting of a panel in the roof of a closed car which can be opened. This arrangement, once very popular, is less used since the adoption of unitary construction.

Cars intended for normal use on the roads have at least two seats, one for the driver and another for a passenger beside him. These are usually two separate seats which are carried on *rails* or *runners* fixed to the floor in such a manner that the seats can be moved forward or backwards—to suit different drivers or passengers—and securely locked in position. Sometimes adjustment for height and for the angle of the seat and the back is also provided. In some vehicles these two seats are provided on a single *bench type* seat which extends the full width of the body, and this type may sometimes provide room for three people.

Most cars have additional seats behind those already mentioned. These are usually non-adjustable, and may provide for either two or three people. Large cars are sometimes provided with additional seats—called *occasional* seats—which fold away into a *division* across the car behind the front seats.

Some years ago legislation was introduced requiring vehicles to be fitted with seat belts for the occupants of the front seats in order to minimise the risk of severe injury if the car is involved in an accident. These belts must be anchored to a substantial part of the vehicle structure in such a way that the anchorages will not be torn out when an accident occurs.

The body, besides housing the occupants, also provides enclosed accommodation for their luggage in a compartment known as the *boot,* usually at the rear of the car. A type of body which has become very popular is the one called the *station waggon.* Alternative names for this are *shooting brake* and *estate car.* Its main feature is the continuation of the roof to the extreme rear of the car, where doors give access to the interior. There is considerable space for luggage or other articles behind the rear seats: an example of this type of body is shown in Fig. 1.2.4.

VANS

These are small commercial vehicles used for the conveyance of relatively light goods usually over short distances, such as, for

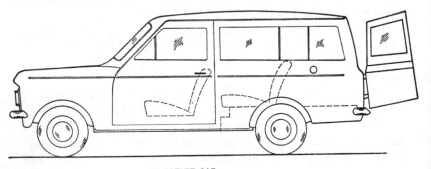

AN ESTATE CAR

FIG. 1.2.4

example, that which a grocer would use for making deliveries to his customers. Generally, vans are similar to private cars but have van bodies instead of the normal car bodywork. In some cases, although the same engine, transmission system and suspension components are used, they are rearranged by moving the engine slightly towards the nearside to make room for the driver to sit alongside the engine and rather higher than is usual in a private car. Often there is provision for seating the driver only but sometimes an additional seat may be provided on the nearside, or a bench-type seat for three. An illustration of a typical small van is given in Fig. 1.2.5: in this case

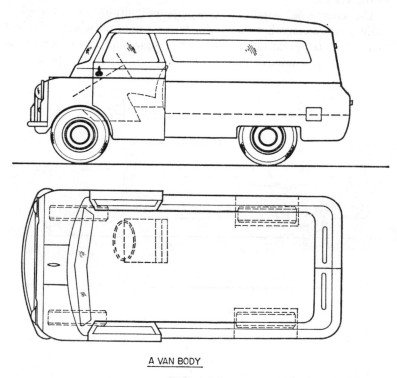

A VAN BODY

FIG. 1.2.5

the two front doors open by sliding backwards instead of hinging. Where a closed body is not required—e.g. for a house decorator to carry his materials and equipment—an open body is used, the vehicle then being called a *light truck* or *pick-up*.

LORRIES

These are much more robustly constructed vehicles, designed for carrying loads from about 3 tons, about 3000 kilograms. (In their smaller sizes they are often called trucks.)

A large flat platform is needed to carry the load: since this can only be provided above wheel height, no special effort is made to lower the frame, which usually consists of two straight and deep side-members joined by several cross-members. This frame supports the main components of the vehicle as well as the platform which forms the basis of the body, and the driver sits in a *cab* at the front of the vehicle.

The engine is usually a compression-ignition, or oil engine. (Briefly this means that the engine burns a light oil which is ignited by the high temperature produced by compressing air to a very high pressure in the engine cylinders: it is described in detail on page 257.)

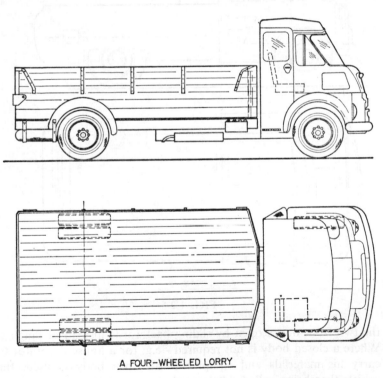

A FOUR-WHEELED LORRY

FIG. 1.2.6

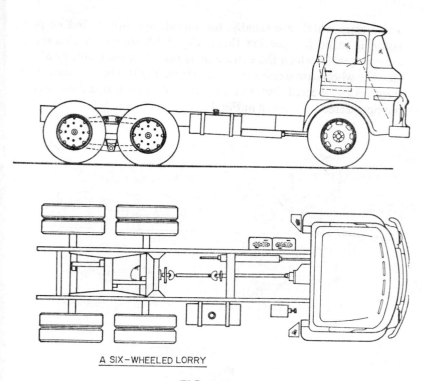

A SIX–WHEELED LORRY

FIG. 1.2.7

It is fitted at the front, and the driver sits high up at one side of it. with his mate at the other side. Thus the whole of the space from the engine rearwards is available for carrying the load.

To carry heavy loads the rear wheels either have *twin tyres*—fitted side by side—or special wide section single tyres. Vehicles exceeding a certain total loaded weight are required to have six wheels carried on three axles, whilst even heavier vehicles are required to have eight wheels, two on each of four axles. These legal requirements are laid down in *Construction and Use Regulations* drawn up by Parliament: since they are constantly liable to revision students seeking further details of maximum permitted weights and dimensions of vehicles are advised to consult the regulations currently in force. Fig. 1.2.6 shows a four-wheeled truck or light lorry.

When six wheels are used the two extra wheels may be carried on an additional axle at the rear of the vehicle, as shown in Fig. 1.2.7.

These extra wheels are usually, but not always, driven, but no provision is made for steering them. Fig. 1.2.8 shows an alternative arrangement in which the extra axle is placed at the front, in which case the wheels are steered but not driven. Eight-wheelers have two front axles—steered but not driven—and two rear axles—driven but not steered—as shown in Fig. 1.2.9.

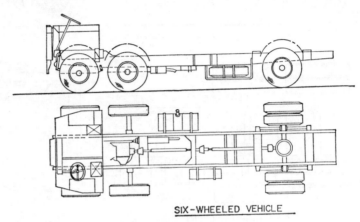

SIX-WHEELED VEHICLE

FIG. 1.2.8

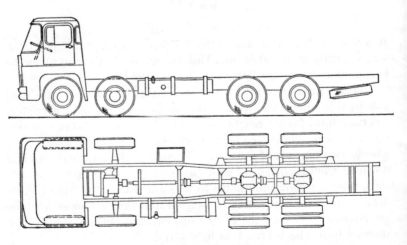

EIGHT-WHEELED VEHICLE

FIG. 1.2.9

Lorries are allowed to tow a trailer on which an additional load can be carried. There is, in addition, a type of vehicle which consists of two parts: a four- or six-wheeled tractor (which does not itself carry any load) to which is attached, by a special turntable coupling, the front end of a semi-trailer having two or four wheels at its rear end. In this way some of the weight carried by the semi-trailer is supported by the tractor. The combination of tractor and semi-trailer is called an articulated vehicle. The trailer has retractable wheels on which its front end can be supported: this enables the tractor to be uncoupled and used with another trailer while its former trailer is being loaded or unloaded. An example of an articulated vehicle is shown in Fig. 1.2.10.

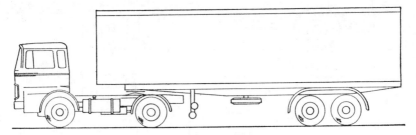

ARTICULATED VEHICLE

FIG. 1.2.10

OMNIBUSES

These vehicles are designed to transport fairly large numbers of passengers. Up to about forty may be carried on a single floor or deck. Fig. 1.2.11 shows a single-decked bus which has its entrance at the front, where the driver can see passengers boarding or alighting from the vehicle. (Doors are not always fitted, but when they are they are often power-operated by the driver or conductor to prevent passengers getting on or off when the bus is moving.) In order to make room for the front entrance the engine is often laid on its side below the frame, as shown in the drawing of the chassis (Fig. 1.2.12).

A double-decked omnibus capable of seating about sixty passengers is shown in Fig. 1.2.13. The *Construction and Use Regulations* stipulate a maximum height for the vehicle and a minimum ceiling height for both upper and lower decks. This means that the floor of the lower deck must be fairly close to the ground, at least along the

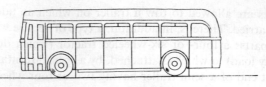

SINGLE-DECK BUS

FIG. 1.2.11

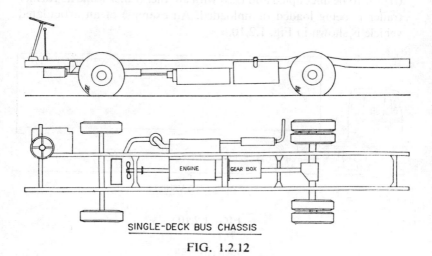

SINGLE-DECK BUS CHASSIS

FIG. 1.2.12

DOUBLE-DECK OMNIBUS

FIG. 1.2.13

central gangway between the seats: to permit this the final-drive gears are not at the centre of the rear axle, but are moved to one side, so that the gangway does not have to clear the highest point of the axle casing.

The engine is placed well forward directly over the front axle, and slightly to the nearside to allow the driver to sit beside it, leaving all the space behind the front wheels free for the accommodation of passengers. The gearbox is separately mounted on the nearside some way behind the engine, where it can be low enough to be completely below floor level, and the two propeller shafts—one between engine and gearbox and the other between gearbox and rear axle—are clear of the gangway. In towns and cities there are usually short distances between stops, and speed of loading and unloading passengers is very important. At the rear of the bus is a large platform little more than a foot above ground level and an easy step up from the edge of the pavement. From this platform another step up leads into the lower deck and a staircase leads to the upper deck. The arrangement of the chassis (Fig. 1.2.14) shows how the rear end of the frame is shaped to support this platform.

An objection to this arrangement is that the driver is unable to see passengers getting on and off except with the aid of mirrors, which do not give an adequate view of people on the platform or running to catch the bus. It is the conductor's responsibility to see passengers safely on and off, but at busy times it is not easy for him to do this. By placing the platform at the front the driver can have a direct view of passengers boarding and alighting, as in the case

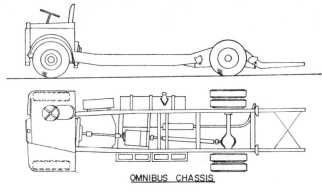

OMNIBUS CHASSIS

FIG. 1.2.14

of the single-decked bus shown in Fig. 1.2.11. In the case of a double-decker the engine cannot be placed beneath the floor, so the forward platform necessitates placing the engine transversely at the extreme rear, and this layout is sometimes used.

The double-deck omnibus is seldom used outside Great Britain; large single deckers, with fewer seats but more space for standing passengers, seem to be preferred. Buses of this kind, having separate entrance and exit doors remotely controlled by the driver and adapted for automatic issue of tickets (thus enabling the bus to be operated by one man) are replacing double-deck buses in some parts of Great Britain and their use seems likely to increase.

COACHES

Vehicles of this type are designed to carry between thirty and forty passengers over fairly long distances in greater comfort than is provided in omnibuses. Speed of loading and unloading is less important, but a fair amount of luggage accommodation is required. A chassis similar to that shown in Fig. 1.2.12 is generally used, but more comfortable seats are provided. The entrance is either at the front or behind the front wheels.

Some buses and coaches are made with the body structure forming the main frame. Though this is not very common it has the advantage of reducing total mass.

The Petrol Engine

2.1

MAIN PARTS AND WORKING PRINCIPLES

THE MAIN PARTS

Fig. 2.1.1 shows the main parts of an elementary engine. They are:

(1) *The cylinder.* In its simplest form this is a tube of circular cross-section, closed at one end.

(2) *The piston* fits closely inside the cylinder. Ideally it would be perfectly gas-tight yet perfectly free to move up and down inside the cylinder.

(3) *The connecting rod* connects the piston to the crankshaft. At the piston end is a pin called the *gudgeon pin* which is fitted into holes in the piston and the connecting rod to couple them together.

(4) *The crankshaft* is the main shaft of the engine and is carried in bearings in the *crankcase*. Offset from the main part of the shaft is the *crank pin* on which the connecting rod is fitted and is free to turn.

The arrangement is such that rotation of the crankshaft causes the piston to move up and down inside the cylinder: the lines *A* and *B* (Fig. 2.1.1) indicate the limits of travel of the top of the piston. As the piston moves upwards the space between its top surface and the closed end of the cylinder is reduced—i.e. the gas trapped in this space is *compressed*. As the piston moves downwards the space above it is increased—i.e. the gas in this space *expands*.

The crankshaft can be rotated by pushing the piston up and down in the cylinder. Starting with the position shown in Fig. 2.1.1, the crankshaft rotates clockwise as the piston is pushed downwards until the piston reaches the lowest point of its travel. At this point the crank pin will be directly under the centre of the crankshaft, and the centres of the gudgeon pin, crank pin and crankshaft will all lie in

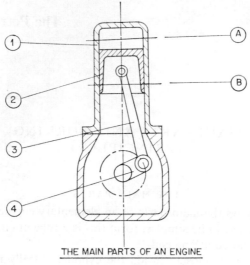

THE MAIN PARTS OF AN ENGINE

FIG. 2.1.1

a straight line. In this position pressure on the piston will have no turning effect on the crankshaft, and this position is therefore called a *dead centre*. Another dead centre occurs when the piston is at the extreme top of its travel. These two dead centres, which are known as *bottom dead centre* (b.d.c) and *top dead centre* (t.d.c) respectively, mark the extreme limits of the piston's travel. They are illustrated in Fig. 2.1.2. Movement of the piston from one dead centre to another is called a *stroke*, and there are two strokes of the piston to every revolution of the crankshaft.

METHOD OF WORKING

The piston is pushed down the cylinder by applying pressure to its upper surface. The method by which the pressure is produced is based upon the fact that if a gas is heated in a confined space its pressure will increase. Fig. 2.1.3 illustrates a simple demonstration of this fact: the apparatus is very simple and you should try it for yourself. Bore a hole in the cork of a bottle and into this hole push one end of a glass tube bent into a U-shape. Partly fill this tube with water, and then push the cork into the bottle, holding the bottle upside-down as shown. The difference in pressure between the air

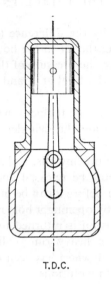

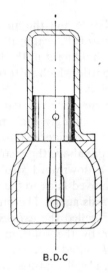

T.D.C.   B.D.C

THE DEAD CENTRES

FIG. 2.1.2

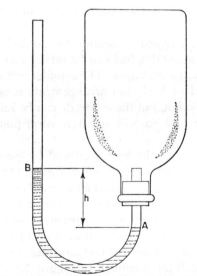

DEMONSTRATION OF INCREASE OF PRESSURE OF
AIR WITH RISE IN TEMPERATURE

FIG. 2.1.3

in the bottle and the air outside is shown by the difference (h) in the levels of the water at A and B. Warming the air in the bottle—even by holding it in the hand—will increase the pressure of the air in the bottle which in turn will push down the level at A and raise the level at B.

In an engine the air can be heated to a very high temperature and a correspondingly high pressure created inside the cylinder, thus exerting a considerable force on the piston.

Pressure above the piston can only push it downwards, and at the end of a downward stroke the pressure must be released and the piston moved back to the top of the cylinder before it can be pushed downwards again. The pressure is released by opening a hole in the cylinder called the *exhaust port*, and the piston is returned up the cylinder by the rotation of a wheel with a heavy rim—called a *flywheel*—fitted to the crankshaft. Once this flywheel has been made to turn, it will continue to rotate for several revolutions.

The air inside the cylinder can be heated by playing a flame on the outside of the cylinder. To reach the air inside, however, the heat would have to pass through the wall of the cylinder, so that the air could be made no hotter than the cylinder. Much of the heat used would be lost by heating the cylinder and the air outside it.

This waste can be lessened by heating the air inside the cylinder directly: to do this a suitable fuel can be mixed with the air in the cylinder and burnt *inside the engine*. The cylinder will still, of course, absorb a good deal of heat, and arrangements must be made to prevent it getting too hot, but the air inside can be raised to a much higher temperature and so will reach a correspondingly higher pressure.

Any engine which uses the heat produced by burning a fuel to develop mechanical power is called a *heat engine*. One in which the fuel is burnt *inside* the engine is called an *internal-combustion engine*. Internal-combustion engines can use any one of a variety of fuels. Petrol is a liquid refined from crude petroleum, and is particularly suitable as a fuel for motor vehicles. It is clean to handle and relatively cheap. It is liquid at normal temperatures, and a vehicle can carry, in quite a small tank, enough to take it 200 or more miles. It gives off an inflammable vapour even at quite low temperatures, enabling the engine to be started from cold with little difficulty.

CYCLE OF OPERATIONS

Before petrol can be burnt it must be vaporised and mixed with a suitable quantity of air. This mixture must then be introduced into the cylinder, and this is done through a hole called the *inlet port*. Once inside the cylinder the mixture is compressed before burning, since this greatly increases the pressure after burning. After compression the vaporised fuel is ignited by an electric spark, which, at the appropriate moment, jumps across a small gap on a *sparking plug*, screwed into the top of the cylinder.

After the fuel has burned and the resulting pressure has pushed the piston down the cylinder, the burned gases are released, as already mentioned, through the exhaust port. The inlet and exhaust ports are normally closed, but are opened at the correct times to allow the gases to pass through them (see page 105).

The running of the engine involves the continuous repetition of *four operations* which make up what is called the *cycle of operations*. These operations are continuously repeated, in the following order, as long as the engine is running.

(1) The space in the cylinder above the piston is filled with a mixture of petrol vapour and air.

(2) This mixture is compressed into the top end of the cylinder (called the combustion chamber).

(3) The petrol vapour is burned, and the resulting pressure drives the piston down the cylinder.

(4) The burned gases are expelled from the cylinder.

Notice that the gas helps the piston on its way during only one of these operations. The remaining operations give no direct help, but actually impede the piston's movement, particularly the compressing of the gas. Thus the work of the flywheel is not merely to push the piston back up the cylinder, but to keep the crankshaft turning as steadily as possible between one impulse on the piston and the next.

ENGINE SIZE

The usual method of indicating the size of an engine is to state the volume of air and fuel taken into the engine for each cycle of operations. This is clearly the volume contained in that part of the cylinder between the t.d.c. and b.d.c. positions of the piston.

The volume of a cylinder is given by the formula

$$V = \pi r^2 h \quad \text{or} \quad V = \frac{\pi}{4} d^2 h$$

Where $V=$ the volume of the cylinder
        $r =$ its radius
        $d =$ its diameter
        $h =$ its height or length

The internal diameter of the engine cylinder is called the *bore,* whilst the distance the piston moves between t.d.c. and b.d.c. is called the *stroke.* Representing these by b and s respectively, the above formula can be written:

$$V=\frac{\pi}{4}b^2s$$

Since this is the volume *displaced* or *swept* by the piston, it is called the *displacement volume* or *swept volume* of the cylinder. If the engine has several cylinders, as most have, the total swept volume of the engine is the swept volume per cylinder multiplied by the number of cylinders.

If the bore (b) and stroke (s) are measured in inches the total swept volume (V_t) will be in cubic inches (in³), and if n represents the number of cylinders then

$$V_t=\frac{\pi}{4}b^2sn \quad \text{in}^3$$

If the bore and stroke are measured in millimetres the total swept volume will usually be given in cubic centimetres (cm³) or litres (l). In this case

$$V_t=\frac{\pi b^2sn}{4000} \quad \text{cm}^3$$

$$\text{or} \quad V_t=\frac{\pi b^2sn}{4\,000\,000} \quad litre$$

$$\left[\text{Note: this may also be written} \quad V_t=\frac{\pi b^2sn}{4\times10^6}\right]$$

COMPRESSION RATIO

An important feature of the dimensions of an engine cylinder is the number of times the volume enclosed above the piston before compression is greater than that after compression. When the piston is at t.d.c. a space is left between its top and the end of the cylinder:

the volume contained in this space is called the *clearance volume*. The volume enclosed above the piston at b.d.c. consists of the *clearance volume plus the swept volume* and is called the *total volume*.

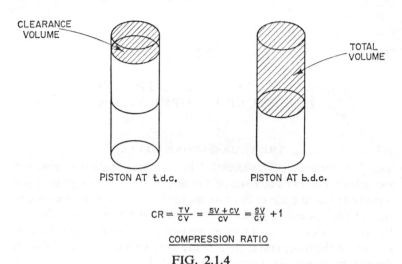

$$CR = \frac{TV}{CV} = \frac{SV+CV}{CV} = \frac{SV}{CV} + 1$$

COMPRESSION RATIO

FIG. 2.1.4

Compression ratio $= \dfrac{\text{total vol.}}{\text{clearance vol.}} = \dfrac{\text{swept vol.} + \text{clearance vol.}}{\text{clearance vol.}}$

$= \dfrac{\text{swept vol.}}{\text{clearance vol.}} + 1$

PRACTICAL APPLICATIONS OF THE CYCLE OF OPERATIONS

THE FOUR-STROKE CYCLE

The first commercially successful internal-combustion engine was made by a Frenchman, Etienne Lenoir, in 1860. It ran on coal gas, but worked on a cycle of operations which did not include compression of the gas before ignition: as a result it was not very efficient. In spite of this it was, in some respects, superior to small steam engines of the time, and a great many were sold and did useful work driving machinery in factories. In 1862 Lenoir made a horseless carriage powered by his engine and possibly drove it on the roads, but he lost interest in this venture and nothing came of it.

A method of carrying out the cycle of operations outlined on page 41 was described in a patent dated 16 January 1862 taken out by a French civil servant, M. Beau de Rochas. Since he did not have the means to develop the patent himself, the patentee offered it to Lenoir who, failing to realise its importance, turned it down.

In Germany Dr. N. A. Otto started manufacturing gas engines in about 1866. His first engines were extremely noisy, though quite effective, but about 1875 he took out a patent describing a method of carrying out the cycle of operations which was identical with that of Beau de Rochas' thirteen years earlier. (It is, however, most unlikely that Otto had heard of the Frenchman or his patent.) Otto's new engine was an immediate success. It was much more efficient than Lenoir's and was very quiet, a characteristic which led to its being named 'Otto's silent gas engine'.

Lenoir, realising his mistake, began to manufacture engines working on the same principle. Otto, of course, sued him for infringing his patent rights, but Lenoir had no difficulty in proving that his engines were made under the earlier patient of Beau de

Rochas, which had by now lapsed. The court proceedings at last brought poor Beau de Rochas the fame he deserved, and he was awarded a sum of money by the Academy of Sciences in Paris in recognition of his invention. Even so, the method of operation which he was the first to describe, and which is the one used in most modern engines, was for many years (and sometimes still is) known as the *Otto cycle*.

In this method one complete stroke of the piston is used to carry out each of the four operations forming the cycle of operations. To complete the cycle, therefore, *four strokes of the piston*, occupying two revolutions of the crankshaft, are needed: consequently the method is generally known as the *four-stroke cycle*.

The inlet and exhaust ports are normally closed by valves (page 76) which are mechanically opened at the correct times. If the engine runs on petrol, the petrol and air are mixed in the correct proportions by a *carburetter*, fitted to the outer end of the inlet port.

Starting with the piston at t.d.c., as the crankshaft rotates the method of operation is as follows:

First stroke   The piston moves *down* the cylinder with the *inlet port open* and *exhaust port closed*, filling the cylinder with a mixture of petrol vapour and air. This is the *induction stroke*.

Second stroke   The piston moves *up* the cylinder with *both ports closed*, compressing the mixture into the combustion chamber at the top end of the cylinder. This is the *compression stroke*.

Third stroke   At about the end of the compression stroke an electric spark is made to jump across a small gap on a *sparking plug* screwed into the end of the cylinder. This spark ignites the petrol vapour which burns very rapidly, heating the gas in the cylinder to a high temperature and considerably increasing its pressure. The pressure forces the piston *down* the cylinder, both ports remaining closed. This is the *power stroke*.

Fourth stroke   The piston returns *up* the cylinder with the *inlet port still closed* but the *exhaust port open*, expelling the burnt gases from the cylinder. This is the *exhaust stroke*.

At the end of this stroke the exhaust port closes and the inlet port reopens ready for the next induction stroke, which follows immediately.

Fig. 2.2.1 illustrates these four operations. Observe the movements of the piston and operation of the valves as the crankshaft of an actual engine is rotated.

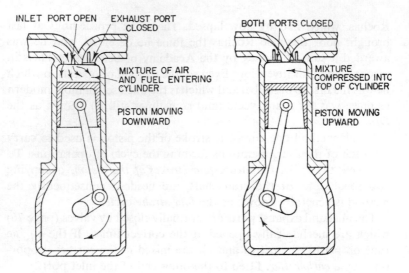

INLET PORT OPEN   EXHAUST PORT CLOSED

MIXTURE OF AIR AND FUEL ENTERING CYLINDER

PISTON MOVING DOWNWARD

THE INDUCTION STROKE

BOTH PORTS CLOSED

MIXTURE COMPRESSED INTO TOP OF CYLINDER

PISTON MOVING UPWARD

THE COMPRESSION STROKE

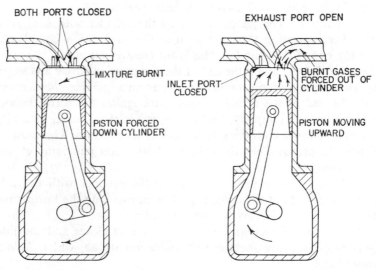

BOTH PORTS CLOSED

MIXTURE BURNT

PISTON FORCED DOWN CYLINDER

THE POWER STROKE

EXHAUST PORT OPEN

INLET PORT CLOSED

BURNT GASES FORCED OUT OF CYLINDER

PISTON MOVING UPWARD

THE EXHAUST STROKE

THE OPERATION OF AN ENGINE ON THE FOUR-STROKE CYCLE

FIG. 2.2.1

THE TWO-STROKE CYCLE

It has always been considered a disadvantage of the four-stroke cycle that there are three 'idle strokes' to every 'working stroke'. Between 1878 and 1881 a Scotsman, Dugald Clerk, developed an engine in which the cycle of operations was completed in only *two strokes* of the piston, thus providing a power stroke for every revolution of the crankshaft. This engine used a second cylinder and piston to force the fresh mixture into the working cylinder.

In 1891 Joseph Day invented a modified form of Clerk's engine, in which he dispensed with the second cylinder by using the space in the crankcase *underneath* the piston to perform the same function. He also avoided the use of valves by using the piston itself to cover or uncover the ports.

The operation of this engine, which is illustrated in Fig. 2.2.2, is as follows.

Beginning with the piston about half-way on its upward stroke, all three ports are covered. The upward movement of the piston compresses a fresh charge of mixture in the *top* of the cylinder, and at the same time decreases the pressure *under* the piston below the pressure of the atmosphere (the crankcase being sealed). Near the top of the stroke the *lower* edge of the piston overruns the *inlet* port, allowing the pressure of the atmosphere to fill the lower part of the engine with fresh mixture from the carburetter.

At about the top of the stroke the mixture above the piston is ignited in the same way as in the four-stroke engine, and with the same result: the high pressure of the burned gases drives the piston down the cylinder. A little below t.d.c. the piston *covers the inlet port*, and further downward movement compresses the mixture in the crankcase. Near the bottom of the stroke the *top* edge of the piston overruns the *exhaust port*, allowing the burnt gases to begin to rush out of the cylinder under their own pressure.

Slightly further down the stroke the *transfer port* is uncovered, and the mixture compressed *below* the piston flows into the cylinder above the piston, where it is deflected upwards by the specially shaped piston. This prevents it shooting straight across the cylinder and out of the exhaust port.

As the piston rises on its next stroke the transfer and exhaust ports are covered and the cycle of operations begins again.

In modern engines of this type the deflector on the crown of the

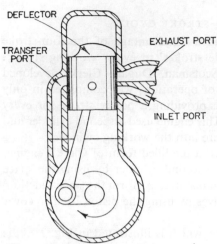

DEFLECTOR

TRANSFER PORT

EXHAUST PORT

INLET PORT

① PISTON RISING, COMPRESSING MIXTURE ABOVE, DECREASING PRESSURE BELOW. ALL PORTS CLOSED.

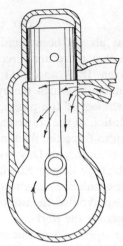

② PISTON PASSING t.d.c., MIXTURE ABOVE PISTON IGNITED, FRESH MIXTURE ENTERING CRANKCASE.

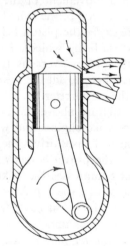

③ PISTON MOVING DOWNWARD. THE FRESH MIXTURE IN THE CRANKCASE HAS BEEN COMPRESSED. THE PISTON HAS JUST UNCOVERED THE EXHAUST PORT, AND IS ABOUT TO UNCOVER THE TRANSFER PORT.

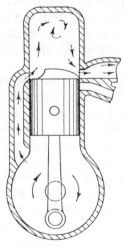

④ PISTON PASSING b.d.c. EXHAUST AND TRANSFER PORTS OPEN. FRESH MIXTURE ENTERING CYLINDER VIA TRANSFER PORT, DIRECTED TO TOP OF CYLINDER BY DEFLECTOR ON PISTON, DRIVING OUT BURNT GAS THROUGH EXHAUST PORT.

THE OPERATION OF AN ENGINE ON THE TWO-STROKE CYCLE

FIG. 2.2.2

piston has been dispensed with, and the transfer port or ports (there are usually two) are shaped and aimed so as to direct the fresh mixture towards the top end of the cylinder away from the exhaust port.

It might be expected that the two-stroke engine would develop twice the power of a four-stroke engine of the same size, but experience does not confirm this. The operations are less effectively carried out, and, despite the deflector on the piston, mixing the fresh charge with burnt gas cannot be avoided: there is usually some loss of fresh mixture through the exhaust port and incomplete scavenging of burnt gas from the cylinder. The main advantages of the two-stroke engine, therefore, are its greater simplicity and smoothness It is commonly used for the smaller sizes of motor-cycles and is seldom used for motor-cars.

CRANKSHAFTS

MAIN FEATURES

The crankshaft of an engine is formed of a number of 'sections' such as that illustrated in Fig. 2.3.1. The *main journals* rotate in the main bearings (a part of a shaft which rotates in a bearing is called a *journal*), and the *crank pin* or *crank journal*, to which the connecting rod is fitted, is offset from the main journals by a distance called the *crank radius*. The *webs* connect the main journals to the crank pin, and where the journals join the webs a *fillet* or *radius* is formed to avoid a sharp corner, which would be a source of weakness. This is of vital importance in crankshafts which are subjected to particularly heavy loads.

BALANCE WEIGHTS

In some cases the webs are extended to form *balance masses* which are used in certain types of engine to ensure that the rotating parts are balanced as effectively as possible and will cause no vibration, or as little as possible, when the engine is running. It is not possible to balance completely the rotating parts of all types of engine; this is, for instance, one of the objections to the use of a single-cylinder engine, which is impossible to balance perfectly, though it can be made satisfactory for certain purposes.

In some engines in which the rotating parts are perfectly balanced, masses similar to balance masses may still be used: centrifugal force acting on the crank pins causes heavy loading of the adjacent main bearings at high speeds, and by extending the webs to form balance masses a counter-centrifugal force is applied in opposition to that on the crank pin, thus reducing the bearing loading. Masses used in this way are more properly known as *countermasses*.

Throw

There appears to be some confusion as to the meaning of this term. It is often used as an alternative to *crank radius*, but old books on steam engines define the throw as the *diameter* of the crank pin circle—i.e. the throw is equal to the stroke of the piston. It might, therefore, be better to avoid the use of the word 'throw' in this sense and clarify what is intended by using the terms *crank radius* or *crank circle diameter* as appropriate.

The same word 'throw' is also used in a slightly different sense: it is the name given to a crank pin together with its adjacent webs and main journals. Thus Fig. 2.3.1 illustrates a single throw crankshaft.

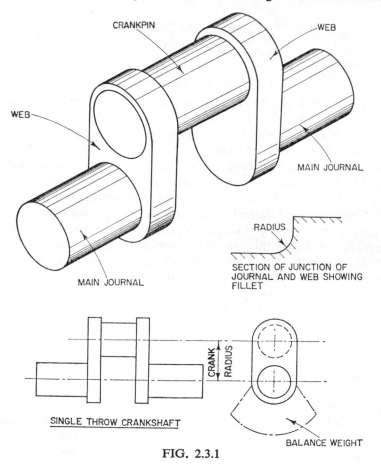

FIG. 2.3.1

Crank pins do not always have a main journal on *both* sides. Fig. 2.3.2 illustrates a *two-throw* crankshaft having only two main journals, the crank pins being connected together by a *flying web*.

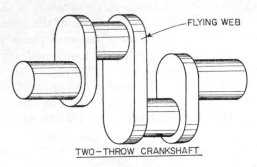

FLYING WEB

TWO–THROW CRANKSHAFT

FIG. 2.3.2

FLYWHEEL ATTACHMENT

The flywheel is usually attached to the rear end of the crankshaft. The attachment must be perfectly secure, and it should be possible to assemble the flywheel in one position only, partly because the flywheel is often marked to indicate the position of the no. 1 crank pin, but more particularly because the crankshaft and flywheel, besides being balanced separately, are also balanced as an assembly, and if the flywheel is not fitted in the same position as that in which the assembly was balanced, some imperfection of balance may arise which may cause vibration. (It is possible that the crankshaft itself may be balanced within the limits permitted, but not perfectly; the flywheel may also have a small but 'tolerable' unbalance. Should the crankshaft and flywheel be assembled so that the unbalance of the crankshaft and of the flywheel are 'additive' the resulting vibration might be eliminated by turning the flywheel through 180° on the crankshaft, and this latter position would be the 'correct' one.)

Fig. 2.3.3 illustrates one method of attaching the flywheel. The end of the crankshaft is extended, and this extension is tapered (usually 1 in 10 on diameter). A slot, called a *keyway*, is cut in the tapered part of the shaft, and a further parallel extension of the shaft, of slightly smaller diameter, is threaded to take a nut. (The end of the shaft is sometimes drilled and tapped to take a large screw instead of a nut.) The flywheel has a central boss which has a tapered hole matching the taper on the shaft, and a keyway extends the full length of this hole. The wedging effect of the tapers gives a very secure attachment and the key, which fits closely in the keyways (except at the top of the key, which must have some clearance), gives additional security and ensures correct assembly. The nut (or screw) is locked by a tab-washer or other means to prevent it coming undone.

Fig. 2.3.4 shows a more common method. A flange is formed on the end of the crankshaft which is a close fit into a counterbored

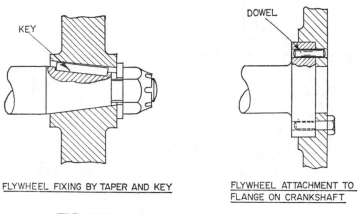

FLYWHEEL FIXING BY TAPER AND KEY

FLYWHEEL ATTACHMENT TO FLANGE ON CRANKSHAFT

FIG. 2.3.3   FIG. 2.3.4

hole in the centre of the flywheel. The flywheel is then secured by a number of screws, which pass through holes drilled axially through the face of the flywheel and screw into threaded holes in the crank-shaft flange. One or more dowels are fitted to relieve the screws of shearing loads, and the dowels, or screws, are often unevenly spaced to permit assembly in one position only. Bolts are sometimes used instead of screws; a suitable locking arrangement is provided for the nuts or screws.

OILWAYS

Engine lubrication systems are dealt with in Section 5, but it is necessary to mention here the method by which oil is supplied to the crank pins. Oil is delivered under pressure to the main bearings, where it is fed into a groove running around the bearing at about the middle of its length. A hole is drilled through the crankshaft (as shown in Fig. 2.3.5) running from the main journal, through the web to the surface of the crank pin. The main-journal end of the hole moves around the groove in the main bearing as the shaft rotates, allowing a continuous supply of oil to pass to the crank pin.

Some large crankshafts have their crank pins and journal bored out to reduce the weight of the shaft. The ends of these hollow pins and journals are usually closed by caps or plugs held in place by bolts (see Fig. 2.3.6) to prevent the escape of oil.

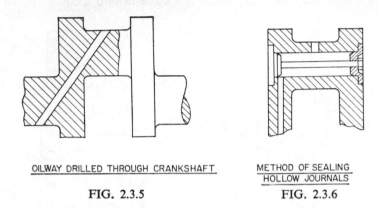

OILWAY DRILLED THROUGH CRANKSHAFT

FIG. 2.3.5

METHOD OF SEALING
HOLLOW JOURNALS

FIG. 2.3.6

OIL RETAINERS

The crankshaft projects from the rear end of the crankcase, and some of the oil which is pumped into the rear bearing to lubricate it will escape from the rear end of the bearing to the outside of the crankcase and be wasted, besides making a mess of the engine and possibly getting into the clutch where it would be very undesirable. Fig. 2.3.7(a) shows two methods of preventing this escape of oil. Immediately behind the rear journal a thin ring or fin of metal is formed around the circumference of the shaft. Oil reaching this ring from the rear bearing is flung off by centrifugal force as the shaft rotates, and is caught in a cavity from which a drain hole leads the oil back inside the crankcase.

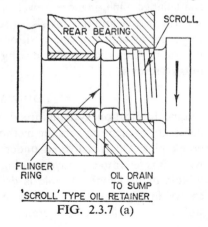

'SCROLL' TYPE OIL RETAINER

FIG. 2.3.7 (a)

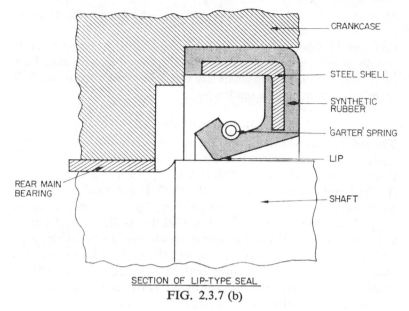

CRANKCASE

STEEL SHELL

SYNTHETIC RUBBER

'GARTER' SPRING

LIP

SHAFT

REAR MAIN BEARING

SECTION OF LIP-TYPE SEAL

FIG. 2.3.7 (b)

Behind this flinger ring a square-section helical groove or scroll, rather like a coarse screw thread, is machined in the surface of the shaft. The outer surface of the shaft has a small clearance inside an extension of the rear bearing housing, and any oil which reaches this part of the shaft will tend to be dragged round with the shaft but at the same time be held back by the stationary housing: as a result the oil will be drawn along the groove, the *hand* of which is such as to return it to the *inside* of the crankcase. In most cases both the methods illustrated and described are used on the crankshaft: sometimes only one may be considered sufficient.

Fig. 2.3.7(b) shows a section of a *lip-type* seal. Seals of this type have been used for many years in axles and gearboxes and are finding increasing use at both ends of the crankshaft. The seal consists of a specially shaped synthetic rubber ring supported by a steel shell and fitting into a recess in the crankcase or timing case. The ring has a shaped *lip* which is held in light contact with the shaft by a *garter spring*. This type of seal usually replaces both the scroll and the flinger ring.

CLUTCH SHAFT SPIGOT BEARING

The power developed by the engine is transmitted through the clutch to the gearbox, and the shaft on which the driven part of the clutch is fitted is usually supported at its forward end in a bearing in the rear end of the crankshaft. This bearing, called a *spigot bearing*, usually consists simply of a bronze bush pressed into an axial hole in the rear end of the crankshaft (see Fig. 2.3.8), but sometimes a ball or roller bearing may be used.

FRONT END OF SHAFT

The mechanism which operates the valves is driven from the crankshaft by gears or chains, and the drive is usually taken from the front end of the shaft, although in a few cases it is taken from the flywheel end. The front end of the shaft is extended beyond the front main journal, the extension being parallel or sometimes *stepped*—i.e. the forward part is of slightly smaller diameter than the rearward part. On to this extension are pressed the *timing gear* which drives the valve mechanism, and the pulley which drives the fan, water pump and dynamo: both are located on the shaft by *Woodruffe keys*. They are secured by a nut or screw threaded onto or into the end of the shaft: the nut or screw is sometimes provided with 'dogs' or claws with which a starting handle can be engaged (see Fig. 2.3.9).

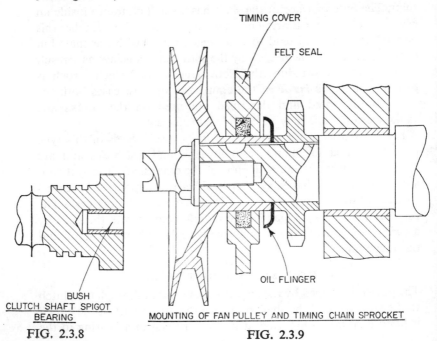

BUSH
CLUTCH SHAFT SPIGOT
BEARING

FIG. 2.3.8

MOUNTING OF FAN PULLEY AND TIMING CHAIN SPROCKET

FIG. 2.3.9

The timing gear is enclosed inside a cover called the *timing case*, but the pulley is outside this case. Oil-retaining arrangements, similar to those at the rear, are provided at this point, though the oil flinger is usually a separate part gripped between the timing gear and pulley bosses, and the scroll is formed on a rearward extension of the pulley boss.

Fig. 2.3.9 illustrates an alternative type of seal which consists of a felt strip packed into a groove in the timing cover and bearing on the shaft. Another alternative is a lip-type seal.

Crankshafts are invariably made of steel, but there are two alternative methods of manufacture—forging and casting.

Forging gives greater strength, but stiffness is of more importance than mere strength, and a shaft which has sufficiently large journals and webs to be stiff enough will usually have ample strength. This makes it possible to use the casting process for forming the shaft, a method which has certain advantages. It is less expensive, and produces a surface which, after machining or grinding, goes very well with the bearing surface. Not many manufacturers make their own castings or forging, but those who have their own foundry for producing the main engine body castings can also easily cast their own crankshafts.

The crankshaft casting or forging is machined and ground to give a suitable surface and accurate size of main journals, crank pins, etc. In a few cases the webs also are machined, but the general practice is to leave them rough.

In a few cases the crank pin and journal surfaces are hardened, depending upon the type of bearings in which they are to run. This is only done when absolutely necessary, since it both increases cost and makes reconditioning of worn shafts more difficult and expensive. This may be done by a process called *nitriding* which consists of heating the shaft to a temperature of about 500°C in an atmosphere of ammonia gas for several hours. During this time the surface of the steel absorbs nitrogen from the ammonia, forming a hard surface of *iron nitride*. An alternative method of hardening is an electrical process called *induction hardening*.

Crankshafts for Multi-cylinder Engines
These will be described in chapter 10, which deals with multi-cylinder engines.

CONNECTING RODS

GENERAL DESIGN

Fig. 2.4.1 shows a simple connecting rod. Owing to limitations of space inside the piston, the end which fits on the gudgeon pin is smaller than that which fits on the crankshaft, and these ends are called the *small-end* and *big-end* respectively.

The load due to gas pressure on the piston has a buckling effect on the shank of the rod: in the direction of the crankshaft axis this tendency to buckle is resisted by the support provided by the gudgeon pin and the crankshaft, but no such support is provided to counteract buckling sideways. The shank of the rod is therefore generally made of H section, which gives the greatest possible resistance to sideways buckling, without excessive weight.

THE BIG-END

The connecting rod shown in Fig. 2.4.1 has a one-piece or *solid-eye* big-end. This can only be used if the crankshaft is of *built-up* construction, i.e. if the shaft is made in sections assembled and suitably fixed together, allowing the big-end to be slipped over the end of the crank pin before the shaft is assembled. While this practice was once common in single-cylinder motor-cycle engines and has even been used in a few multi-cylinder car engines it is much heavier and more expensive than the usual one-piece crankshaft construction described in chapter 3, and is seldom or never used in modern motor-vehicle engines.

It is therefore necessary to split the big-end across the centre of the crank pin and bolt the two halves together after assembly onto the crank pin. The detachable portion is called the *big-end cap*. The bolts used are of *high-tensile steel*: their heads are specially formed to prevent their rotating while the nuts are being tightened, and the nuts are usually locked by split pins, tab-washers, or some other arrangement.

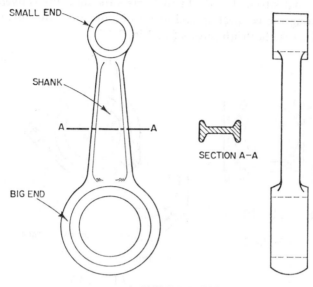

A SIMPLE CONNECTING ROD

FIG. 2.4.1

Whenever possible the split is made at right angles to the length of the connecting rod (Fig. 2.4.2), as this gives the best combination of lightness and strength. The piston and connecting rod are usually assembled together and the assembly then placed in position in the engine, either by passing the connecting rod through the cylinder from the top end, or entering the piston into the cylinder from the lower end. The removal of the piston and connecting rod assembly is made in the reverse way. If the crankshaft is in position it is often impossible to get the piston past the crankshaft, especially if the shaft has balance weights; and though it would be quite practicable for the engine manufacturer to insert the pistons and connecting rods before fitting the crankshaft into its bearings, it is often necessary during repair work to remove one or more pistons; if the crankshaft also had to be removed just for this, a great deal of extra work would be needed.

On many modern high-speed engines the size of the crank pins required to give the crankshaft the necessary stiffness makes the

big-end so large that it is impossible for the connecting rod to be
assembled or withdrawn through the cylinder if the big-end is split
at right angles to its length. In such cases the difficulty is overcome
by splitting the connecting rod at an oblique angle and fixing the
two parts together with screws (see Fig. 2.4.3).

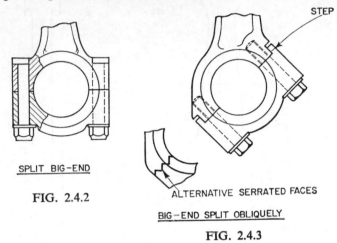

SPLIT BIG-END

FIG. 2.4.2

ALTERNATIVE SERRATED FACES

BIG-END SPLIT OBLIQUELY

FIG. 2.4.3

At high engine speeds large inertia forces act on the piston and
impose loads on the connecting rod, tensile around t.d.c. and compressive around b.d.c. When the big-end is split perpendicularly the
inertia forces around t.d.c. impose high tensile loads on the big-end
bolts. On the other hand, when the rod is split obliquely, the forces
also tend to slide the cap sideways across the rod, and impose heavy
shearing loads in addition to the tensile loads on the screws securing
the cap. To relieve the screws of these shearing loads the joint faces
of the rod and cap have steps machined in them (see Fig. 2.4.3).
Alternatively the joint faces may be serrated.

Big-end Bearing

To provide a suitable bearing surface to run on the steel crank pin,
the inside surface of the big-end eye is lined with a thin coating of
a special *bearing metal*. This is described in Section 6.

SMALL-END

The construction of the small-end of the connecting rod varies
according to the method of securing the gudgeon pin, which may

either be fixed in the small-end or free to move. In the latter case a solid-eye small-end is used, and this is generally lined by a bronze bush pressed in. One or more oil holes are drilled from the top of the rod to allow oil to reach the bearing surface: in some cases a hole is drilled, through a thickening of the web of the shank, to carry oil from the big-end to the small-end under pressure from the big-end. A bushed solid-eye small-end is shown in Fig. 2.4.4.

If the gudgeon pin is fixed in the small-end it is usually done in one of the two ways illustrated in Fig. 2.4.5, (a) being the more

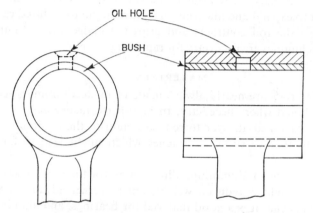

CONNECTING ROD SMALL-END, FOR FULLY-FLOATING GUDGEON PIN

FIG. 2.4.4

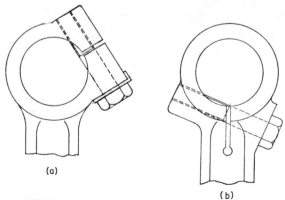

METHODS OF CLAMPING GUDGEON PIN IN SMALL-END

FIG. 2.4.5

common. The screw is arranged so that a small groove must be made in the surface of the gudgeon pin to allow the screw to be fitted; this provides positive endwise location of the pin independently of the clamping action of the screw, besides ensuring correct assembly. The screw is locked after tightening by some method such as the tab-washer illustrated in Fig. 2.4.5.

In many engines a third method of securing the semi-floating gudgeon pin is adopted. This consists of making the pin an inter-ference fit in the unbushed solid-eye of the connecting rod small-end. Assembly is usually carried out by heating the small-end of the rod causing it to expand and allowing the gudgeon pin to be fitted easily. On cooling the rod contracts and grips the gudgeon pin securely. Special techniques are necessary for removing the pin.

MATERIALS

Connecting rods are nearly always made from steel forgings, accur-ately machined where necessary. In high-performance engines they are often machined all over to reduce weight to the minimum, and polished to remove surface scratches which might lead to fatigue failure.

In a few cases an aluminium alloy is used for the rods. The main advantage sought is reduced weight, but a further advantage with aluminium is that it is a good material for bearings, and aluminium rods can be used without any bush in the small-end or lining in the big-end. (A lined big-end is usually—but not always—used with aluminium alloy rods.)

PISTONS, RINGS AND GUDGEON PINS

THE PISTON: MAIN FEATURES

Fig. 2.5.1 shows the main features of a piston. The *crown* forms the upper surface on which the gas pressure acts, and the force due to this pressure is equal to the cross-sectional area of the cylinder multiplied by the gas pressure. This force, which acts along the centre-line of the cylinder, is transmitted through the structure of the piston to the *gudgeon pin bosses* and thence through the *gudgeon pin* to the connecting rod.

During the greater part of the stroke the connecting rod operates at an angle to the centre-line of the cylinder. This causes a side force to be applied by the piston to the cylinder wall (Fig. 2.5.2), and it is necessary to provide bearing surfaces on the piston to carry this side force: these bearing surfaces are formed on the *skirt*.

To allow the piston to move freely in the cylinder it must have some clearance. This in turn allows gas to leak from the combustion chamber past the piston. Since the greatest leakage occurs when pressures are highest and the gas is hottest, much of the oil film lubricating the piston will be burnt away or carbonised. After combustion the gases contain water vapour, carbon dioxide and, probably, small amounts of sulphur dioxide which may contaminate the lubricating oil and lead to corrosion of the engine parts. To reduce the leakage as much as possible *piston rings* are fitted into grooves formed on the piston just below the crown.

The crown of the piston is directly exposed to the full heat of the burning gases during combustion. These gases are still extremely hot during the power and exhaust strokes: the piston absorbs a great deal of heat from these hot gases and will reach a very high temperature unless heat is removed from the piston quickly enough to keep its temperature within reasonable limits. The piston can pass this heat on to the cylinder walls through the piston rings and skirt, and it can do this better if the metal of which the piston is made is a good conductor of heat.

Most metals expand with a rise in temperature, and since the piston gets hotter than the cylinder (which can be cooled more effectively), under running conditions it will expand more and the clearance between cylinder and piston will become smaller as the engine parts heat up. Thus, the clearance allowed when the engine is assembled must be large enough to allow for the decrease in

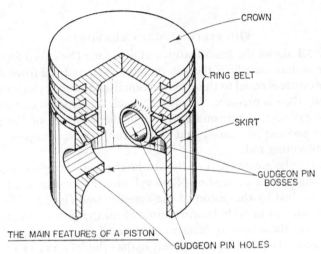

THE MAIN FEATURES OF A PISTON

FIG. 2.5.1

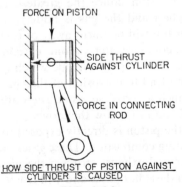

HOW SIDE THRUST OF PISTON AGAINST
CYLINDER IS CAUSED

FIG. 2.5.2

clearance which occurs at running temperature, and the material used for the piston should preferably have a low coefficient of thermal expansion. Large clearances allow excessive side-to-side movement of the piston as the crank passes the dead centres and the connecting-rod angle changes, and this causes a noise called *piston slap*, which is objectionable.

MATERIALS

Cast iron Early engines had pistons made of cast iron. This has good strength and hardness at operating temperatures and forms a good bearing surface against the cylinder wall. But it is relatively heavy, rather brittle and liable to develop cracks, and is not a particularly good conductor of heat. It has a coefficient of expansion comparable with that of the cylinder, allowing quite small clearances to be used when cold, thus avoiding slap.

Aluminium This material was first used for pistons by W. O. Bentley in a D.F.P. car which he was using for racing and record-breaking towards the end of 1913, and he subsequently pioneered its use in aero-engines during the 1914–18 War. In its pure state aluminium is relatively soft and weak, and the alloy originally used contained 12% copper. Since that time great improvements have been made in the properties of aluminium alloys for pistons.

The main advantages resulting from the use of aluminium alloys for pistons are:

(1) Improved thermal conductivity, which makes for lower piston crown temperatures. This in turn causes less heating of the fresh mixture during the induction stroke, so that the mixture filling the cylinder is cooler and denser, leading to improved power output.

(2) Reduced mass of the piston due to the lower density of aluminium, permitting the engine to run at higher speed and so develop more power.

(3) Because of its lower melting point it can be cast in steel moulds or *dies*. This gives greater accuracy of casting and reduced costs if the pistons are made in large numbers.

(4) Aluminium alloys are usually softer than cast iron and are easier to machine.

The chief disadvantages are:

(1) Greater coefficient of thermal expansion. This necessitates the use of larger clearances when cold, resulting in piston slap.

This can be minimised by special construction of the piston skirt and by the use of alloys which have a relatively low coefficient of expansion.

(2) Aluminium is not as strong as cast iron, particularly at high temperatures. It is thus necessary to use a greater thickness of metal to avoid distortion under load. Whilst this reduces the saving of mass resulting from its lower density, it does increase the ability of the piston to conduct heat.

(3) Aluminium is also softer than cast iron, especially at high temperatures; this may lead to excessive wear of the ring grooves. Improved alloys have been developed and in some cases other methods have been adopted to overcome this difficulty.

(4) Aluminium is more expensive than cast iron, though this is to some extent offset by its greater ease of casting and machining.

Magnesium This metal is lighter than aluminium but in other respects it is inferior and is more expensive. A few engines have used magnesium alloy pistons but its use has never been extensive, and it is now seldom or never used.

Composite construction Attempts to combine the low weight and good heat conductivity of aluminium with the small clearances when cold permissible with cast iron or steel resulted in a two-piece construction in which the crown and gudgeon-pin bosses were made of aluminium and the skirt of cast iron or steel. This construction seems now to be obsolete.

PISTON DETAILS

The Crown

In its simplest form the crown is flat and at right angles to the cylinder axis, and this involves only the simplest of machining operations.

In some cases the crown is slightly *dished* (Fig. 2.5.3). One reason for this is to make possible the use of higher compression ratios,

CONCAVE PISTON CROWN

FIG. 2.5.3

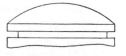

DOMED PISTON CROWN

FIG. 2.5.4

should this become desirable, simply by reducing or eliminating the 'dish'. It is sometimes done to provide a particular form of combustion chamber.

Certain designs of combustion chamber require the piston crown to be made a particular shape, such as the *domed* crown (Fig. 2.5.4).

Note that, whatever the shape of the crown, the effective force on the piston due to gas pressure is always given by multiplying the pressure by the cross-sectional area of the cylinder bore; i.e. if $b=$ cylinder bore in inches and $P=$ gas pressure in lbf/in², then:

$$\text{effective force on piston} = \frac{\pi b^2 P}{4} \text{ lbf}$$

Or, if $b=$ cylinder bore in millimetres and $P=$ gas pressure in newtons per square metre, then

$$\text{effective force on piston} = \frac{\pi b^2 P}{4\,000\,000} \text{ N}$$

$$\text{which may also be written } \frac{\pi b^2 P}{4 \times 10^6} \text{ N}$$

The Ring Belt

It is most important that this part of the piston be accurately made. In particular, each ring groove should lie in a plane at right angles to the cylinder axis. This part of the piston is generally given more clearance in the cylinder than the skirt, and does not normally bear against the cylinder. The *ridges* which separate the grooves are called *lands*.

There are usually three or four of these grooves above the skirt, and often one in the skirt below the gudgeon pin. These are discussed in greater detail on pages 69 and 70 in connection with piston rings.

Gudgeon-pin Bosses

These must be connected to the piston crown in such a way that the loads which result from gas pressure are transmitted from crown to gudgeon pin without any possibility of distortion of the piston. The bosses are usually connected directly to the crown by substantial struts or thick webs.

It is also important that the gudgeon-pin holes should be bored accurately and with an extremely fine surface finish.

The Skirt

The simplest form of this is illustrated in Fig. 2.5.1, in which the skirt forms a downward tubular extension below the ring belt: this arrangement is called a *solid skirt*. It is the strongest form of skirt and is always used for engines where the loads on the piston are particularly great.

To permit the use of small clearances with aluminium alloy pistons when cold, special types of skirt construction are used which involve some degree of flexibility of the skirt. For example, the skirt may be almost completely separated from the ring belt except at the gudgeon-pin bosses, and split down one side. This allows it to fit in the cylinder with very little clearance when cold; expansion due to rise in temperature is taken up by reducing the width of the split. The split usually extends the full length of the skirt and is at a slight angle, to avoid leaving a ridge on the cylinder as wear occurs.

Diametral expansion is sometimes even further controlled by casting plates of a special alloy steel which has an extremely low coefficient of expansion (*Invar* steel) into the gudgeon-pin bosses so that these plates connect opposite sides of the piston skirt and limit expansion in a direction at right angles to the gudgeon pin.

The split sometimes extends for only half the length of the skirt, either the upper or lower half.

PISTON CLEARANCE

The clearance left between the cylinder and piston when the engine is assembled will depend upon the metal of which the piston is made and the size and design of the piston. For any particular engine the manufacturer's workshop manual should be consulted, but the table below gives some guide to the clearances that may be expected.

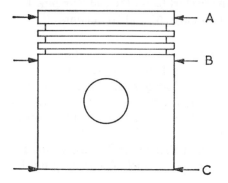

Type and Material	Approximate clearance					
	inches per inch dia.			microns per mm dia		
	A	B	C	A	B	C
Cast Iron	0·0035	0·0010	0·0008	3·50	1·00	0·80
Aluminium, solid skirt	0·0060	0·0015	0·0025	6·00	1·50	1·25
Aluminium, split skirt	0·0060	0·0008	0·0006	6·00	0·80	0·60

N.B. When assembling split-skirt pistons it is important that the split side of the skirt is on that side which bears against the cylinder during the compression stroke, so that the unsplit—and stronger—side takes the greater side-thrust during the power stroke.

PISTON RINGS

It was mentioned on page 63 that the purpose of these is to prevent gas leakage through the clearance which must be left between piston and cylinder to allow the piston to move freely.

Fig. 2.5.5 shows the main features of a piston ring: it is rectangular in section, and the *nominal diameter* is the diameter of the cylinder into which it is to fit. (This is measured on the ring with the gap

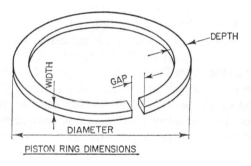

PISTON RING DIMENSIONS

FIG. 2.5.5

closed, using a steel tape which is passed around the ring and pulled tight.) A radial cut is made in the ring so that it can be placed in position in the groove on the piston. When in position in the cylinder the gap between the ends of the ring, called the *working gap*, needs to be large enough to ensure that the ends of the ring do not actually touch, however hot the ring may get. When out of the cylinder the actual diameter of the ring is larger than its nominal diameter. The gap, now called the *free gap*, is also larger than the working gap: this ensures that when in position in the cylinder the ring will exert an outward pressure against the wall of the cylinder along its whole circumference.

Fig. 2.5.6 shows a section of the ring in position in its groove and filling the clearance between the cylinder wall and piston. The depth of the ring should be slightly less than the depth of the groove, to ensure that side forces acting on the piston are transferred to the cylinder via the bearing surfaces on the skirt and not through the piston rings, and also to ensure that the clearance between the inner surface of the ring and the bottom of the ring groove is not less than the correct piston clearance.

The width of the ring must also be slightly less than the width of the groove, to ensure that the ring will be perfectly free to move about in its groove. If the ring is too close a fit in its groove it is liable to become securely stuck by carbonised oil after a period of use.

Fig. 2.5.6 shows that the ring has a rectangular cross-section. In some cases this is slightly modified in one of three ways:

(1) The *outer surface* of the ring is given a slight taper towards the top (about 1°). The purpose of this is to speed up the 'bedding in' process when the ring is new (Fig. 2.5.7(a)).

(2) The *top inner corner* of the ring is cut away, leaving the cross-section of the ring like a thick letter L. This serves the same purpose as the taper-faced ring above (Fig. 2.5.7(b)).

(3) The *top outer corner* of the ring is cut away (Fig. 2.5.7(c)). This ring should be used when new top rings are fitted to worn cylinders. The cut-away portion avoids contact with the ridge which develops at the upper limit of ring travel in a worn cylinder.

Oil-control or Scraper Rings

The piston rings so far described are fitted for the purpose of preventing the escape of gas through the clearance between cylinder and piston, and are called *compression rings*, *pressure rings* or *gas rings*. Piston rings also control the oil film on the cylinder wall, in order to permit adequate lubrication without excessive quantities of oil getting past the piston and into the combustion chamber. In the

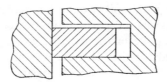

PLAIN RECTANGULAR-SECTION PISTON RING

FIG. 2.5.6

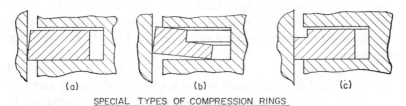

(a)　　　　　　(b)　　　　　　(c)

SPECIAL TYPES OF COMPRESSION RINGS

FIG. 2.5.7

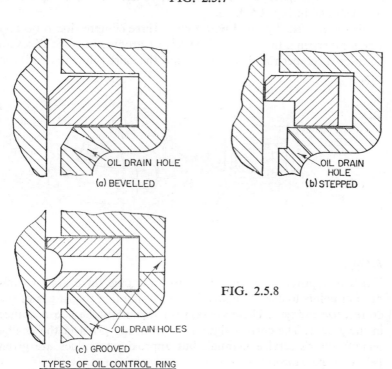

OIL DRAIN HOLE

(a) BEVELLED

OIL DRAIN HOLE

(b) STEPPED

FIG. 2.5.8

OIL DRAIN HOLES

(c) GROOVED

TYPES OF OIL CONTROL RING

combustion chamber the oil would be decomposed and partly burnt, forming deposits of carbon on the combustion chamber walls and causing smoke in the exhaust gas. Special types of ring have been developed for this purpose which are intended to glide over the oil film as the piston moves upward, but to scrape off all but a very thin film of oil on the downward stroke. Provision is made, usually by holes at the back of the ring groove or by *chamfering* the land immediately below the groove and drilling oil drain holes from this chamfer to the inside of the piston, to return oil collected by the scraper ring to the underneath of the piston. Fig. 2.5.8 shows sections of several types of oil control rings and their grooves. The bevelled scraper is the least severe in its action, the grooved type the most severe.

Another form of oil control ring consists of two narrow steel *rails* separated from one another by a specially shaped spacer and pressed into contact with the cylinder wall by an expander ring. In some cases the spacer and expander are combined into a single unit, as illustrated in Fig. 2.5.9.

Pistons are usually fitted with two or three compression rings and one scraper ring, the latter in the lowest groove. In some cases an additional scraper ring is fitted around the skirt below the gudgeon pin.

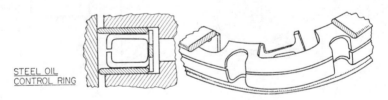

STEEL OIL
CONTROL RING

FIG. 2.5.9

Fit of Piston Rings

When new piston rings are fitted to an engine there are two important points to check—apart from ensuring that the ring is of the correct size and type. These are (a) the gap, and (b) the side clearance in the groove. The correct figures for these are given in the engine manufacturer's service manual, but approximate values are given below for guidance.

Working gap per in diameter
Water-cooled engines 0·003–·004 in
Air-cooled engines 0·004–·006 in
Side clearance in groove 0·0015 in

Or, in S.I. Units,

Working gap per mm diameter
Water-cooled engines 3–4 μm
Air-cooled engines 4–6 μm
Side clearance in groove 0·375 mm

Measurement of working gap

This gap is measured by putting the ring, removed from the piston, into its cylinder and *squaring it up* by pushing it up against the end of the piston also placed inside the cylinder. The gap between the ends of the ring is then measured by feeler gauges. If the cylinder is worn, the ring should be in the *least worn* part of the bore when this measurement is made. Too small a gap can be rectified by carefully filing or grinding one end of the ring, preferably in a special jig which ensures squareness of the ends.

Piston Ring Materials

The most important properties of the material used for piston rings are:

(1) Wear-resistance, especially—in the case of the compression rings —under conditions of somewhat scanty lubrication.

(2) Elasticity, to ensure that the ring will maintain sufficient outward pressure against the cylinder wall to maintain contact with the surface of the cylinder.

(3) These properties must not be adversely affected by the temperatures to which the ring is subjected in use.

The material which most nearly fulfils these requirements is cast iron. In some cases the wear-resistance is improved by chromium-plating the outer face of the ring by a special process, but rings of this type are normally only used for the top compression ring.

In some oil control rings the material used is steel, generally chromium plated on the edges which bear upon the cylinder wall.

GUDGEON PINS

These are of two types, depending upon the method of locating them in position. To provide the strength necessary to carry the high loads imposed upon them by gas pressure on the piston, and a wear-resistant surface, they are made of steel, usually alloyed with 3%–4% of nickel to increase toughness, and case-hardened to obtain a wear-resistant surface. Clearly the ends of the hardened pin must be prevented from rubbing against the cylinder wall—otherwise it would soon score deep grooves in the cylinder surface.

The two types of gudgeon pin are:

(1) *Semi-floating* These are securely fixed in either the piston or the connecting rod, usually the latter, as described on pages 61 and 62. Although it was at one time common practice to fix the gudgeon pin in the piston by means of a screw threaded into one of the gudgeon-pin bosses, this practice has been discarded in favour of fixing the pin in the connecting rod. Movement is therefore confined to oscillation of the pin in the piston.

(2) *Fully-floating* This type is free to turn in both piston and connecting rod, and is generally used in engines in which the loads are particularly high. The pin is shorter than the cylinder diameter and is prevented from contacting the cylinder by one of the methods illustrated in Fig. 2.5.10. The method shown at (a) consists of a spring-steel ring called a *circlip*, which is sprung

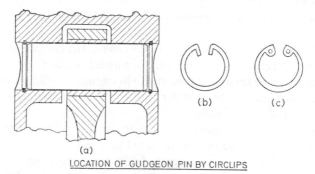

LOCATION OF GUDGEON PIN BY CIRCLIPS

FIG. 2.5.10

into a groove inside the gudgeon-pin hole after the gudgeon pin has been fitted—one at each end of the pin. The circlip is some-times made of round-section steel wire and may have its ends bent inwards as shown at (b) to make it easier to fit and remove with pointed-nose pliers. Some circlips do not have the bent-in ends: in this case the ends of the gudgeon pin are slightly chamfered as shown at (a) (this helps to prevent the circlip being forced out of its groove by endwise forces), and small notches are cut in the piston so that a pointed instrument can be inserted behind the circlip to remove it. Another type of circlip often used is the *Seeger circlip* (c) which is stamped from spring-steel sheet. Special circlip pliers are used for fitting and removing this type.

Gudgeon pins are usually made tubular to reduce weight, and when this is the case an alternative method of preventing scoring of the cylinder involves fitting mushroom-shaped pads of soft metal such as aluminium or brass. The 'stem' of the mushroom is a press fit in the bore of the gudgeon pin. This method is seldom used in modern engines.

Gudgeon Pin Fit

The gudgeon pin is usually made a tight push fit in the piston when cold: this eases off slightly when the piston reaches normal running temperature. You must not use force to remove a tightly fitting pin unless you do it very carefully, and great care must be taken to ensure that no force whatever is applied to the connecting rod, to avoid the risk of bending it. If possible, heat the piston in hot water or oil: if the piston cannot be immersed in oil or water, you can wrap rags soaked in hot water round the piston, after which the gudgeon pin can be pushed out easily without risk of damage.

A recent development is the use of an interference fit of the gudgeon pin in the small end of the connecting rod. This is in effect a semi-floating pin in which the interference fit is relied upon to hold the gudgeon pin in place. See page 62.

2.6

VALVES AND VALVE-OPERATING GEARS

THE FUNCTIONS OF VALVES

The gases enter and leave the working cylinder through ports, but these ports must be open *only* during that part of the cycle of operations when gas is required to pass through them. At all other times they must not only be closed, but closed sufficiently tightly to prevent the passage of gas at considerable pressure. *It is the function of the valves to close the ports except when they are required to be open.* (Note that in the case of two-stroke engines the ports can be closed by covering them with the piston, but a little thought will show that this method cannot be successfully used on an engine working on the four-stroke cycle.)

In performing this function the valves must

(1) make a completely gas-tight seal in the ports when closed
(2) offer no opposition to the flow of gases when open
(3) require the simplest possible mechanism to operate them
(4) operate with the minimum of friction.

TYPES OF VALVE

During the development of internal-combustion engines, several types of valve have been used. The chief of these are:

(1) *The poppet valve* This was already in use on steam engines before successful internal-combustion engines were developed, and was used on the early types of such engines. It has proved so successful that its use has continued and it is almost the only type to be used in modern engines.
(2) *The slide valve* This too was very commonly used on some early internal-combustion engines, but proved less satisfactory than the poppet valve and is now obsolete.

(3) *The sleeve valve*   Several versions of this type of valve have been used. The two most successful were the Knight and the Burt-McCullum.

The *Knight* type originated in about 1905 and consisted of a sleeve free to slide inside the cylinder with a second sleeve free to slide inside it, the piston moving within the inner sleeve. The sleeves were moved up and down inside the cylinder, and ports cut in the sleeves were arranged to uncover the cylinder ports at the correct times.

This valve was used by the Daimler Company from about 1909 until about 1933: it was also used by a number of Continental manufacturers such as Panhard, Minerva, Voisin, Peugeot and on a few Mercedes models.

The *Burt-McCullum* sleeve valve consisted of a single sleeve which was given a combination of up-and-down motion and part-rotary motion inside the cylinder, ports in the sleeve uncovering the cylinder ports at the appropriate times. This was developed in about 1909 and was first used on the Argyll car in 1911. It has also been used in a few other cars, but its greatest success has been in aircraft engines, chiefly the large engines made by the Bristol Aeroplane Co beginning about 1935. It was also used in the famous Napier 'Sabre' engine, a twenty-four-cylinder engine developing about 3500 hp, and in the last of the Rolls-Royce piston-type aero-engines, the 'Eagle', also a twenty-four-cylinder engine developing over 3000 hp.

Although these types of valve seemed to have many advantages over the cruder poppet valve they have not survived in motor-vehicle engines. Their main drawback was a relatively high oil consumption and a smoky exhaust.

(4) *The rotary valve*   Several types of rotary valve have been developed and some have given very good results. They consist of rotating 'plugs' fitted across the ports, having holes which, at the correct times, uncover the ports and allow gas to pass.

The only type of valve at present in use in motor-vehicle engines is the poppet valve and this is the only type which will be described in detail.

The Poppet Valve

A poppet valve, with its immediate attachments, is shown in

Fig. 2.6.1. The valve itself consists of a disc-shaped *head* having a *stem* extending from its centre at one side. The edge of the head on the side nearest the stem is accurately ground at an angle—usually 45° but sometimes 30°—to form the *face*. When the valve is closed, the face is pressed into contact with a similarly ground *seating* at the inner end of the port. Beyond the seating the port curves smoothly away clear of the valve.

The condition of the face and seating is of vital importance in ensuring the gas-tightness of the valve. They are ground on special machines and the valve face is sometimes *lapped in* to its seating with a very fine abrasive. Whether this is necessary or even advisable if the grinding is sufficiently accurate is often in dispute.

When, after a considerable period of use, the condition of face and seating deteriorates and allows leakage, they must be reground. Special grinding machines have been developed for this purpose.

Fig. 2.6.2 shows the face and seating in more detail. The seating is narrower than the face, to reduce the risk of trapping particles of carbon between face and seating, and to ensure a surface pressure great enough to provide a gas-tight seal. The thickness of the head indicated by the arrows is most important: a sharp edge, particularly in the case of the exhaust valve, is liable to become excessively hot and may cause '*pre-ignition*' (ignition of the mixture inside the cylinder *before* the spark occurs).

In a few cases the exhaust valve face is ground to an angle about $\frac{1}{2}$° less than the seat angle, as shown in Fig. 2.6.3. There are three reasons for this:

(1) The hottest part of the valve, under running conditions, is the stem side of the head, and the additional expansion of this side makes the face and seat angles equal at running temperatures.

(2) The exhaust valve gets very hot (often red hot when the engine is running at full throttle) and is then less strong. Under these conditions the spring load tends to cause the head to dish slightly, which can lift the inner edge of the face (nearest the combustion chamber) clear of the seating if the angles are the same when cold.

(3) It reduces the risk of trapping carbon between face and seating. In this case the face and seating cannot be lapped in.

VALVE GUIDE

The valve slides in a hole in the cylinder or cylinder head called the *valve guide*. This must be perfectly true with the seating, and a small

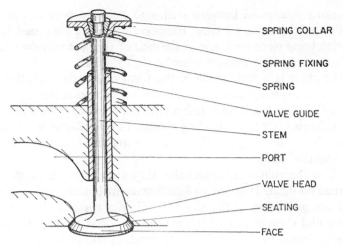

SPRING COLLAR

SPRING FIXING

SPRING

VALVE GUIDE

STEM

PORT

VALVE HEAD

SEATING

FACE

A POPPET VALVE

FIG. 2.6.1

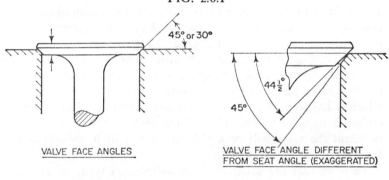

45° or 30°

VALVE FACE ANGLES

FIG. 2.6.2

44½°

45°

VALVE FACE ANGLE DIFFERENT
FROM SEAT ANGLE (EXAGGERATED)

FIG. 2.6.3

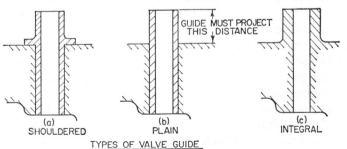

GUIDE MUST PROJECT
THIS DISTANCE

(a)
SHOULDERED

(b)
PLAIN

(c)
INTEGRAL

TYPES OF VALVE GUIDE

FIG. 2.6.4

clearance is allowed between stem and guide to prevent any possibility of the valve sticking. Excessive clearance may lead to the seating being worn oval, and in the case of the inlet valve will allow air to leak into the mixture entering the cylinder.

The guide is usually made in the form of a detachable sleeve to permit easy renewal when worn, but in some cases it is integral with the cylinder or head, since this assists the transfer of heat from the hot exhaust valve to the cooling system. In this case wear is rectified by boring or reaming out the guide slightly and fitting a valve with an 'oversize' stem.

When the guides are detachable they sometimes have a shoulder formed on them. They are an interference fit in the cylinder or head and are pressed in to the shoulder. Guides without shoulders are easier and cheaper to make: when fitting, press these in to leave a definite length projecting from the head, as shown in Fig. 2.6.4(b).

THE VALVE SPRING

The spring returns the valve to its seat after it has been opened, and holds it there (assisted by gas pressure during the compression and power strokes) until it is next opened.

The spring must be strong enough to close the valve quickly at maximum engine speeds. The spring strength needed depends upon the weight of the valve and any other part of its operating gear which it has to move, and upon the maximum speed at which the engine is required to run. If the force exerted by the spring is insufficient the valve will be *late* in closing at high rev/min and so limit maximum engine speeds.

Valve springs are usually of the *helical coil* type, as shown in Figs. 2.6.1 and 2.6.5(a). Such springs are liable to *surging* at certain engine speeds, when the centre coils vibrate in a direction parallel to the valve stem. In extreme cases this can lead to breakage of the springs, and can also allow the valves to *bounce* off their seatings after closing. This may be overcome in several ways:

(1) The springs are so designed that when the valve is fully open they are compressed until adjacent coils almost touch, so preventing the building up of excessive surging.

(2) The coils are spaced closer together at one end than the other (Fig. 2.6.5(b)). Springs of this kind must be fitted with the 'close' coils nearest the cylinder head.

(3) Two (or occasionally three) springs are used, one inside the other.

This does not prevent surging, but the two springs will not both surge at the same engine speed, and 'valve bounce' will be prevented. Also, if one spring breaks the second one will maintain pressure on the spring attachment and prevent the valve dropping into the cylinder.

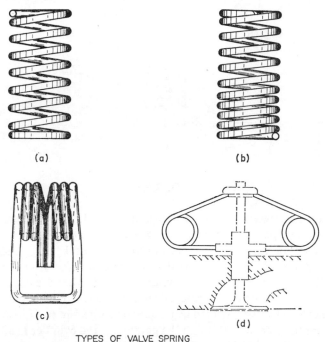

(a) (b)

(c) (d)

TYPES OF VALVE SPRING

FIG. 2.6.5

Another type of spring occasionally used is the *hairpin* spring shown in Figs. 2.6.5(c) and (d). This is not liable to surge, but is more difficult to fit into the space available.

Valve Spring Fixing

Several different methods have been used to attach the spring to the end of the valve stem. Some commonly used methods are shown in Fig. 2.6.6.

MATERIALS

The exhaust valve is exposed to the full heat of the burning gas during combustion, and when the hot gases are released from the

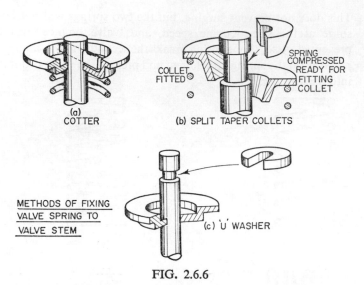

(a) COTTER

(b) SPLIT TAPER COLLETS

COLLET FITTED

SPRING COMPRESSED READY FOR FITTING COLLET

METHODS OF FIXING VALVE SPRING TO VALVE STEM

(c) 'U' WASHER

FIG. 2.6.6

cylinder they sweep past the exhaust valve head. The exhaust valve is the hottest part of the engine, and it is estimated that under full power conditions it reaches a temperature of around 650°C (1200°F). A rather special steel is required to operate satisfactorily for long periods, and alloys have been developed for this purpose containing varying amounts of manganese, silicon, nickel and chromium.

The exhaust valve is cooled by passing on its heat in two directions: (1) along the stem and through the guide into the cylinder head, and (2) directly into the cylinder head from the face to the seating when it is closed. For extreme operating conditions the valve stem is sometimes made hollow and partly filled with sodium, which is a very soft metal having a melting point of 98°C. Under running conditions it is molten, and in splashing from end to end of the valve stem it assists the transfer of heat from the hot head. This is an expensive form of construction and is only used when absolutely necessary.

Detachable valve guides are usually made of cast iron, though bronze is sometimes used, particularly for exhaust valves, because of its better heat-conducting properties.

Valve springs are made of *spring steel*. This contains about 0·6 to 0·7% carbon and usually small amounts of silicon, manganese and vanadium.

VALVE POSITION

The position of the valve in the cylinder depends upon the design of the combustion chamber which is discussed on page 113. It is sufficient for the present to list the possible positions of the valves, as follows:

(1) *Side valve or L-head*   Both valves are at one side of the cylinder, heads uppermost with the stems approximately parallel to the cylinder axis. To accommodate the valves in this position the combustion chamber is extended sideways from the top of the cylinder forming a shape similar to an inverted letter L (Fig. 2.6.7(a)). This arrangement is not used on modern engines.

(2) *Side valve or T-head*   This is like the above except that inlet and exhaust valves are fitted at opposite sides of the cylinder. This arrangement, though common on early engines, has been obsolete for many years.

(3) *Vertical overhead valves*   Both valves are fitted over the top of the cylinder with their stems approximately vertical and parallel (Fig. 2.6.7(b)), usually in a single row.

(4) *Overhead inlet and side exhaust or F-head*   The inlet valve is arranged as in (3) above and the exhaust as in (1) (Fig. 2.6.7(c)).

(5) *Inclined overhead valves*   Both valves are fitted over the top of the cylinder head, but in two rows inclined at an angle to one another (Fig. 2.6.7(d)).

VALVE-OPERATING GEAR

It has already been explained that the valves are moved to, and held in, their closed position by their springs. They are opened by *cams* carried upon one or more *camshafts,* which are driven by suitable gearing from the crankshaft. The cams do not usually act directly upon the valves since their rotary motion would impose a side force upon the end of the valve stem: to combat this side force *cam followers* are interposed betwen the cam and the valve. These followers may take one of two forms:

(1) *tappets* which rest upon the cams and are guided so as to move in a straight line, and

(2) *rockers* or levers which rock upon fixed pivots. If the cams are placed close to the ends of the valves no additional mechanism may be needed, but in the case of overhead valves this would involve a long and possibly complicated driving gear between camshaft and crankshaft. In many engines it is considered pre-

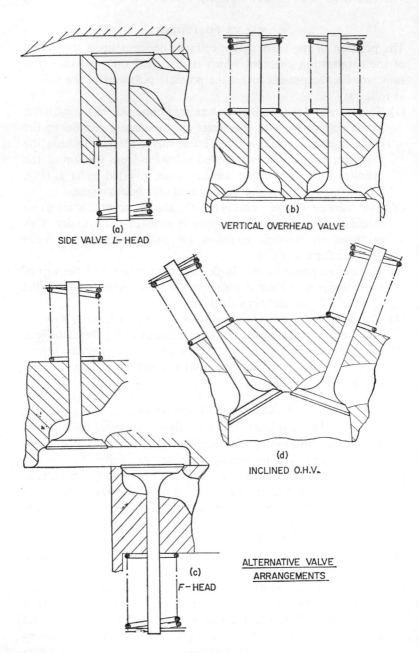

(a)
SIDE VALVE *L*-HEAD

(b)
VERTICAL OVERHEAD VALVE

(d)
INCLINED O.H.V.

(c)
F-HEAD

ALTERNATIVE VALVE
ARRANGEMENTS

FIG. 2.6.7

ferable to place the camshaft reasonably near the crankshaft, so that a short and simple driving gear can be used. In such cases the motion of the tappets is conveyed to the valves through *push rods* and overhead rockers.

VALVE CLEARANCE

A valve is closed when its face is pressed into contact with the seating by the full force of the spring.

Fig. 2.6.8 shows a simplified arrangement of valve, tappet and cam, and at (a) the valve is shown in the fully open position. As the cam rotates, the valve moves under the action of its spring (not shown) towards its closed position. At (b) a condition is shown in which the tappet has reached the *base* of the cam before the face of the valve has come into contact with the seating. Since the tappet cannot move downwards any further *the valve cannot completely close.*

At (c) the tappet is shown in the same position on the cam, but the valve face has reached the seating *before* the tappet has reached the base of the cam, leaving a gap or clearance between the end of the valve and the tappet. This is called *valve clearance* or *tappet clearance*, and it is clear that in this case the tappet cannot prevent the valve from closing properly.

There must always be a small clearance in the valve-operating gear when the valve is in its closed position *to ensure that the valve will close completely.* When the clearance is checked, allowance

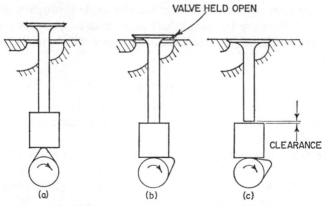

VALVE HELD OPEN

CLEARANCE

(a)   (b)   (c)

ILLUSTRATING THE NEED FOR VALVE CLEARANCE

FIG. 2.6.8

must be made for the fact that under different running conditions the amount of clearance will be altered by different temperatures—and therefore different amounts of expansion—of the valves, cylinder block and valve-operating gear. The valve clearance and the engine conditions under which it should be measured (i.e. engine hot or cold) are specified by the engine manufacturer, and it is most important that the clearance should be correct under the specified conditions. Excessive clearance will result in noisy operation and excessive wear. Too little clearance may result in the valve not fully closing under certain conditions. This causes loss of pressure in the cylinder and burnt exhaust valves (since one of the paths for the escape of heat is cut off if the valve does not close properly, and gas at a very high temperature will be forced at high speed through the gap between valve face and seating).

There is always provision for adjusting the valve clearance during assembly, usually (but not always) by means of an adjusting screw. In most cases the clearance should be checked at intervals to ensure that it has not been altered by wear.

It is often assumed that the valve clearance is decreased as the engine becomes hotter, but this is by no means always the case. It is suggested that students should themselves check the valve clearances of a number of engines both hot and cold, and note the results.

It should be noted that incorrect clearance will affect the angle of the cam at the instant the valve leaves or returns to its seat. Excessive clearance will cause the valve to leave its seat *later* and return to it *earlier* in terms of cam rotation: i.e. the angle through which the cam—and therefore the crankshaft also—rotates while the valve is open will be *shortened*. Insufficient clearance will have the reverse effect.

CAMS AND CAMSHAFTS

A cam is a component so shaped that by its rotation it causes another part in contact with it to move in a different manner. There are very many types of cams in use in all manner of machines.

The type of cam used to operate the valves of a motor-vehicle engine is a relatively simple one such as is illustrated in Fig. 2.6.9. The cam follower remains stationary during that part of the cam's rotation when it rests upon the *base circle*, and its 'lift' begins at the point where the *opening flank* joins the base circle. At the *peak* of the cam the lift is maximum, and the follower falls as the *closing*

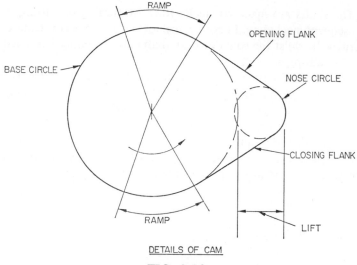

RAMP

OPENING FLANK

BASE CIRCLE

NOSE CIRCLE

CLOSING FLANK

RAMP

LIFT

DETAILS OF CAM

FIG. 2.6.9

flank passes beneath it. By the time it is again in contact with the base circle at the end of the closing flank it will have returned to its original position.

In some engines there may be fairly large variations of clearance under different running temperatures, and to ensure quiet operation even when the clearances are large the flanks are joined to the base circle by *ramps* which extend over about 30° of cam rotation. When checking valve clearances it is most important that the cam follower should be resting on the base circle of the cam. One way of ensuring this is to turn the engine to the position where the valve whose clearance is to be adjusted is *at full lift*, and then turn the engine *one complete revolution*. A simpler method is to note that in most multi-cylinder engines (see chapter 10) the pistons are arranged to move up and down together in pairs, so that if one of a pair is moving, say, upwards on its exhaust stroke, the other will also be moving upwards but on its compression stroke. Thus, to get any valve in the correct position for adjusting its clearance, *turn the engine to the position where the corresponding valve in the other cylinder of the pair is at maximum lift.*

All the cams for an engine are usually formed on a single shaft called the *camshaft*, although in some cases separate shafts may be used for the inlet and exhaust valves.

The shafts are made of steel, either by forging or casting, with subsequent machining. Forged camshafts usually have the cams case-hardened, whilst the cams of cast shafts are generally hardened by *chilling* during casting.

The camshafts are carried in suitable bearings. These are usually plain bearings, but in some cases ball or roller bearings may be used. In most engines the shaft is moved into position from the front end of the engine, and to enable this to be done the bearings are larger than the cams. The shaft is located endwise by some such arrangement as that shown in Fig. 2.6.10, which also shows one of the methods used to secure the camshaft driving gear.

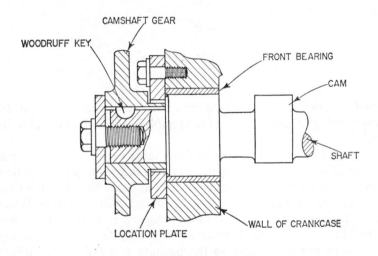

ATTACHMENT OF CAMSHAFT TIMING GEAR

FIG. 2.6.10

CAMSHAFT DRIVES

In an engine working on the four-stroke cycle each valve must open once every two revolutions of the crankshaft, which makes it necessary for the camshaft to rotate at half crankshaft speed. In the majority of engines the camshaft is fitted in the crankcase quite close to the crankshaft, so that a short and simple driving gear can be used. The usual arrangement consists of a chain running over sprockets fitted on the crankshaft and camshaft, the latter have twice as many teeth as the former to provide the two-to-one speed reduction (Fig. 2.6.11(a)).

It was at one time common practice to drive the camshaft by spur gears, a gear keyed to the crankshaft engaging with one twice its size on the camshaft, sometimes with an intermediate *idler* gear. This arrangement is still used, though it is rather rare (Fig. 2.6.11(b)). The camshaft is sometimes carried on the cylinder head. While this gives the advantage of reducing the weight of the valve-operating mechanism, permitting better functioning at high rev/min, it involves a longer and more complex driving arrangement for the camshaft, and one in which allowance must be made for expansion of the engine structure as it warms up in use. Chain drive is the most common, and sometimes the drive is arranged in two stages. Fig. 2.6.11(c) shows a single-stage chain drive to a single overhead camshaft. Fig. 2.6.11(d) shows a two-stage drive, the first stage being by spur gears which incorporate the two-to-one reduction. In both cases a *Weller* tensioner, consisting of a curved spring-steel blade bearing against the 'slack' side of the chain, is used to maintain chain tension constant although the distance between camshaft and crankshaft may vary because of cylinder-block expansion. The fibre pad prevents noise and damps 'flutter'.

Fig. 2.6.11(e) illustrates an arrangement of the chain drive to twin overhead camshafts. In a few cases an all-gear drive is used, whilst another alternative is bevel or skew gears and vertical shafts. Another alternative worth mentioning is the *eccentric and coupling strap* arrangement, which has been used on several engines, though it is by no means common.

Fig. 2.6.11(f) illustrates a type of camshaft drive which is coming into increasing favour. Belt drive cannot normally be used for camshafts because 'belt slip' would occur and the correct timing of the valves would be lost. The notches on this type of belt and pulleys prevent slip occurring.

In the case of overhead-camshaft engines the drive to the camshaft (or shafts) must be disconnected whenever the cylinder head is removed, and arrangements are usually made so that the correct valve timing is automatically obtained on reassembly.

When connecting up the camshaft drive the valves must be *timed* so that they open and close at the correct positions of the crankshaft. The cams are made so that if the opening point is correct the closing point will be correct also. The timing of the valves can usually be

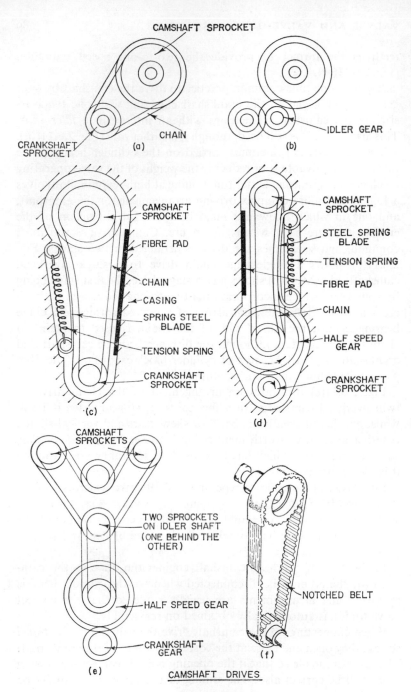

CAMSHAFT DRIVES

FIG. 2.6.11

adjusted in steps of one tooth of the gear or sprocket, but sometimes a *Vernier* device is used to provide a finer adjustment.

TAPPETS

As mentioned on page 83 tappets are one form of cam follower, and some common types of tappet are shown in Fig. 2.6.12; (a) and (b) show *barrel* type tappets, which are made of cast iron, the bottom surface being *chilled* in the casting process to provide a hard surface bearing against the cam. They are hollow and usually have 'windows' which help to reduce weight and assist lubrication. The tappet shown at (a) is suitable for a side valve and has a hardened adjusting screw to adjust the valve clearance. That shown at (b) is suitable for an o.h.v. engine and operates a push rod, the lower end of which is located in the small hollow formed inside the base of the tappet. Both these types of tappet operate directly in the cylinder block.

Fig. 2.6.12(c) shows an older type of tappet for a side-valve engine. This type is usually made of steel and is carried in a detachable tappet block attached to the cylinder block by screws.

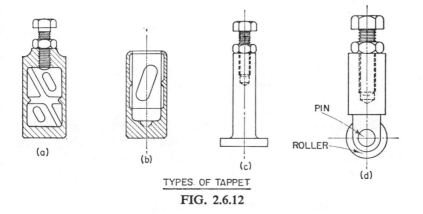

(a) (b) (c) (d)

TYPES. OF TAPPET

FIG. 2.6.12

These three types of tappet, and all tappets having a flat base, are used with cams which have convex curved flanks. Some cams have straight flanks, and these operate on followers having curved ends. In some cases the tappet has a roller rotating on a pin, as shown in Fig. 2.6.12(d). This type is now seldom used, since for high-speed engines the roller must revolve much more rapidly round the flanks

and nose than it does around the base circle, and at high engine
speeds the angular accelerations of the roller involved are greater
than can be achieved, and a considerable amount of skidding occurs.
This being so, the more expensive roller construction might just as
well be dispensed with and a plain rounded tappet base substituted.
An additional weakness of this roller type is the pin, which is subjected to high shearing loads: increasing the pin diameter to make it
stronger raises the rubbing speed between pin and roller, and little
is gained compared with a plain tappet. For low-speed engines,
however, a roller tappet may have advantages.

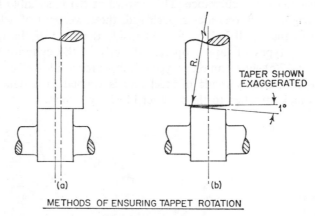

METHODS OF ENSURING TAPPET ROTATION

FIG. 2.6.13

Flat-based tappets are usually allowed to rotate in their guides;
indeed they are encouraged to do so since this reduces the rubbing
speed between cam and tappet and spreads the wear over the whole
of the tappet base. Rotation of the tappet is encouraged by offsetting
the tappet from the centre-line of the cam (Fig. 2.6.13(a)) or by
grinding the cams with a very slight taper (about 1°) in which case
the foot of the tappet is ground very slightly convex, forming part of
a sphere of large radius R (Fig. 2.6.13(b)). Roller tappets and curved-
ended tappets must not, of course, rotate on their axes, and some
means of positively preventing rotation must be provided, such as
an axial groove in the tappet engaging a fixed peg in the guide
(Fig. 2.6.14(a)) or a slotted extension to the guide engaging flats on
the tappet foot (Fig. 2.6.14(b)).

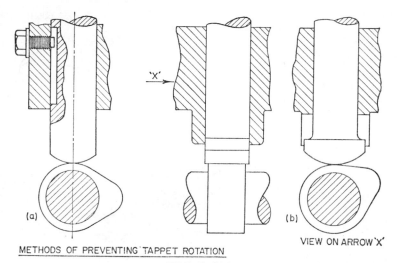

(a)

(b)

VIEW ON ARROW 'X'

METHODS OF PREVENTING TAPPET ROTATION

FIG. 2.6.14

ROCKERS AND PUSH RODS

Rockers are sometimes used instead of tappets between camshaft and valve, with either a side camshaft or an overhead camshaft arrangement. Valve clearance may be adjusted by a hardened screw in the rocker, or by mounting the rocker pivot (or the bush) eccentrically. Fig. 2.6.15 illustrates two types. In Fig. 2.6.15(a) an adjusting screw is shown as the means of adjusting the valve clearance. In the arrangement shown in Fig. 2.6.15(b) the eccentric bush is a close fit in the rocker, but can be rotated in the rocker by a hexagonal flange at one end. The other end of the bush is threaded, and the bush is locked in the rocker by tightening a nut on this threaded end. To adjust the clearance, slacken the nut, rotate the bush to give the correct clearance, and re-tighten the nut.

Most modern engines have overhead valves operated by a camshaft in the crankcase, close to the crankshaft. This arrangement necessitates the use of push rods and overhead rockers to transmit the motion from the tappets to the valves, the usual arrangement being as illustrated in Fig. 2.6.16(a). The rockers pivot on a common rocker spindle supported in pillars attached to the cylinder head, and the rockers are spaced apart on the spindle by distance pieces, or springs, or both. Valve clearance is adjusted by a hardened ball-ended screw in the end of the rocker, the screw fitting into a small cup formed in the top end of the push rod; the cup retains oil to

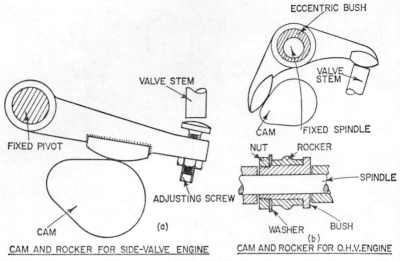

VALVE STEM

FIXED PIVOT

ADJUSTING SCREW

CAM

(a)

CAM AND ROCKER FOR SIDE-VALVE ENGINE

ECCENTRIC BUSH

VALVE STEM

CAM   FIXED SPINDLE

NUT   ROCKER

SPINDLE

WASHER   BUSH
(b)

CAM AND ROCKER FOR O.H.V.ENGINE

FIG. 2.6.15

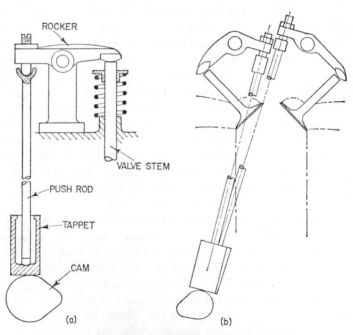

ROCKER

VALVE STEM

PUSH ROD

TAPPET

CAM

(a)

(b)

PUSH-ROD OPERATION OF OVERHEAD VALVES

FIG. 2.6.16

ensure lubrication at this point. The lower end of the push rod is ball-ended and is located in a cup formed in the tappet. The push rod may be made of a solid steel rod, the two ends being suitably 'formed' from the rod iself. Alternatively the push rod may be tubular, of either steel or aluminium alloy, with separate hardened steel ends pressed on.

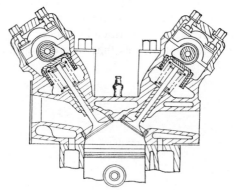

TWIN OVERHEAD CAMSHAFT OPERATION OF VALVES
IN A HEMISPHERICAL COMBUSTION CHAMBER

FIG. 2.6.17(a)

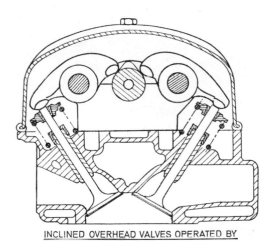

INCLINED OVERHEAD VALVES OPERATED BY
A SINGLE OVERHEAD CAMSHAFT

FIG. 2.6.17(b)

The rocker is usually made from a steel forging, but is sometimes formed from a steel pressing, and some are made in a special type of cast steel.

When the valves are arranged as shown in Fig. 2.6.7(d), it is generally preferred to operate them by a camshaft immediately over each row of valves, as illustrated in Fig. 2.6.17(a), or by a single overhead camshaft and rockers as shown in Fig. 2.6.17(b). Sometimes, however, a designer may prefer to retain the advantages of a camshaft mounted in the crankcase close to the crankshaft, in which case the valves may be operated by a more complicated system of push rods and rockers such as that shown in Fig. 2.6.16(b).

2.7

THE CYLINDER BLOCK
AND CRANKCASE

Once the early motor vehicle engines had developed beyond the
initial experimental stage, design settled down to a type which had
up to four or even more separate cylinders mounted upon a separate
crankcase. This arrangement was probably dictated by the limitations imposed by the foundry practice and machine tools then
available, which made complicated castings difficult to produce and
to machine. Furthermore, bearing in mind the unreliability of early
engines, it was no doubt thought desirable to be able to get at any
individual piston without having to disturb too much of the engine.
The cylinders, which had to resist wear from the pistons and valves,
were made of cast iron, whilst the crankcase was generally made of
aluminium to save weight. (It should be remembered that at the
beginning of this century aluminium was a relatively new metal and
the art of alloying it with other metals to improve its properties had
not been developed to anything like its present state.)

As manufacturing techniques improved, it became possible to
cast and machine cylinders in *blocks* of two, three or four, and it
eventually became the practice to cast up to six or even eight cylinders
in one block, but still separate from the crankcase.

This arrangement of having all the cylinders of an engine in one
casting was known as *monobloc* construction: its chief merits compared with the previous practice of having separate cylinders were:
(1) a reduction in the number of machining operations, (2) simplification of assembly, and (3) (most important), increased rigidity of
the engine structure.

Carried to its logical conclusion, this development brings us to the
arrangement, now almost universal, in which the cylinders and
crankcase are contained in a single casting which forms the main

structure of the engine. Fig. 2.7.1 illustrates the cylinder block and crankcase for four-cylinder engine. The chief advantages gained by this construction are: (1) it provides the greatest possible rigidity of the engine structure, (2) it reduces machining and assembly operations to the minimum, and (3) it reduces cost (for the reasons given in (2)).

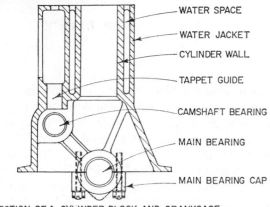

SECTION OF A CYLINDER BLOCK AND CRANKCASE

FIG. 2.7.1

The arrangement has, of course, some disadvantages, the chief being that it makes a large and heavy component, particularly on large engines, which may necessitate lifting-tackle to hand it in the factory and workshop.

Early engines usually had the cylinders made with integral cylinder heads, but when the monobloc construction was adopted there were advantages, both in manufacture and in maintenance, in making all the cylinder heads in a single separate casting secured to the cylinder block by screws or studs and nuts. In manufacture, for instance, it is easier to bore the cylinders if they are open at both ends, and assembly of the engine is simplified. In maintenance, the combustion chambers, piston crowns and valves are more easily accessible for decarbonising. In spite of these advantages, however, *fixed* or non-detachable cylinder heads continued to be used in a few engines.

There are difficulties in obtaining a gas- and water-tight joint between head and block. Sufficient thickness of metal has to be left in the region of the joint to accommodate the screws or studs by which the head is secured to the block, and this impedes the circulation of cooling water in a region where free flow is very important. Unless the bosses into which the studs are screwed are substantial and very carefully positioned, the upper surface of the block will be distorted by the tightening of the nuts and a gas-tight joint will be impossible to maintain. The use of fixed cylinder heads simplifies the problem of water flow around the ports and sparking plugs and avoids distortion and gas- and water-leaks.

The adoption of the unit cylinder block and crankcase construction makes the detachable cylinder head a necessity, and this is now the universal practice.

The cylinder casting of a side-valve engine is somewhat complicated by the ports and valve seats which lie at the side of the cylinders, though the cylinder head casting is simpler than that necessary on o.h.v. engines.

The crankshaft main bearings are carried in webs which lie transversely across the crankcase. One of these webs forms the front wall of the crankcase and another the rear wall, whilst the others stiffen the structure besides acting as supports for the main bearings. These bearings are usually split across their diameters to permit assembly of the crankshaft. The machining of the block is simplified if its lower face is level with the centre of the main bearings.

In some engines the crankcase walls are extended below the centre of the main bearings. This stiffens the structure by making it deeper, but more machining operations are involved: the bearing housings must be machined flat across a diameter, and the detachable half of the bearing housing—called the *cap*—must be securely attached by studs and nuts: thus the lower face of the crankcase comes at a different level, complicating the machining operation. If the front and rear main bearing caps are machined flush with the crankcase joint face, the attachment of the *sump* which closes the bottom of the crankshaft is simplified.

The sump, which usually contains the supply of oil used for lubricating the engine, is attached to the lower face of the crankcase by a number of screws or bolts and nuts. If the joint is at the level of the main bearing centres, the sump and the front and rear bearing caps must be specially shaped to permit an oil-tight seal. A cork gasket is generally fitted between sump and crankcase to assist in making the joint oil-tight. The sump is usually made as a steel pressing, though in a few cases it may be an aluminium casting.

CYLINDER LINERS

The wearing surface of the cylinder must be made of a relatively hard material which is resistant to wear. Cast iron is most commonly used because it is both reasonably hard and can be cast into complicated shapes. There are, however, many different varieties of cast iron, and those which have the best casting properties are not necessarily the best for wear-resistance. Furthermore, wear-resistant cast iron may not only be more difficult to cast but also more difficult to machine. This difficulty can be overcome by making the main cylinder block casting of a type of iron having good casting and machining properties, and making the wearing surfaces of the cylinders in the form of *sleeves* or *liners* of a harder material. These cylinder liners are of two main types:

(1) *Dry liners* The cylinder block is made in the normal way but the cylinders are lined with thin sleeves of harder material—usually a high-quality cast iron but sometimes steel. The liners are made an interference fit in the block and are inserted by means of a press, the operation usually being assisted by heating the block to expand the bores or by freezing the liners in liquid air to contract them. Fig. 2.7.2 shows a liner of this type fitted in position in its cylinder bore.

Owing to the interference fit the liners shrink slightly in fitting. It is thus necessary for them to be accurately bored to the correct diameter after they have been fitted. To eliminate the necessity for this operation and to simplify fitting and removing the liners, some engines have liners which have no interference fit and which can be pushed in with only a slight pressure—in some cases *hand pressure*. Such liners are called *slip* liners, and these can be *pre-finished* to the correct size before fitting. They are prevented from moving when the engine is running by a flange at their upper ends which is clamped by the cylinder head into a recess, machined at the top of the cylinder block.

(2) *Wet liners* When this type of liner is used the cylinder bores are omitted from the cylinder block casting. Each bore is made separately in the form of a relatively thick liner, which is fitted into the block in a suitable manner—Fig. 2.7.3. shows two methods in common use. At (a) a liner is shown clamped between the cylinder head and the bottom of the water jacket, in which holes are bored to allow the lower ends of the liners to pass

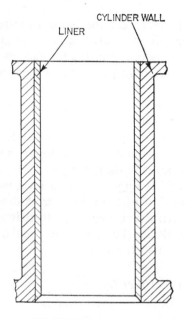

DRY CYLINDER LINER

FIG. 2.7.2

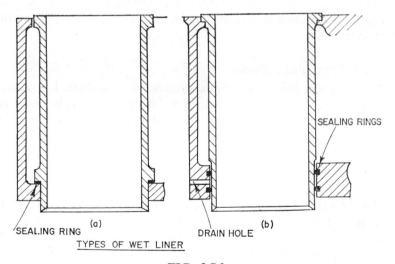

TYPES OF WET LINER

FIG. 2.7.3

through. A shoulder near the bottom of the liner seats on a gasket or sealing ring to make a water-tight joint. At the top the liner stands slightly proud of the top face of the block, so that it is clamped securely in position and a gas-tight joint with the head is ensured.

In the arrangement shown at (b) the top of the liner is a light press fit in a recess in the top face of the block: the top face of the liner stands slightly proud of the block face to hold the liner firmly and ensure a sound joint. The lower end of the liner passes through a hole bored in the lower part of the block, and a seal is made by two rubber rings fitted in grooves which may be either in the block (as shown) or in the liner. A drain hole leads from the space between the sealing rings, to reduce the risk of water entering the crankcase should the upper seal leak, and to provide visible evidence of such leakage.

Comparison of Dry and Wet Liners

The main advantages of wet liners over dry are:
(1) they can be pre-finished to correct size
(2) they are easily fitted and removed
(3) their outer surfaces are in direct contact with the cooling water.

There are two objections to wet liners: the most obvious is the risk of water leakage into the crankcase, and the other is the reduced rigidity of the main engine casting due to the omission of the cast-in cylinder walls.

Aluminium Cylinder Blocks

When cylinder liners are used the cylinder block and crankcase may be made of aluminium alloy, thus reducing weight. Advantage is taken of this only where low weight is important, for aluminium is more expensive than cast iron, is less strong and is softer. If dry liners are used in an aluminium block they may be cast in position.

AIR-COOLED ENGINES

The cylinder blocks so far described have all incorporated water cooling of the cylinders. Air-cooled cylinders have *fins* formed on their outer surfaces, and it is necessary that the cylinders should be made separately from the crankcase and often separate from one another, or in blocks of two.

CYLINDER HEADS

In the case of *in-line* engines (those in which the cylinders are arranged in a single row or *bank* with their axes parallel) the cylinder head is generally made in a single casting containing the upper surfaces of all the combustion chambers.

If the engine has *side valves* the cylinder head is merely a cover incorporating the water jackets (or fins if the engine is air-cooled) with suitably placed holes into which the sparking plugs are screwed. In the case of *overhead-valve* engines the head casting will also have to incorporate the ports and valve seatings with suitable provision for the valve-operating gear. Whenever possible the top face of the cylinder block is machined flat and square to the cylinder axis, although there are some engine designs in which this surface has to be at some other angle. The lower surface of the cylinder head is also machined flat, and the head is securely fastened to the block by a number of screws or studs and nuts.

Gaskets

To ensure a gas- and water-tight joint it is necessary to fit a *gasket* between the head and the block. For many years the type of gasket used consisted of a thin sheet of asbestos protected on either side by thinner sheets of copper, with suitable holes to clear the combustion chambers, water holes and studs. This type is still in use, but a later type which seems to be replacing the older one consists of a thin sheet of metal—such as stainless steel—with corrugations formed around the holes to assist in making a good seal.

When the cylinder head is being tightened down, two points in particular must be carefully observed:

(1) After tightening *all* the screws or nuts finger-tight, tighten them further *a little at a time in the order specified by the manufacturer.*

(2) Do the final tightening using a *torque wrench* to the tightness recommended by the engine manufacturer, and check the tightness again after the engine has been run for some time.

The object of this procedure is to avoid distorting the joint faces, and it follows that equal care should be taken in slackening the nuts when removing the head.

Materials

As with the cylinder block, the head is usually made of cast iron, but in some cases aluminium alloy is preferred. This gives the advantages of reduced weight and better heat conductivity, the latter resulting in lower and more uniform temperatures of the combustion chamber walls, permitting the use of a slightly higher compression ratio than is possible with a cast iron head.

When aluminium is used for the cylinder head it is generally necessary to fit *inserts* of harder material—usually cast iron or bronze—for the valves to seat on and for the sparking plugs to be screwed into.

THE FOUR-STROKE CYCLE IN DETAIL:
VALVE AND IGNITION TIMING

In chapter 2 of this section the operation of an engine on the four-stroke cycle was described. We must now consider this more closely, particularly in connection with the opening and closing of the valves.

The first point to be appreciated is the fact that it is not possible for a valve to move from closed to fully open or vice-versa *instantaneously*. In fact, the opening and the closing movements will each be spread over a considerable angle of crankshaft rotation. Thus, if a valve is required to be *effectively* open at the *beginning* of a stroke it must begin to open *before* the dead centre: similarly, if it is required to be *effectively* open at the *end* of a stroke it must not *close completely* until *after* the dead centre.

Even if the valves *could* be opened and closed instantaneously, the dead centres would not be the best points at which they should open and close except at very low engine speeds. The engine will give its best performance when the greatest mass of air and fuel is passed through the combustion chamber and burnt effectively. Consider an engine running reasonably fast. The most suitable point at which to open the inlet port depends upon conditions at the end of the exhaust stroke, and we will begin our study with the piston moving down the cylinder on the induction stroke and the inlet port already wide open (Fig. 2.8.1). The downward movement of the piston reduces the pressure inside the cylinder so that the pressure of the atmosphere forces air through the carburetter and along the inlet pipe—i.e. the flow of air along the pipe is *accelerated*. The *inertia* of this air (its resistance to change of speed) causes it to lag behind the piston movement, so that by the time the piston has reached its maximum speed (about half-way down the stroke) the

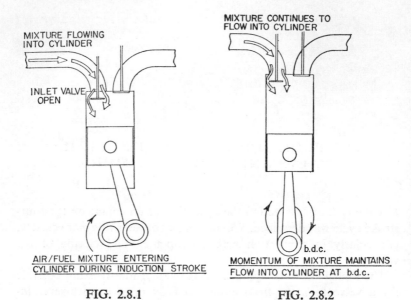

MIXTURE FLOWING
INTO CYLINDER

INLET VALVE
OPEN

AIR/FUEL MIXTURE ENTERING
CYLINDER DURING INDUCTION STROKE

FIG. 2.8.1

MIXTURE CONTINUES TO
FLOW INTO CYLINDER

b.d.c.
MOMENTUM OF MIXTURE MAINTAINS
FLOW INTO CYLINDER AT b.d.c.

FIG. 2.8.2

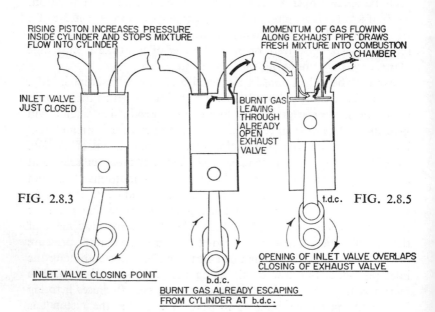

RISING PISTON INCREASES PRESSURE
INSIDE CYLINDER AND STOPS MIXTURE
FLOW INTO CYLINDER

INLET VALVE
JUST CLOSED

FIG. 2.8.3

INLET VALVE CLOSING POINT

BURNT GAS
LEAVING
THROUGH
ALREADY
OPEN
EXHAUST
VALVE

b.d.c.
BURNT GAS ALREADY ESCAPING
FROM CYLINDER AT b.d.c.

FIG. 2.8.4

MOMENTUM OF GAS FLOWING
ALONG EXHAUST PIPE DRAWS
FRESH MIXTURE INTO COMBUSTION
CHAMBER

t.d.c.   FIG. 2.8.5

OPENING OF INLET VALVE OVERLAPS
CLOSING OF EXHAUST VALVE

pressure inside the cylinder is well below atmospheric pressure, but during the second half of the stroke, when the piston speed is decreasing, the air flow is able to catch up with the piston and the pressure inside the cylinder rises towards atmospheric pressure.

At b.d.c. the direction of piston movement reverses, but the momentum of the air flow along the inlet pipe *towards* the cylinder causes it to continue entering the cylinder until the piston has moved some way up the next stroke—provided the valve remains open (Fig. 2.8.2). At some point during this stroke the upward movement of the piston increases the pressure inside the cylinder sufficiently to stop the inward flow of air and to begin to force air *out* of the cylinder (Fig. 2.8.3), and the greatest possible amount of air will be trapped inside the cylinder if the inlet valve closes at this point. This will always be *after* b.d.c. How much after will depend upon engine speed, upon the length and diameter of the inlet pipe, and throttle opening.

At about the end of the compression stroke the fuel is ignited and burnt, the gas pressure increases and the piston is forced down the cylinder on its power stroke. During the downward movement of the piston, the increasing volume lowers the pressure of the gas, but if the exhaust valve remains closed the pressure will still be well above atmospheric when the piston arrives at b.d.c. This pressure will offer a good deal of opposition to the upward movement of the piston during the exhaust stroke, even though the exhaust valve may now be open. Moreover, as the piston approaches b.d.c., the leverage exerted by the connecting rod on the crankshaft decreases rapidly and the pressure on the piston thus has a rapidly decreasing turning effect on the crankshaft. By opening the exhaust valve *early*, i.e. *before* the piston reaches b.d.c., a good deal of the burnt gas is allowed to escape before the piston begins its upward exhaust stroke, and the pressure during this stroke—and consequently the opposition to the piston's upward movement—is very much reduced (see Fig. 2.8.4). The point at which the exhaust valve opens must be carefully chosen so as to sacrifice as little as possible of the effect of the pressure in driving the piston downwards during the power stroke, whilst ensuring that as much gas as possible will escape before b.d.c. to reduce to a minimum the opposition to the piston's upward movement during the exhaust stroke.

Thus the exhaust gas is already moving out of the cylinder and along the exhaust pipe before the piston starts its exhaust stroke.

During the stroke the piston increases the gas velocity along the exhaust pipe. Thus, as the piston approaches t.d.c. and its upward velocity decreases, the momentum of the gas rushing along the exhaust pipe creates a partial vacuum inside the cylinder. As soon as the pressure inside the cylinder falls below the pressure in the inlet manifold, fresh mixture will begin moving into the cylinder if the inlet valve is opened. This can usually occur *before* the piston has reached t.d.c.—i.e. by opening the inlet port before the exhaust port has closed, the momentum of the exhaust gas can be used to start the flow of fresh gas into the cylinder without any help from the piston (Fig. 2.8.5).

The fresh gas entering the cylinder will, of course, be drawn towards the exhaust port, displacing burnt gas. Placing the valves on opposite sides of the combustion chamber makes the fresh gas sweep right across the chamber on its way from inlet port to exhaust port. This ensures that the combustion chamber is thoroughly *scavenged*, or cleared of exhaust gas and filled with fresh gas. If the ports are very close together it is possible for fresh gas to reach the exhaust port without displacing *all* the burnt gas from the cylinder. The correct moment to close the exhaust port is the moment the fresh gas reaches it.

Thus the opening point of the inlet valve and the closing point of the exhaust valve depend upon:

(1) the velocity of the flow of exhaust gases along the exhaust pipe. This in turn depends upon engine speed, throttle opening, the length and diameter of the exhaust pipe and the restricting effect of the silencer.

(2) The pressure in the inlet manifold, which is dependent upon engine speed and throttle opening

(3) the position of the ports in relation to the combustion chamber and to each other.

The inlet valve usually opens a little *before* t.d.c. and the exhaust valve remains open a little *after* t.d.c. Thus, for some angle of crankshaft rotation around t.d.c. *both valves are open at the same time*. The opening of the inlet valve *overlaps* the closing of the exhaust valve: this is the period of *valve overlap*.

Whilst a large valve overlap may be beneficial at high engine speeds if the ports are arranged on opposite sides of the combustion chamber, it will make it impossible for the engine to *idle* or run slowly at light load. At low engine speeds and small throttle openings the pressure in the inlet manifold is well below atmospheric pressure (as a vacuum gauge connected to the manifold will show). The quantity of gas exhausted from the cylinder is small and moves slowly, having very little momentum, so that it does not reduce the pressure in the cylinder appreciably below atmospheric pressure. Under these conditions, opening the inlet valve before the exhaust valve has closed will result in a rush of exhaust gas into the inlet manifold. Hence, on the following induction stroke the cylinder will be filled *with a lot of exhaust gas and very little fresh mixture*, which will almost certainly fail to be ignited when the spark occurs. If the engine will never be required to run slowly (e.g. a racing engine), this may not matter, but all engines used in normal motor vehicles are frequently called upon to idle smoothly and reliably, and for such engines the amount of valve overlap must be strictly limited.

To sum up, therefore:

(1) The inlet valve remains open *after* the piston has passed b.d.c. at the end of the induction stroke. This is called the *inlet valve closing lag*.

(2) The exhaust valve opens *before* the piston reaches b.d.c. at the end of the power stroke *(exhaust valve opening lead)*.

(3) The exhaust valve usually remains open *after* t.d.c. at the end of the exhaust stroke *(exhaust valve closing lag)*.

(4) The inlet valve usually opens *before* the exhaust valve has closed (valve overlap) and usually *before* t.d.c. *(inlet valve opening lead)*.

(5) The amount of lead or lag of valve opening or closing points and the amount of overlap will depend upon the design of the engine—particularly the port arrangement and inlet and exhaust systems—and upon the performance characteristics the engine is required to have.

The opening and closing points of the valves in relation to piston and crankshaft position are called the *valve timing,* and the correct timing for an engine—that selected by the engine manufacturers—is given either in the form of a table or by means of a *valve timing diagram*. Some examples of valve timing tables and diagrams are given in Fig. 2.8.6, together with brief details of the engine to which they refer: students should make similar tables and diagrams for other engines.

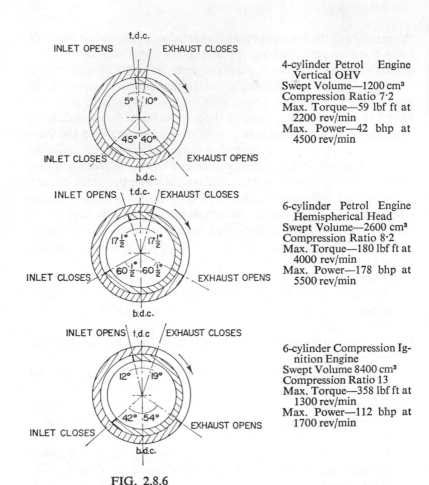

4-cylinder Petrol Engine
Vertical OHV
Swept Volume—1200 cm³
Compression Ratio 7·2
Max. Torque—59 lbf ft at
2200 rev/min
Max. Power—42 bhp at
4500 rev/min

6-cylinder Petrol Engine
Hemispherical Head
Swept Volume—2600 cm³
Compression Ratio 8·2
Max. Torque—180 lbf ft at
4000 rev/min
Max. Power—178 bhp at
5500 rev/min

6-cylinder Compression Ignition Engine
Swept Volume 8400 cm³
Compression Ratio 13
Max. Torque—358 lbf ft at
1300 rev/min
Max. Power—112 bhp at
1700 rev/min

FIG. 2.8.6

TIMING THE VALVES OF AN ENGINE

During the process of assembling an engine the drive between the
crankshaft and the camshaft must be connected up so that the valves
will open and close at the correct times in relation to the crankshaft
and piston. This operation is known as *timing the valves*. There
are three main stages to this operation:
(1) Set the crankshaft in the position where one of the valves should
open or close. (It is usual to work on the opening point of the
inlet valve, but any other point can be used.)

(2) Set the camshaft in the position where it is about to open the inlet valve (or whatever point is chosen).

(3) Connect up the drive to the camshaft.

If the engine has more than one camshaft each one will have to be timed individually.

Suitable parts of the engine are usually marked, to assist in timing the valves. The timing gear or sprocket is keyed to the crankshaft and can be fitted in one position only: the camshaft gear or sprocket is similarly fixed to the camshaft in such a way that it can be attached in one position only. By lining up marked teeth on these gears the crankshaft and camshaft are placed in the correct positions for connecting up the camshaft drive. These gears are hidden inside the *timing cover* when the engine is assembled. To enable the timing to be checked without removing the cover, the flywheel is usually marked in a position corresponding to t.d.c. in one of the cylinders. If the flywheel is not marked in this way, the t.d.c. position can be found by any one of several methods, of which the following is an example.

On most modern engines the piston can be felt by inserting a rod through a sparking-plug hole. Turn the engine until the piston is approximately half an inch below its highest position, and file a notch on the rod exactly opposite the top of the plug hole when the end of the rod is resting on the piston. Mark the rim of the flywheel opposite some suitable fixed reference point. Now turn the engine crankshaft so that the piston passes t.d.c. and begins to move down the cylinder: stop when the mark on the rod reaches the top of the plug hole, and put a second mark on the flywheel opposite the fixed reference mark. Mark the mid-point of the distance between the two marks on the flywheel. The piston is at t.d.c. when this last mark is opposite the fixed reference point.

Valve timing marks can also be made on the flywheel. If the circumference of the flywheel is divided by 360, a figure is obtained which represents the distance measured round the flywheel rim equivalent to one degree. For example if the circumference of the flywheel is 30 inches and the inlet valve opening point is 9° before t.d.c., the distance to be measured round the flywheel rim is:

$$\frac{30 \times 9}{360} = \frac{3}{4} \text{ inch}$$

Or, if the circumference of the flywheel is 0·8 metre the distance to be measured round the flywheel rim is:

$$\frac{0\cdot8\times9}{360} = 0\cdot02\,\text{m} = 22\,\text{mm}$$

There are several ways by which the opening point of the valve can be found. First of all the valve clearance must be correct, since variation of clearance causes a considerable variation in timing, as a little experimenting will show. (Some manufacturers stipulate a different clearance for valve timing from that used for running.) If the valves are push rod operated and the end of the push rod is accessible, it can be spun easily between finger and thumb while the valve is on its seat, but becomes stiff to turn as soon as the valve begins to open. If this method is not practicable, a feeler gauge inserted in the clearance between the rocker (or tappet) and the valve stem will be nipped at the moment the valve begins to open: in this case *the valve clearance must be increased by an amount equal to the thickness of the feeler used.*

IGNITION TIMING

In describing the cycle of operations in chapter 2, it was stated that the mixture was ignited 'at about the end of the compression stroke', and that after ignition the mixture 'burns very rapidly'. It is clear that the rate at which the mixture burns must be very high, because if it is not, the piston will have moved most of the way down the cylinder before maximum pressure is developed. To have its maximum effect the pressure must be developed as early as possible after t.d.c. Since, however, the mixture does take some time—however short—to burn and develop maximum pressure, the spark which starts combustion must be timed to occur *before* the piston reaches t.d.c.—i.e. the timing of the spark must be *advanced*.

The amount of advance necessary to give best results varies with engine speed and throttle opening, and it is the usual practice to fit automatic devices to regulate the ignition timing according to conditions (see pages 545 and 546), but it is necessary to 'time the ignition' correctly to set the automatic controls in their correct basic setting.

COMBUSTION CHAMBERS

COMBUSTION

The process of combustion in an engine is considered on page 262. For the purposes of this chapter it is sufficient for the student to understand that:

(1) the rate of burning must be rapid, but not excessively so
(2) the rate is influenced by several factors, of which temperature, pressure and *turbulence* are the only ones which concern us here
(3) the higher the compression ratio of the engine the higher is its theoretical efficiency.
(4) *Detonation* is a form of extremely rapid combustion which is liable to occur under certain conditions. It is harmful and must be avoided. It occurs if the mixture is heated and compressed to an excessive extent during combustion. It is also influenced by the quality of the fuel.

GENERAL PRINCIPLES OF COMBUSTION CHAMBER DESIGN

The power which can be obtained from an engine depends upon:

(1) the amount of air which can be passed through the engine per minute—i.e. the *volumetric efficiency*
(2) the efficiency with which the air can be mixed with fuel and burnt to release heat—i.e. the *thermal efficiency*
(3) the efficiency with which the energy released by the burning fuel can be converted into mechanical work at the driving end of the crankshaft, i.e. the *mechanical efficiency.*

Whilst the design of the combustion chamber can have little direct influence on the mechanical efficiency it has a great deal to do with both the volumetric and thermal efficiencies. It has, however, an indirect influence on the mechanical efficiency.

Requirements for High Volumetric Efficiency

The chief requirements for high volumetric efficiency are:

(1) large and unobstructed ports offering the minimum obstruction to the flow of gases

(2) the most suitable valve timing for the engine speeds and throttle openings at which the engine will most be required to operate

(3) a mixture temperature as low as possible at the moment the inlet valve closes. (Because of thermal expansion the cylinder will hold a smaller *mass* of mixture if it is hot.)

Requirements for High Thermal Efficiency

The chief of these are:

(1) the highest possible compression ratio which can be used without *knocking* (detonation)

(2) the minimum loss of heat to the combustion-chamber walls. This depends upon the temperature difference between the hot gases and the walls, and upon the surface area of the walls. Since a high temperature is necessary to produce high pressure it is important to reduce the surface area—i.e. to make the combustion chamber as compact as possible. This compactness has a further benefit—it reduces the time taken by the gas to burn, by reducing the distance the flame has to travel. This can be assisted by placing the sparking plug as near the centre of the combustion chamber as possible.

Possibly the most important consideration in the use of a high compression ratio is the *anti-knock rating* (octane number) of the fuel used. Since *high-octane* fuels are more expensive, a compression ratio must be chosen which balances thermal efficiency against fuel cost, bearing in mind the purpose for which the engine is to be used. (Whilst a high compression ratio will result in a lower fuel consumption for a given amount of work done, any gain may be entirely offset if the extra cost of the high-octane fuel necessitated by so high a ratio results in an increase in overall running costs. If running cost is of no importance, the fuel with the highest octane rating available may be used with a correspondingly high compression ratio.)

The design of the combustion chamber can also contribute to the suppression of knocking. The risk of detonation is greatest in the last gas to burn—what is called the *end gas*—and this risk can be reduced in two ways:

(1) by getting the gas burnt as quickly as possible
(2) by arranging that the end gas is burnt in the coolest part of the combustion chamber: it is easier to do this by placing the sparking plug nearer to the exhaust valve (which gets very hot) than to the inlet valve (which keeps relatively cool).

Turbulence

The rate at which the flame travels through stagnant gas is much too low to be of use in a high-speed engine, and it was realised many years ago that a violent agitation or *turbulence* of the gas is necessary to help spread the flame rapidly thoughout the mixture of air and fuel. There are two ways of creating turbulence:
(1) by arranging the inlet port so that the mixture enters the cylinder obliquely and at high velocity, setting up a swirling motion which persists during the compression stroke. This is known as *induction turbulence*, and, though helpful, it is not by itself sufficient
(2) by designing the combustion chamber so that at t.d.c. the piston approaches *part* of the cylinder head very closely, displacing mixture from this region with some violence. This action has been given the very descriptive name of *squish*, and turbulence created during the compression stroke (which is not, however, always due to squish) is known as *compression turbulence.*

Mechanical Efficiency

The positioning of the valves is one consideration in the design of the combustion chamber, and depending upon this the valve-operating gear will be more or less complicated. The greater the complication of the valve gear the more friction will be absorbed in operating the valves. This will also influence the cost of manufacturing the engine, and the maintenance it is likely to need.

With the foregoing in mind, some of the commoner types of combustion chamber can be considered.

THE L-HEAD COMBUSTION CHAMBER

Volumetric efficiency is not particularly high in this design (Fig. 2.9.1). The arrangement of the valves at one side of the cylinder restricts valve size to about half cylinder diameter or less, and there are sharp bends through the ports and into the cylinder.

The chamber is not very compact, but there is a good deal of

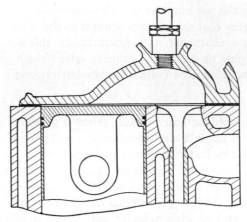

TYPICAL SIDE-VALVE DESIGN

FIG. 2.9.1

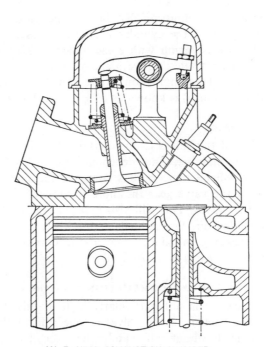

AN *F*-HEAD COMBUSTION CHAMBER

FIG. 2.9.2

freedom in the choice of plug position to obtain the best results. The compression ratio is limited to about 7:1, as it is necessary to leave sufficient space above the valves to allow them a reasonable lift.

By bringing the surface of the head down close over the piston at t.d.c., leaving a suitable passage between the offset combustion chamber and the cylinder, both induction and compression turbulence are improved: it is, in fact, easy to get too much turbulence causing rough running through excessively rapid combustion.

The position of the valves makes possible the use of the very simplest valve-operating gear, and mechanical losses are the least possible.

Though popular at one time, this combustion chamber is now obsolete in motor vehicle engines on account of its low volumetric efficiency and restriction on compression ratio.

THE F-HEAD COMBUSTION CHAMBER

By placing the inlet valve over the top of the cylinder (Fig. 2.9.2) larger valves can be used, a better flow of gas *into* the cylinder is produced, and a more compact combustion chamber results. However, as the compression ratio is raised beyond 7:1, some of the difficulties encountered in L-head engines become apparent in this engine too.

The flow of exhaust gas, and cooling around the exhaust valve seat, are improved by inclining the exhaust valve away from the cylinder. This also makes possible a well-shaped, compact combustion chamber. It is, however, less suitable than other types, particularly if the cylinder bore is large in relation to the piston stroke.

THE 'BATH-TUB' COMBUSTION CHAMBER

The valves are placed vertically over the top of the cylinder (Fig. 2.9.3), giving a better port shape leading directly into the cylinder. Thus the gas flow—and volumetric efficiency—are much better than in the L-head design. The valves are arranged in line, slightly offset from the cylinder centre, and the sides of the combustion chamber form a shape like an inverted bath (from which the name derives). Almost the only position for the sparking plug is the one shown, but this happens to fit in well with requirements, and the plug can be slightly nearer the exhaust valve than the inlet.

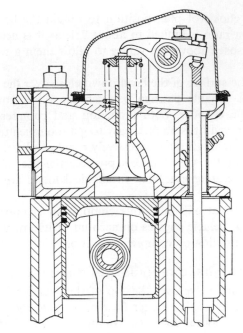

A 'BATH-TUB' COMBUSTION CHAMBER WITH VERTICAL VALVE

FIG. 2.9.3

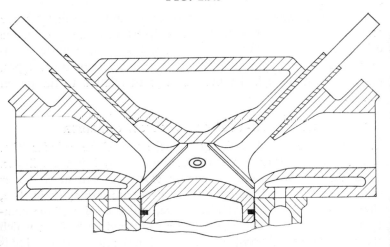

HEMISPHERICAL COMBUSTION CHAMBER

FIG. 2.9.4

The chamber is reasonably compact, and in some cases the bath-tub shape is somewhat bent to make the chamber roughly heart-shaped when seen from below.

There is little induction turbulence, but this is made up for by the very good compression turbulence produced by the squish effect. The *squish area*, as it is called, is placed on the side of the combustion chamber opposite to the sparking plug, to ensure a thorough sweep of fresh gas over the sparking plug as the piston approaches t.d.c.

The valves are often inclined towards the port side of the cylinder head, to give a slightly reduced bend to the ports. This also gives a wedge-shaped combustion chamber, which makes for more effective control of flame speed. The sparking plug is fitted at the thick end of the wedge, thus giving a large area of flame front during the early stages of combustion and speeding up the first part of this process. As combustion proceeds the flame area is reduced, thus reducing somewhat the speed of the final stages of combustion and minimising the risk of detonation.

THE HEMISPHERICAL COMBUSTION CHAMBER

It is commonly believed that the ideal shape for a combustion chamber is a perfect sphere. This belief is based upon the fact that the sphere has the smallest surface area per unit of volume and thus the heat loss to the combustion chamber walls is reduced to the minimum. In most other ways, however, this shape is most unsuitable. For instance, if the bore and stroke of the engine are equal, and the spherical combustion chamber is formed half in the piston and half in the cylinder head, the compression ratio is only $2\frac{1}{2}$:1, which is absurdly low. For a compression ratio of 8:1 and a similar form of combustion chamber the stroke would need to be $4\frac{2}{3}$ times the cylinder bore. This would severely limit engine rev/min and place an unacceptable restriction on valve size.

However, a combustion chamber, the upper surface of which consists of a hemisphere formed in the cylinder head, has several important benefits to offer. By inclining the valves at about 45° on opposite sides of the centre-line (Fig. 2.9.4) the valve diameter is much increased and an excellent port shape is obtained, giving excellent volumetric efficiency. This advantage is so important that where high power output is the main consideration this type of cylinder head is almost invariably chosen.

To obtain a high compression ratio the piston crown must be

domed, giving the combustion chamber a shape like the peel of half
an orange having a high surface area per unit of volume, quite the
opposite of the 'ideal' spherical shape. However undesirable this
may be, it is of little importance compared with advantages gained.

Induction turbulence can be arranged by having the inlet port
at a slight angle to a cylinder diameter, and compression turbulence
can be obtained by a suitable shape of piston crown.

The chamber is of a shape easy to machine all over, giving accurate
control of compression ratio. Although the sparking plug cannot
be fitted in the ideal position, it can be placed near the centre of the
cylinder head, where good results are obtained.

The greatest drawback to this type of combustion chamber is
undoubtedly the complication necessary in the valve-operating gear.
The best method is twin overhead camshafts (Fig. 2.6.17(a) (page
95), one directly over each row of valves, but this is also the most
complicated and expensive. Alternative arrangements are:

(1) single overhead camshaft with rockers (Fig. 2.6.17(b) (page 93)
(2) double side camshaft, push rods and rockers.
(3) single side camshaft, push rods and rockers (Fig. 2.6.16(b)
    (page 94).

With improved designs, materials and lubrication the objections
to the use of the hemispherical head are becoming less important,
and the increasing emphasis on engine power output, even for
'production' cars, is resulting in the use of the twin overhead camshaft layout (which has been used for practically all racing-car
engines since about 1912).

2.10

MULTI-CYLINDER ENGINES

Practically all motor vehicle engines have more than one cylinder. To understand the reasons for this it is necessary to consider the limitations of the single-cylinder engine and the ways in which the use of a number of cylinders overcomes these limitations.

Irregular Torque Output
The torque exerted upon the crankshaft of a single-cylinder engine by the gas pressure acting on the piston fluctuates widely during each cycle of operations. As shown in Fig. 2.10.1, the torque reaches its maximum value during the power stroke, and during the exhaust, induction and compression strokes some effort has to be applied to the crankshaft to keep it turning. The energy necessary to do this is taken from the energy stored in the flywheel during the power stroke. Thus, although the *maximum* value of the torque developed may be high, its *average* or *mean* value is very much lower. (The *mean torque* is that steady value of torque which would do the same amount of work per minute as the actual fluctuating torque.)

The driving effort developed by the engine is, therefore, rather jerky, especially at low speeds: a heavy flywheel is necessary to give acceptable smoothness. Moreover the transmission system must be capable of transmitting the *maximum* torque developed, and is therefore undesirably heavy in relation to the *mean torque*. Fig. 2.10.2 shows that if *four* cylinders are used, working in succession, the mean torque is little less than the maximum torque, and this increased mean torque can be transmitted by the same transmission system as was needed for the single-cylinder engine.

Balance
The inertia forces which are caused by the acceleration of the reciprocating parts of the engine tend to cause vibration. To balance

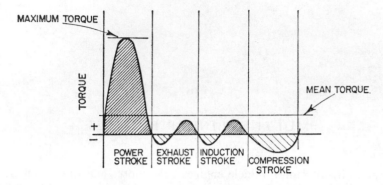

TORQUE FLUCTUATIONS IN SINGLE-CYLINDER ENGINE

FIG. 2.10.1

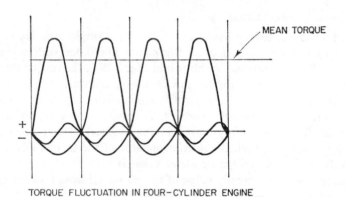

TORQUE FLUCTUATION IN FOUR-CYLINDER ENGINE

FIG. 2.10.2

these forces and neutralise their effects, equal and opposite forces must be introduced. This can only be done by additional reciprocating parts making similar movements but in the opposite direction. While a single-cylinder engine cannot be perfectly balanced, it should be possible to arrange that, in multi-cylinder engines, the vibratory forces are neutralised.

Power Output

The power which an engine can develop is determined by the amount of air it can consume per minute—i.e. upon its swept volume and the speed at which it runs. The maximum speed is limited by the inertia forces on the reciprocating parts of the engine, and these forces depend upon the mass of these parts and their acceleration: this in turn depends upon piston stroke and the *square* of the engine speed.

For a given swept volume the bore and stroke of a multi-cylinder engine are smaller than those of a single-cylinder. The size and mass of each piston will be smaller and the stroke will be shorter, and so at the same engine speed the inertia forces on the reciprocating parts of a multi-cylinder engine will be considerably less than those in a single-cylinder: the multi-cylinder can safely run at higher speed and develop greater power.

Shape of Engine

The shape of a single-cylinder engine cannot be altered very much, and its size will depend upon its swept volume. This does not leave the designer much scope for making the engine more compact so as to fit it into a smaller space in the vehicle. When several cylinders are used the designer has a choice of several different cylinder arrangements, by means of which the engine shape can be varied to suit the space into which it must fit.

LIMITATIONS ON CYLINDER NUMBERS

The advantages resulting from the use of a number of cylinders are not gained without some sacrifices. One of the chief objections to the multi-cylinder engine is the greater cost and complication due to the increased number of parts which have to be made and assembled. Other difficulties arise in connection with carburation and ignition systems. For these reasons the majority of motor vehicles use engines having either four, six or eight cylinders. A few small vehicles have two-cylinder engines, whilst some large cars have used twelve or even sixteen cylinders, but these are exceptional.

CYLINDER ARRANGEMENTS

There are four arrangements which may be used for the cylinders of an engine.

(1) *In line*   The cylinders are arranged in a single row, side-by-side and parallel to one another. They may be either vertical, horizontal or inclined at any convenient angle.

(2) *Vee*   The cylinders are arranged in two rows at an angle to one another. For two, four and eight-cylinder engines, the V-angle

is usually 90°, and for six and twelve-cylinder engines it is usually 60° or occasionally 120°. There are, however, exceptions to this: for instance most of the modern examples of V-four engines have used a V-angle of 60° and a number of older engines used a V-angle of about 13°–14°. In each case the crankpins were suitably offset in order to equalise the intervals between firing impulses.

(3) *Opposed* This could be regarded as a V-type engine in which the V-angle is 180°. The cylinders are usually placed horizontally.

(4) *Radial* The cylinders are placed radially with the crankshaft as centre. This arrangement is not very convenient for motor vehicles and has only been used experimentally. Its chief merit is the extreme shortness of the engine: it is particularly suited to air-cooling because of the wide spacing of the cylinders.

CYLINDER NUMBERING

The cylinders of an engine are identified by giving them numbers. When there is only one row of cylinders they are usually numbered from one end towards the other, but in the case of other arrangements there is considerable variation in practice. A method put forward by the British Standards Institute (B.S. 1599 of 1949) may be summarised as follows: The cylinders of *in-line* engines should be numbered 1, 2, 3, etc., commencing from the 'free' or non-driving end. In the case of Vee or opposed engines, each group of cylinders should be numbered in the same manner, but groups of cylinders should be identified by letters A, B, etc. The order of the lettering should be clockwise, looking at the 'free' or non-driving end of the engine, beginning at '9 o'clock' or the first after. This method is seldom used by motor-vehicle manufacturers: in V-type and opposed-type engines the two groups of cylinders are sometimes identified as Left (L) or Right (R): sometimes one group of cylinders contains even numbers and the other odd; sometimes one group of cylinders is numbered consecutively, followed by the cylinders in the other group.

FIRING ORDER

The cylinders of a multi-cylinder engine are arranged to have their power strokes in succession, and the order in which the cylinders work is called the *firing order* of the engine. For smoothest running the power strokes should be spaced at equal intervals, each interval being equal to the number of degrees per cycle of operations (720°

for a four-stroke engine) divided by the number of cylinders. For a four-cylinder engine the interval will be $\dfrac{720°}{4} = 180°$ and for a six-cylinder, $\dfrac{720°}{6} = 120°$.

The firing order of an engine is determined by *two* things:
(1) the disposition of the cylinders and the cranks on the crankshaft. (This determines the *possible* firing orders.)
(2) the arrangement of the cams on the camshaft. (This must be in accordance with *one* of the possible orders.)

Firing orders for some of the common types of engine are discussed in a little more detail in the following pages.

FOUR-CYLINDER IN-LINE ENGINES

Fig. 2.10.3 shows in the form of a line diagram the arrangement of cylinders and cranks in an engine of this type. Power strokes occur at intervals of 180° and the pistons move in pairs, nos. 1 and 4 forming one pair and 2 and 3 the other. Suppose no. 1 piston is commencing its power stroke. Then no. 4 piston will move *down* its cylinder on its induction stroke. No. 2 piston will move *upwards* on either its exhaust or compression stroke, and no. 3 on either its compression or exhaust. We can now make up a table showing the four strokes made by each piston during one cycle of operations.

cylinder no.	1	2	3	4
1st stroke	P	C or E	E or C	I
2nd stroke	E	P or I	I or P	C
3rd stroke	I	E or C	C or E	P
4th stroke	C	I or P	P or I	E

P — power stroke   E — exhaust stroke
I — Induction stroke   C — compression stroke

From this table we see that there are two possible firing orders for a four-cylinder engine. These are 1243 and 1342. Both are in common use.

SIX-CYLINDER IN-LINE ENGINES

Fig. 2.10.4 is a line diagram of the cylinder and crank arrangement. (a) and (b) show alternative crankshaft arrangements as viewed from

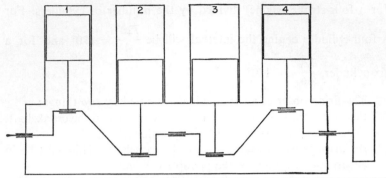

ARRANGEMENT OF CYLINDERS AND CRANKSHAFT IN 4-CYLINDER IN—LINE ENGINE

FIG. 2.10.3

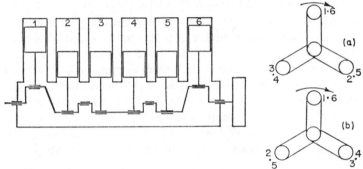

ARRANGEMENT OF CYLINDERS AND CRANKSHAFT IN 6-CYLINDER IN-LINE ENGINE

FIG. 2.10.4

the front. In arrangement (a), commencing with pistons 1 and 6 at
t.d.c., the next pair to come to t.d.c. will be nos. 3 and 4, followed
by nos. 2 and 5, and then 1 and 6 again. If no. 1 piston is commencing its power stroke, the next power stroke will occur in either
no. 3 or no. 4 cylinder, and the next in either no. 2 or no. 5. There
are thus *four* possible firing orders:

132645 . . . , 135642 . . . , 145632 . . . , 142635 . . .

In the first three of these, all three cylinders in one half of the
engine fire during one revolution and the three in the other half
during the next revolution. In the last one, cylinders in opposite
halves of the engine fire alternately. This arrangement is generally
preferable as it helps to obtain good 'distribution' of the air/fuel

mixture (see page 183): it is the only one in common use, though others have been used in rare cases.

If the cranks are arranged as shown at (b) the pistons come to t.d.c. in the order 1 and 6, 2 and 5, 3 and 4, followed by 1 and 6 again. In this case the four possible firing orders are:

123654 . . . , 124653 . . . , 154623 . . . , 153624 . . .

Once again it is only in the last one that cylinders in opposite halves of the engine fire alternately, and this is the one in common use.

Both alternative crank arrangements are used, and there are thus *two* alternative firing orders for a six-cylinder engine in common use—142635 and 153624.

V-EIGHT ENGINES

Fig. 2.10.5 shows the arrangement of cylinders in this type of engine: the cylinders are shown numbered in accordance with B.S. 1599. The earliest engines of this type used a crankshaft similar to that used in the in-line four-cylinder engine, as shown at (a). Later the crank arrangement shown at (b) was adopted because it gives better balance. Power strokes occur at intervals of 90° in both cases, and the 'pairs' in which the pistons move are, for arrangement (a), 1A and 4A, 1B and 4B, 2A and 3A, 2B and 3B, giving *eight* possible firing orders. In the case of arrangement (b) the 'pairs' are 1A and

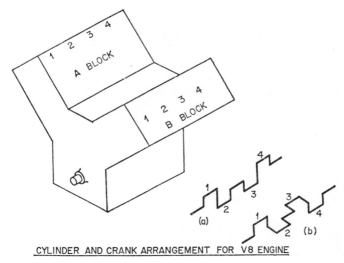

CYLINDER AND CRANK ARRANGEMENT FOR V8 ENGINE

FIG. 2.10.5

2B, 1B and 3A, 3B and 4A, 4B and 2A, also giving eight possible firing orders. It is suggested that the reader works out these sixteen possible firing orders for himself.

DETERMINATION OF FIRING ORDER

It is necessary to know the firing order of an engine in order to be able to connect up the sparking-plug leads correctly. There are several methods by which it may be found. It is sometimes marked on the engine, or on a plate on or near the engine. It is invariably given in the workshop manual. If the engine is not marked and the workshop manual is not available the following method can be used:

(1) Remove the valve gear covers and note which are the inlet valves and which the exhaust.

(2) Rotate the engine in the direction in which it runs and watch the order in which *one* set of valves, inlet *or* exhaust, operate. This will give the order in which the inlet strokes or exhaust strokes occur, and the power strokes occur in the same order.

The Fuel System

3.1

THE FUEL SUPPLY SYSTEM

The fuel supply system consists of the fuel tank and the means for delivering fuel to the carburetter.

THE TANK

A variety of constructional methods are used for making fuel tanks, of which the following are examples.

(1) *Soldered* The walls of the tank are made from tinned-steel sheets cut and bent to shape. The seams are either rolled or riveted before soldering, and the tank walls are internally supported at intervals by stiffeners. These consist of sheets which divide the tank into compartments but are pierced with large holes, so that although they allow fuel to pass from one compartment to another they prevent the fuel 'surging' from side to side of the tank.

(2) *Welded* This construction uses steel pressings for walls and stiffeners, with joints and seams welded. The tank is often coated inside, and sometimes outside also, with tin or lead.

(3) *Plastic* In recent years the use of plastics has been applied to tank construction, giving the advantages of lightness and complete immunity from corrosion.

Location of Tank

It was at one time common practice on small and some medium-sized cars to fit the tank as high as possible in the *scuttle* (between the engine bulkhead and the base of the windscreen). With the carburetter mounted fairly low at the side of the engine the fuel could be allowed to flow to the carburetter by gravity, providing a simple and reliable system (see Fig. 3.1.1).

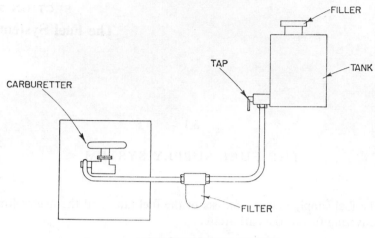

GRAVITY-FEED FUEL SYSTEM

FIG. 3.1.1

In large cars and commercial vehicles, a tank of sufficient size could not conveniently be accommodated in the scuttle. Furthermore, any leakage would allow fuel to drip into the interior of the driving compartment, with consequent risk of fire, and in case of accident a split tank would allow petrol to leak onto the exhaust pipe at a point where the pipe might be hot enough to ignite the fuel. Various alternative positions for the tank were tried, the most popular for cars being at the rear of the vehicle. For commercial vehicles, the tank is usually attached to a chassis frame side-member below floor level. Almost all modern cars, large and small, have the fuel tank at the rear.

In this position the tank is below the carburetter level and it is necessary to provide some means of lifting fuel from tank to carburetter. This usually takes the form of a pump in which the pumping element is a flexible diaphragm: it may be operated either mechanically or electrically.

When mechanically operated, it is mounted on the engine and worked by a special cam on the engine camshaft. As the engine is carried on flexible mountings, it is necessary to include a length of flexible piping in the pipeline connecting the pump to the tank, as shown in Fig. 3.1.2(a).

When electrically operated, the pump may be mounted in one of two positions. The first of these is on the engine bulkhead: the pump is connected to the tank by a rigid pipeline, but a flexible pipe connects the pump to the carburetter to allow for engine movement on its flexible mountings. With the pump in this position, one difficulty which is sometimes met is the formation of bubbles of fuel vapour in the pipe between tank and pump. There are two main causes for this—heat and reduced pressure. If the fuel pipe is heated by passing near the exhaust pipe it should be rearranged, but if the heating is merely due to hot weather little can be done. The trouble is aggravated by the fact that the pipeline between tank and pump, being on the suction side of the pump, is operating under a pressure less than atmospheric, a condition which encourages the formation of vapour. Thus the alternative position for an electric fuel pump is close to the tank so that the main length of the pipeline is under pressure and the formation of vapour is discouraged. Both these positions are shown in Fig. 3.1.2(b).

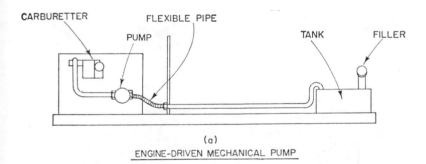

(a)
ENGINE-DRIVEN MECHANICAL PUMP

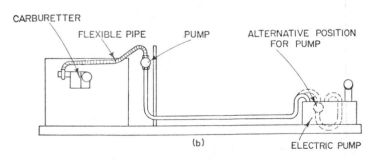

(b)

PUMP-FEED FUEL SYSTEM

FIG. 3.1.2

Some cars use a small centrifugal pump—like a very small coolant pump—driven by an electric motor, the whole assembly being sealed and submerged below the fuel *inside* the tank.

MECHANICAL FUEL PUMP

The constructional features of a pump of this type are shown in Fig. 3.1.3. The upper part of the body (16) contains the inlet connection (1), the inlet valve (2), the outlet valve (3) and the outlet connection (4). The circular diaphragm (5) (made of fabric impregnated with synthetic rubber) is clamped around its edge between the upper (16) and lower (15) parts of the body. It is also clamped at its centre between two dished circular plates attached to the upper end of the diaphragm pull rod (6). A spring (7) fitted between the lower diaphragm plate and the lower body pushes the diaphragm

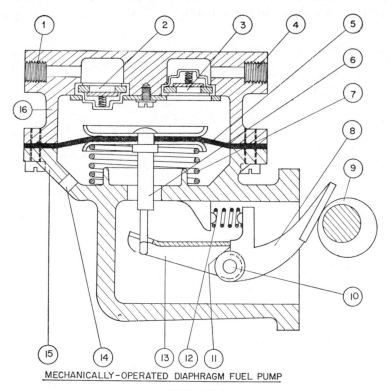

MECHANICALLY-OPERATED DIAPHRAGM FUEL PUMP

FIG. 3.1.3

upwards. The pump is bolted to the wall of the crankcase. The lever (8) passes through an aperture to bear against an eccentric (9) on the engine camshaft, the end of the lever being pressed lightly against the eccentric by the spring (12). The lever pivots on a pin (10) on which is also pivoted a ⊓ section link (13), the other end of which engages the lower end of the diaphragm pull rod.

When the engine is running, the lever (8) is rocked on its pivot. Movement of the lever *towards* the pump causes the step (11) on the lever to engage the link (13), which it moves about the pivot (10), so pulling down the diaphragm and compressing the diaphragm spring (7). Movement of the lever (8) *away* from the pump allows the diaphragm to be moved upwards by the spring (7).

Downward movement of the diaphragm increases the volume of the pumping chamber above the diaphragm, holding the outlet valve (3) on its seat, but opening the inlet valve (2) and drawing fuel from the tank through the inlet connection into the pumping chamber. On the upward stroke of the diaphragm, pressure is applied to the fuel in the pumping chamber by the spring (7), closing the inlet valve but forcing the outlet valve off its seat and delivering fuel through the outlet connection (4) and a pipe to the carburetter.

When the carburetter is full of fuel a valve in the carburetter closes (see page 145), preventing the entry of any more fuel, and consequently fuel will now be unable to leave the pump. The diaphragm will thus be held in its lowest position by the fuel in the pumping chamber under the loading of the spring (7), although the lever (8) will maintain contact with the eccentric (9) through the influence of the spring (12). The pressure at which fuel is delivered to the carburetter is determined by the force exerted by the spring (7). This force in turn depends upon the dimensions of the spring and the extent to which it is compressed when the diaphragm is in its lowest position. Within limits this may be varied by selecting a suitable thickness of packing to place between the pump mounting-flange and the engine crankcase, a greater thickness reducing the pressure slightly and a lesser thickness increasing it.

Should the diaphragm develop a leak, fuel can escape through a number of drain holes (14) drilled through the wall of the pump body.

ELECTRIC FUEL PUMP

A sectional view of an example of this type of pump is given in

Fig. 3.1.4. For convenience of description the pump may be divided into three main sections, viz. the pumping section, the magnet section and the contact-breaker section.

The *pumping section* is similar in both construction and operation to the corresponding section of the mechanical pump, differing only in detail. It consists of the outlet connection (1), the pump body (2), the outlet valve (3), the inlet valve (4), the inlet connection (6) and inlet filter (5), and the diaphragm (30).

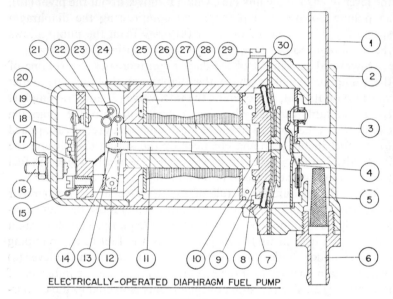

ELECTRICALLY-OPERATED DIAPHRAGM FUEL PUMP

FIG. 3.1.4

The *magnet section* is contained within the magnet housing (26), and consists of the central iron core (27), the solenoid winding (25) which surrounds this core, and the armature (9) which is clamped to the central region of the diaphragm. The edge of the diaphragm is clamped between the body (2) and the magnet housing. To support and centralise the diaphragm and armature assembly, a number of brass centralising rollers (8) are fitted between the armature plate and the end of the magnet housing. The spring (28) acts upon the back of the armature and pushes the diaphragm towards the pump body.

A hole passes centrally through the core (27) and in this hole is a freely-fitting armature spindle (11), one end of which is screwed into the armature plate.

The *contact-breaker section* is enclosed under the bakelite cover (20). The end of the armature spindle (11) is screwed into the trunnion (14), which is pivoted in the channel-section inner rocker (13). This rocker rocks about the hinge pin (12), and carried on the same hinge pin is the outer rocker (22). These two rockers are connected through the toggle-spring assembly (23), which consists of a pair of springs attached by pivot pins to the ends of the two rockers.

A tungsten point (19) is fixed to an extension of the outer rocker and, in the position shown, makes electrical contact with another tungsten point carried on a spring blade (18). As shown, the outer rocker is held by the toggle springs against the bakelite pedestal (21) deflecting the spring blade away from the pedestal and ensuring a firm contact between the contact points. The terminal (16) is electrically connected to one end of the solenoid winding. The other end of the winding is connected to the spring blade (18) through the tag (15). When the points are closed (as shown) the solenoid circuit is completed through the outer rocker, the wire (17), and a screw securing the contact-breaker assembly to the magnet housing. If the pump is not bolted to an earthed part of the vehicle, an earthing lead must be connected from a good 'earth' to the earthing screw (29).

When the pump is switched on the solenoid winding is energised, attracting the armature (9) and moving the diaphragm (30) away from the body (2). This draws in fuel from the tank via the inlet connection and valve (4). As the diaphragm moves, the spindle (11) also moves, taking the inner rocker with it. At a certain point in the rocker's movement the toggle spring will move the outer rocker (22) sharply away from the pedestal, separating the tungsten points and interrupting the flow of current through the solenoid winding. The movement of the outer rocker is limited by the fibre rollers (24) making contact with the magnet housing. The solenoid being now de-energised, the spring (28) will move the diaphragm towards the body (2). This expels fuel from the pumping chamber via the outlet valve (3) and the outlet connection (1) to the carburetter. The spindle (11), moving with the diaphragm, will return the inner rocker to its original position, whereupon the toggle springs will move the outer rocker back and re-make contact between the tungsten points.

This action will continue until the carburetter is full of fuel, when the diaphragm will be unable to make its return stroke, holding the tungsten points open until the carburetter requires more fuel. The pressure at which the fuel is delivered to the carburetter is governed by the strength of the spring (28).

FILTERS

All carburetters have a number of passages and small holes through which petrol must flow, and tiny pieces of dirt or blobs of water can obstruct the flow and prevent the correct functioning of the carburetter.

The petrol companies take a great deal of trouble to ensure that the petrol delivered by their pumps at filling stations is clean, but it is possible for dust to enter the tank of the car any time the filler cap is open, even for short periods. As fuel is taken out of the tank and delivered to the carburetter, air must be allowed to enter the tank. It does this through a vent hole or pipe, and it may take in dust or moisture with it, the moisture subsequently condensing inside the tank. A small sump is usually formed at the lowest point of the fuel tank, with a drain plug to enable any water collected in the sump to be drained. The fuel supply to the engine is taken from above sump level to minimise the possibility of dirt and water getting into the pipelines and eventually into the carburetter.

It is, however, a sensible precaution to fit one or more filters in the fuel system to trap dirt and water, preventing them entering the fuel pump—where they might prevent a valve from closing properly —or the carburetter. Filters may be fitted in one or more of the following positions:

(1) around the outlet from the fuel tank
(2) at the fuel pump inlet (see Fig. 3.1.4)
(3) at the carburetter inlet
(4) at any convenient point in the pipeline connecting tank to carburetter.

Fuel filters usually consist of brass wire gauze of a mesh sufficiently fine to trap those particles of dirt which are large enough to cause trouble in fuel pumps and carburetters, and of an area large enough to pass more than the maximum fuel flow. If previously damped with petrol such filters will also trap water.

Fig. 3.1.5 illustrates a type of filter suitable for connecting in a fuel pipeline. A cast body (4) has a drilled lug (1) by which it can be secured to a suitable position on the vehicle. A cylinder of fine-mesh brass gauze (7), closed at its lower end, is soldered at its top

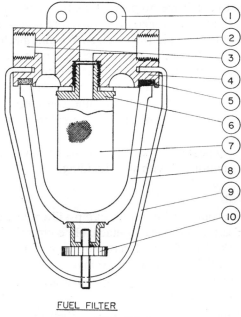

FUEL FILTER

FIG. 3.1.5

edge to a fitting (6) which screws into the under side of the body. A
hole drilled through this fitting communicates with the outlet connection (2). A glass bowl (8) is clamped below the body by a stirrup
(9) and a clamping nut (10), and seats on a cork washer (5) to
prevent leakage.

Fuel enters at the inlet connection (3) directly into the bowl and
passes through the gauze to the outlet connection, leaving dirt and
water in the bowl. The filter will need cleaning at suitable intervals.

There are several alternatives to brass gauze as a filtering element.

PIPELINES

For many years the pipes used to convey the fuel from tank to
carburetter were made of copper, a metal of great ductility, which
enables it to be easily bent to shape, and possessing good resistance
to corrosion. Copper, however, is relatively expensive and has been
almost entirely replaced on modern vehicles by tinned steel.

Practically all modern vehicles have their engines supported on
flexible mountings which permit fairly extensive movement of the

engine relative to the frame, to prevent the transmission of vibration to the bodywork and passengers. It is therefore necessary to include a length of flexible piping in the pipeline. When a mechanical pump is used, this is fitted on the engine, and a length of flexible pipe connects the pump with the rigid part of the pipe which is secured to the frame. In the case of an electric pump, which is normally mounted on the engine bulkhead, the rigid pipeline continues as far as the pump inlet, and a length of flexible pipe is used to connect the pump outlet to the carburetter.

These flexible pipes are made of plastic material, often transparent and sometimes reinforced with wire braiding.

Pipe Connections

Where pipes are connected to tanks, pumps, filters and carburetters, some form of secure but easily detachable connection is required. This usually takes the form of screwed connectors such as those shown in Fig. 3.1.6. That shown at (a) involves soldering the nipple onto the end of the pipe, but the type shown at (b) requires no soldering, the olive being compressed between the coned surfaces of the union and the screw as the latter is tightened. Since the olive is made of a relatively soft brass it contracts onto the pipe making a

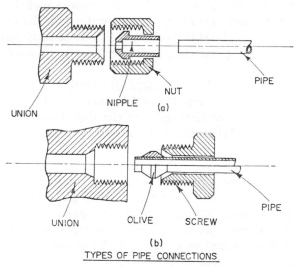

TYPES OF PIPE CONNECTIONS

FIG. 3.1.6

fuel-tight connection. In a third type, not shown, the end of the pipe is flared out to mate with a suitable conical seating on the union.

With the increasing use of flexible plastic pipes a very simple connection is being used, in which the end of the plastic pipe is simply pushed on to a tightly-fitting tubular extension on the union (such as that shown in Fig. 3.1.4), sometimes with the use of a petrol-proof adhesive.

THE FUNCTIONS OF
A CARBURETTER

It has been seen in Section 2, chapter 1, that the driving force in an internal-combustion engine is the pressure resulting from the heating of a gas by burning a fuel inside the engine cylinder. During one cycle of operations the pressure acting on the piston varies widely, but it has an 'average' value which is called the *mean effective pressure*. The effort exerted by the engine is clearly proportional to the mean effective pressure (m.e.p.), which depends upon engine design, compression ratio, and the temperature to which the gas is heated by combustion.

COMBUSTION OF PETROL

Petrol is a fuel which is particularly suitable for use in motor vehicles. It is a clean liquid which is easily stored (although reasonable precautions against fire are necessary) and which flows freely. It gives off an inflammable vapour at quite low temperatures and when burnt liberates quite a large amount of heat.

Before petrol can be burnt it must be vaporised and mixed with a suitable quantity of air, since combustion is a process involving the chemical combination of a fuel with oxygen.

Crude petroleum, from which petrol is obtained, is a mixture of various compounds of hydrogen and carbon (called *hydrocarbons*) and petrol consists of these constituents of the crude petroleum which have boiling points between the temperatures of, roughly, 30° to 200°C.

CALORIFIC VALUE

The amount of heat liberated by complete combustion of unit mass of a fuel is called the *calorific value* of the fuel. For an average sample of petrol the calorific value is about 19 000 Btu/lb (42 000 Kj/kg).

MIXTURE STRENGTH

The mass of air per pound (or kg) of fuel in a mixture of air and fuel gives the air/fuel ratio of the mixture and, as already noted, the A/F ratio for complete combustion—called the *chemically correct* mixture —is about 15 in the case of petrol.

A mixture having a greater proportion of fuel—i.e. a *lower* A/F ratio than 15—is called a *rich* mixture, whilst one having a greater proportion of air—i.e. a *higher* A/F ratio than 15—is a *weak* mixture. Within limits both rich and weak mixtures will burn, but will produce different results.

INFLUENCE OF A/F RATIO

Mixtures having A/F ratios of less than about 8 or more than about 22 cannot normally be ignited in petrol engine cylinders, and within this range variation of A/F ratio has a considerable influence on the engine's performance. (It should be emphasised that the mixtures referred to are those in which the fuel is completely vaporised and thoroughly mixed with the air so that the proportions of air and fuel are the same throughout the whole bulk of the mixture. This is rarely the case in an engine cylinder under running conditions.)

It might be expected that the chemically correct mixture ought to give the best results, but this is not necessarily the case. As indicated in the preceding paragraph, for instance, it is impossible, under normal running conditions, to ensure that the fuel is evenly distributed throughout the air, and under some conditions the fuel is not all completely vaporised when combustion occurs.

The main effects of variation of A/F ratio are upon:

(1) *The mean effective pressure* This is found to reach maximum values with a slightly rich mixture. The upper curve of Fig. 3.2.1 gives some idea of the way in which m.e.p. varies with A/F ratio.

(2) *The rate of combustion* The speed of travel of the flame through the mixture varies in a manner roughly similar to the variation of m.e.p., being fastest with slightly rich mixtures and slowing down markedly as the mixture is weakened and to a lesser extent as it is enriched. One result of this is a tendency for the engine to run hotter if the mixture is weak.

(3) *The rate of fuel consumption* This is called the *specific fuel consumption* (s.f.c.) and it is found to be lowest with mixtures which are slightly weaker than the chemically correct mixture as shown by the lower curve of Fig. 3.2.1.

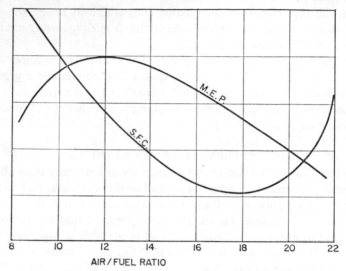

AIR / FUEL RATIO

EFFECTS OF VARIATION OF AIR/FUEL RATIO ON MEAN
EFFECTIVE PRESSURE AND SPECIFIC FUEL CONSUMPTION

FIG. 3.2.1

(4) *Composition of exhaust gas* If an engine is supplied with the chemically correct mixture the exhaust gas should consist of a mixture of carbon dioxide, water vapour and nitrogen. Due to imperfect mixing of the air and fuel, however, it is found that there are in fact small amounts of both oxygen and carbon monoxide in addition to the other gases. If the mixture is made richer the proportion of carbon dioxide in the exhaust gas decreases whilst the amount of carbon monoxide increases, and a small amount of unburnt hydrogen is also found. As the limit of combustibility is approached some unburnt carbon appears as *sooty black smoke* in the exhaust gas, and this is always a sign of excessive richness.

If the mixture is weakened from the chemically correct the proportion of carbon dioxide in the exhaust gas again decreases.

Carbon monoxide is absent once the mixture has been weakened slightly, but the proportion of oxygen increases.

These changes in the composition of the exhaust gas can be used to estimate the A/F ratio on which the engine is running. A sample of exhaust gas can be analysed chemically: though this impracticable in a repair shop an alternative is available in the form of an instrument called an *exhaust gas analyser* which, by detecting changes in the proportions of carbon dioxide electrically, can indicate the A/F ratio on a scale.

VAPORISATION

Since it is petrol *vapour*, and not the liquid, which burns, it is important that all the petrol supplied to the engine should be vaporised before combustion occurs. As liquids change into vapours they absorb heat (called *latent heat*) which they obtain from their surroundings. If petrol were to be vaporised in the carburetter the latter would be chilled by the heat taken from it to vaporise the petrol, and moisture in the air passing through the carburetter would be condensed, deposited on the throttle and choke tube, and frozen. In this way the passage through the carburetter would become blocked by ice and the engine would stop.

This could, of course, be prevented by arranging for the carburetter to be supplied with hot air drawn through a muff around the exhaust pipe, but this is unsatisfactory for two reasons:

(1) It reduces power output. Since petrol vapour occupies a considerably greater volume than the equivalent quantity of liquid, a much smaller mass of petrol and air can be got into the cylinder if the petrol is in vapour form than if it is liquid. If the air is heated any more than is absolutely necessary to prevent the formation of ice there is a further loss of power due to the density of the air (and hence the mass of air in the cylinder) being reduced by the rise in temperature, and it is not easily possible to regulate the extent to which the air is heated.

(2) If the petrol can be vaporised *inside the cylinder* the heat absorbed during vaporisation will have a beneficial cooling effect on the inside of the combustion chamber, particularly when the engine is developing full power.

Thus best results will be obtained if the fuel can be induced into the cylinder in liquid form *provided it can all be vaporised before combustion*. Since vapour is given off from the *surface* of a liquid, the rate of evaporation can be increased by breaking up the liquid into a fine spray of minute droplets. (A millimetre cube has a volume of 1 cubic millimetre and a surface area of 6 square millimetres. The cube can be cut up into eight smaller cubes each having sides ½ millimetre long and a surface area of 1½ square millimetres, giving a total area of 12 square millimetres for the same total volume. Hence, the smaller the size of the droplets forming a spray of fuel the greater the surface area for a given volume.)

A liquid broken up into an extremely fine spray is said to be *atomised*, and petrol in this state will evaporate exceedingly rapidly: under running conditions some evaporation will take place in the manifold, but at high engine speeds the greater proportion of the fuel entering the cylinder will still be liquid, especially if the manifold is short.

FUNCTIONS OF THE CARBURETTER

These can now be summarised as:
(1) To mix air and petrol in suitable proportions to obtain the desired performance from the engine.
(2) To atomise the liquid fuel.

THE SIMPLE CARBURETTER

The term *simple carburetter* refers to the basic type of carburetter. Whilst it might be suitable for certain types of engine, it is not satisfactory for modern motor-vehicle engines, and modifications to this basic type are necessary. These modifications will be described in later chapters.

A carburetter consists essentially of two parts:

(1) The means for regulating the entry of fuel to the carburetter according to the rate at which the fuel is used. This usually takes the form of a *float chamber*.

(2) The means for atomising the fuel and mixing it with the necessary amount of air. This part is known as the *mixing chamber*. These two parts are not necessarily separate from one another.

THE FLOAT CHAMBER

The action of this is based upon the principle of the simple U-tube, which is illustrated in Fig. 3.3.1. Diagram (a) shows a U-tube partly filled with liquid: so long as the pressures acting at A and B are equal, the levels of liquid in the two limbs of the tube will be at the same height, but if the pressure at A exceeds that at B, the level of liquid in limb A will be forced down and that in B raised. Thus there will be a difference in the height of the two levels, h, proportional to the difference in the two pressures, as illustrated in diagram (b). Note that it is not the *actual* pressures which matter, but their *difference*, and the same effect will be produced by either an *increase* of pressure at A or a *decrease* at B, or by a combination of both.

Fig. 3.3.2 shows the U-tube modified for use in the carburetter, the modifications consisting of an enlargement of the size of limb A and a shortening of limb B. (It can easily be demonstrated that this

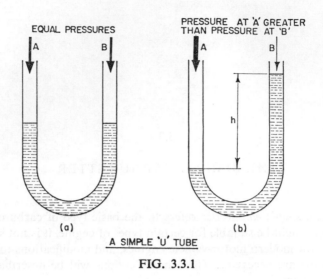

EQUAL PRESSURES

PRESSURE AT 'A' GREATER
THAN PRESSURE AT 'B'

h

(a)   (b)

A SIMPLE 'U' TUBE

FIG. 3.3.1

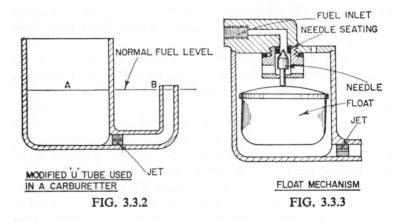

NORMAL FUEL LEVEL

A   B

MODIFIED 'U' TUBE USED
IN A CARBURETTER   JET

FIG. 3.3.2

FUEL INLET
NEEDLE SEATING

NEEDLE
FLOAT
JET

FLOAT MECHANISM

FIG. 3.3.3

does not affect the principle in any way whatsoever.) Under normal conditions the limb or chamber A is open to the pressure of the atmosphere, and is kept full of fuel to the level of the top of the limb B, or slightly below. If this level can be kept constant and the limb B subjected to a pressure lower than that of the atmosphere, fuel will be drawn out from B at a rate which depends upon the difference in pressures and the opposition which the liquid encounters in flowing from A to B. It is a simple matter to provide the necessary opposition to flow by fitting, at any convenient point in the tube *B*, a plug with a small hole, and different sizes of hole will clearly regulate the rate of flow for any given pressure difference.

These drilled plugs are known as *jets*, and they are carefully calibrated and numbered by carburetter manufacturers to indicate the rate at which fuel flows through them under standardised conditions. The jets are externally threaded to screw into position and are easily interchangeable.

Fig. 3.3.3 illustrates the manner in which the level in the chamber *A* is kept constant. The top of the chamber is closed by a lid in which there is a small hole or air vent, by means of which atmospheric pressure is maintained on the liquid in the chamber. The lid also has a connection for the pipe from the fuel pump, and this connection leads to a hole entering the top of the chamber. Inside the chamber is a float which may be made of hollow brass pressings soldered together, or cork coated with a fuel-resisting varnish, or a suitable plastic material. Attached to the top of the float is a needle, the pointed end of which enters the hole by which the fuel comes into the chamber.

When the chamber is empty the float lies on the bottom of the chamber and the fuel inlet is open. Operation of the fuel pump delivers fuel to the chamber; as this fills, the float rises on the fuel level, bringing the end of the needle into contact with a seating at the end of the fuel inlet hole and cutting off any further entry of fuel until some fuel is drawn away through the jet, when the needle valve reopens as the fuel level falls to admit more fuel. The height of fuel in the chamber at which the needle valve cuts off the supply is arranged to be slightly below the top of the discharge nozzle.

THE VENTURI

This device consists simply of a tube of which the bore diminishes smoothly to a *throat* and then smoothly enlarges to its original size, as illustrated in Fig. 3.3.4. A fluid (i.e. a liquid or a gas) flowing along this tube will have to move faster as it passes through the throat than at other points. The result of this is that the pressure of the fluid will be reduced as its velocity increases, and will rise again as the velocity falls.

This can easily be demonstrated by the simple piece of apparatus shown in Fig. 3.3.5. The tube can be made of any suitable material, preferably perspex, and of rectangular section, with double-ended

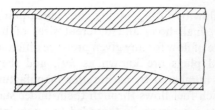

VENTURI

FIG. 3.3.4

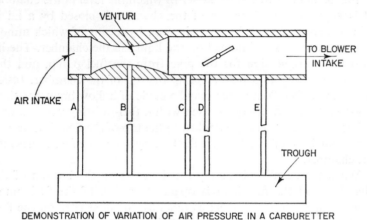

DEMONSTRATION OF VARIATION OF AIR PRESSURE IN A CARBURETTER

FIG. 3.3.5

wedges to form the throat of the venturi. Narrow glass tubes, *A*, *B*, *C*, *D* and *E*, are fitted into holes drilled at the positions shown, and dip into coloured water in a small trough. One end of the tube is connected to the intake side of a *blower* (like that in a vacuum cleaner), which will draw air through the tube. When there is no flow through the tube the levels in the tubes *A*, *B* and *C* are at the height of the water in the trough, but when the blower is switched on, air is drawn through the tube and the levels in the glass tubes will rise. It will be found that the level in tube *B* will be higher than those in tubes *A* and *C*, showing that the pressure at the throat of the venturi is lower than that in the larger parts of the tube. It will also be seen that the level in *B* *rises* as the blower speeds up after switching on, and *falls* as the blower slows down on switching off. This shows that the pressure drop at the throat of the venturi is related to the rate of air flow through it.

The mixing chamber of a carburetter consists of a venturi fitted on to the end of the induction pipe leading to the inlet valve of the engine. Thus when the engine is running air is drawn through the venturi on its way into the engine and a *depression* or drop in pressure occurs at the throat of the venturi. The fuel discharge nozzle is inserted into the throat of the venturi, which is generally known as the *choke tube*.

THE COMPLETE CARBURETTER

Fig. 3.3.6 shows the complete carburetter. The only component not so far mentioned is the *throttle valve*, the purpose of which is to regulate the engine power by controlling the air flow to the engine. The action of the carburetter is as follows.

When the fuel supply is turned on, fuel enters the float chamber (11) through the inlet connection (7), and rises in both the float chamber and also the fuel discharge nozzle through the passage (12). As the level rises, the float (10) also rises, and lifts the needle (9) into the needle seating (8). This cuts off the entry of fuel when the level is just below the top of the discharge nozzle. If the engine is rotated, air is drawn in through the air intake (5) and choke tube (3), producing a pressure drop or depression inside the choke tube. This depression draws fuel from the float chamber via the passage (12) and the jet (4) into the mixing chamber. The rush of air through the choke tube will, if its velocity is great enough, atomise the fuel as it issues from the discharge nozzle. The mixture of air and atomised fuel will be drawn into the engine at a rate which depends upon engine speed and the extent of opening of the throttle valve (2). The driver controls the throttle by the lever (1) and a suitable linkage to the accelerator pedal.

As the rate of air flow increases, because of either an increase in engine speed or a wider throttle opening or both, the depression in the choke tube also increases, thus drawing more fuel from the jet.

The size of the choke tube is selected so that the air velocity through it is sufficient to atomise the fuel at the lowest speed at which the engine is required to run. The desired mixture can be obtained by using a size of jet (4) which allows the correct amount of fuel to flow and join the air stream.

Attitude of Choke Tube
In Fig. 3.3.6 the axis of the choke tube is horizontal. It does not

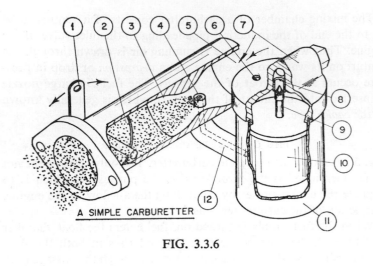

A SIMPLE CARBURETTER

FIG. 3.3.6

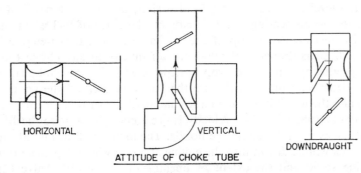

HORIZONTAL

VERTICAL

ATTITUDE OF CHOKE TUBE

DOWNDRAUGHT

FIG. 3.3.7

matter whether the choke tube is horizontal, vertical, or at some intermediate angle (so long as the float chamber remains vertical) and carburetters are made with the choke tube in any of these attitudes, as shown in Fig. 3.3.7.

The downdraught arrangement is most common on modern engines, for two main reasons: (1) the flow of mixture into the manifold is assisted by gravity, and (2) it enables the carburetter to be fitted in a very accessible position on top of the engine.

METHODS OF MIXTURE CORRECTION

The simple carburetter described in the previous chapter is not suitable for use with modern motor vehicle engines. The physical laws governing the flow of fluids take account of the density of the fluid—i.e. its mass per unit volume. Since the volume of a given mass of gas varies with its pressure, its density also varies with pressure. This is not the case with liquids.

To cause a flow of air into the engine the pressure inside the cylinder and inlet manifold must be reduced below atmospheric pressure, and the rate of air flow will increase as the pressure difference increases. To increase the velocity of the air flow requires an increase in the pressure difference, but since this is accompanied by a decrease in the air density, the mass of air entering the cylinder is not increased in the same proportion as the velocity. Thus the mixture of air and fuel delivered by the simple carburetter becomes *richer* as speed is *increased*, and *weaker* as it is *decreased*.

Thus, by selecting suitable sizes of choke tube and jet the carburetter can be adjusted to deliver the chemically correct mixture at one rate of air flow. At higher rates the mixture will become richer and at lower speeds weaker.

To make the carburetter suitable for motor vehicle engines, which have to operate over a wide range of speeds and loads, this variation of mixture strength must be *corrected*. The term *correction* as applied to carburation refer to the prevention of variation in air/fuel ratio with variation in air flow.

A corrected jet or carburetter is one which supplies a constant air/fuel ratio at all engine speeds and loads. One which supplies a mixture which becomes *richer* as air flow increases is *uncorrected* or *under-corrected*, whilst one which supplies a mixture which becomes *weaker* as air flow increases is *over-corrected*.

OVER-CORRECTION

In the simple carburetter the jet is subjected to atmospheric pressure on the float chamber side and to choke tube pressure on its other side. In the arrangement illustrated in Fig. 3.4.1, both sides of the jet are open to atmospheric pressure, for on the side remote from the float chamber it feeds into a well open to atmospheric pressure: from the well a discharge tube leads to the throat of the choke tube. With the engine stationary and the fuel supply turned on, fuel will fill the float chamber to a level determined by the float mechanism.

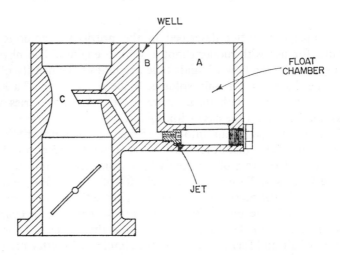

AN OVER-CORRECTED CARBURETTER

FIG. 3.4.1

It will also flow through the jet and fill both the well and the discharge tube to the same level, since when the engine is not running the pressures at A, B and C are equal (atmospheric).

If the engine is now started and set to run slowly, the pressure at C will fall according to the rate of flow through the choke tube. Regarding the jet discharge tube and the well as a simple U-tube, this will result in a fall in the level of the fuel in the well proportional to the pressure difference between B and C. The fuel drawn from the well issues from the discharge tube and mixes with the air drawn through the choke tube to form the mixture delivered to the engine.

There is now a difference in level between the fuel in the well and that in the float chamber: this will cause fuel to flow through the jet *at a rate determined by the size of the jet and the difference in level between A and B.* Fuel will be drawn away at *C* at the same rate as it passes through the jet, thus keeping the level in *B* constant so long as the pressure at *C* remains constant. As engine speed is increased the air flow through the choke is increased, lowering the pressure at *C*, thus in turn lowering the level in *B* and consequently increasing the flow through the jet.

The pressure of the atmosphere (about 15 lbf/in² or 10⁵ N/m²) can support a column of petrol about *forty feet* (or about 12 metres) high, whilst the distance of the jet below the level of fuel in the float chamber is only an inch or two (about 25–50 mm). Thus a *very small* pressure drop at *C* will empty the well to the level where the discharge tube leads off, and thereafter *the difference in level between A and B cannot be increased any more.* This condition will occur at quite a low engine speed and produces the maximum possible flow of fuel through the jet, so that any further increase in engine speed, while decreasing the pressure at *C*, cannot increase the fuel flow. Increase in engine speed now results in a *weakening* of the mixture, since air flow increases without a corresponding increase in fuel flow, giving the characteristic of an *over-corrected jet.*

Compound Jet

Fig. 3.4.2 shows a carburetter using two jets. The main jet is a simple uncorrected jet as described in the last chapter, whilst the compensating jet is of the over-corrected type just described. It seems reasonable to suppose that it should be possible to select sizes of main and compensating jets which match up in such a way that the richening mixture delivered by the main jet as air flow increases is exactly balanced by the weakening mixture supplied by the compensating jet under the same conditions. This arrangement was a feature of Zenith carburetters for many years.

Air Bleed

Return for a moment to Fig. 3.4.1. If the well is blocked up at a point above where the jet discharge tube leads off, the arrangement is identical with the simple carburetter, since the jet is connected directly between the float chamber and the choke tube, and gives a mixture which becomes richer as air flow increases. Complete block-

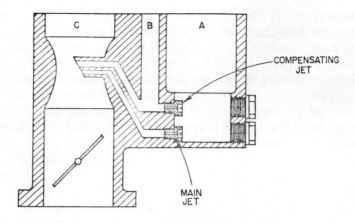

THE COMPOUND JET ARRANGEMENT

FIG. 3.4.2

ing up of the well can change the characteristic of the carburetter from one extreme to the other. Thus it is to be expected that there should be some restriction on the opening of the well to atmosphere which would give an intermediate characteristic whereby neither richening nor weakening would occur as air flow was increased. Since the fuel in the discharge tube is subjected to a pressure lower than atmospheric, air will *bleed* into the fuel passing along this passage, entering through the hole communicating from the well to atmosphere. This arrangement is used in many modern carburetters, and is known as the *air bleed system*.

Fig. 3.4.3 illustrates a typical arrangement. The air correction jet forms the opening of the well to atmosphere, and is screwed into the top of a *diffuser tube* dipping into the fuel in the well. The lower end of this tube is drilled with a number of small holes through which the air is bled into the fuel. Thus the air forms an *emulsion* of tiny bubbles of air in the liquid fuel, so assisting with the atomisation of the fuel when it enters the mixing chamber.

Some variation of this arrangement is used in most modern carburetters. The degree of correction can be varied to suit different engines by fitting different-sized air correction jets, whilst the mixture strength can be altered by fitting a larger or smaller main fuel jet.

The arrangements so far described incorporate choke tubes of fixed size in which the depression varies with air flow. They are there-

AIR — CORRECTION JET

DIFFUSER TUBE

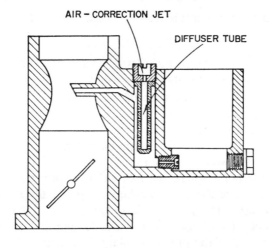

AN AIR BLEED SYSTEM

FIG. 3.4.3

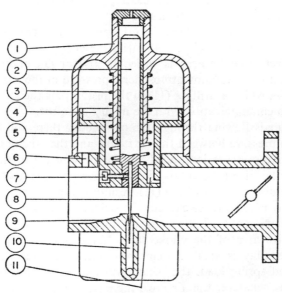

A CONSTANT DEPRESSION CARBURETTER

FIG. 3.4.4

fore known as *constant choke, fixed choke,* or *variable depression* carburetters.

CONSTANT DEPRESSION CARBURETTERS

An alternative way of tackling the problem of mixture correction takes the form of a choke tube of variable area in which the depression is maintained constant. Fig. 3.4.4 shows the constructional features of an instrument of this type.

The main air passage is of constant diameter, apart from a slightly raised *bridge* (9) which passes transversely across the floor of the passage at the point where the fuel jet (10) enters the air passage. Immediately above the jet the effective area of the air passage is varied by a piston (5) free to slide vertically across the passage, so forming, in effect, a choke tube of variable area.

The upper end of the piston is enlarged to form a disc (4) which has a clearance fit inside a suction chamber (1). This clearance is as small as possible (to minimise air leakage) without permitting actual contact between the outside of the disc and the inside of the chamber (thus eliminating friction and wear at this point). The piston is guided by a rod (2) sliding in a bearing in the top of the chamber, and this can be lubricated by a *thin* oil.

A tapered needle (8) attached to the piston by a screw (7) passes through the jet orifice (10), and varies the effective area of the jet as the effective choke area is varied by rise or fall of the piston. An air vent (6) maintains atmospheric pressure in the space below the disc (4), whilst a drilling (11) in the piston puts the space above the disc in communication with the mixing chamber.

When air is flowing through the carburetter there will be a difference in pressure between the air intake and the mixing chamber.

Air-intake pressure is applied via the air vent (6) to the underneath of the disc (4), and mixing-chamber pressure to the space above the disc via the drilling (11), resulting in an upward force on the disc. When this force exceeds the weight of the piston assembly plus the loading of the light spring (3), the piston will rise, increasing the effective area of the choke tube. If the upward force on the piston assembly is smaller than the downward force because of weight and spring load, the piston will fall, decreasing the choke area. Thus, whatever the air flow, the piston assembly will take up a position in which the upward force due to pressure difference just balances the downward force due to piston weight and spring load, and since the downward force is virtually constant it is clear that the pressure difference will also be constant. There are two important results of this.

(1) The piston rises to increase the choke area as rate of air flow increases, and falls as the flow decreases: i.e. choke area is varied according to air flow.

(2) As the piston rises, the needle (8) is withdrawn from the jet, and since the needle is tapered this increases the effective jet size. Similarly, the jet size is reduced as the piston falls.

It is, therefore, only necessary for the taper of the needle to be suitable to ensure that air flow and fuel flow are kept within the desired relationship. When a carburetter of this type is first applied to an engine, tests are carried out to determine the necessary taper of the needle, and if similarly tapered needles are fitted to the carburetters of similar engines the best air/fuel ratio for all conditions will automatically be obtained.

In some carburetters of this type a synthetic rubber diaphragm is used in place of the suction disc, but the operation is exactly the same.

3.5

SLOW-RUNNING SYSTEMS

The rate of air flow through a carburetter can be varied in two ways:
(1) by varying the engine speed, leaving the throttle position fixed,
and (2) by varying the amount of throttle opening, engine speed
remaining constant.

Under most running conditions, of course, these two factors do
not operate independently, and a change of throttle opening will
usually result in a change in engine speed, but this is not always the
case; e.g. when climbing hills it will be necessary to open the throttle
wider to maintain the same speed as on a level road.

Decreasing air flow results in a reduction in the air velocity at the
choke tube, and consequently the pressure at this point rises nearer
to atmospheric. If the carburetter is properly corrected this will not
alter the mixture strength, but it will result in a progressive coarsening
of the spray owing to the reduced velocity of the air flow. Also, as the
air flow is reduced, the velocity will eventually become insufficient
to maintain the fuel droplets in suspension, owing both to their
increased size and the low air velocity in the manifold.

There will, therefore, be a speed below which the engine will not
run, and this will depend primarily upon the size of the choke tube
and, to a lesser extent, upon the diameter and length of the inlet
manifold. The conditions necessary for good low-speed operation
are quite unsuitable for developing reasonably high power at
high speeds, and there is obviously a limit to the extent to which
power at high rev/min can be sacrificed to obtain good low-speed
operation.

The extreme condition of low air velocity through the choke tube
occurs when the engine is running but not driving the car, and therefore has merely to develop sufficient power to overcome its own

internal friction losses. This is the case whenever the vehicle is stationary but may be required to move at any moment, as, for instance, when halted in traffic or at traffic lights. For economy and comfort, the engine should run slowly and quietly, but respond instantly to the opening of the throttle when the time comes for it to drive the vehicle.

This condition of engine operation is known as *slow running*, *ticking over* or *idling*. The air flow through the choke tube is then not only too slow to atomise the fuel, but there is insufficient depression in the choke tube to draw fuel from the jets.

To pass the amount of mixture needed to keep the engine running at idling speed, the throttle is barely open, and the air velocity is greatest where it passes through the very small gap around the edge of the throttle. A vacuum gauge will show that the depression in the manifold is at its highest (about 15–18 inches or 380–450 mm of mercury below atmospheric).

To provide a suitable mixture for slow running, therefore, an arrangement similar to that shown in Fig. 3.5.1 is used. A passage (1) connects with the float chamber via the main jet at its lower end, and a jet (2) called the *slow-running jet* or *idling jet* is fitted in this passage. It connects with another passage (4) which leads to the mixing chamber at a point opposite the edge of the throttle (5). The other end of passage (4) is open to the atmosphere through a small hole, which is partly closed by the pointed end of a screw (3).

When the engine is idling there is a strong depression on the engine side of the throttle, which draws fuel through passage (1), jet (2) and passage (4) into the manifold. Mixed with this fuel will be a small amount of air drawn past screw (3) and forming an emulsion of air and fuel in passage (4). This emulsion emerges into the air passing the throttle at the point where the air velocity is very high, thus ensuring thorough atomisation of the fuel. The mixture reaching the engine thus consists of fuel drawn past the jet (2), air entering at the hole (3), and the air passing the throttle edge. The speed at which the engine runs is determined primarily by the extent of throttle opening, and this is adjustable by a screw which contacts the lever attached to the throttle spindle, thus preventing it from closing fully. The strength of the mixture delivered by the slow-running system can be adjusted by means of the screw (3) within limits, although the size of the jet (2) and the amount of throttle opening also play their parts.

MIXTURE STRENGTH FOR SLOW RUNNING

It was shown on page 108 that the valve timing must be selected to give good results over a wide speed range: it cannot be suitable for both high speeds *and* low speeds, and in the interests of reasonable performance the timing will be quite unsuitable for idling conditions, particularly on account of *overlap*. For idling, the engine needs a mere whiff of gas, so that the pressure developed during combustion and the amount of exhaust gas to be disposed of during the exhaust stroke are correspondingly small. This, combined with the very low speed of the engine, results in a small quantity of exhaust gas being wafted gently along the exhaust pipe. It therefore possesses little or no momentum and consequently will not reduce the pressure in the cylinder appreciably below atmospheric. As a vacuum gauge will show, the pressure inside the inlet manifold will be well below atmospheric when the engine is idling, so that when the inlet valve opens there will be a rush of burned gas from the exhaust pipe into the inlet manifold which will continue until the exhaust valve closes. It is this which limits the amount of overlap which can be permitted if the engine is to be expected to idle smoothly and reliably, and it will occur to some extent even with a very few degrees of overlap. Thus, during the succeeding induction stroke the cylinder will take in from the induction manifold a good deal of already burnt gas followed by a small amount of fresh mixture, and to ensure combustion the mixture provided by the carburetter needs to be much richer than normal.

Slow-running Adjustment

The screw (3) (Fig. 3.5.1) is provided to permit the slow-running mixture strength to be adjusted to suit the particular engine to which the carburetter is fitted. At medium and high speeds the most suitable mixture is provided by the main jet system by fitting a choke tube and jets of a fixed size, as determined by careful testing during the development stage of the engine. The tolerances allowed on the sizes of engine parts are so small that there will be little discernible difference in the running of individual engines of the same make and type at normal running speeds, but under idling conditions the situation is a little different.

Since the pressure inside the manifold is always below atmospheric pressure when the engine is running, any leakage in the manifold will be of air leaking *into* the manifold and weakening the

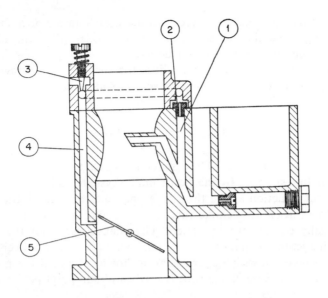

A SIMPLE SLOW-RUNNING SYSTEM

FIG. 3.5.1

mixture. The chief points of leakage are the clearances which must necessarily be allowed between the inlet valves and their guides, and there will in addition be some leakage past the piston rings. Moreover, this leakage will increase as these parts become worn. The leakage will be greatest when manifold pressure is lowest, i.e. during idling, and will have its greatest effect on mixture strength when the leak is into the smallest quantity of mixture taken in by the cylinder, which also occurs when idling. It is thus not possible to ensure the most suitable strength of mixture for idling without some simple adjustment which can be made to suit the individual engine, and which can be readjusted as valve guides and cylinders wear.

The operation of adjusting the idling system may vary slightly with different engines, but the following are the main points:

(1) Check that sparking plugs and contact breaker are clean and correctly adjusted and ignition correctly timed.
(2) Start the engine and warm it up to its normal running temperature.
(3) Adjust the throttle stop screw to obtain the desired engine rev/min.
(4) Adjust the air screw (3) (Fig. 3.5.1) to the best position. This

can be made easier by use of either a tachometer or a vacuum
gauge, and the correct setting is that which gives the highest
rev/min or vacuum gauge reading.

(5) It may be necessary to readjust the throttle stop screw after
operation (4), and these two screws should be adjusted alternately until the best results are obtained.

'PICK UP' FROM IDLING

As the throttle is opened, more air passes it: At the same time
manifold pressure rises. These two effects result in a weakening of
the mixture supplied by the slow-running system, and this gradually
goes out of action as the throttle is opened. At the same time, the
air flow through the choke tube increases and the main jet system
gradually comes into operation. The changeover from the slow-
running jet to the main jet should take place smoothly, but this does
not always occur with the arrangement shown in Fig. 3.5.1, especially
if a relatively large choke tube is used to obtain good performance
at higher engine speeds.

This difficulty is overcome by the arrangement illustrated in
Fig. 3.5.2. The idling system discharges through two holes so

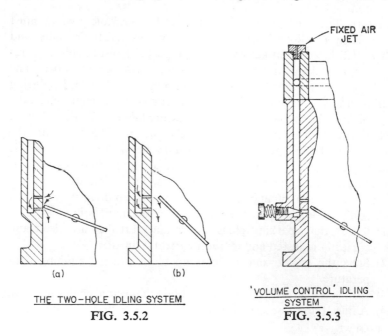

(a)   (b)

THE TWO-HOLE IDLING SYSTEM
FIG. 3.5.2

'VOLUME CONTROL' IDLING
SYSTEM
FIG. 3.5.3

disposed that when the throttle is in the idling position (a), one hole is slightly on the engine side of the throttle edge and the other on the choke tube side. With this setting of the throttle, the pressure on the choke tube side of the throttle will be practically atmospheric, and air will enter the small hole on this side and issue with the mixture from the other. Slight opening of the throttle (b) allows greater air flow past it, but now *both* holes come under the influence of manifold pressure, cutting off the entry of air to the upper hole and drawing fuel from *both* holes. This prevents excessive weakening of the mixture and extends the range of operation of the slow-running system until the main jet system can take over.

This arrangement is known as the *two-hole* idling system. The hole nearest the choke tube is sometimes made in the form of a detachable and interchangeable jet—called the *progression jet*—in order that the most suitable size for any engine can be selected. The arrangement is otherwise as shown in Fig. 3.5.1.

VOLUME CONTROL

The slow-running system described above is sometimes called the *quality-controlled system,* since adjusting the screw (3) regulates the quality or strength of the mixture discharged into the mixing chamber. An alternative system is shown in Fig. 3.5.3. Here the screw (3) of Fig. 5.3.1 is replaced by a fixed air jet, and the main idling hole (i.e. the one on the engine side of the throttle) is made adjustable by means of a pointed screw. The effect of this adjustment is to regulate the *quantity* or *volume* of mixture discharged by the slow-running system: hence the name *volume-controlled system.*

The main advantages claimed for this system are that it cannot deliver neat petrol to the mixing chamber (as the other system might if the adjusting screw were screwed hard in): that it prevents siphoning of petrol when the engine is not running (which can occur in downdraught carburetters): and that it is less critical and therefore easier to adjust.

ECONOMISERS, POWER JETS
AND ACCELERATION PUMPS

ECONOMISERS

Motor vehicle engines spend little of their lives at full throttle, and in most cases low fuel consumption is considered of great importance. This being so, it is not reasonable to adjust the carburetter to give the slightly rich mixture necessary to provide maximum power, bearing in mind that this results in a higher fuel consumption than is obtainable with a weaker mixture. If, however, it were possible to obtain maximum economy when maximum power is not required, but yet have maximum power when necessary, most vehicle users would consider it an advantage.

To achieve this, it is necessary to set the carburetter to provide the best mixture for economy when the throttle is not fully opened, but to richen the mixture to that giving maximum power for full-throttle operation. Since weak mixtures cause higher running temperatures, overheating of the engine and burnt exhaust valves are likely to result from full-throttle running on the best mixture for economy.

Many carburetters are therefore fitted with means for enriching the mixture when the throttle approaches the fully open position, thus permitting the use of *economy* mixture at part throttle: arrangements of this kind are called *economisers, enrichment devices* or *power jets*.

These devices generally function in one of two ways. Either (1) an additional jet is normally closed by a valve, but opened as full throttle is approached, or (2) the size of the air-bleed jet, or air supply to the well of a compound jet, is reduced at full throttle.

In each case the enrichment device may be brought into operation either by a direct mechanical link to the throttle or by an arrangement operated by manifold pressure.

Fig. 3.6.1 shows an enrichment jet which is brought into operation by a mechanical connection to the throttle. The mixture for part-throttle operation is supplied by the main jet (7). Alongside this is the enrichment jet (6) which is closed by the valve (5) being pushed up by spring (8) so that the coned head of the valve seats in the orifice of the jet. A lever (9) attached to the throttle spindle is connected by a link (4) to a second lever (2) on the end of which is a roller (1). As the throttle approaches the fully-open position, the link (4) pulls down lever (2) until the roller (1) touches the end of the rod (3), after which further opening of the throttle opens the enrichment. jet.

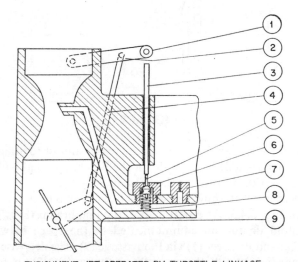

ENRICHMENT JET OPERATED BY THROTTLE LINKAGE

FIG. 3.6.1

Fig. 3.6.2 illustrates a similar valve-controlled jet, but operated by manifold depression instead of by a mechanical linkage.

A diaphragm (3) is clamped around its circumference under a cover (1). The space under the diaphragm is open to the float chamber via hole (5), and the float chamber is vented to atmosphere. The space above the diaphragm is subjected to manifold pressure via the passage (11). At part throttle the manifold pressure is appreciably below atmospheric pressure, and the diaphragm is held upwards against the loading of the spring (2).

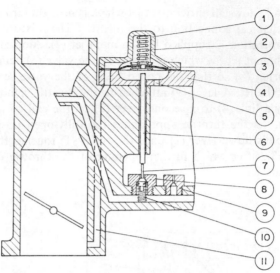

ENRICHMENT JET CONTROLLED BY MANIFOLD PRESSURE

FIG. 3.6.2

At full throttle manifold pressure increases almost to atmospheric and the spring is able to push down the diaphragm and with it rod (6) and valve (7), so opening the enrichment jet (8).

The arrangement shown in Fig. 3.6.3 is a modification of that shown in Fig. 3.4.3. At part throttle, the diaphragm (3) is held up by manifold depression communicated to the space between the diaphragm and its cover (1) via the passage (9). The decreased manifold depression at full throttle allows the spring (2) to push the diaphragm down so that the disc valve (4) closes off the main air-bleed hole (6) leaving open only the smaller hole (5), thus enriching the mixture delivered by the main jet (8).

ACCELERATION

For best acceleration the mixture which reaches the cylinders should be the slightly rich mixture which gives maximum power. Whatever mixture the carburetter is adjusted to deliver under steady conditions, the effect of suddenly opening the throttle is an immediate weakening of the mixture reaching the cylinders.

The main reason for this is the greater inertia of petrol compared with air, which prevents the flow of fuel increasing as rapidly as the air flow increases, so that the mixture is weaker than that normally provided until steady conditions are again reached. If the carburetter is already set to deliver the slightly weak mixture necessary for economy, the weakening on opening the throttle will cause poor acceleration, possibly accompanied by spluttering at the carburetter.

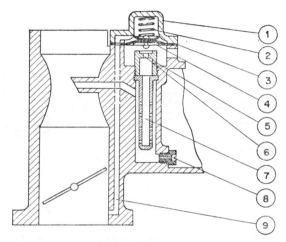

AIR—BLEED SYSTEM WITH ENRICHMENT DEVICE OPERATED BY
MANIFOLD PRESSURE

FIG. 3.6.3

This is overcome by fitting an *acceleration pump* which delivers an additional controlled amount of fuel to the mixing chamber when the throttle is opened. There are two main types, one operated by a direct mechanical linkage to the throttle spindle, the other operated by inlet manifold pressure. Either or both of these can be used to operate the enrichment device as well as the acceleration pump.

Acceleration Pumps
Fig. 3.6.4 illustrates an acceleration pump mechanically linked to the throttle. When the throttle is opened, the lever (10) pulls down the link (2) and lever (1), thus causing the pump rod (4) to push down the plunger (6). The reverse action takes place as the throttle is closed, the plunger being pushed up by spring (7), causing fuel to enter the pump cylinder from the float chamber through the non-return valve (8), the ball-valve (5) closing onto its lower seat.

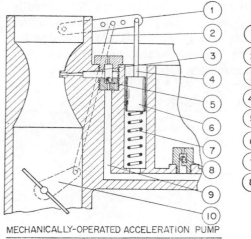

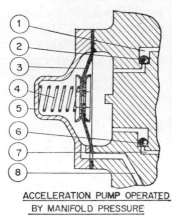

MECHANICALLY-OPERATED ACCELERATION PUMP

ACCELERATION PUMP OPERATED
BY MANIFOLD PRESSURE

FIG. 3.6.4   FIG. 3.6.5

Gradual opening of the throttle causes the plunger (6) to be moved slowly down the cylinder, and the non-return valve (8) closes to prevent the return of fuel to the float chamber. The plunger has sufficient clearance in its cylinder to eliminate any possibility of sticking and fuel will, of course, leak past the plunger through this clearance and so back to the float chamber. During *slow* downward movement of the plunger, a large proportion of the fuel in the cylinder can leak in this way, and the fuel which *is* pumped up passage (9) is moving so slowly that it merely lifts the ball-valve (5) off its lower seating, leaving the upper hole open. This allows a good deal of the fuel passing the ball-valve (5) to return to the float chamber through the upper hole, and very little fuel is ejected from the pump jet (3).

Rapid opening of the throttle displaces fuel from the pump more quickly so that less fuel leaks past the plunger in the shorter time available: more fuel is pumped more quickly up passage (9), causing the ball-valve (5) to be lifted to its upper seating where it closes the hole at the top of the valve body, preventing the return of fuel to the float chamber. Thus nearly all the fuel displaced by the pump is ejected into the air stream via the pump jet (3).

The main function of the hole at the top of the valve body is to vent the pump jet to the top of the float chamber when the pump is not being operated, thus preventing fuel being drawn through the accelerating pump by the depression in the choke tube at steady speeds.

The quantity of fuel delivered can be varied by fitting the upper end of the link (2) into a different hole in the lever (1), thus altering the plunger stroke.

Fig. 3.6.5 shows a diaphragm type of acceleration pump operated by manifold pressure. At small throttle openings the low manifold pressure is applied behind the diaphragm via the passage (8) which communicates with the space on the engine side of the throttle. This draws the diaphragm to the left against the spring force, filling the pumping chamber with fuel from the float chamber via passage (7) and non-return valve (6).

Opening the throttle raises manifold pressure and therefore the pressure behind the diaphragm also, allowing the spring (4) to move the diaphragm to the right, expelling fuel from the pumping chamber via non-return valve (2) and passage (1), either into the main spraying nozzle or through a separate pump nozzle: in either case additional fuel is ejected into the air entering the cylinders.

3.7

STARTING FROM COLD

There are two main problems to be solved in ensuring that an engine will start readily when cold. These are:

(1) the speed at which the starter motor turns the engine does not draw air through the choke tube fast enough to draw fuel from the main spraying system. In cold weather this is aggravated by the extra drag of cold oil in the bearing surfaces, which reduces still more the speed at which the engine can be turned, and even the idling system may not function at such low speed.

(2) there is no heat to assist in vaporising any fuel that may be delivered, so that the *effective* mixture of fuel *vapour* and air will be much too weak to be readily ignited by the spark.

The simplest solution of these two problems is to supply temporarily an excess of fuel sufficient to ensure that the proportion of the fuel which does vaporise at the prevailing temperature will form an ignitable mixture with the air drawn in.

If this can be achieved, and if everything else is in good order, the engine should start, but to keep it running, some excess of fuel will still be required until the engine warms up, and a greater *quantity* of mixture will be required to offset the increased oil drag until the oil warms up.

The excess of fuel which does not evaporate will be deposited on cylinder walls, and whilst a small amount of this may be helpful by thinning down the oil film, it will be harmful if it washes oil off the cylinder walls. Thus any excess fuel must be no more than is absolutely necessary and must be discontinued as soon as possible.

Fig. 3.7.1 shows one method of providing the necessary excess fuel. Fitted in the carburetter air intake is a butterfly type of valve similar to the throttle valve, but with two differences:

(1) the spindle is not across a diameter, but is offset to one side

(2) the lever (4) is connected to the valve spindle through a spring which moves it towards its closed position shown by the full line (3), but the valve can be opened against the spring load, as shown by the chain-dotted line (2).

Its operation is as follows:

The valve, called a *choke* or *strangler*, is normally held positively in the open position (1) by the cam which is spring-loaded to the

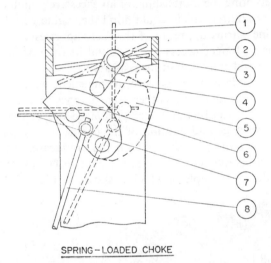

SPRING−LOADED CHOKE

FIG. 3.7.1

position shown by the dotted line (5). For starting, the cam is moved to the position shown by the full line (6) by the control wire (7), the spring moving the lever (4) and valve to the closed position shown by the full line (3), in which position the valve almost completely blanks off the air intake. Thus, when the engine is rotated by the starter, a strong depression is imposed on the main jet system, and draws from it almost neat fuel, which mixes with a small amount of air leaking past the edge of the valve (3). This fuel is deposited on the floor of the manifold, and any fuel that evaporates forms a combustible mixture with the air, of proportions such that it can be

ignited in the cylinder by the spark at the plug. At the same time the
main throttle is slightly opened by the rod (8) so that when the engine
starts it runs at a speed rather higher than its normal idling speed,
to counter the drag of the cold oil in the bearings.

This higher engine speed imposes a higher depression on the main
jet system which would quickly flood the engine with liquid fuel,
making the mixture too rich to fire. This is prevented by the offsetting of the choke spindle. The depression thus imposes a greater
force on the choke valve on the side of the spindle having the greater
area than upon the other side, thus opening the valve slightly, as
shown by the chain-dotted line (2). This allows additional air to
pass, so preventing the establishing of an excessively high depression
inside the carburetter which would flood the engine with liquid fuel.
As the engine warms up, more of the fuel vaporises and the use of
the choke is no longer necessary: it should be fully opened as soon
as the engine will run without its assistance.

This is a simple and inexpensive arrangement which gives good
results if properly used. It has the disadvantages that no attempt is
made to atomise the fuel and that prolonged use of the choke results in fuel wastage and dilution of the engine oil, by unvaporised
fuel getting past the pistons and into the crankcase. An improvement in both respects can be obtained by a rather more elaborate
arrangement, one example of which is shown in Fig. 3.7.2.

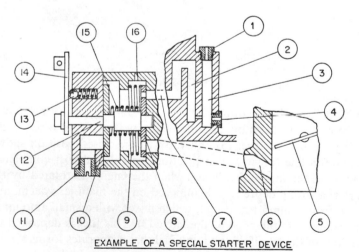

EXAMPLE OF A SPECIAL STARTER DEVICE

FIG. 3.7.2

A special starter jet (4) supplies fuel from the float chamber to a well (3), at the top of which is an air jet (1). From the bottom of the well, fuel passes through an orifice into a passage (2), from which a drilling (7) leads through the body of the carburetter to a chamber mounted on the side of the carburetter. This contains a spring-loaded disc valve which has three holes, two of which are shown. The disc valve can be rotated by the spindle (12) and the lever (14), which is operated by a suitable control wire. The valve is shown in the starting position, in which one hole opens the chamber to passage (7), while the second hole, which is elongated, opens the chamber to passage (6), which leads to a point on the engine side of the throttle. A second disc valve (10) is loaded by the spring (15) to close off an opening to atmosphere via the air jet (11). When the engine is being started, the throttle (5) *is left in its normal idling position.*

With the engine stationary, fuel fills the well (3) and the passage (2) to the level determined by the float mechanism. When the engine is rotated by the starter, fuel is drawn from the well along the passage (2) and drilling (7) into the chamber, where it mixes with air drawn in through hole (16). The fuel and air form an emulsion which passes along passage (6) into the manifold where it mixes with air drawn past the almost closed throttle (5) to form a mixture of air and fuel of such proportions as will enable the engine to start. The proportions of air and fuel in this mixture are controlled mainly by the sizes of jet (4) and air hole (16) and by the throttle opening. It must be emphasised that opening the throttle will weaken the starting mixture and may prevent the engine starting.

Once the engine has started it will run at a higher speed than the starter motor can turn it, thus increasing the depression in the manifold and in the chamber. This draws disc (10) off its seat against the loading of its spring, admitting additional air through jet (11). At the same time air is drawn through air jet (1) to mix with fuel drawn through jet (4) and form an emulsion, which passes along passage (2) and drilling (7). Thus jets (1) and (11) now admit additional air to dilute the mixture to proportions suitable to enable the engine to continue running.

As the engine warms up, an increasing proportion of the fuel supplied is vaporised and the mixture will soon become excessively rich. The lever (14) can now be moved to an intermediate position, located by the spring-loaded ball (13) engaging a depression drilled in the lever (14). This moves the disc (8) to a position where a third (smaller) hole is brought opposite drilling (7), thus reducing the amount of fuel supplied to the engine. The elongated lower hole in disc (8) keeps passage (6) open.

Further warming up of the engine enables the starting device to be put out of action by moving lever (14) and disc (8) to blank off both drilling (7) and passage (6).

Other devices to achieve the same results as the arrangement described are used and in some cases put into or out of operation automatically, either mechanically by a bi-metal spring heated by the exhaust system, or electrically by a thermostatic switch in the cooling system of the cylinder head.

You should look at the leaflets issued by carburetter manufacturers for detailed descriptions of the construction and functioning of actual carburetters.

For example, Fig. 3.7.2 is based on a device used on Solex carburetters. This is not the only type used on Solex carburetters. Other manufacturers have similar devices working on slightly different principles.

INLET MANIFOLDS

FUNCTION OF THE INLET MANIFOLD

Put as simply as possible, the function of the inlet manifold is *to distribute the mixture of air and fuel from a single carburetter to the individual cylinders of a multi-cylinder engine.* There are, however, several difficulties to be overcome in designing a satisfactory induction manifold, difficulties so complex that the designer of a very famous engine has remarked that 'a certain amount of what can only be termed "witchcraft" is apparent' in the development of the induction manifold. These difficulties will be considered very briefly in two stages.

Air Flow

If a single, straight, open-ended pipe is connected to the inlet port of a single-cylinder engine, and the engine driven by, say, an electric motor, the engine will draw air through the pipe during its induction stroke. It was explained in Section 2 chapter 8, that towards the end of the induction stroke the momentum of the gas in the inlet pipe causes the gas to continue to flow towards the cylinder even after the piston has passed b.d.c. This inward flow of gas, combined with the upward movement of the piston at the beginning of the next stroke, causes a rise in pressure of the gas in the cylinder, which stops the inward flow of gas. This is the point at which the inlet valve should close. If the valve timing is 'correct', therefore, the pressure at the port end of the inlet pipe will be higher than the pressure at the open end, and this will cause the air to *rebound* away from the port, setting up an air flow along the pipe *away* from the closed valve. If the valve closes too late this *reverse flow* will already have started before the valve closes, while if it closes too early the

momentum of the gas will cause it to build up pressure at the valve
end of the port still further, producing the same result—a reverse
flow. During this reverse flow the gas will acquire momentum which
will cause the flow to continue until the pressure at the port end of
the pipe falls below atmospheric, and this will in turn cause a second
rebound of gas *into* the port. These reversals of air flow in the pipe
will continue for some time if there is little or no opposition to flow,
the time for one complete oscillation depending upon the length of
the pipe.

By selecting a suitable length of pipe it is possible to arrange that,
at the moment the inlet valve opens, the gas in the pipe is moving
towards the cylinder. The result is that more gas will get into the
cylinder than would be the case if the gas were moving away from
the port at the moment the valve opened, and a useful gain in power
will be obtained. This, however, will only occur at one engine speed,
and at other speeds the reverse effect will be produced. Whilst this
can be very usefully applied to engines required to deliver high
power outputs over a very narrow speed range, such as racing engines, it is impractical for engines such as those used in ordinary
motor vehicles which are expected to give good results over a wide
range of speeds. To achieve this object, the inlet manifold should
not be too long, and the length of pipe between the carburetter and
each cylinder should be as nearly as possible the same.

Finally, to obtain the best flow of gas into the cylinder, the pipe
should be of large diameter and all bends should be gentle.

Behaviour of Fuel Spray

It is the presence of the fuel spray in the air passing along the
manifold that is responsible for most of the difficulties. Since liquid
fuel is much denser than air it has a much greater disinclination to
change either its speed or direction, so that where changes of speed
or direction occur in the manifold the air responds to these changes
much more quickly than the fuel does.

Unless the speed of the flow of mixture along the manifold is
kept at a fairly high level the fuel spray tends to settle out on the
floor and walls of the manifold, and fuel will then not reach the
cylinders in a form in which it can easily be vaporised.

It is thus clear that the cross-sectional area of the manifold must
be small enough to ensure that the flow of mixture through it is
sufficiently rapid to maintain the fuel spray in suspension in the air,

even at low engine speeds: this is contrary to what is required to obtain the best filling of the cylinders.

There are three other factors which influence the extent to which the fuel remains in suspension in the air stream. These are:

(1) the fineness of atomisation of the fuel
(2) the pressure (or depression) in the manifold
(3) the temperature of the mixture in the manifold.

The finer the atomisation the less likely are the fuel particles to separate out from the air, but the greater the amount of evaporation which takes place in the manifold. Evaporation within the manifold is undesirable because it reduces the weight of air and fuel which can be got into the cylinder, and the internal cooling due to vaporisation of the fuel inside the cylinder, as explained on page 143, is lost. Since the fineness of the spray depends upon the speed of air flow through the choke tube, the spray is coarsest when the speed of the mixture through the manifold is lowest—i.e. both conditions are at their worst at low speeds, and any attempt to improve either or both at low speeds merely reduces the possible power output at high speeds.

The lower the pressure—or the higher the depression—in the manifold the more rapidly does the fuel evaporate in the manifold. Here again, conditions are worst at low speeds and wide throttle openings.

Heating of the mixture encourages evaporation in the manifold and so helps to keep the fuel in suspension in the air, but it also reduces the possible power output, for the reason stated above and because it reduces the density of the air. In this case, however, conditions are rather better, provided the heating is applied via the walls of the manifold, because the faster the mixture travels through the manifold the less time it has to absorb heat, and the mixture will pick up more heat under those conditions when it will be most helpful—i.e. at low speeds.

FEATURES OF MANIFOLD DESIGN

Enough has been said to indicate that manifold design is so complex that it is not possible to design one which gives satisfaction under all conditions, and it is to be expected that a great deal of variation in manifold design will be found on motor vehicle engines.

For what may be called the normal types of motor vehicle engines, smoothness and economy are of more importance than sheer power.

Thus the manifold will be designed to provide the best possible distribution of mixture, both as to quantity and equality of air/fuel ratio, among the individual cylinders. Features which contribute to this are:

(1) Not too large a size of pipe, to maintain reasonably high mixture speeds at low engine speeds.

(2) Sharp corners rather than gentle bends where changes in direction occur. The turbulence created at these sharp corners assists in keeping the fuel in suspension in the air.

(3) A fairly short manifold to avoid marked gain in power at one part of the speed range at the expense of a marked loss at some other speed.

(4) Some means of applying heat to the manifold walls.

There are two methods of heating the manifold walls, (a) by using heat from the exhaust manifold, and (b) by circulating water from the cooling system through a jacket surrounding the inlet manifold.

(a) Exhaust-heated Manifold

The temperature of the exhaust manifold varies with the load on the engine, and it may reach almost dull-red heat when climbing long, steep hills. Heating from this source is generally fairly intense, and takes the form of bolting the inlet manifold to the exhaust manifold, usually at one point and over a relatively small area. The point invariably chosen for this *hot spot* (as it is called) is immediately opposite the connection to the carburetter, as shown in Fig. 3.8.1.

The inlet and exhaust ports are both on the same side of the cylinder head (7), the inlet manifold (3) being mounted above the exhaust manifold (6). Apertures formed at the centre of each manifold are separated by a stainless-steel plate (4) at the point where the manifolds are bolted together and a heat pick-up plate (5) welded to the plate (4) projects into the exhaust gas stream and conducts heat to the centre of the hot spot plate. This plate forms the floor of the inlet manifold immediately below the connection to the carburetter (1), at the point where fuel spray from the carburetter is most likely to be deposited. From this point the two arms of the manifold lead approximately horizontally fore-and-aft to the inlet port connections.

To enable the excess fuel necessary for starting from cold and warming up to be dispensed with as soon as possible, it is important that the hot spot plate be heated by exhaust gas as quickly as

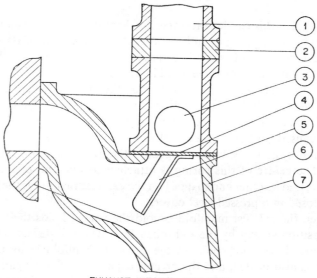

EXHAUST-HEATED HOT SPOT

FIG. 3.8.1

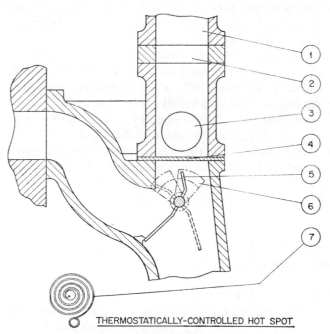

THERMOSTATICALLY-CONTROLLED HOT SPOT

FIG. 3.8.2

possible, but this can lead to excessive heating of the hot spot when the engine is working at full throttle. A modification of the above arrangement which is sometimes used is shown in Fig. 3.8.2. It consists of a butterfly type valve fitted in the exhaust manifold, so that in the position shown in unbroken lines the flow of exhaust gas is deflected *towards* the hot spot plate, but in the position shown in the dotted line exhaust gas is deflected *away from* the hot spot. The valve (5) is caused to move by a spiral bi-metal spring (7) consistings of steel and brass strips brazed together, the brass being on the outer side. The centre of this spring is attached to one end of the valve spindle, and its outer end to a peg on the exhaust manifold: the spring is enclosed in a pressed-steel cover.

When the exhaust manifold is cold the spring holds the valve in the position shown by the unbroken line, where it deflects exhaust gas towards the hot spot. As the exhaust manifold heats up, the spring is also heated, and the greater expansion of brass causes the spring to 'wind up' and move the valve to the dotted line position, where it deflects exhaust gas away from the hot spot. A counterweight (6) is usually fitted to the end of the valve spindle remote from the spring, to bias the valve to one or other extreme end of its travel and so stop valve flutter.

In exhaust-heated hot spot systems, the inlet manifold itself is heated in the region of its connection to the carburetter, which may lead to heat being conducted to the carburetter itself (especially when the engine is running at full load), causing the fuel to boil in the float chamber. This is prevented by a thick asbestos washer (2) fitted between the carburetter and inlet manifold.

The main objection to the use of exhaust-heated spots is the extreme and rather rapid temperature variations. The inlet manifold can become undesirably hot when the engine is running at full throttle, as when climbing steep hills. On the other hand, it may cool down excessively if the car runs down a long hill with the throttle closed. A further criticism is that it cannot easily be applied to an engine in which the inlet ports emerge from the side of the head opposite to the exhaust ports.

(b) *Water-heated Manifold*

The alternative method of heating the manifold consists of circulating hot water from the cooling system through a jacket surrounding all or part of the manifold. This system was popular during the

1920s, but fell into disfavour because of the long time taken by the cooling system to warm up after a cold start. With the development and application of reliable and inexpensive thermostats for the cooling system, this objection was removed, and the method is now fairly common. In some cases the whole, or the greater part of, the inlet manifold is formed inside the water jacket around the cylinder head. Since the maximum temperature is much lower than in the case of exhaust heating, a relatively large area of manifold is enclosed in the water jacket.

SOME TYPICAL MANIFOLDS

Fig. 3.8.3. shows one form of inlet manifold used on four-cylinder engines. The valves are arranged in the order: exhaust, inlet, inlet, exhaust, exhaust, inlet, inlet, exhaust. This brings the inlet valves of cylinders 1 and 2 adjacent to one another, so that the inlet ports leading to these cylinders can be joined together, or *siamesed*. The inlet ports for cylinders 3 and 4 are treated in the same manner. This simplifies the casting of the cylinder head and leaves more room for the cooling water jacket around the head, besides making possible a simple 'two-branch' inlet manifold.

To simplify the sketch, only the inlet valve (2) of each cylinder (1) is shown. The siamesed inlet ports (3) formed in the cylinder head

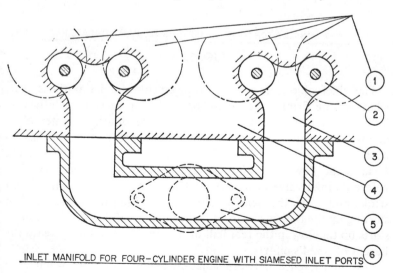

INLET MANIFOLD FOR FOUR–CYLINDER ENGINE WITH SIAMESED INLET PORTS

FIG. 3.8.3

(4) are joined by the inlet manifold (5), and the carburetter is bolted to a flange, (6) (shown dotted) at the centre of the manifold. This flange, positioned on the upper face of the manifold, would be suitable for a downdraught carburetter, but a horizontal carburetter might be used with a flange positioned as shown in Fig. 3.8.4. An exhaust-heated hot spot would be placed directly opposite the carburetter flange.

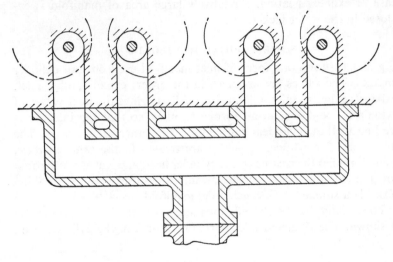

INLET MANIFOLD FOR FOUR–CYLINDER ENGINE WITH SEPARATE INLET PORTS

FIG. 3.8.4

The chief objection to this arrangement of inlet ports is that, whatever the firing order used, one cylinder of each pair has its induction stroke immediately following the other: an interval of almost one engine revolution then follows before the first has its next induction stroke. Thus, if the firing order is 1243, cylinder no. 1 starts the flow of mixture towards the front pair of ports, but before its inlet valve has closed, cylinder no. 2 begins its induction stroke and reaps the benefit of the work which no. 1 has done in starting up the flow in the front half of the manifold. Similarly, no. 4 starts up the flow in the rear half of the manifold and no. 3 reaps the benefit of no. 4's efforts.

Less interference between adjacent cylinders occurs when each inlet valve has its own port, as shown in Fig. 3.8.4. This helps all cylinders to obtain a more nearly equal share of mixture as regards quantity, although there is still some tendency for the two end cylinders to get a somewhat richer mixture than the two centre ones. This is because the momentum of the fuel spray causes it to *overshoot* the manifold branches to the centre ports. The chief drawback to the 'separate port' arrangement is the greater complication of both manifold and cylinder head casting, resulting in some increase in both mass and cost.

Fig. 3.8.5 shows a manifold arrangement suitable for a six-cylinder engine having three pairs of siamesed inlet ports. An awkward

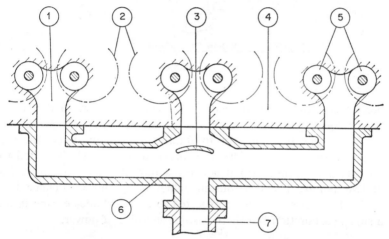

INLET MANIFOLD FOR SIX—CYLINDER ENGINE WITH SIAMESED INLET PORTS

FIG. 3.8.5

feature of this arrangement is that the siamesed port for the two centre cylinders is directly in line with the connection to the single central carburetter, and to prevent these two cylinders getting more than their fair share of mixture, a baffle (3) is sometimes fitted in the manifold. The central region of the manifold is heated by an exhaust hot spot, or, alternatively, all but the two end branches are enclosed in a jacket around which hot water from the cooling system can be circulated.

Fig. 3.8.6 illustrates a manifold for a six-cylinder engine differing in several ways from the above. Each inlet valve (2) has its own port branching from the main manifold (3) which is cast into the cylinder

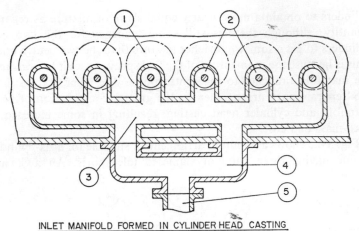

INLET MANIFOLD FORMED IN CYLINDER HEAD CASTING

FIG. 3.8.6

head and entirely surrounded by the cooling water, so that once the engine has warmed up the inlet manifold temperature will be fairly constant. In an attempt to obtain good distribution of the air/fuel mixture to all cylinders, the single carburetter (5) is bolted to an external manifold (4) which feeds into the main manifold (3) at two points. The distribution achieved by this arrangement is probably as even as can be expected in a six-cylinder engine using a single carburetter, but there is some sacrifice of power.

USE OF MULTI-CARBURETTERS

It is impossible to ensure perfect distribution of the air/fuel mixture from a single carburetter to all the cylinders of a multi-cylinder engine. Thus, this arrangement cannot give the best possible results either in power or economy, since *all* cylinders cannot be supplied with the most suitable mixture. It is possible to obtain perfect distribution of the moisture to the different cylinders by using a separate inlet port and carburetter for each cylinder, and this layout is used where maximum power is the main consideration, and complication and expense are no drawback.

A compromise which is very commonly used is the fitting of several carburetters to one engine. A four-cylinder engine having siamesed ports, as shown in Fig. 3.8.3., is fitted with one carburetter directly attached to each port, while a six-cylinder engine having a

similar port arrangement (Fig. 3.8.5) is treated in the same manner
—i.e. two carburetters are fitted to the four-cylinder engine and
three to the six.

When each inlet valve has its own separate port, there is more
scope for variation of multi-carburetter layout. Where a single carburetter supplies two cylinders, it is an advantage if the induction
impulses are equally spaced. To obtain this in a four-cylinder engine,
one carburetter would supply cylinders 1 and 4, and the other
cylinders 2 and 3. While this is occasionally done, it requires a
greater length of inlet manifold, and it is not always easy to arrange
an equal length of pipe to each cylinder, so that the alternative
arrangement of supplying cylinders 1 and 2 from one carburetter
and cylinders 3 and 4 from the other is generally adopted.

In the case of a six-cylinder engine, the pairs of cylinders having
equally-spaced induction impulses are nos. 1 and 6, 2 and 5, and 3
and 4. This is a much more difficult layout to arrange than that for
a four-cylinder engine. Thus, when three carburetters are used on
a six-cylinder engine, one is used for each of the pairs 1 and 2, 3
and 4, and 5 and 6, as when siamesed ports are used. If each inlet
valve has a separate port, or if only two pairs of ports are siamesed
(the remaining two inlet ports being separate), it is possible to use
two carburetters, one supplying cylinders 1, 2 and 3, and the other
4, 5 and 6.

A manifold such as that shown in Fig. 3.8.6 could be converted
to use two carburetters simply by removing the single carburetter
and external manifold (4) and fitting a carburetter to each of the
cylinder head ports.

When constant-depression carburetters are used in multi-
carburetter layouts, it is necessary to provide a balance pipe between
the parts of the manifold served by the different carburetters. The
size of this balance pipe has an important influence upon the operation of the system, and is determined by careful tests.

MULTI-CHOKE CARBURETTERS

Some carburetters have two, three or even four choke tubes. This
is often a convenient way of saving space and cost, since a double-
choke carburetter can be used to replace two single-choke instru-
ments. Each choke tube has its own jet system, but all are supplied
from a single float chamber. There is, however, a variation of the
double-choke type in which the two throttles, instead of opening

simultaneously, are coupled together in such a way that one remains closed until the other has been opened about two thirds, the linkage being arranged so that both reach the fully-opened position together. This arrangement is an attempt to maintain good atomisation of the fuel at low engine speeds, by concentrating the air flow in one choke tube, without excessive restriction on air flow at high speeds and wide throttle openings.

AIR CLEANERS AND SILENCERS

In the course of only one day's running, an engine breathes in a considerable volume of air, which may contain a large proportion of dust. This dust will find its way into the engine cylinders and mix with the lubricating oil to form an abrasive compound which will cause wear of pistons, cylinders and bearings. In an attempt to reduce such wear, filters are generally fitted to the carburetter air intake to remove the dust particles.

These filters are often combined with silencers which eliminate or reduce the noise created by the air flow through the carburetter. This noise varies from an intense hiss at small throttle openings to a roar at full throttle.

Fig. 3.9.1 illustrates the construction of one type of air cleaner and silencer. Air first passes through the filtering element (1) which collects as much as possible of the dust, and then passes down the central tube (3), and into the carburetter through the connection (4). The sound waves produced in the carburetter are absorbed in the resonance chambers (2).

The filtering element shown in this diagram consists of a somewhat tangled mass of fine wire which is wetted with oil. As air threads its way through the wire mesh, dust sticks to the oil and the cleaned air passes on. Periodically (more often in very dusty conditions), the element should be thoroughly swilled in a can of paraffin (kerosine) to remove the trapped dirt. After drying, it should be dipped in clean oil and drained: this will leave a thin film of oil adhering to the wire mesh to collect more dirt.

An improved filtering element is composed of a special grade of paper through which the air passing to the engine is drawn. A considerable area of paper surface is necessary to avoid restriction of

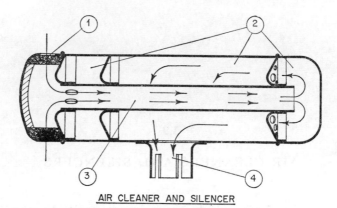

AIR CLEANER AND SILENCER

FIG. 3.9.1

the air flow, and the necessary area is provided within a filter of reasonable size by making the paper into a large number of fine pleats as shown at (2) in Fig. 3.9.2. This paper filtering element is surrounded by a pressed-steel frame and fitted into the lower part of the filter casing (4), and is enclosed by the cover (3) which is held in place by clips or screws. Air enters through the tube (6), passes through the paper element (2) and thence to the carburetter through

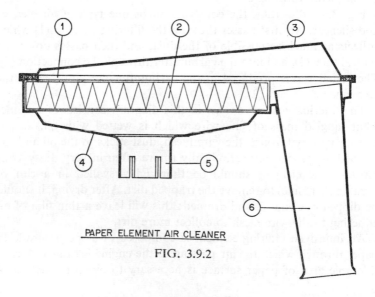

PAPER ELEMENT AIR CLEANER

FIG. 3.9.2

the connection (5). A silencing action is produced partly by the form of the tube (6) and also by the absorption of sound waves from the carburetter by the paper element itself. An additional advantage of this type of filter is its small overall height.

Other materials used for filtering elements are cloth and felt. These, like paper, cannot normally be cleaned and should be replaced at intervals as specified by the engine manufacturer.

EXHAUST SYSTEMS

The exhaust system consists of three main parts:

(1) The exhaust manifold, which collects the exhaust gases from a number of cylinders and leads them to a single pipe.
(2) The exhaust pipe, which conducts the exhaust gases to a suitable point before discharging them into the air. This point is usually at the rear of the vehicle, but certain special types of vehicle (such as petrol tankers) may be required by law to discharge their exhaust gases at some other point.
(3) The silencer.

Exhaust Manifolds

When an engine is running at full throttle, the temperature of the exhaust gases may reach 800°C or more. To withstand such temperatures, exhaust manifolds are generally made of iron castings or fabricated from steelpipes and plate by welding.

The chief problem in the layout of an exhaust manifold is possible interference between cylinders. Consider the manifold shown in Fig. 3.9.3, which is fitted to a four-cylinder engine having the firing order 1243. At the moment when no. 1 piston is approaching t.d.c.

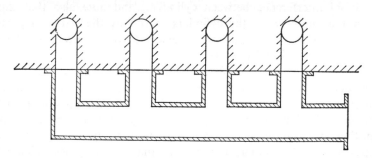

SIMPLE EXHAUST MANIFOLD

FIG. 3.9.3

at the end of its exhaust stroke and the momentum of the gas moving along the exhaust pipe should be helping to scavenge the burnt gas from the cylinder, the exhaust valve of no. 2 cylinder opens and discharges into the manifold a cylinderful of burnt gas at high pressure. The shape of the manifold will clearly result in some of this gas discharged from no. 2 cylinder entering no. 1 cylinder, which will thus retain an unduly large proportion of burnt gas when its exhaust valve closes.

The manifold shown in Fig. 3.9.4 is an improvement on that of Fig. 3.9.3. since the entry of each port into the manifold is curved

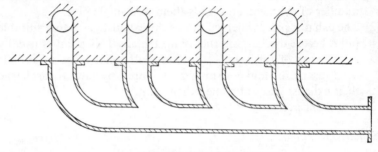

IMPROVED EXHAUST MANIFOLD

FIG. 3.9.4

so as to maintain an outward flow from each port rather than permitting one port to blow back into another.

Exhaust ports are sometimes siamesed to simplify and cheapen the cylinder head casting, a common arrangement being that shown in Fig. 3.9.5. Note the shaping of the end branches of the manifold to avoid interference between cylinders, and note also that this cannot occur between the cylinders served by the siamesed ports since, on a four-cylinder engine, exhaust strokes occur in these cylinders one revolution apart.

Interference can be completely avoided by having a separate pipe for each cylinder, but for ordinary cars and commercial vehicles this is too bulky and expensive. Furthermore, it is possible to use the gas pulsations from one cylinder to assist the flow of gas from another at certain engine speeds. This is done by joining separate pipes from each cylinder, first in pairs, making two pipes which are then joined into one. The lengths of the various sections of pipes are important, depending upon the engine speed at which the

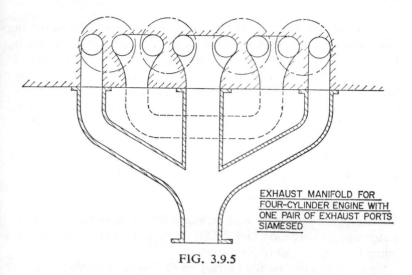

EXHAUST MANIFOLD FOR
FOUR-CYLINDER ENGINE WITH
ONE PAIR OF EXHAUST PORTS
SIAMESED

FIG. 3.9.5

greatest benefit is desired; in a four-cylinder engine the pairs of
pipes to be joined are nos. 1 and 4, and 2 and 3. Thus, when performance is an important consideration, a pipe layout similar to
that shown diagrammatically in Fig. 3.9.6 is used for a four-cylinder
engine.

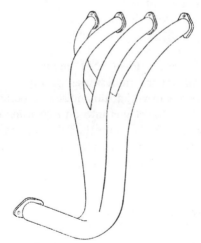

HIGH EFFICIENCY EXHAUST MANIFOLD FOR FOUR-CYLINDER
ENGINE

FIG. 3.9.6

For six-cylinder engines the cylinders which should be *paired* in this manner are nos. 1 and 6, 2 and 5, and 3 and 4, but this is much more difficult to arrange compactly and neatly than in the case of a four-cylinder engine. It is, however, easy and convenient to use two manifolds, one for cylinders 1, 2 and 3, and the other for cylinders 4, 5 and 6, each of which groups have equally spaced firing intervals. The pipes from these two manifolds usually join at some distance from the manifolds, but in a few cases two completely independent exhaust systems are used, one for each group of three cylinders.

Exhaust Pipes

These pipes are made of steel tubing which is, in some cases, protected against corrosion and oxidation by being coated with aluminium by a metal-spraying process.

Since engines are usually carried on flexible mountings, provision must be made for their movement relative to the frame. In some cases, there is a length of flexible exhaust piping between the pipes or manifolds bolted to the ports and the rear part of the pipe which is attached to the frame by rigid brackets. Alternatively, the whole exhaust system is made up of rigid pipes and connections but is supported from the frame by flexible attachments, usually incorporating bonded rubber blocks.

Silencers

The exhaust noise of an 'unsilenced' engine is due to the release of gas into the atmosphere in a series of high-pressure pulsations. There are three ways in which this noise can be reduced:

(1) by leading the exhaust gas into an *expansion chamber* having a capacity several times greater than the capacity of each cylinder. Gases leave this expansion chamber through a pipe of approximately the same diameter as the main exhaust pipe, but the pressure pulsations in this pipe are considerably reduced by the expansion chamber.

(2) by fitting *baffles* inside the expansion chamber which to some extent restrict the flow of the exhaust gas and make it leave the expansion chamber in a steady stream. This, however, creates pressure—called *back pressure*—in the exhaust pipe which reduces the engine's power output, and it cannot be satisfactorily silenced without an unduly great sacrifice in power.

(3) by leading the exhaust gas through a perforated tube which is
   surrounded by sound-absorbing material (such as glass fibre)
   contained in an outer casing. The casing is often divided into
   compartments of different sizes, each compartment absorbing
   sound waves of a particular frequency range. If enough compartments are used, most of the noise produced by the exhaust
gases can be absorbed with very little back pressure. It is sometimes more convenient to use two or even three silencers of this
type in preference to a single large one, which may be difficult to
fit into the space available.

The Cooling System

4.1

THE FUNCTION OF THE COOLING SYSTEM

During combustion, and when the engine is operating at full throttle, the maximum temperature reached by the burning gases may be as high as 1500–2000°C. The expansion of the gases during the power stroke lowers their temperature considerably, but during the exhaust stroke the gas temperature may still be not far short of 800°C (Fig. 4.1.1). All the engine parts with which these hot gases come in contact will absorb heat from them in proportion to the gas temperature, the area of surface exposed and the duration of the exposure; this heat will raise the temperature of the engine components. The temperature of even the exhaust gases is above red heat and much above the melting point of such metals as aluminium. Unless steps are taken to limit the temperature of the engine parts, a number of more or less serious troubles will arise.

(1) The combustion chamber walls, piston crown, the upper end of the cylinder and the region of the exhaust port are exposed to the hottest gases and will reach the highest temperatures. The resulting thermal expansion of these parts will distort them from their correct shape, causing gas leakage, loss of power, valve burning, and possibly even cracking of cylinder or head.

(2) The oil film which should lubricate the piston and cylinder walls will be burnt or carbonised, causing excessive wear and even seizure of the piston.

(3) Power will be reduced by the heating of the fresh gas entering the cylinder, so reducing its density. The increased temperature of the fresh gas will also increase the liability to detonation, thus making a reduction in compression ratio necessary.

(4) Some part of the surface of the combustion chamber may become hot enough to ignite the fresh gas before the spark occurs: this

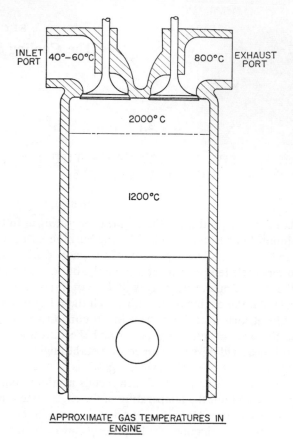

INLET PORT · 40°–60°C · 800°C · EXHAUST PORT

2000° C

1200°C

APPROXIMATE GAS TEMPERATURES IN ENGINE

FIG. 4.1.1

is called *pre-ignition*, and will result in serious damage to the engine if it persists.

The function of the cooling system is to remove heat from the engine parts at a high enough rate to keep their temperature within safe limits and so avoid these troubles.

It is, however, important not to overcool the engine, or other troubles will be encountered:

(1) Heat is necessary to assist in vaporising the fuel inside the cylinder during the compression stroke. Unvaporised fuel will be deposited on cold cylinder walls, and besides being wasted it will dilute the lubricating oil and destroy its lubricating properties.

(2) Water vapour formed during combustion will condense on the cold cylinder walls, forming a sludge with the lubricating oil and corroding engine parts. Thus the rate of wear is considerably greater when an engine is cold than when hot.

Experience suggests that the temperature of the cylinder head must be kept below about 200–250°C if overheating is to be avoided.

There are two main systems in use, both of which dissipate heat removed from the cylinder into the surrounding air.

(1) *Direct Air Cooling*

In this system, more simply called *air cooling*, heat is radiated from the cylinder and head directly into the surrounding air. The rate at which heat is radiated from an object depends upon:

(a) the difference in temperature between the object and the surrounding air

(b) the surface area from which heat is radiated.

Since (a) must be limited, the surface area of the cylinder and head exposed to the air must be increased, and this is done by forming *fins* on their external surfaces (Fig. 4.1.2). It is also necessary to

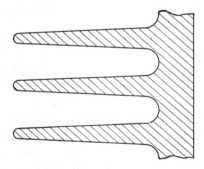

SECTION OF FINS FOR AIR-COOLED CYLINDERS

FIG. 4.1.2

remove the heated air from around the cylinder and deliver a constant supply of cool air around and between the fins. This means that the cylinders must be sufficiently widely spaced to permit a suitable depth of finning all around them, and the engine must be placed in an exposed position where the motion of the vehicle can provide the necessary supply of cool air. If it is necessary or desirable to enclose the engine, for the sake of protection or appearance, a fan must be used to supply the air, and suitable cowls to direct the air where it is needed.

(2) *Liquid Cooling*

In this system the outer surfaces of the cylinder and head are enclosed in a casing or *jacket,* leaving a space between cylinder and jacket through which a suitable liquid is circulated. The liquid generally used is water, which is in many ways the most suitable for this purpose, though it has certain drawbacks. During its passage through the jacket, the water absorbs heat from the cylinder and head, and it is cooled by being passed through a *radiator* before being returned to the jacket.

COMPARISON OF AIR- AND WATER-COOLING SYSTEMS

Air cooling has several points in its favour:

(1) An air-cooled engine should generally be lighter than the equivalent water-cooled engine.

(2) The engine warms up to its normal running temperature very quickly.

(3) The engine can operate at a higher temperature than a water-cooled engine.

(4) The system is free from leakage problems and requires no maintenance.

(5) There is no risk of damage due to freezing of the coolant in cold weather.

It has, however, a number of disadvantages:

(1) A fan and suitable cowls are necessary to provide and direct the air flow. The fan is noisy and absorbs a fairly large amount of power. The cowling makes it difficult to get at certain parts of the engine.

(2) The engine is more liable to overheating under arduous conditions than a water-cooled engine.

(3) Mechanical engine noises tend to be amplified by the fins.

(4) The cylinders usually have to be made separately to ensure proper formation of the fins. This makes the engine more costly to manufacture.

(5) Cylinders must be spaced well apart to allow sufficient depth of fins.

(6) It is more difficult to arrange a satisfactory car-heating system.

The chief points in favour of *water cooling* are:
(1) Temperatures throughout the engine are more unform, thus distortion is minimised.
(2) Cylinders can be placed close together and the engine made more compact.
(3) Although a fan is usually fitted to force air through the radiator, it is smaller than that required in an air-cooling system and is thus quieter and absorbs less power.
(4) There is no cowling to obstruct access to the engine.
(5) The water and jackets deaden mechanical noise.
(6) The engine is better able to operate under arduous conditions without overheating.

Its main disadvantages are:
(1) Weight—not only of the radiator and connections but also of the water: the whole engine installation is likely to be heavier than an equivalent air-cooled engine.
(2) Because the water has to be heated, the engine takes longer to warm up after starting from cold.
(3) If water is used, the maximum temperature is limited to about 85–90°C to avoid the risk of boiling away the water.
(4) If the engine is left standing in very cold weather, precautions must be taken to prevent the water freezing in the cylinder jackets and cracking them.
(5) There is a constant risk of leakage developing.
(6) A certain amount of maintenance is needed, e.g. checking water level, anti-frost precautions, cleaning out deposits, etc.

4.2

MAIN FEATURES OF
AN AIR-COOLING SYSTEM

The volume of air required to conduct a given amount of heat away from the cylinders of an air-cooled engine is about 2000 times the volume of water necessary to remove the same amount of heat, and in order to provide the necessary air flow around the cylinders of an enclosed engine, a powerful fan is essential. Fig. 4.2.1(a) shows a fan of the simple curved-blade type, known as an *axial-flow* fan

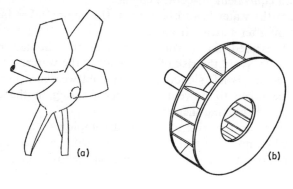

TYPES OF FAN

FIG. 4.2.1

because the direction of air flow is parallel to the axis of the fan spindle. This type of fan is sometimes used, but the *radial-flow* or centrifugal type, shown in Fig. 4.2.1(b), is more often used since it is more effective and a fan of smaller diameter can be used for a given air flow. This type of fan consists of a number of curved radial vanes mounted between two discs, one or both having a large central hole. When the fan is rotated, air between the vanes rotates with it and is thrown outwards by centrifugal force.

Fig. 4.2.2 shows a simple air-cooling system for a four-cylinder in-line engine. A centrifugal fan (4), driven at approximately twice crankshaft speed, is mounted at the front of the engine and takes in air through a central opening (5) in the fan casing (6). From the fan the air is delivered into a cowl (3), from which it passes over

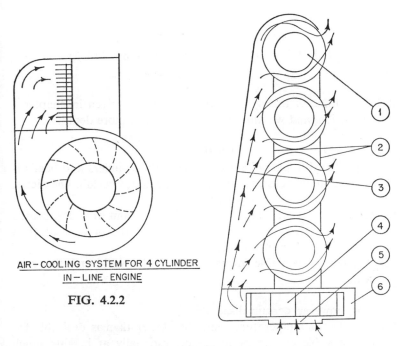

AIR-COOLING SYSTEM FOR 4 CYLINDER
IN-LINE ENGINE

FIG. 4.2.2

the fins on the engine cylinders (1). Baffles (2) direct the air flow between the fins, from which the air picks up heat, so cooling the cylinders.

The in-line type of engine shown is not the most suitable for air-cooling, since the cylinders have to be placed further apart than would otherwise be necessary, in order to allow enough air to flow between the cylinders. Vee-type engines, or horizontally opposed types, are better in this respect since the cylinders have to be spaced far enough apart to leave room for the crankshaft bearings: this allows a good air flow between the cylinders while keeping the total engine length short.

MAIN FEATURES OF A
SIMPLE LIQUID-COOLING SYSTEM

A brief outline of this system has already been given in chapter 1 of this section, and we must now consider it in more detail.

COOLANT

The liquid used to carry heat away from the cylinders and heads is almost invariably water, to which may be added certain chemicals. The chief advantages of water are:
(1) It has a high specific heat—i.e. a given amount of water, heated through a given temperature range, absorbs more heat than almost any other substance.
(2) It is readily available in *most* parts of the world at little or no cost.

It has, however, certain disadvantages:
(1) It boils at a temperature somewhat lower than is desirable for best possible engine performance, especially at heights much above sea level.
(2) It freezes at temperatures often encountered in winter in many parts of the world. Since ice expands with fall in temperature, there is a considerable risk of cracking the cylinder blocks if freezing is allowed to occur.
(3) There may be some trouble with corrosion of the metals with which it comes in contact.

These objections can be wholly or partly overcome in the following ways:
(1) The temperature at which the coolant boils can be raised by

operating the system under pressure. The way this is done will be described later, but the boiling temperature is raised by 1·5°C for every 1 lbf/in² increase in pressure (or about 0·215°C for every 1 kN/m²).

(2) The freezing temperature of the coolant can be lowered by adding an *anti-freeze* chemical. The one most commonly used is ethylene glycol, and a solution containing about 20% of this in water is sufficient to give complete protection in Britain. The strength of the solution can be checked by means of a suitable hydrometer.

(3) The risk of corrosion can be reduced or eliminated by the addition of suitable chemicals. These are usually included in the anti-freeze solution.

CIRCULATION

The coolant must be made to circulate around the cooling system so that heat absorbed by the coolant around the cylinders can be dissipated in the radiator. The simplest method of producing this circulation relies upon the convection currents in the coolant. These result from the reduction in density caused by expansion of the coolant with increase in temperature. A system using this method of circulation is known as a *natural circulation* system, or a *thermosyphon* system, and is illustrated in Fig. 4.3.1.

The cylinders (6) are surrounded by a jacket (7) enclosing spaces around the cylinders. The top of the jacket is connected to the top of the radiator by a flexible hose connection (5), and the bottom of the radiator is connected to the bottom of the jacket by a similar connection (8). The radiator, which will be described in more detail in chapter 5 of this section, consists of a large number of tubes (10) through which the coolant passes, while air circulates around the outside of the tubes. This air movement is caused by the forward movement of the vehicle, sometimes assisted by a fan (not shown in this diagram, but see Fig. 4.4.1).

A *header tank* (1), usually incorporated in the top of the radiator, maintains a sufficient supply of coolant and ensures that the jacket and radiator are kept full to about the level indicated at (3), an air space being left above this level to allow for expansion of the coolant as its temperature rises. The level must not be allowed to fall below that indicated by the line (4) or the coolant will not be able to circulate. A smaller tank (9) collects the coolant passing through the

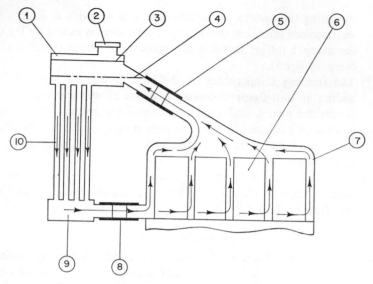

THERMO-SYPHON SYSTEM OF WATER CIRCULATION

FIG. 4.3.1

radiator tubes (10). The system is filled through the filler (2).

Coolant in the jackets absorbs heat from the cylinders and expands as its temperature rises. This causes a reduction in its density which makes it rise to the highest part of the system, the header tank (1). The temperature of the coolant is lowered by heat given up to the air passing over the tubes (10); as it cools, the coolant contracts, becomes denser, and sinks to the lowest part of the system.

To ensure efficient circulation in this system it is necessary to arrange that the cylinders are low in relation to the radiator so that coolant heated in the jacket will rise into the top of the radiator, and coolant cooled in the radiator will sink into the jacket. The circulation produced in this way will not be very rapid, and a relatively large quantity of coolant must be carried. Furthermore there must be the least possible opposition to coolant movement, which calls for large passages and connections. Provided these conditions can be satisfied, this system works well, and it was once very popular for small vehicles on account of its simplicity. In vehicles with large engines, however, it is not convenient to mount the radiator at a sufficient height above the engine; an undesirably large amount of coolant would be required and excessively large coolant passages and connections would be necessary. For such engines, some more positive method of circulation, such as a pump, is generally used, and this method is now usually adopted for small engines as well in order to make the installation as compact as possible.

4.4

PUMP CIRCULATION

Practically all modern engines of all sizes use a pump to provide
positive circulation of the coolant, and Fig. 4.4.1 shows a typical
arrangement. The radiator incorporates the header tank (1), the
filler (2), the tubes (9) and the bottom tank (8). It is identical to that
used in a thermo-syphon system except that it may be smaller for
a given size of engine and may be fitted lower in relation to the
cylinders. In the arrangement shown, the pump draws water from
the bottom of the radiator and delivers it to the bottom of the jacket
around the cylinders, from where it circulates through the spaces

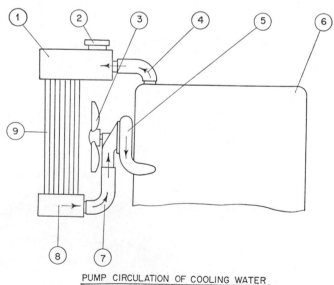

PUMP CIRCULATION OF COOLING WATER

FIG. 4.4.1

around the cylinders and head and then into the header tank and radiator tubes. Flexible hose connections (4) and (7) join the radiator to the engine at the top and to the pump at the bottom.

There are two alternative arrangements in addition to the one shown in Fig. 4.4.1. In one, the pump delivers coolant to a tube fitted into the cylinder head which extends the complete length of one side of the head (Fig. 4.4.2). Holes (2) formed in this tube (1) direct jets of coolant around the outside of the exhaust valve seats to ensure rapid circulation around a very hot part of the engine. Holes in the joint faces of the cylinder block and head admit coolant to the jacket around the cylinders, but convection currents are relied upon to provide circulation around the cylinders where the heating is less intense.

In the second alternative, the pump is fitted at the front of the cylinder head, drawing coolant from the head and delivering it to the header tank.

The pump spindle is often extended to carry a fan which ensures positive circulation of air around the radiator tubes. Pump and fan are generally driven by a reinforced rubber V-belt from the crankshaft: this drive is not shown in Fig. 4.4.1.

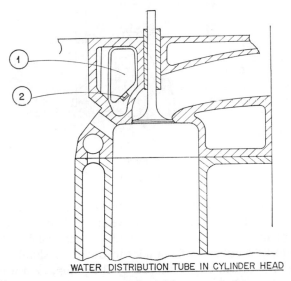

WATER DISTRIBUTION TUBE IN CYLINDER HEAD

FIG. 4.4.2

THE WATER PUMP

Fig. 4.4.3 shows a representative type of water circulating pump. The body of the pump (1) is a casting (usually of iron or aluminium, but occasionally of bronze) in which the spindle (5) is carried in a special type of ball bearing (7) which is located by a set screw (11). The impeller (4) is a tight press fit on one end of the spindle and is located by a Woodruff key: it takes the form of a disc, on one face of which is a number of radial vanes which are often curved (see Fig. 4.4.4), and it is usually made of cast iron or bronze. The body fits closely around the impeller at front and back: the inlet connection (9) leads to a space around the centre of the impeller, whilst the outlet (2) leads tangentially away from an annular space around the outside of the impeller.

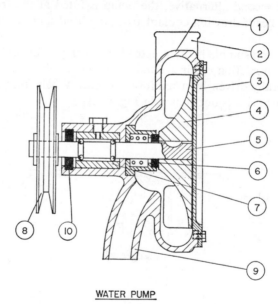

WATER PUMP

FIG. 4.4.3

With the pump full of water, the rotating impeller carries with it the water contained in the spaces between the impeller blades and the casing: this water is thus subjected to centrifugal force which causes it to flow outwards from inlet to outlet. It should be noted that very little pressure is developed by the pump, even if its outlet is completely blocked up.

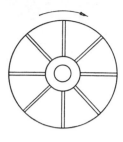RADIAL VANES

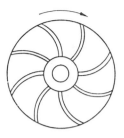CURVED VANES

FACE OF WATER PUMP IMPELLERS

FIG. 4.4.4

A carbon ring (6), bonded to a rubber sleeve fitting into the housing, is pressed by a spring into light contact with a machined face on the impeller. This acts as a seal and prevents the escape of water from the pump along the spindle.

The pump is driven by belt from the crankshaft, a pulley (8) being fitted at the front end of the spindle: this pulley often has bolted to it the fan which induces the air flow through the radiator. A seal (10) is fitted in front of the bearing (7) to keep in the grease with which the bearing is packed and to exclude dirt.

In the arrangement shown in Fig. 4.4.3 the impeller is assembled through an opening in the back of the body which is then closed by a cover (3). In some cases this cover may be formed by the front wall of the cylinder block or head, and there are other variations in the construction.

The pump is sometimes fitted at the front of the cylinder head from which it draws out water and pumps it to the radiator. In such a case the pump outlet is shaped to accommodate the thermostat (see pages 213–16).

RADIATORS

Figs. 4.3.1 and 4.4.1 show the general layout of a radiator which incorporates a header tank. The *core* or *matrix* of the radiator—that part through which the heat is transferred from the water to the air—may be made in a variety of ways, of which two examples are given.

(1) *Tube and Fin* (Fig. 4.5.1)

The tubes through which the water flows are of a flattened oval section and made of brass about 0·005 in (0·125 mm) thick. They are arranged in two, three or four rows and spaced about ½ in (12·5 mm) apart; they pass through continuous copper fins about 0·003 in (0·075 mm) thick spaced about $\frac{3}{16}$ in (5 mm) apart. The whole assembly is dipped in solder to bond tubes and fins together.

To allow for expansion and contraction of the water with changes in temperature, a header tank is fitted at the highest point in the system, usually the top of the radiator. This tank is made of brass sheet with folded and soldered seams, the bottom of the tank being pierced with holes to take the upper ends of the tubes, as shown in Fig. 4.5.1. A larger tube connects with the cylinder head or water pump outlet. A filler, closed by a cap, is fitted to the header tank and, in the simplest type of system, a vent pipe leading from just below the filler maintains atmospheric pressure in the system and provides an overflow to guard against overfilling the system.

A similar but smaller tank is fitted to the bottom of the radiator core to collect the water leaving the tubes, and this connects with the cylinder block or pump inlet.

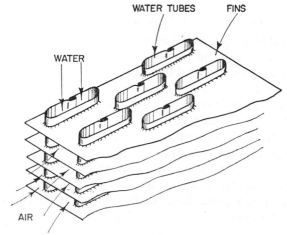

TUBE AND FIN RADIATOR CONSTRUCTION

FIG. 4.5.1

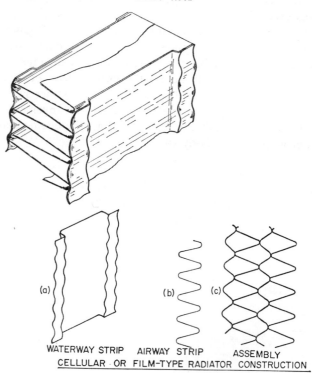

CELLULAR · OR FILM-TYPE RADIATOR CONSTRUCTION

FIG. 4.5.2

(2) *Cellular or Film Type* (Fig. 4.5.2)

Two forms of strip are used in this construction.

(a) The *waterway* strip (shown somewhat simplified) is a shallow trough with corrugated flanges. Two of these are fitted together to form a water tube.

(b) The *airway* strip is deeply corrugated, and one of these is fitted between two water tubes.

These two types of strip are assembled together as shown at (c) and dipped in a solder bath to bond the assembly together and seal the waterway against leakage. The airway strip conducts heat from the water tubes and presents a large surface to the air passing through the radiator. Upper and lower tanks are fitted to the core as with the tube and fin type.

CROSS-FLOW RADIATORS

On the older type of vehicle, particularly if thermo-syphon circulation was used, the radiator was taller than it was wide, but with modern wide and low bonnets and the universal use of pump circulation, a low, wide radiator is more suitable. To avoid a large number of short, vertical water tubes the radiator may be arranged so that the water flows horizontally across the core instead of vertically. In this case the core has a small collecting tank at either side, and it is necessary to use a separate header tank. This arrangement allows the radiator to be fitted at a lower level than the engine and may fit in better with modern body styles.

TEMPERATURE CONTROL OF
THE COOLING SYSTEM

The cooling system must be capable of keeping the engine temperature within safe limits under the most arduous conditions, such as when climbing long, steep hills at full throttle in hot climates. Since these conditions represent a very small proportion of the running time of most vehicles, it is clear that the cooling system will overcool the engine most of the time unless some method of reducing the effectiveness of the system when necessary is adopted.

There are two ways in which this may be done:

(1) By controlling the circulation of the water. This is the commonest method and is done by a temperature-sensitive valve called a *thermostat*.

(2) By controlling the air flow through the radiator by shutters or blinds. It is more difficult to arrange reliable automatic operation of these, and they are consequently less common. When used they are generally manually operated, and so a temperature gauge is needed to tell the driver when adjustment is necessary.

THERMOSTATS

There are two types in common use.

(1) *The Bellows Type* (Fig. 4.6.1)

The operating element is a sealed, flexible metal bellows (8) partly filled with a liquid which has a boiling point somewhat lower than the boiling point of water (such as alcohol, ether or acetone). Air is excluded from the bellows, which consequently contains the liquid and its vapour only, so that the pressure inside the bellows is due to the vapour pressure of the liquid. This varies with temperature, being equal to atmospheric pressure at the boiling temperature of

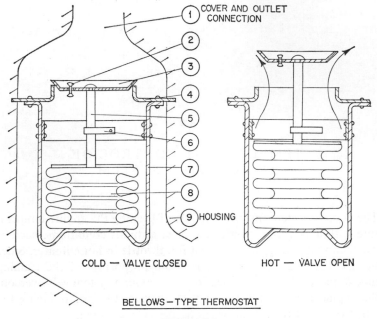

1 COVER AND OUTLET CONNECTION
2
3
4
5
6
7
8
9 HOUSING

COLD — VALVE CLOSED   HOT — VALVE OPEN

BELLOWS—TYPE THERMOSTAT

FIG. 4.6.1

the liquid: it is less at lower temperatures and greater at higher temperatures.

The lower end of the bellows is fixed to a frame (7) which is attached at its upper end to a circular flange (4), by which the thermostat is supported in its housing (9) which is usually formed in the outlet from the cylinder head to the radiator. A poppet type valve (3) attached by a stem (5) to the top of the bellows controls a circular opening in the flange to regulate the flow of water. A flat spring blade (6) holds the stem in light contact with a V-shaped groove in a cross-member of the frame which supports the stem, and provides sufficient friction to prevent flutter of the valve.

At low temperatures the pressure inside the bellows is lower than atmospheric pressure outside it and the bellows is contracted, holding the valve closed and preventing water circulating through the radiator.

As the water temperature increases, the hot water will collect around the thermostat which is usually in the water pump outlet connections, heating the liquid in the bellows and so increasing the pressure inside the bellows. At about the boiling temperature of the liquid in the bellows, the internal and external pressures will be equal, and the bellows will begin to extend and open the valve. This occurs at a temperature of about 70–80°C and by the time the temperature has reached about 85–90°C the internal pressure in the bellows will have extended it sufficiently to open the valve fully.

The thermostat will, therefore, perform two important functions: (a) it will shorten the time required to get the engine warmed up after a cold start, and (b) it will prevent the temperature falling below about 70°C when the engine is running at light loads.

A small hole (2) drilled in the valve acts as a vent to prevent air being trapped underneath the valve when the system is being filled, and a loosely fitting *jiggle-pin* prevents this hole becoming clogged.

The 'free length' of the bellows is such that when internal and external pressures are equal, the valve is open: thus, should the bellows develop a leak, the valve will remain open, i.e. the thermostat will *fail safe*.

(2) *The Wax Element Type* (Fig. 4.6.2)

This depends for its operation upon the considerable change in volume which occurs in certain types of wax at around melting point. The operating element is a substantial metal cylinder or capsule (7) filled with wax into which is inserted a thrust pin (2). A flexible rubber sleeve (8) surrounds the pin and is sealed into the top of the capsule to prevent the escape of wax. Expansion of the wax during melting forces the thrust pin out of the capsule.

The thermostat is supported in its housing by the flange (5) in a similar manner to the bellows type, and the thrust pin (2) is attached to a bridge (1) spanning the flange. The valve (3) is attached to the capsule (7) and closes against an opening in the flange, being held in the closed position by the spring (6) when cold. Expansion of the wax during melting forces the thrust pin out of the capsule, so opening the valve.

The useful life of this thermostat is claimed to be over 100,000 miles; it is limited by a tendency for its opening temperature to increase because of deterioration of the rubber sleeve. It is much more robust than the bellows type so that sudden and complete failure is extremely unlikely. This is just as well since failure would generally cause the valve to remain closed, resulting in overheating

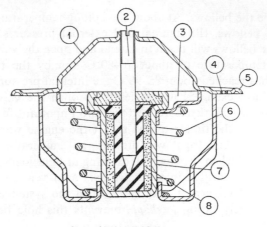

COLD — VALVE CLOSED

<u>WAX ELEMENT THERMOSTAT</u>

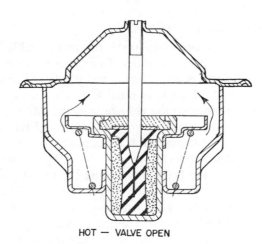

HOT — VALVE OPEN

FIG. 4.6.2

of the engine, but if a leak develops in the rubber sleeve (8) below the thrust pin, the valve will stick open.

The hole (4) serves the same purpose as the hole (2) in the bellows type (Fig. 4.6.1), and usually has a jiggle-pin also.

RADIATOR BLINDS

A very simple arrangement for controlling the air flow through the radiator is illustrated in Fig. 4.6.3. A spring-loaded roller blind (4) is carried at the lower end of a rectangular channel-section frame secured to the front of the radiator. A cable control enables the blind to be raised to blank off as much of the radiator as may be necessary to maintain the required temperature. The end of the cable is taken into the driving compartment of the vehicle and incorporates some means of fixing the blind at a suitable height. It is desirable that a temperature gauge should be fitted to indicate to the driver the temperature of the cooling water.

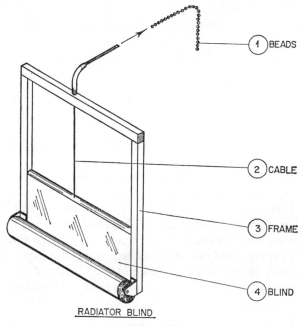

1 BEADS
2 CABLE
3 FRAME
4 BLIND

RADIATOR BLIND

FIG. 4.6.3

RADIATOR SHUTTERS

This rather more complex arrangement for regulating the air flow through the radiator is illustrated in Fig. 4.6.4. A rectangular frame fixed to the front of the radiator supports about twelve horizontal rods, each of which carries a metal strip about $1\frac{1}{2}$ in wide. When these strips are all vertical they blank off the air flow through the

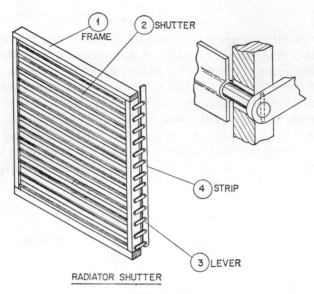

RADIATOR SHUTTER

FIG. 4.6.4

radiator, but by turning them through 90° a free passage for air is provided.

Small levers fitted to one end of each spindle are connected to a vertical strip which may be raised or lowered to open or close the shutters. This may be operated manually as in the case of the blind, but the short movement necessary makes possible the use of a thermostat device. Shutters such as these were once fitted to some of the more expensive types of car and operated by a bellows type thermostat immersed in the radiator header tank. They fell into disuse because the spindle bearings either wore loose and rattled, or corroded and seized, the bellows thermostat being unable to exert sufficient force to overcome stiff bearings. The use of nylon bushes for the spindle bearings coupled with a wax capsule thermostat should overcome these difficulties, and shutters of this type are being fitted to some heavy commercial vehicles.

FANS

In the simplest type of water-cooling system, the forward motion of the vehicle is alone relied upon to force sufficient air through the radiator. However, a positively-driven fan gives a bigger air flow so that a smaller radiator can dissipate the required amount of heat. The simplest method of driving the fan is by belt, usually the same belt which drives the dynamo and the water pump: the fan is, in fact, usually mounted on an extension of the water-pump spindle. Except when the engine is approaching maximum power, or when vehicle speed is low such as in heavy traffic or hill-climbing, the fan may well be unnecessary, but being continuously driven will still be absorbing power. There are several methods of arranging for the fan to be driven only when necessary, the two commonest being:

(1) *Electric motor drive*   The fan is driven by a separate electric motor which is only switched on when the cooling water reaches a pre-determined temperature. The switch is usually thermostatically operated by the temperature of the cooling water.

(2) *Special fan couplings*   These consist of two parts, a rotating member positively driven by belt from the engine and a free member carrying the fan: these two parts are connected or disconnected according to temperature.

In one type the connection is made magnetically by passing a current through a coil of wire carried by the rotating member. The current is supplied to the coil by carbon brushes via a thermostatic switch, so that the action is completely automatic.

In a second type, the surfaces of the rotating and free members are separated by a small clearance, and drive is transmitted by introducing a viscous fluid into this clearance. A bi-metallic spiral is mounted on the front of the fan where it is subjected to the temperature of the air after it has passed through the radiator. When this temperature is low the fluid is retained in a small reservoir in the cover of the unit. As the temperature rises, the bi-metallic spiral moves a valve which lets the fluid into the clearance between the two members, so taking up the drive to the fan. If the temperature drops, the bi-metallic spiral closes the valve and opens another which allows the fluid to escape from the clearance and return to the reservoir.

A fan coupling of this type saves the power wasted in driving the fan unnecessarily, thus reducing fuel consumption.

USE OF ANTI-FREEZE MIXTURES

One of the disadvantages of water as a coolant is the fact that temperatures may drop to freezing point during the winter months in many parts of the world.

Water is peculiar in that its maximum density occurs at a temperature of 4°C and from this point it expands with either rise or fall in temperature. So long as it remains liquid this has no very serious consequences, but solid ice expands on cooling and will transfer its expansion to its container: if this happens to be the brittle cast iron cylinder block, it is very likely to crack.

The freezing point of water can be lowered by dissolving some other substance in it. The one most commonly used is a liquid, *ethylene glycol*. The effect of this substance in lowering the freezing point of water is shown in Fig. 4.6.5. A solution of about 20%

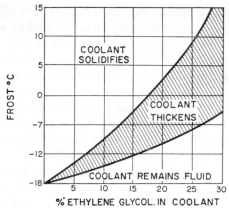

EFFECT OF ETHYLENE GLYCOL ON FREEZING POINT OF WATER

FIG. 4.6.5

ethylene glycol in water will give protection from frost damage during winter months in Great Britain.

Since the specific gravity of ethylene glycol differs from that of water, it is possible to check the proportion of glycol in the engine coolant by using a suitable hydrometer.

Ethylene glycol has the disadvantage of decomposing in use, forming acid which causes corrosion of parts of the cooling system with which it comes in contact. To combat this, suitable chemicals (called *corrosion inhibitors*) are added to the anti-freeze mixture.

PRESSURISED COOLING SYSTEMS

Another disadvantage of water as a coolant is the fact that its boiling point is lower than the most efficient engine-operating temperature, and to prevent boiling and the formation of steam pockets around exhaust ports and sparking-plug bosses, it is necessary to keep the temperature of the water leaving the cylinder head below 85–90°C.

The temperature at which a liquid boils rises with the increase of the pressure on it. In the case of water, the variation of boiling point with pressure is shown in the graph of Fig. 4.6.6.

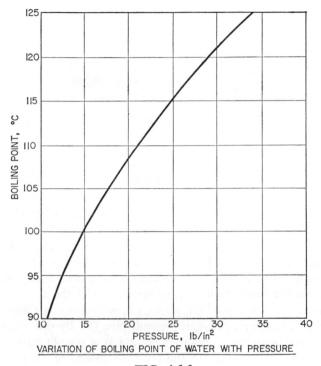

VARIATION OF BOILING POINT OF WATER WITH PRESSURE

FIG. 4.6.6

Pressure can easily be imposed on the water in a cooling system by sealing it off from the atmosphere, so that any steam formed by the boiling of the water will raise the pressure and suppress further boiling until the temperature has risen still further. There is obviously a limit to the pressure which a radiator and rubber hoses can stand, and a pressure relief valve, such as that illustrated in Fig. 4.6.7, is necessary. The one illustrated is incorporated in the header-tank filler cap.

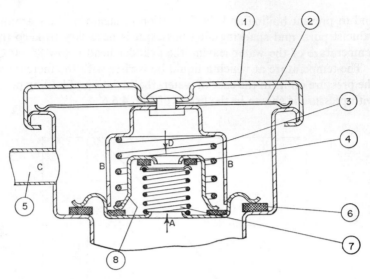

PRESSURE CAP FOR COOLING SYSTEM

FIG. 4.6.7

Starting from cold, the header tank will contain some air above the water at a pressure approximately that of the atmosphere. As the water is heated it expands, compressing the air, and if the temperature rises sufficiently for boiling to begin, the steam formed will raise the pressure still further. This suppresses the boiling until the pressure in the header tank rises sufficiently to lift the pressure valve (8) against the loading of the spring (3), whereupon air and steam will be able to escape through the vent pipe (5). By this means the system may be operated without boiling at a temperature slightly below that corresponding to the pressure needed to lift the valve.

If pressures greater than about 7 lb/in^2 (48 kN/m^2) above atmospheric are to be used, the radiator and hoses will need to be strengthened. Systems operating at up to about 4 lb/in^2 (28 kN/m^2) are common, whilst others operating at up to 7 lb/in^2 (48 kN/m^2) are coming into greater use. With suitably strengthened radiators and hoses, systems operating at pressures up to 15 lb/in^2 (100 kN/m^2) are also used. The setting of the pressure relief valve is stamped on the header-tank cap.

When the engine is stopped and allowed to cool down, condensation of vapour and contraction of the water will reduce the pressure in the header tank. Should this pressure fall appreciably below atmospheric, there is a risk of the hoses and even of the header tank collapsing. To prevent this, a vacuum valve (4) is fitted in the centre of the pressure valve and acting in the opposite direction—i.e. it is closed by a spring (7) assisted by positive pressure inside the header tank, but opens against the spring loading if header-tank pressure falls about 1 lb/in² (7 kN/m²) below atmospheric.

The advantages to be gained by using a pressurised cooling system are:
(1) elimination of coolant loss by surging of the coolant during heavy braking
(2) prevention of boiling during long hill climbs, particularly, for example, in regions much above sea level
(3) raising the working temperature improves engine efficiency
(4) allows a smaller radiator to dissipate the same amount of heat as a larger one operating at a lower temperature.

Never remove the cap when the coolant temperature is above 100°C, since the release of pressure will allow the water to boil violently: the resulting jet of steam and water from the open filler can cause serious scalds. At temperatures below this, the cap should be released *slowly*: it is designed so that the spring disc (2) (which is riveted between the cover (1) and the frame which contains the valves) remains seated on the top of the filler neck until *after* the seal (6) has lifted, so allowing pressure to escape through the vent pipe (5) before it can escape from the main opening.

Since bellows type thermostats are sensitive to pressure changes, they are unsuitable for use in pressurised cooling systems. The wax-element type does not have this disadvantage.

SEALED COOLING SYSTEMS

A further refinement of the cooling system consists of an arrangement whereby the system is kept completely full of coolant, expansion of the coolant being accommodated by providing an *expansion tank* into which the displaced coolant can pass and from which it can return to the system as the coolant in the system contracts on cooling. There are several variations of the arrangement, of which two are briefly described.

Fig. 4.6.8 shows an addition to the pressurised system already described, the modification consisting of leading the vent pipe from the filler neck to the bottom of an expansion tank. A vent pipe is

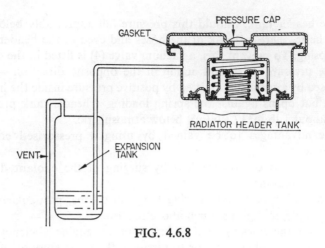

FIG. 4.6.8

fitted to the top of the expansion tank, which may—though not necessarily—have a drain tap and a filler cap.

The pressure cap differs from that shown in Fig. 4.6.7 only in having a sealing gasket fitted between the filler neck and the spring disc (2).

The system is completely filled with coolant up to the top of the filler neck and the cap fitted. As the engine warms up the coolant expands, lifting the pressure valve off its seating, and some coolant passes into the expansion tank. Air displaced from the expansion tank escapes through the vent pipe. The expansion tank is seldom more than about half full under normal conditions.

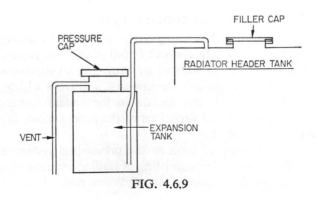

FIG. 4.6.9

As the engine cools down after stopping, the coolant in the system contracts withdrawing coolant from the expansion tank back into the system through the filler cap vacuum valve—hence the necessity for the gasket under the spring disc.

A variation of this system uses a plain, airtight filler cap on the header tank, the pressure and vacuum valves being contained in a small housing permanently attached to the header tank.

Fig. 4.6.9 shows an alternative system in which the pressure cap is fitted on the expansion tank which is connected to the top of the header tank by a small pipe. The filler neck on the header tank is sealed by a plain cap. The header tank is completely filled with coolant and a small amount of coolant is also put into the expansion tank. As the system warms up coolant expands into the expansion tank which in this case is under pressure. As the system cools down coolant from the expansion tank is drawn back into the header tank.

The advantages claimed for sealed systems are:

(1) It eliminates coolant loss by expansion.
(2) It eliminates the need for periodic topping up, and prevents possible damage by neglecting to top up.
(3) By excluding air from the main system it considerably reduces corrosion of the components in the cooling system and deterioration of the anti-freeze additives.

Engine Lubrication

5.1

THE FUNCTIONS AND PROPERTIES OF LUBRICANTS

FRICTION

When two surfaces are in contact, there is an opposition to relative movement between them which is called *friction*. If the surfaces are clean and dry, the force needed to overcome friction depends upon
(1) the materials of which the surfaces are made
(2) the surface finish, i.e. whether rough, smooth or polished, and
(3) the load pressing the surfaces together.

For any one pair of clean dry surfaces it can be shown by simple experiments that the ratio

$$\frac{\text{resistance to movement}}{\text{load pressing surfaces together}}$$

is a constant number: it is called the *coefficient of friction* for those surfaces.

When friction is overcome and movement between two surfaces occurs, work is done against friction and an equivalent amount of heat is generated at the surfaces. In a continuously running bearing, this heat must be dissipated into the surrounding air to keep the bearing temperature within reasonable limits.

Another result of movement between dry surfaces is wear of the surfaces. The rate of wear depends upon the materials and also varies with the load and speed, but in a high-speed machine it is likely to be so rapid as to render the mechanism useless within a very short time.

If the surfaces can be kept apart neither friction nor wear can occur, and the primary function of a lubricant is to separate the moving surfaces. Lubricants may be solid, liquid or gaseous, but liquids are by far the commonest and are almost universally used in motor vehicles.

VISCOSITY

When the moving surfaces are *completely separated* by a film of liquid lubricant, the only resistance to motion is due to the *viscosity* of the lubricant. Viscosity is a property of fluids by which they resist flow: the greater the viscosity the greater the resistance and vice-versa. Thus the 'friction' in a lubricated bearing depends upon the viscosity of the lubricant. But the viscosity also influences the rate at which the lubricant is squeezed out from between two surfaces when load is applied: i.e. the greater the viscosity the greater the lubricant's ability to withstand load. Hence the lubricant should have a high enough viscosity to withstand the maximum load to be carried without causing excessive resistance to movement.

Viscosity Index

The viscosity of lubricants decreases as the temperature is raised, and the extent of this change is measured by the *viscosity index*. A high index indicates a relatively small change in viscosity whilst a low index indicates a large change. The lubricant used should have a suitable viscosity at its normal operating temperature in the engine. This means that when the engine is cold, the viscosity will be unnecessarily high, leading to poor circulation of the lubricant and excessive friction (oil drag), possibly even to the extent of making the engine difficult to start.

OIL

The lubricant used for motor vehicle engines—and most other components—is oil. Oils are obtained from three main sources:

(1) *Animal* Purified and suitably treated animal fats, such as tallow and whale oil, are used for certain purposes, but decompose too readily to be suitable lubricants in motor vehicle engines.

(2) *Vegetable* These also decompose too readily to be satisfactory, though one example, castor oil, was used quite extensively at one time. Its chief merit is ability to lubricate under arduous conditions, but after a fairly short time treacle-like deposits are formed, and it is now very seldom used.

(3) *Mineral* Oils of this type are refined from crude petroleum and are far more stable than the other types. They form the basis of practically all modern lubricants, and though by no means

perfect, they can be improved by the addition of certain chemicals known by the general name of *additives*.

Additives

Among the most important of these for use in engines are:

Oxidation inhibitors At high temperatures mineral oils tend to oxidise, forming hard deposits on the hottest parts with which they come in contact (e.g. the underside of the piston crown) and varnish-like deposits on parts not quite so hot (e.g. the piston skirt). Other products of oxidation may be carried in the oil and deposited in other parts of the engine: if they settle in oil passages, they may eventually reduce the oil flow to a dangerous extent. Oxidation inhibitors (or anti-oxidants) are added to the oil to reduce oxidation.

Detergents In use the oil becomes contaminated with oxidation products and with burnt or partly burnt products of combustion which escape past the pistons. These usually consist of extremely small and relatively soft particles which will not harm the bearings, but which tend to settle out and block up oil passages: around piston rings they become baked hard and restrict the free movement of the rings, eventually sticking them completely in their grooves.

The function of detergent additives is to keep these oxidation products in suspension in the oil so that they are not deposited inside the engine. The oxidation products are removed from the engine with the dirty oil when the oil is changed.

Viscosity index improvers Certain chemicals have the property of reducing the change in the viscosity of mineral oil caused by change in temperature.

Anti-foam agents Some engines suffer from the formation of foam or froth in the oil, and suitable additives are used to reduce this tendency.

Oil as a Coolant

In modern engines, the oil helps to cool such parts as pistons and bearings. In its passage around the engine, the oil picks up heat from the hot parts with which it comes in contact, and to prevent excessive oxidation and loss of viscosity, the oil itself must be cooled. In most normal types of engine the circulation of air around the engine and the oil reservoir is sufficient for this purpose, but on high-performance cars and some commercial vehicles it is necessary to fit an oil cooler.

THE LUBRICATION SYSTEM

The function of the lubrication system of an engine is to distribute the lubricant to all the surfaces needing lubrication. In the very early motor vehicles, simple—even crude—lubrication systems were considered quite satisfactory. These usually consisted of a tank to hold a supply of oil, from which one or more pipes could convey the oil to the engine by gravity. The rate of flow of oil to the engine was adjustable by tapered needles, and sight glasses were included to enable the flow to be observed. Once in the engine, the oil was splashed around by the moving parts and beaten up into a coarse mist, some of which, settling on cylinders walls, lubricated the piston. Oil splashed onto the crankcase walls was caught in troughs which led into crankshaft bearings. Holes drilled in the upper side of the big-ends led oil to the big-end bearings, and in all bearings grooves helped to distribute the oil about the bearing surfaces. The oil eventually escaped from engine either by leaking out where shafts protruded from the crankcase, or by getting past the pistons and being burnt in the combustion chambers—oil-control rings not being known or considered necessary at that time.

This arrangement was superseded by one in which the main oil supply was carried in a *sump* forming the bottom of the crankcase. From the sump, oil was supplied to troughs immediately below each big-end, and a 'spike' projecting from the bottom of each connecting rod dipped into the trough as it passed b.d.c., thus splashing oil about the engine: the oil eventually drained back into the sump. The oil was picked up from the sump by some moving part such as the flywheel and delivered through channels to the troughs: later a pump was used to deliver oil to the troughs.

As early as 1905, Lanchester used a system in which a pump forced oil under pressure into the crankshaft bearings, and this has developed into the typical modern system, of which an example is

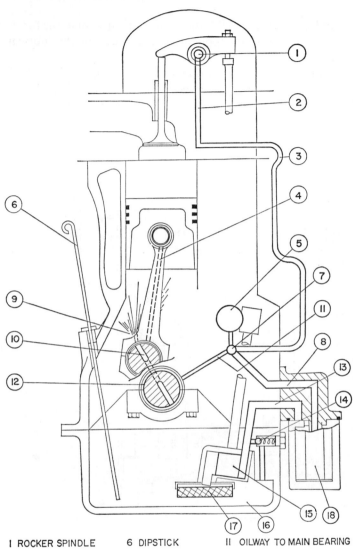

1	ROCKER SPINDLE	6	DIPSTICK	11	OILWAY TO MAIN BEARING
2	OILWAY TO ROCKER SPINDLE	7	MAIN OIL GALLERY	12	GROOVE ROUND MAIN BEARING
3	PIPE TO ROCKER SPINDLE	8	OUTLET FROM PRESSURE FILTER	13	PASSAGE FROM PUMP TO FILTER
4	OILWAY TO GUDGEON PIN	9	OIL JET TO CYLINDER WALL	14	PRESSURE RELIEF VALVE
5	CAMSHAFT BEARING	10	OILWAY TO BIG END	15	PUMP
				16	SUMP
				17	INLET STRAINER
				18	MAIN FILTER

LUBRICATION SYSTEM

FIG. 5.2.1

shown in Fig. 5.2.1. Fig. 5.2.2 shows the same system in the form of a diagram, omitting all components not included in the lubrication system.

The oil is carried in the sump (16) (Fig. 5.2.1), in which the level must be high enough to cover the pump inlet but not so high that the crankshaft dips into the oil. A dip-stick (6) is a simple means of

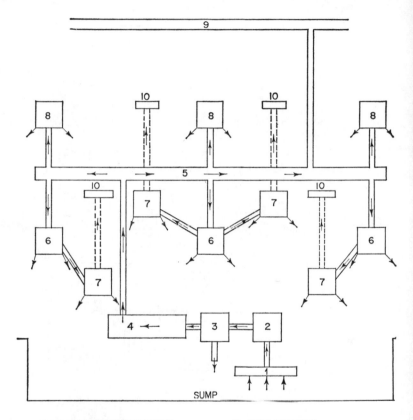

1	SUCTION STRAINER	6	MAIN BEARINGS
2	PUMP	7	BIG-END BEARINGS
3	PRESSURE RELIEF VALVE	8	CAMSHAFT BEARINGS
4	MAIN FILTER	9	ROCKER SHAFT
5	MAIN OIL GALLERY	10	GUDGEON PINS

BLOCK DIAGRAM OF LUBRICATION SYSTEM

FIG. 5.2.2

checking the level of oil in the sump, though other means, such as a float indicator or an electric gauge, may be used. A mechanically driven pump (15) draws oil from the sump and delivers it via the main filter (18) to the main oil gallery (7). A rather coarse strainer (17) is fitted over the pump inlet to protect the pump from small hard objects which would damage it.

From the main oil gallery, oil is supplied to the main crankshaft bearings and the camshaft bearings through passages drilled through the crankcase walls. A feed is also taken through an external pipe (3) and a drilled oilway (2) to the hollow rocker shaft on the cylinder head. Radial holes in the rocker shaft convey oil to the rocker bearings, and oil seeping through the bearings is splashed about the valve chamber to lubricate valve stems, push rods, etc. This oil eventually drains back to the sump via the push-rod enclosure, lubricating the tappets on its way. It is usual to have a restrictor in the supply to the valve gear, and oil seals are generally fitted to inlet-valve stems to prevent oil being drawn into the combustion chambers through the inlet ports.

Holes (10) drilled through the crankshaft convey oil from a groove (12) round the main bearing to the big-end: the groove is supplied from the main gallery (7) via the oilway (11), so that there is an uninterrupted supply to each big-end.

A small hole (9) drilled in a suitable position in the big-end bearing allows an intermittent jet of oil to spray onto the cylinder, and in some engines a hole (shown in dotted lines) is drilled through the shank of the connecting rod to take an intermittent supply to the small-end bearing.

Oil splashed off the crankshaft lubricates the remaining parts, and eventually drains back to the sump.

The quantity of oil delivered into the system by the pump depends upon the pump capacity and the speed at which it is driven. Exactly the same quantity must escape from the system, and this can normally happen only through the bearing clearances. As engine speed increases, the pressure in the system increases in order to force a greater quantity of oil through the constant bearing clearances. The pressure must be sufficient to ensure an adequate flow through the bearings at relatively low speeds, so that at higher speeds the pressure will be unnecessarily high, with risk of burst pipes or joints and excessive power loss in driving the pump. The pressure in the system is therefore limited by using a pressure relief valve (14). (See page 236.)

OIL PUMPS, PRESSURE RELIEF VALVES AND FILTERS

PUMPS

Several types of pump have been used:

Plunger Type

These are rarely used in modern engines and will not be described here.

Gear Type

For many years this type was almost universal, and it is still in common use. As shown in Fig. 5.3.1, it consists of a pair of gear wheels meshing together in a casing (1) which fits closely around the tips of the teeth and the ends of the gears. One gear (2) is fixed to the driving spindle (3) and drives the other gear (7), which rotates idly on a fixed spindle (6). Inlet (4) and outlet (5) ports are cut in the casing on either side of the meshing point of the gears. When the gears rotate they carry oil from inlet to outlet in the spaces between the teeth. As a tooth of one gear moves out of mesh with a space between two teeth of the other gear, oil flows in through the inlet to fill the void left. On the outlet side, oil is displaced through the outlet as a tooth of one gear moves into the space between two teeth of the other. Note particularly the direction of the oil flow and the direction of rotation of the gears, shown by arrows.

Eccentric-Rotor Type (Fig. 5.3.2)

The casing (1) has a cylindrical bore in which is fitted the outer rotor (2). The outer surface of this is cylindrical, but a number of lobes are formed on its inner surface. The inner rotor (3) has lobes

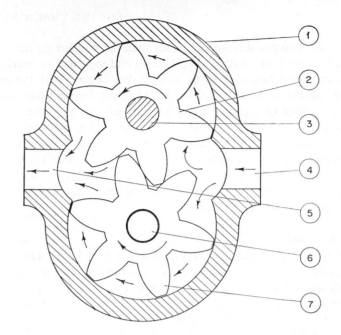

GEAR-TYPE OIL PUMP

FIG. 5.3.1

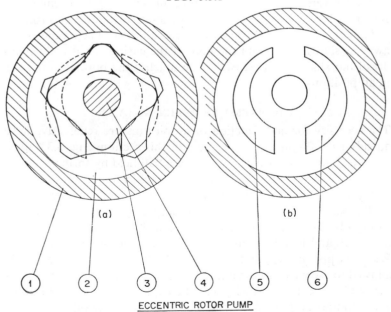

(a)

(b)

ECCENTRIC ROTOR PUMP

FIG. 5.3.2

formed on its outer surface, one fewer than the number on the outer rotor. It is fixed on the driving spindle (4) and mounted eccentrically in the casing so that each of its lobes makes contact with the inner surface of the outer rotor, dividing the space between the rotors into a number of separate compartments of varying size: i.e. the size of each compartment varies as the rotors turn. Inlet and outlet ports are cut in the end plate of the pump, and positioned so that the pumping compartments sweep over the inlet port (6) as they increase in size and over the outlet ports (5) as they decrease. The pump is shown assembled at (a): sketch (b) shows the rotors removed to reveal the ports more clearly.

Eccentric-Vane Type (Fig. 5.3.3)

The earlier form of this pump is shown in Fig. 5.3.3(a). The casing (1) has a cylindrical bore in which is fitted the rotor (2) mounted on a shaft eccentric to the casing bore and touching it at one place. Spring-loaded vanes (4) are a close sliding fit in a slot cut diametrically through the rotor, their outer edges being kept in contact with the casing bore by the spring (3). Oil is carried from the inlet (5) to the outlet (6) as the rotor turns.

A later version of this pump used on some modern engines is shown in Fig. 5.3.3(b). This has two one-piece vanes each fitting in a diametral slot at right angles to one another. Each vane is cut away as shown at (7) and the bore of the casing is not truly cylindrical but shaped so that each vane touches the bore at both ends in all positions.

OIL PRESSURE RELIEF VALVES

The necessity for and function of an oil pressure relief valve have already been discussed in chapter 2 of this section. Fig. 5.3.4 illustrates a simple type, which consists of a ball held by spring pressure over a hole drilled into the main oil channel leading from the pump to the bearings. The pressure of oil in this channel exerts a force on the ball (5), tending to lift it off its seat against the load of the spring (3). The spring load is adjustable by screwing the cap (1) in or out, and locking it in the correct position by the locknut (2). When oil pressure is great enough to lift the ball off its seat, oil is allowed to escape from the main oil channel, thus relieving the pressure and preventing further rise. Oil escaping past the valve returns either to the sump or the pump inlet via the passage (4).

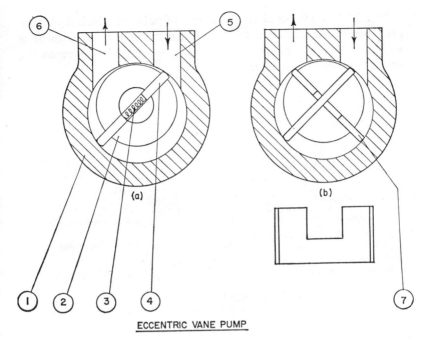

ECCENTRIC VANE PUMP

FIG. 5.3.3

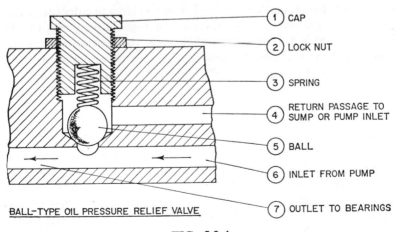

1. CAP
2. LOCK NUT
3. SPRING
4. RETURN PASSAGE TO SUMP OR PUMP INLET
5. BALL
6. INLET FROM PUMP
7. OUTLET TO BEARINGS

BALL-TYPE OIL PRESSURE RELIEF VALVE

FIG. 5.3.4

Fig. 5.3.5 shows an alternative type of valve in which a plunger (4) replaces the ball, and an alternative method of adjustment is shown. In this case the spring load is adjusted by adding or removing shims (2) above the spring.

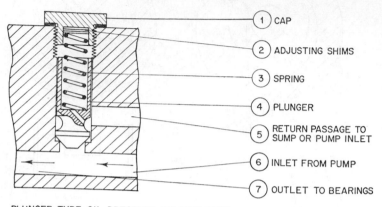

1 CAP

2 ADJUSTING SHIMS

3 SPRING

4 PLUNGER

5 RETURN PASSAGE TO SUMP OR PUMP INLET

6 INLET FROM PUMP

7 OUTLET TO BEARINGS

PLUNGER-TYPE OIL PRESSURE RELIEF VALVE

FIG. 5.3.5

FILTERS

The purpose of the filters in a lubrication system is to remove from the oil abrasive particles which would cause rapid wear of the bearings. If a fluid containing solid particles is passed through a porous material the solid particles will either be too large to enter the pores, or will become lodged in the tortuous passages of the pores, or will pass completely through, depending upon the relative sizes of the pores and the particles. Clearly the finer the pores the smaller the particles the filter will remove from the fluid, but its resistance to the flow of the fluid will be correspondingly greater. Thus a very fine filter will need to have a very large surface area if the flow of oil to the engine bearings is not to be restricted.

A rather coarse wire-mesh strainer is usually fitted at the pump intake to protect the pump against odd nuts, etc., lying about in the engine, or hard objects large enough to damage the pump. On the pressure side of the system a much finer filter is used. A filter capable of removing *all* the abrasive particles from *all* the oil delivered by the pump would be inconveniently large: there are, therefore, two 'compromise' types of filter which may be used.

The Full-flow Filter

This filters *all* the oil delivered to the bearings, but is not so fine as to restrict unduly the flow of oil, *provided the filter is clean and the oil is not excessively viscous*. It is connected in the system as shown in Fig. 5.3.6.

The pressure on the pump side of the filter is kept approximately constant by the pressure relief valve, but on the bearing side the pressure will be somewhat lower, depending on how easily the oil can pass through. When the oil is hot and the filter is clean the pressure drop across the filter will be very small. However, when the oil is cold or the filter clogged with dirt, the pressure on the bearing side of the filter may fall so low as to reduce to a dangerous extent the supply of oil to the bearings. To avoid this, a *by-pass valve* is fitted which opens when the pressure drop across the filter exceeds about 10 lbf/in² (70 kN/m²), thus allowing oil to pass directly to the bearings: even though it is unfiltered it is preferable to too little oil.

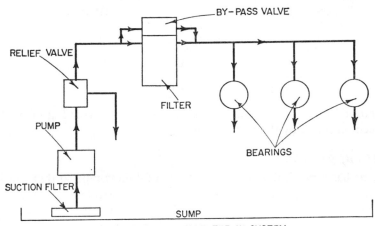

POSITION OF FULL—FLOW FILTER IN SYSTEM

FIG. 5.3.6

The construction of a filter of this type is shown in Fig. 5.3.7. The element usually consists of one or more layers of felt carried on a wire-mesh frame of star formation to provide the largest possible surface area: a plastics-impregnated paper may be used instead of felt. The filter is constructed so that the element can easily be re-

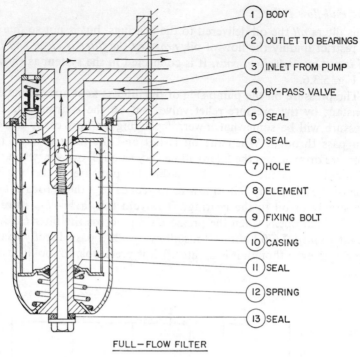

1. BODY
2. OUTLET TO BEARINGS
3. INLET FROM PUMP
4. BY-PASS VALVE
5. SEAL
6. SEAL
7. HOLE
8. ELEMENT
9. FIXING BOLT
10. CASING
11. SEAL
12. SPRING
13. SEAL

FULL—FLOW FILTER

FIG. 5.3.7

moved: it should be discarded and replaced by a new one at intervals recommended by the manufacturers.

The By-pass Filter

This has a much finer element than the full-flow type so that it will remove finer particles, but will offer much greater resistance to flow. It is, therefore, connected in the system in the manner shown in Fig. 5.3.8, so that it is constantly filtering a *proportion* of the oil delivered by the pump, but *not* the oil delivered to the bearings. If the resistance offered by the element is not great enough to restrict the flow through the filter to a sufficiently *small* proportion of the pump output, a restrictor is sometimes fitted on the output side of the filter. Oil passing through the filter returns directly to the sump.

Fig. 5.3.9 illustrates the construction of a by-pass filter. It is similar to the full-flow type; it has a finer element but no by-pass valve, since blockage of the filter does not restrict the flow to the bearings.

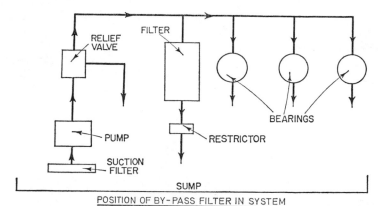

POSITION OF BY-PASS FILTER IN SYSTEM

FIG. 5.3.8

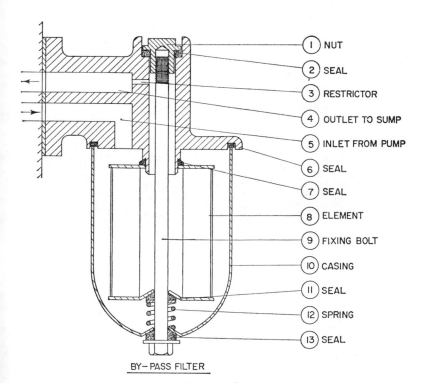

1	NUT
2	SEAL
3	RESTRICTOR
4	OUTLET TO SUMP
5	INLET FROM PUMP
6	SEAL
7	SEAL
8	ELEMENT
9	FIXING BOLT
10	CASING
11	SEAL
12	SPRING
13	SEAL

BY-PASS FILTER

FIG. 5.3.9

Bearings

6.1

PLAIN BEARINGS

A bearing is a part of a mechanism which supports and guides a moving part. By far the commonest type of bearing is that used to support a rotating shaft.

Plain bearings are those in which the moving surfaces are in sliding contact with one another, apart from a film of lubricant, and nearly all engine bearings are of this type.

BUSHES

The simplest type of bearing consists of a plain hole in the supporting component in which the shaft rotates. In order to provide a suitable combination of materials to minimise friction and wear, and to provide a simple and inexpensive way of repairing a worn or damaged bearing, a sleeve—called a *bush*—is fitted in the hole. Bushes are usually made an interference fit in the hole so that all movement and wear takes place between the bore of the bush and the shaft. There is, however, a type of bush which has a clearance fit in its housing as well as on the shaft; when correctly fitted, this bush rotates at about half the speed of the shaft, thus reducing the rubbing speed of the surfaces. This type is not often used.

Fig. 6.1.1 shows three types of bush. Type (a) is a plain bush and is used to support a shaft where radial loads only—i.e. loads acting at right angles to the shaft—are carried.

Type (b) has a flange at one end which, in conjunction with a collar or shoulder on the shaft, will resist an end force—or axial load—on the shaft in one direction. It also has one end closed or *blind*, to prevent lubricant escaping or dirt getting in.

Type (c) shows a popular and inexpensive type of bush made from metal strip bent into cylindrical shape. It is called a *wrapped* bush.

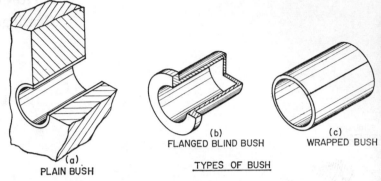

(b)
FLANGED BLIND BUSH

(c)
WRAPPED BUSH

(a)
PLAIN BUSH

TYPES OF BUSH

FIG. 6.1.1

SPLIT BEARINGS

A bush can only be used when the part of the shaft which runs in it can be inserted from one end. If the shaft is of such a shape that this is not possible—e.g. an engine crankshaft—the bearing must be split as illustrated in Fig. 6.1.2, the two halves of the bearing being held together by bolts, screws or studs and nuts. In this case the equivalent of the bush is known as a *pair of bearing shells, or half bearings.*

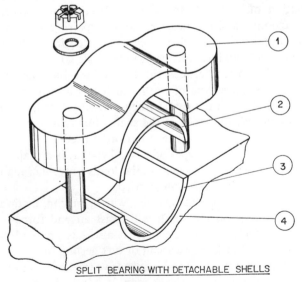

SPLIT BEARING WITH DETACHABLE SHELLS

FIG. 6.1.2

The lower part (4) is the housing in which the bottom shell (3) is fitted. The top shell (2) fits in the cap (1).

As in the case of a bush, the shells are prevented from turning in the housing by an interference fit. When a shell is pressed down into its housing, its edges should stand slightly proud of the housing faces, and similarly for the shell fitted in the cap. If the cap is now fitted in place and the two nuts screwed down *finger-tight*, there will be a small clearance between the faces of the cap and housing, although the edges of the shells are touching, as shown (much exaggerated) in Fig. 6.1.3. The gap—or *nip*—is actually only a few

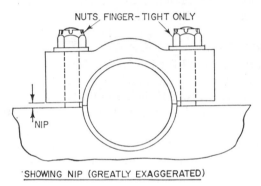

NUTS FINGER-TIGHT ONLY

NIP

SHOWING NIP (GREATLY EXAGGERATED)

FIG. 6.1.3

thousandths of an inch (hundredths of a millimetre), the exact amount depending upon the size of the bearing and the materials of which the housing and cap are made. When the nuts are correctly tightened down, the nip disappears and the shells are tightly held.

Location Devices

These are provided to ensure correct positioning of the shells during assembly, and two common types are illustrated in Fig. 6.1.4. A *dowel* (a) is a short peg, one end of which is made a tight fit in a hole in the housing, the other (protruding) end being a clearance fit in a hole in the shell.

Lugs (b) are pressed out at *one* joint face of each shell and engage with corresponding notches cut in the housing and cap. One lug per shell is used, and the lugs of both shells of a pair are normally arranged at opposite ends of *the same* joint face, as shown in Fig.

6.1.4(c). It is most important that there should be a clearance between the back of the lug and the notch to prevent the shell being pushed inwards and causing local metal-to-metal contact at this point. You can check this by pushing down on the joint face of the shell on the lug side. It should be possible to move it about $\frac{1}{32}$ in (1 mm) lower than the housing face before the lug touches the back of the notch.

It should be emphasised that the shells must be prevented from moving in the housing and cap by their interference fit alone. The dowels or lugs are purely for correct location during assembly and they must not be relied upon to prevent rotation of the shells, though they may contribute to it.

Oil Holes and Grooves

In most bearings, the oil for lubrication is supplied through a hole drilled through the housing, and there must be a corresponding hole in one of the shells. This hole should be placed at that part of the bearing where radial load is least, which is usually the centre of the upper shell. From this hole, oil is carried round by shaft rotation, and pressure causes the oil to spread towards the ends of the bearing. Oil grooves are unnecessary in most pressure-fed bearings and are undesirable in the areas supporting heavy loads, since not only do they reduce the surface area of the bearing but they also let the oil escape easily from the region where it is most important to retain it.

Certain bearings, such as the big-end bearing, are carried on moving parts and cannot conveniently be supplied with oil directly and independently. In such cases the oil is supplied through a drilling in the shaft, and thus there is no need for an oil supply hole in the shells. To ensure a continuous supply of oil to the big-ends, a circumferential groove is formed around the main bearing shells, into which the oil is fed from the main oil gallery (Fig. 6.1.5): the main journal end of the hole through the crankshaft runs around this groove so that the big-end is in constant communication with the main oil gallery. The width and depth of this groove around the main bearing shells should be no more than is sufficient to carry enough to the big-ends.

BEARING MATERIALS

Shafts are almost invariably made of steel or iron, and the surface of the bearing should make a satisfactory combination with the

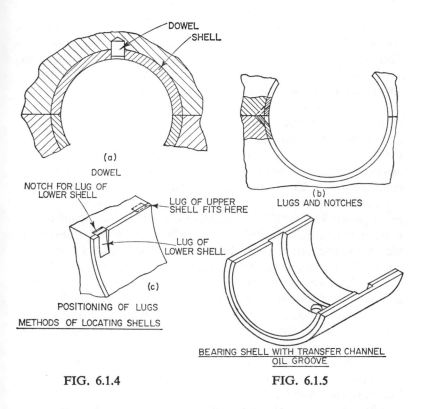

(a)

DOWEL

NOTCH FOR LUG OF
LOWER SHELL

LUG OF UPPER
SHELL FITS HERE

LUG OF
LOWER SHELL

(b)
LUGS AND NOTCHES

(c)

POSITIONING OF LUGS

METHODS OF LOCATING SHELLS

BEARING SHELL WITH TRANSFER CHANNEL
OIL GROOVE

FIG. 6.1.4   **FIG. 6.1.5**

shaft. Some materials used for the housing may be satisfactory in this respect: for instance both cast iron and aluminium are quite satisfactory for many conditions of operation and could be used without bushes or shells. But for operation at high speeds, or heavy loads, or both, some other material is generally preferred. A few are mentioned below.

Bronze

Bronzes are primarily alloys of copper and tin, the exact properties depending upon the proportions and also upon what other elements, if any, are included. A type commonly used contains a small amount of phosphorus and is known as *phosphor bronze*.

Bronzes are fairly hard—though softer than steel—and have good load-carrying capacity, but are less suited than some other materials to high rubbing speeds.

White Metal

This is basically an alloy of tin with small amounts of copper and antimony. In any bearing lubricated with oil under pressure there is always the risk of abrasive particles being carried into the bearing with the oil; hence the importance of filtration. An important property of white metal is its softness, which permits abrasive particles to become embedded in it flush with the surface, thus minimising the harm they can do. The shaft must be hard enough to resist, as far as practicable, wear due to such abrasive particles as are not completely embedded in the white metal.

Another important property of white metal is its low melting point (about 300° to 350°C). Should the supply of lubricant to the bearing fail, metal-to-metal contact will occur with considerable increase in friction: thus the bearing and shaft surfaces will suffer a considerable rise in temperature and the bearing will be liable to 'seize up', which may wreck the engine. This cannot happen in the case of white metal, which will melt and be flung out of the bearing, thus leaving sufficient clearance to prevent seizure. This results in a warning clatter: the engine should not, of course, be allowed to continue running until a new bearing has been fitted.

The softness of white metal, which has already been mentioned as an advantage, is also one of its chief limitations, in limiting its load-carrying capacity.

White metal may be used in the form of a lining bonded direct to the bearing housing. This method, though once popular, has now been superseded by the use of modern types of detachable shells. The use of shells has always been popular, chiefly because of easy replacement, the shells being made of steel or bronze with a lining of white metal bonded in. In the earlier types of shell the white metal lining was relatively thick, and was finally bored to the correct size when all the shells were fitted in their housings. This was done by a *line-boring machine*, which ensured correct alignment of the bearing surfaces independently of the alignment of the housings.

The modern type of shell consists of a 'backing' of steel (approximately 0·080 in thick) (2 mm) with a lining of white metal approximately 0·005 in (0·1 mm) thick bonded in. Shells of this type are called *thin-walled* shells, and they are precision-manufactured in large numbers at relatively low cost. The chief advantages of this construction are:

(1) Being pre-finished to fine tolerances they do not require any skilled fitting—merely careful assembly.
(2) The ability of the white metal to carry heavy loads is greatly increased by the support given by the steel backing, because the white metal lining is thin.
(3) Being mass-produced in large numbers and using very little of the expensive metal, tin, they are relatively cheap.

Copper-lead

This has greater load-carrying capacity than white metal and is used for most heavy commercial vehicle engines and high-performance car engines. Being harder and therefore less able to 'embed' abrasive particles, it generally requires a harder shaft than could be used with white metal.

It is generally used in the form of a steel-backed thin-wall shell as already described, and is often given a thin coating of tin about 0·0002 in (0·005 mm) thick to assist in running-in, the tin layer usually wearing away during the running-in process.

Some copper-lead bearings are given a very thin coating of pure lead followed by an even thinner *flash* of indium. The lead and indium diffuse into one another, giving a coating to the copper-lead which not only assists running-in but protects it from corrosion. This coating is intended to last the life of the bearing.

Lead Bronze

This material is slightly superior to copper-lead in load-carrying ability, but is otherwise similar. It is commonly applied to a steel backing for making wrapped bushes.

THRUST WASHERS

Shafts usually need to be located endways, usually against a certain amount of end thrust. Bushes may be flanged (see Fig. 6.1.1(b)) in conjunction with shoulders or collars on the shaft, and shells may be flanged in a similar manner. In the case of wrapped bushes and thin-wall shells it is more usual to use separate thrust washers or half washers. These have steel backs faced with white metal, copper-lead or lead bronze, and are located in a recess in the bearing housing (see Fig. 6.1.6).

In many cases only one half washer is used, and it is prevented from rotating by letting its ends abut the unrecessed edge of the

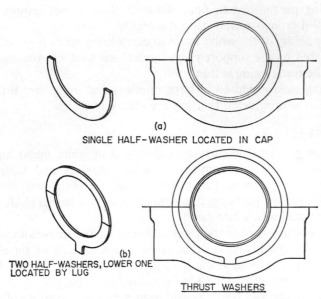

(a)
SINGLE HALF-WASHER LOCATED IN CAP

(b)
TWO HALF-WASHERS, LOWER ONE
LOCATED BY LUG

THRUST WASHERS

FIG. 6.1.6

housing half which does not have a half washer. When a pair of half washers is used, one has a lug which engages a notch in the housing to prevent rotation.

Shafts are usually located endways by one bearing only, thrust washers being fitted at both ends of this bearing but omitted from all others.

6.2

BALL AND ROLLER BEARINGS

In this class of bearing, rolling motion is substituted for sliding by interposing rolling elements between the shaft and its housing. By this means friction is reduced, especially when the speed of rotation is low and no continuous supply of oil under pressure is available.

A complete bearing consists of four components:

(1) An inner race which is fixed on the shaft. (In a few cases the shaft itself may form the inner race if it is made of suitable material, but replacement may then be more costly when excessively worn.)

(2) An outer race which is fixed in the housing. (As with the inner race, this may sometimes be formed by the housing itself.)

(3) A suitable number of balls or rollers.

(4) A cage to prevent adjacent balls or rollers from rubbing against one another.

The races and balls or rollers are made from a special quality steel, suitably hardened. There may be slight variations in the composition and heat treatment of the steel between different manufacturers and for different types of bearing. Cages may be made of bronze, aluminium or mild steel.

There are four main types of bearing, classified by the shape of the rolling elements as ball, cylindrical roller, spherical roller and taper roller.

BALL BEARINGS

Fig. 6.2.1 shows cross-sections of three examples of ball bearing.

(a) is a *single-row* bearing with the balls running in grooves in the races. This type is intended for carrying mainly radial loads, but can also support some axial load in both directions. Double-row

(a)

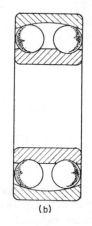

(b)

(c)

TYPES OF BALL BEARINGS

FIG. 6.2.1

bearings of this type are also made and are capable of carrying heavier loads.

(b) is a *self-aligning* bearing. The inner race has two ball tracks and both rows of balls run in an outer race whose inner surface forms a section of a sphere having its centre at the shaft centre. This allows the shaft axis to run at a small angle to the axis of the housing, and bearings of this type are used for applications where precise alignment of shaft and housing cannot be maintained.

(c) is an *angular contact* ball bearing which is capable of taking axial loads comparable with the radial loads, but in one direction only. Bearings of this type are generally used in pairs one at each end of a shaft, and care must be taken when fitting the bearings to ensure that they are fitted the correct way round.

CYLINDRICAL ROLLER BEARINGS

An example of this type is shown in Fig. 6.2.2. These are capable of carrying greater radial loads than ball bearings, *but no axial load.* The guiding flanges may be either on the inner or outer races.

Where heavy radial loads have to be carried at low speeds, or where the motion is of an intermittent or oscillating nature, specially long rollers of small diameter—called *needle rollers*—may be used.

SPHERICAL ROLLER BEARINGS

As shown in Fig. 6.2.3, this is the roller bearing equivalent of the self-aligning ball bearing. It is constructed on similar principles and used for similar applications, but is capable of carrying greater loads.

TAPER ROLLER BEARINGS

An example of this important and useful type is shown in Fig. 6.2.4. The working surfaces of both races and rollers are conical, the taper being such that the cones, of which races and rollers form a part, each have their apex at a common point on the axis of the shaft.

They are always used in pairs facing opposite ways, and are capable of dealing with considerable axial loads as well as radial loads. Different taper angles may be used, depending upon the amount of axial load to be carried. They are provided with some means of axial adjustment to control the amount of end play or pre-load allowed.

A single-row bearing as illustrated can only deal with thrust in one direction (hence the need for using two) but double-row types, each row having its taper facing opposite ways, are also made and are capable of taking thrust in *both* directions.

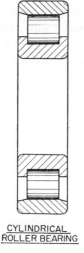

CYLINDRICAL
ROLLER BEARING

FIG. 6.2.2

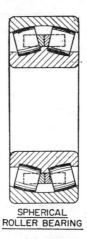

SPHERICAL
ROLLER BEARING

FIG. 6.2.3

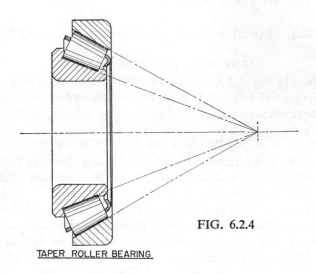

FIG. 6.2.4

TAPER ROLLER BEARING

FITTING BEARINGS

Cleanliness is vitally important. Do not unwrap new bearings from their packages until the last possible moment. The bearings are coated with preservative and this need not be removed.

In most cases the races are an interference fit both in housings and on shafts. The best way to fit the bearings is by pressing them into place with a press, using a mild steel tubular drift of correct diameter for each race. *Under no circumstances should pressure be applied to one race in order to press the other into place*—i.e. the pressure must be applied directly to the race being fitted. Where a press is not available, strike the drifts carefully with a suitable hammer.

REMOVING BEARINGS

Unless the bearing is to be scrapped, the same care must be exercised in removing as in fitting it. Using a suitable extractor, drift and press or hammer, force must be applied directly to the race being removed. In many cases, special extractors are available for this purpose.

BEARING ADJUSTMENT

Where adjustment is provided it may be made by nuts, threaded rings or by distance pieces and shims. For many applications the ideal adjustment is that there should be no end float and no pre-load (or over-tightening). For certain applications, however, such as rear-axle pinion shafts, correct meshing of the gears demands complete elimination of play, and the bearings are generally *pre-loaded*—i.e. they are tightened slightly beyond the point of elimination of play. Specific instructions are given in workshop manuals on this point.

LUBRICATION

The bearings are lubricated with oil or grease depending upon the component into which they are fitted. In engines, gearboxes and final-drive gears, oil is used and the design ensures a constant supply to each bearing. In other parts of the vehicle, such as wheel hubs, bearings are grease-lubricated by packing the bearings and the inside of the hub cavity with a suitable grease. Details as to the type of grease to be used, and the amount to be put into the housing, are given in the service manual for the vehicles.

The Compression-Ignition Engine

7.1

CYCLE OF OPERATIONS

HISTORY

This type of engine is often called a *Diesel* engine; the name is derived from the German engineer, Dr. Rudolf Diesel, who in 1892 took out a patent (No. 7241) on an engine which relied on the heat generated during compression to ignite a fuel of coal dust. This fuel was blasted into the cylinder by air pressure at the end of the stroke. The aim of the design, which was successfully applied to an engine five years later, was to achieve a higher thermal efficiency or improved fuel consumption by using a compression ratio higher than that employed on petrol engines. In those early days, pre-ignition (ignition before the spark) occurred in a petrol engine if the compression ratio exceeded a given value.

Many authorities do not recognise Diesel as the inventor of the engine which was the forerunner of the modern compression-ignition engine. They state that the patent (No. 7146) taken out in 1890 by a British engineer, Herbert Ackroyd-Stuart, and put into commercial production two years later, contained all the fundamental features of the modern unit. This patent, which was the result of practical development work on low-compression oil engines, included the induction and compression of air, and the timed injection of a liquid fuel by means of a pump.

To avoid taking sides in this controversy, the terms *compression-ignition* (C.I.) or *oil engine* are often used.

FOUR-STROKE OPERATION

In many ways, this operation is similar to the four-stroke petrol cycle; both occupy 720 degrees, or two revolutions of the crank, to complete the four strokes—induction, compression, power and exhaust.

Fig. 7.1.1 shows the sequence of operations, and also the main constructional differences between petrol and C.I. engines: that is, the elimination of the carburetter and the substitution of a fuel injector in place of the sparking plug. A difference which is not apparent is the compression ratio, which is much higher in the case of the C.I. engine. Some engines have ratios as low as 11:1, or as high as 26:1, whereas petrol engines seldom use a ratio greater than 10:1.

The sequence is as follows:

Induction   The descending piston increases the cylinder volume and decreases the pressure. Atmospheric pressure forces *air* through the open inlet port into the cylinder.

Compression   Both valves are closed and so the ascending piston compresses and raises the temperature of the air. For a compression ratio of 14:1, the final temperature and pressure will be 500 lbf/in² (3·5 MN/m²) and 650°C respectively.

Power   Just before t.d.c., fuel oil, having a self-ignition temperature of 400°C, is injected into the cylinder at a high pressure [e.g. 175 atmospheres, 2500 lbf/in² (17·2 MN/m²)] by means of a jerk type pump. After a short delay, the fuel begins to burn and liberates heat which raises the pressure to 900 lbf/in² (6·2 MN/m²), providing the thrust necessary for the power stroke: the amount of power is controlled by the period of injection, i.e. the quantity of fuel injected.

Exhaust   As the piston nears the end of the power stroke, the exhaust port is opened. The ascending piston pumps out the burnt gas in readiness for the new cycle.

(The pressures and temperatures quoted are approximate and are only intended as a guide, since engine design and other factors can alter conditions considerably.)

TWO-STROKE OPERATION

Although the two-stroke C.I. engine is not so popular as the four-stroke unit, some manufacturers regard the two-stroke engine's smoother torque, simpler construction and smaller unit as supreme advantages. Originally, this type was restricted to low-speed industrial and marine applications, but nowadays high-speed units are fitted to commercial vehicles. The great disadvantage of the two-stroke petrol engine—the loss of fuel to the exhaust when both ports are open—does not apply to the C.I. engine, since the cylinder only contains air: therefore it may be stated that the two-stroke cycle is most suitable for C.I. operation.

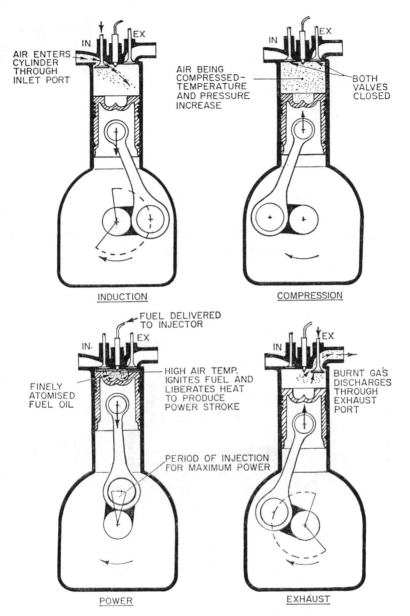

AIR ENTERS
CYLINDER
THROUGH
INLET PORT

AIR BEING
COMPRESSED—
TEMPERATURE
AND PRESSURE
INCREASE

BOTH
VALVES
CLOSED

INDUCTION

COMPRESSION

FUEL DELIVERED
TO INJECTOR

FINELY
ATOMISED
FUEL OIL

HIGH AIR TEMP.
IGNITES FUEL AND
LIBERATES HEAT
TO PRODUCE
POWER STROKE

PERIOD OF INJECTION
FOR MAXIMUM POWER

BURNT GAS
DISCHARGES
THROUGH
EXHAUST
PORT

POWER

EXHAUST

4-STROKE COMPRESSION-IGNITION ENGINE

FIG. 7.1.1

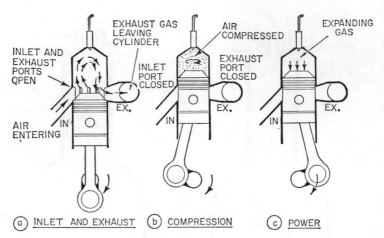

INLET AND EXHAUST PORTS OPEN

AIR ENTERING

EXHAUST GAS LEAVING CYLINDER

INLET PORT CLOSED

IN

EX.

AIR COMPRESSED

EXHAUST PORT CLOSED

IN

EX.

EXPANDING GAS

IN

EX.

(a) INLET AND EXHAUST (b) COMPRESSION (c) POWER

2 – STROKE CYCLE: VALVELESS FORM

FIG. 7.1.2

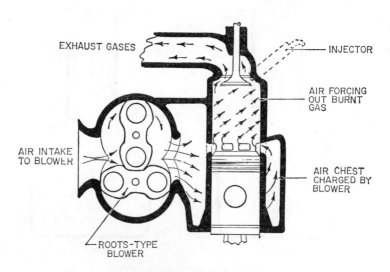

EXHAUST GASES

INJECTOR

AIR FORCING OUT BURNT GAS

AIR INTAKE TO BLOWER

AIR CHEST CHARGED BY BLOWER

ROOTS-TYPE BLOWER

'UNIFLOW'-TYPE 2 – STROKE ENGINE

FIG. 7.1.3

Fig. 7.1.2 shows the sequence of operations for a simple two-port valveless form of engine. Diagram (a) shows the air entering the cylinder through the inlet port, and 'burnt' gas flowing to the exhaust system.

As the piston ascends (diagram (b)) inlet and exhaust ports are closed to provide the compression stroke. After the air has been compressed to a c.r. of 12–16:1, the high temperature will ignite the fuel injected into the cylinder and produce the power stroke (diagram (c)).

Vehicle applications normally employ a blower to pressure-charge the cylinder with air, but it is possible to operate the engine by utilising the pressure waves or pulses in the exhaust system to induce the 'new' air into the cylinder.

Fig. 7.1.3 shows a uniflow type of two-stroke engine which is fitted with an exhaust valve and pressure-charged with a Roots type blower. This arrangement gives excellent cylinder evacuation and recharging, which is claimed to give double the power of a four-stroke engine of the same capacity.

Opening the exhaust valve before uncovering the circumferential air ports allows the remaining gas pressure to start pumping out the exhaust gas. This is followed by an air charge approximately 30% greater in volume than the cylinder capacity, to cool and scavenge the cylinder effectively.

7.2

ENGINE CONSTRUCTION: COMBUSTION CHAMBERS

Combustion in the chamber of a petrol engine originates at the sparking plug and then progresses throughout the cylinder. In the case of the C.I. engine, combustion of the fuel is started by the heat of the air in the chamber. As the fuel 'droplet' passes through the air, it absorbs heat, and, if the temperature is high enough, the fuel will vaporise and ignite. Wide distribution of the fuel occurs during the heating phase and so combustion will begin at many points in the chamber. In the case of one type of direct injection engine, once ignition has taken place, most of the burning will tend to concentrate in zones fairly close to the injector. These zones must be fed with air in order to sweep away the *burnt* gases and supply the oxygen necessary for complete combustion: lack of oxygen in the combustion region leads to black smoke in the exhaust. Since power is governed by the quantity of fuel injected, and this, in turn, is limited by the point at which smoke is emitted, some system must be used to introduce an orderly supply of air to the fuel. This air flow is called *swirl,* a term used in preference to *turbulence*, since this expression implies a disorderly movement.

Diesel Knock

Combustion noise, commonly known as *Diesel knock,* is one of the main disadvantages of the C.I. engine. It is caused by the sudden pressure rise which follows the period termed *ignition delay*, when the injected fuel is being heated to its self-ignition temperature. During this delay period, fuel is still entering the cylinder, and so the chamber contains a large quantity of fuel by the time ignition is begun. Design factors which increase swirl, atomisation and temperature give a shorter delay period, but perhaps one of the most important factors is the ignition quality of the fuel. Unlike petrols, C.I. fuels must be capable of igniting in a heated air mass without the aid of an electrical spark. The ability of a fuel to ignite, or its 'ignition quality', is expressed as a *Cetane Rating*. Classification is obtained by comparing the fuel with a good fuel, cetane, rated at 100, and a poor fuel, alpha-methyl-naphthalene, which is rated as 0. Most of the fuels which are commercially available have a cetane rating of about 50.

TYPES OF COMBUSTION CHAMBER

There are many good designs of C.I. combustion chamber, each arrangement, providing an effective swirl pattern. These designs can be divided broadly into two main classes: (a) direct injection, and (b) indirect injection.

In the former, fuel is injected directly into the closed end of the cylinder, whereas in the latter type, fuel is sprayed into a separate small chamber, which is connected to the cylinder by a small passage or throat.

Direct Injection

This *open type* chamber is used on the majority of heavy C.I. power units fitted to British vehicles. Fig. 7.2.1 shows the essential features of one popular type.

A deep cavity, machined in the piston, contains most of the air, since at t.d.c. the piston is very close to the flat cylinder head. To obtain the necessary compression ratio, overhead valves are essential. Shallow recesses in the piston crown provide clearance for the valve heads. (Inaccurate setting of the valve timing allows the valves to strike the piston.) A multi-hole injector allows finely atomised fuel under high pressure (175 atm) to penetrate the fast-moving air and just enter the cavity of the piston.

Swirl is produced in two planes, vertical and horizontal. The ascending piston causes the air to be directed into the cavity and move in the manner shown in the diagram. As the piston approaches t.d.c., this motion will be speeded up because of the *squish* action of the air between piston and head. Horizontal or rotary swirl can be obtained by inclining the inlet port tangentially to the cylinder, or masking the inlet valve. Fig. 7.2.1(a) shows the latter arrangement, which is the most popular. Combining both swirl movements gives a vortex air flow in the cavity, and ensures a good supply of oxygen to the combustion region.

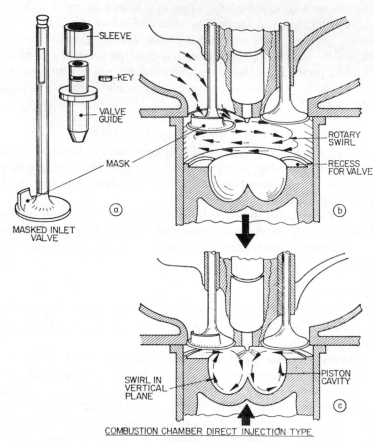

FIG. 7.2.1

Indirect Injection

Although the direct injection type gives excellent fuel economy because of its comparatively small surface area, its rough running qualities, high fuel penetration and high pump pressure requirements render it unsuitable for small power units which have to operate over a large speed range.

These engines normally use an indirect system similar to the type illustrated in Fig. 7.2.2, which shows a swirl chamber. On com-

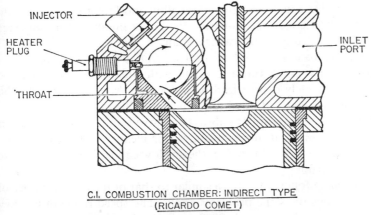

INJECTOR

HEATER PLUG

THROAT

INLET PORT

C.I. COMBUSTION CHAMBER: INDIRECT TYPE
(RICARDO COMET)

FIG. 7.2.2

pression, the air is pumped through a hot throat and set in a high state of swirl in the small antechamber. Into this hot air, fuel is injected in the form of a soft spray by means of a single hole or pintle nozzle. Since the fuel is quickly broken up by the rapidly moving air, only a comparatively low injection pressure (100 atm) is required.

A short ignition delay and high b.m.e.p. (brake mean effective pressure) are achieved with the indirect injection chamber, which also allows the engine to operate smoothly over a greater speed and fuel range.

Larger heat losses, linked with a low engine temperature and cold intake air, give a final compression temperature which is too low to produce ignition of the fuel; therefore, electrical heater filaments (glow plugs) are normally fitted in the swirl chamber, to provide a hot spot in a cold chamber to assist ignition. All C.I. engines require some special provision for cold-starting—generally, a larger quantity of fuel is injected, and in some instances the intake air is heated or, in the case of a Ricardo Comet chamber, a special pintaux injector is fitted.

MAIN COMPONENTS

The higher cylinder pressures of C.I. engines demand stronger components, although for production economy purposes, manufacturers of light C.I. units often use engine components the same as those they employ on the alternative petrol models. The following points apply to heavy C.I. engines.

Pistons are usually of aluminium alloy and long to accommodate the cavity (if direct injection) and the larger number of piston rings which are fitted to resist leakage of air.

A more robust crankshaft with a main bearing of copper-lead between each crank throw is often used. Big-end bearings may be either completely copper-lead or copper-lead/white metal, with the heavier-duty material fitted to the piston half of the bearing.

Induction manifolds are not always employed on C.I. engines. When the item is fitted, it allows a central air cleaner and silencer to be used, and in some light engines the air flow can be utilised to operate a fuel governor.

Valve timing follows a pattern similar to that of the low-speed petrol engine, since the same problems apply. The speed range of a heavy C.I. engine seldom exceeds 2000 rev/min; therefore, an inlet period of 10° before to 40° after, and an exhaust period of 40° before to 20° after, are often used.

Engine Lubrication

High combustion temperatures, and elements such as sulphur in the fuel, make the C.I. engine more prone to deposits of carbon and other combustion products on the piston rings and rubbing surface of the piston. Most manufacturers combat this by recommending the use of a heavy-duty detergent oil.

ADVANTAGES AND DISADVANTAGES OF C.I. ENGINES

Compared with a petrol engine of the same size, a C.I. engine has the following advantages:

(1) Fuel economy—the high compression ratio gives a good thermal efficiency (35–40% indicated) and provides the operator with approximately 30% more miles to the gallon.
(2) Reduced risk of fire—at room temperature, the low volatility of *Derv* (Diesel-Engined Road Vehicle) fuel makes ignition difficult.

The disadvantages are:

(1) High initial cost—due to expensive fuel-injection equipment and more substantial engine construction.
(2) Lower maximum torque and power output.
(3) Lower power/weight ratio.
(4) Noisier in operation.

7.3

THE FUEL SYSTEM

Early C.I. engines used air pressure to deliver the fuel into the cylinder, but nowadays liquid fuel, supplied by a reciprocating plunger pump, is delivered via small-bore steel pipe lines to the injector. The modern jerk pump system, which is shown in simplified form in Fig. 7.3.1, is often termed *mechanical* or *solid injection*, since the ejection of the fuel is brought about by the action of the plunger on a 'solid' column of oil.

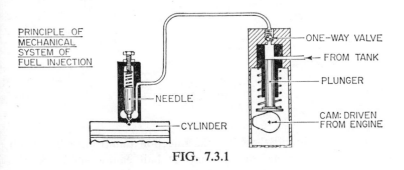

FIG. 7.3.1

The equipment must be capable of metering and delivering the fuel at the correct pressure and precise time. When it is said that the volume of fuel injected into the cylinder per cycle is often less than the volume of a small pin head, and the variation between cylinders must not exceed 2%, you must appreciate that the injector system is a high precision unit. Very close limits and small clearances [e.g. the clearance between plunger and barrel is less than 0·0001 in (3 μm)] demand special precautions to prevent dirt from entering the system. Clean fuel, regular replacement of filters, and close attention to cleanliness during overhaul of equipment are all essential if the apparatus is to perform its exacting task.

A layout of a typical system is shown in Fig. 7.3.2. A low-pressure feed pump or gravity supply ensures that the injection pump receives a continuous flow of clean filtered fuel. The system incorporates many filters: a fine gauze unit(s) is fitted on the inlet side of the pump, and a felt, cloth or paper filter(s) is inserted between feed pump and injection pump. Injection, in the case of a four-stroke, occurs every

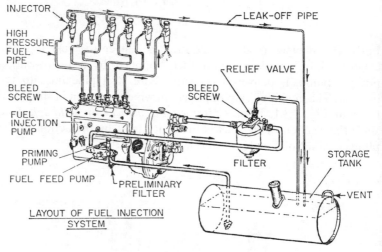

FIG. 7.3.2

other revolution and therefore the injection pump must be driven from the timing gears or camshaft at half engine speed. At the appropriate time, fuel under high pressure is conveyed to the injector by fuel lines, which should be of equal length to maintain an equal injection delay (period between the time when a high pressure builds up in the pump and the time when fuel begins to spray from the injector).

Lubrication of the main working parts of the system is usually done by the fuel oil itself: a pre-determined leakage past the injector needle is directed to waste or returned to the fuel tank.

The pump will not function correctly if air is present in the system, and therefore venting screws or valves are provided at various points to allow air to be bled out. This is necessary after disturbance of supply lines or 'running-out' of fuel. A priming lever, generally fitted to the feed pump, allows the feed pump to be operated manually. With the air vent (bleed screw) open, operation of the feed pump forces a column of fuel through the line and allows the air to be driven from the system.

7.4

THE INJECTION PUMP

Modern C.I. engines are fitted with either an *in-line* pump or a *distributor* pump: the former is similar in basic construction to the pump produced by Robert Bosch over fifty years ago, whereas the distributor pump has only been in production for a few years. The comparatively low initial cost of the latter makes this type attractive to many manufacturers.

Since both pumps are being produced in large numbers, this chapter describes each type.

IN-LINE PUMP

Fig. 7.3.2 shows a six-element (six-cylinder) enclosed camshaft type of pump, and Fig. 7.4.1(a) illustrates the construction of one pumping element. This unit comprises:

(1) *The pumping element* (Fig. 7.4.1(b)) A steel plunger moving through a constant stroke reciprocates inside a close-fitting steel barrel. The plunger is partly machined away to produce a control helix and vertical groove. An inlet and spill port in the barrel communicates with a gallery fed from the fuel tank. Location of the barrel is provided by allowing a screw in the casing to register in a recess adjacent to the spill port.

Partial rotation of the plunger varies the output from zero for stopping the engine, to maximum for starting. Between these limits a variable supply of fuel is necessary to meet the engine power and speed requirements.

The operation of the pumping element is shown in Fig. 7.4.1(c).

Position A When the plunger is at b.d.c. the depression in the pump chamber causes fuel to enter both ports.

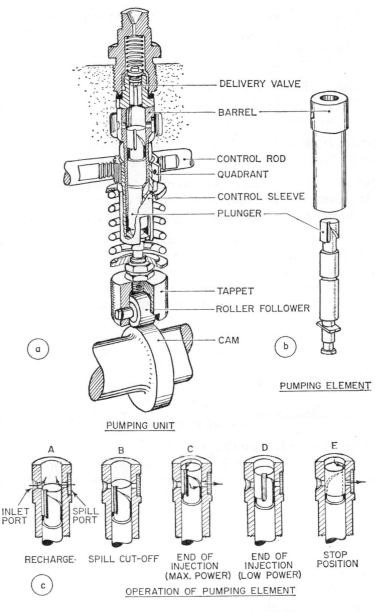

DELIVERY VALVE

BARREL

CONTROL ROD

QUADRANT

CONTROL SLEEVE

PLUNGER

TAPPET

ROLLER FOLLOWER

CAM

(a)

(b)

PUMPING ELEMENT

PUMPING UNIT

A   B   C   D   E

INLET
PORT

SPILL
PORT

RECHARGE·   SPILL CUT-OFF   END OF   END OF   STOP
                            INJECTION   INJECTION   POSITION
                            (MAX. POWER) (LOW POWER)

(c)

OPERATION OF PUMPING ELEMENT

THE FUEL INJECTION PUMP

FIG. 7.4.1

Position B This position, known as the point of port closure (or spill cut-off with this type of pump), is generally regarded as the theoretical point of injection. Both ports have been covered, and so the ascending plunger raises the pressure of the fuel to produce injection.

Position C Injection stops when the edge of the helix uncovers the spill port. Pressure is relieved by fuel passing down the vertical groove, around the waist of the plunger and out of the spill port.

Position D Rotation of the plunger causes the helix to uncover the spill port either earlier or later, to give less or more fuel respectively.

Position E Moving the plunger to make the vertical groove coincide with the spill port means that the port will remain open; therefore no fuel will be delivered and the engine will come to rest.

(2) *The plunger control* Two lugs on the plunger fit into slots in a control sleeve on to which is clamped a toothed quadrant. This quadrant engages a rack cut in the control rod which runs the length of the pump. By moving the quadrant relative to the sleeve, the output from each element can be calibrated or equalised.

(3) *The drive* Symmetrical cams, set to give the appropriate firing order, act on a roller follower and tappet block. A screw or shim adjustment between tappet and plunger allows the time of the start of injection of one element to be varied in respect to the other elements. A four-cylinder engine has a *phase angle*—the interval between injections—of $\dfrac{360°}{\text{no. of cylinders}} = 90°$: the operation for setting this angle is known as *phasing*.

(4) *The delivery valve* (Fig. 7.4.2) This valve performs two duties:

(a) The conical seat acts as a non-return valve preventing the return of fuel from the high-pressure pipeline when the spill port opens. This allows the pump chamber to recharge and also enables air or gas to be purged from the pipeline via the injector.

(b) If air can be eliminated from the high-pressure pipeline the pump will often operate satisfactorily without a delivery valve: on the opening of the spill port the pressure at the injector will fall rapidly to pump inlet pressure giving a sharp closing of the injector. The fitting of a non-return valve, however, traps pressure in the pipeline while the injector is still open. This pressure can only be relieved by fuel continuing to pass the injector

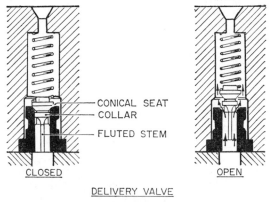

CONICAL SEAT
COLLAR
FLUTED STEM

CLOSED

OPEN

DELIVERY VALVE

FIG. 7.4.2

at a diminishing pressure, resulting in the last few droplets of fuel merely 'dribbling' out, causing incomplete combustion, carbon formation, smoky exhaust and high fuel consumption.

The collar below the conical seat acts as a piston and withdraws a small amount of fuel from the high-pressure pipeline as the valve closes, causing the necessary rapid pressure drop to ensure a sharp cut-off to injection.

DISTRIBUTOR PUMP

Fig. 7.4.3(a) shows a D.P.A. type pump suitable for a four-cylinder engine. Connected to the engine by a flange and driven by a splined shaft, this unit resembles the distributor used on a petrol engine; fuel lines to the injectors occupy the position of the h.t. leads.

A single-element, opposed plunger pumping unit supplies fuel to either a four- or six-cylinder engine; except for the cam and the number of ports, the other parts are the same for both engines. Operated by a non-rotating cam, the single element provides a correctly phased and balanced output over a very large speed range.

The pumping unit, shown diagrammatically in Fig. 7.4.3(b), consists of two plungers mounted in a rotor which turns in a fixed hydraulic head. Ports in the head and rotor line up in certain positions to allow either inward or outward flow of oil. Fig. 7.4.3(b) shows the inlet port open. Pressure from a transfer pump, fitted at the end of the main pump, directs fuel oil along the centre of the rotor to force out the plungers. Fig. 7.4.3(c) shows that the un-

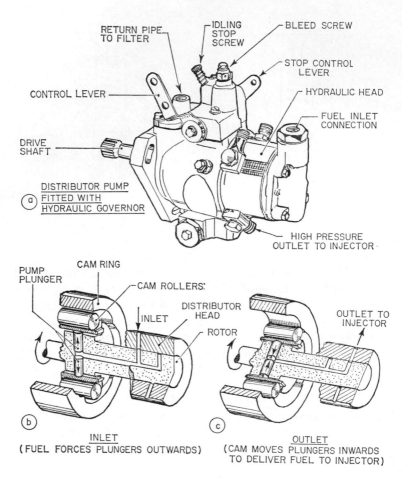

CONTROL LEVER

RETURN PIPE TO FILTER

IDLING STOP SCREW

BLEED SCREW

STOP CONTROL LEVER

HYDRAULIC HEAD

FUEL INLET CONNECTION

DRIVE SHAFT

(a) DISTRIBUTOR PUMP FITTED WITH HYDRAULIC GOVERNOR

HIGH PRESSURE OUTLET TO INJECTOR

PUMP PLUNGER

CAM RING

CAM ROLLERS

INLET

DISTRIBUTOR HEAD

ROTOR

OUTLET TO INJECTOR

(b) INLET (FUEL FORCES PLUNGERS OUTWARDS)

(c) OUTLET (CAM MOVES PLUNGERS INWARDS TO DELIVER FUEL TO INJECTOR)

THE DISTRIBUTOR PUMP

FIG. 7.4.3

covered outlet port will allow the cam to force the plungers together and discharge the fuel to the injector.

Dribble is eliminated by using a special cam design to stop fuel delivery sharply.

Fig. 7.4.4 shows a typical fuel system. A feed pump supplies fuel, via a filter, to a sliding vane transfer pump which directs the oil through a driver-controlled metering valve to the rotor. Transfer pump pressure is limited by a regulating valve, and oil, which escapes from the pumping element, returns to the filter after lubricating the working parts.

The quantity of fuel delivered to the injector is governed by the position of the metering valve. The diagram shows a partly opened valve restricting the flow of oil to the rotor. This reduction in oil flow prevents the full outward travel of the plungers; hence the shortened stroke gives reduced fuel and lower engine power.

On fitting a 'new' pump, it is essential to completely fill the pump with clean fuel oil before attempting to start the engine. Various venting screws are provided to bleed the air from the system.

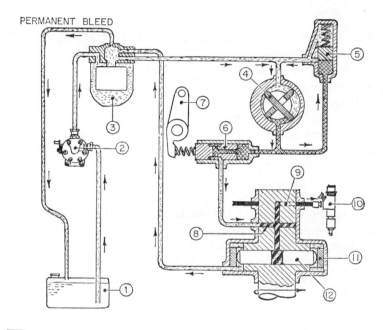

INLET AND RETURN PRESSURE   METERING PRESSURE
TRANSFER PRESSURE   INJECTION PRESSURE

1	FUEL TANK	7	CONTROL LEVER
2	FEED PUMP	8	INLET PORT
3	FILTER	9	DISTRIBUTOR PORT
4	TRANSFER PUMP	10	INJECTOR
5	REGULATING VALVE	11	CAM RING
6	METERING VALVE	12	PLUNGERS

FUEL SYSTEM FOR A DISTRIBUTOR PUMP

FIG. 7.4.4

INJECTORS

The purpose of the injector or sprayer is to break up the fuel to the required degree and deliver it to the combustion region in the chamber. This atomisation and penetration is done by using a high pressure to force the fuel through a small orifice.

Vehicles in this country use a type of injector which incorporates a valve. This *closed* system is responsive to pump pressure—raising the pressure above a predetermined point allows the valve to open, and stay open until the pressure has dropped to a lower value. The 'snap' opening and closing of the valve give advantages which make this system popular.

The complete injector, shown in Fig. 7.5.1(a), consists of a nozzle and holder, which is clamped to form a gas-tight seal in the cylinder head. A spring, compressed by an adjusting screw to give the correct breaking (opening) pressure, thrusts the needle on to its conical seat. Fuel flows from the inlet nipple through a drilling to annular groove above the seat of the needle. A thrust, caused by fuel acting on the conical face X, will overcome the spring and lift the needle when the pressure exceeds the breaking pressure. The opening of the valve permits discharge of fuel until the pressure drops to the lower limit. Any fuel which flows between the needle and body acts as a lubricant for the needle before being carried away by a leak-off pipe.

NOZZLE TYPES

There are three main types of nozzle: (a) single-hole, (b) multi-hole, and (c) pintle.

Single-hole (Fig. 7.5.1(b))   A single orifice, which may be as small as 0·008 in (0·2 mm), is drilled in the nozzle to give a single jet form of spray. When this nozzle is used with indirect injection systems, a

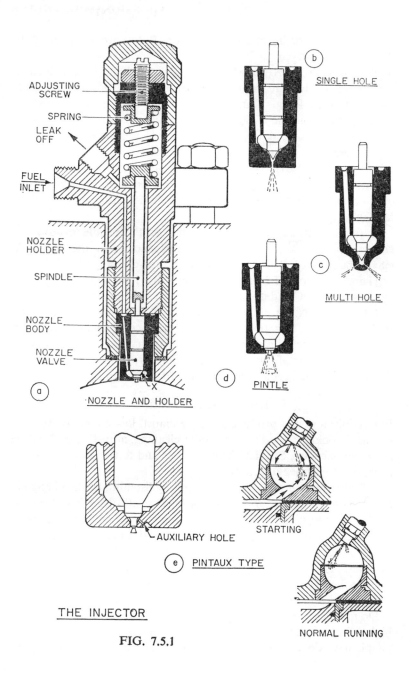

ADJUSTING
SCREW

SPRING

LEAK
OFF

FUEL
INLET

NOZZLE
HOLDER

SPINDLE

NOZZLE
BODY

NOZZLE
VALVE

X

(a) NOZZLE AND HOLDER

(b) SINGLE HOLE

(c) MULTI HOLE

(d) PINTLE

AUXILIARY HOLE

(e) PINTAUX TYPE

STARTING

NORMAL RUNNING

THE INJECTOR

FIG. 7.5.1

comparatively low injection pressure of 80–100 atmospheres (8–10 MN/m²) is employed.

Multi-hole (Fig. 7.5.1(c)) Two or more small orifices, drilled at various angles to suit the combustion chamber, produce a highly atomised spray form. Many engines with direct injection systems use a four-hole nozzle with a high operating pressure of 175 atmospheres (18 MN/m²). A long-stem version of this type simplifies the accommodation of the injector in the head.

Pintle (Fig. 7.5.1(d)) Swirl chambers can accept a *soft* form of spray, which is the form given by a pintle type of nozzle when set to operate at a low injection pressure of 80–100 atmospheres (8–10 MN/m²).

A small cone extension on the end of the needle produces a conical spray pattern and increases the velocity of the fuel as it leaves the injector. This type tends to be self-cleaning.

The elimination of heater plugs on some light indirect injection engines has been made possible by the invention of a special pintle nozzle known as the *pintaux* (pronounced 'pintawks') type, shown in Fig. 7.5.1(e)). Starting conditions produce a small needle lift, and so fuel passes through the small auxiliary hole and is directed to the hottest part of the chamber. Under normal running pressures, the full lift of the needle discharges the fuel through the main orifice.

INJECTOR SERVICING

Faulty injectors can produce a dirty exhaust, low engine power and intense knocking; therefore periodic cleaning, adjusting and testing are recommended. Special cleaning tools and testing equipment are necessary to service injectors.

A faulty injector can often be traced by listening to the change in engine note which occurs when one injector at a time is cut out by slackening the pipeline union. To examine the fuel spray pattern, the injector may be removed from the cylinder head and connected in an inverted manner so that the spray is discharged outside the cylinder. The other injector supply unions are disconnected to prevent the engine firing, and the starter motor is operated. A streaky spray pattern indicates that cleaning is necessary.

Do not let your hands come into contact with the spray, since the high injector pressure enables the fuel oil to penetrate the skin: people have died from getting fuel oil in their bloodstream.

GOVERNORS

Higher gas pressures in the cylinder of a C.I. engine usually demand stronger components than those used in a petrol engine. Strength is normally improved by increasing the component dimensions, but this also increases weight and leads to engine damage if the speed exceeds a given value which is governed by the components' strength/weight ratio.

A pump with a *rising output* characteristic (i.e. for a given control rod setting the output increases with speed) and compression pressures, which are substantially the same at *idling* as at maximum speed, makes it difficult to obtain a steady idling speed—the engine tends either to race or to stall.

Limitation of maximum speed and control of the engine at idling speed are the two main duties performed by the governor. If the unit attends to these two duties only, it is known as an *idling and maximum speed governor*, whereas a unit which regulates throughout the speed range is termed an *all-speed governor*.

There are three main types of governor: (a) mechanical, (b) pneumatic, and (c) hydraulic.

Mechanical The type shown diagrammatically in Fig. 7.6.1 is an *idling and maximum speed* governor, which is often used on heavy vehicle engines. Mounted at the end of the injector pump, it consists of two weights, which are rotated by the pump camshaft. Springs exert a force in an inward direction on the weights, and bell cranks link each weight to the bottom end of a floating lever: the top end of the lever is connected to the control rod and the centre is mounted on an eccentric, which is rotated by the accelerator pedal.

The diagram shows the governor in the *engine-stationary* position, and in this condition the weights are fully retracted to hold the

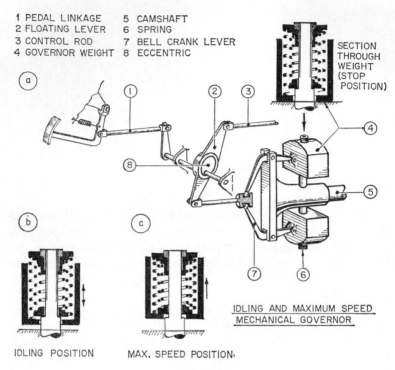

1 PEDAL LINKAGE	5 CAMSHAFT
2 FLOATING LEVER	6 SPRING
3 CONTROL ROD	7 BELL CRANK LEVER
4 GOVERNOR WEIGHT	8 ECCENTRIC

SECTION
THROUGH
WEIGHT
(STOP
POSITION)

IDLING AND MAXIMUM SPEED
MECHANICAL GOVERNOR

IDLING POSITION   MAX. SPEED POSITION.

FIG. 7.6.1

control rod in the *maximum fuel* position in readiness for starting the engine. When the engine fires, rotation of the weights causes the centrifugal effect to overcome the spring and move the weight out to the position shown by diagram (b), which causes the control rod to be withdrawn to the 'idling' setting. In this position the weights are being controlled by the outer (weaker) springs only, so sensitive control is possible.

Assuming the pedal is not depressed, any increase in speed produces a slight outward movement of the weights and this moves the control rod in the direction which reduces the fuel delivery. In a similar way, stalling is prevented by the weights moving inwards, which causes the control rod to increase the fuel delivery.

Between idling and maximum speeds, the weights maintain the same position, and appear to be locked together. During this phase, downward movement of the accelerator pedal rotates the eccentric and moves the control rod in a direction which increases the fuel delivery.

As maximum speed (e.g. 1800–2000 rev/min) is reached, the high centrifugal force acting on the weights will overcome the strong outer springs and move the weights outwards (diagram (c)). This motion, when transmitted to the control rod, decreases the quantity of fuel delivered, and reduces the engine power, irrespective of the position of the accelerator pedal.

A small quantity of engine oil, contained in the separate governor housing, lubricates the moving parts. Check the level at regular intervals [e.g. every 2000 miles (3000 km)].

A number of adjusting nuts, screws and stops are employed with this type of governor. Do not disturb settings, unless you have special tools and the necessary knowledge.

Pneumatic In-line pumps fitted to light C.I. engines often use this *all-speed* type of governor. Holding the accelerator pedal in a set position, the governor will maintain a constant speed up to a point where the load on the engine is too great.

Fig. 7.6.2 shows the main construction of this type. A spring-loaded diaphragm, connected to the control rod, is mounted to seal a chamber which is linked by a pipe to a venturi control unit in the inlet manifold. A butterfly valve, fitted in the waist of the venturi, is directly connected to the accelerator pedal.

When the engine is at rest, the diaphragm spring forces the control rod to the maximum fuel or excess-fuel position. (Many pumps are fitted with an excess-fuel device. This is a manually operated control fitted at the end of the pump which enables extra fuel to be delivered for cold starting. It cannot be operated from the driving position.)

Closing the accelerator pedal after starting produces a depression in the venturi and diaphragm chamber. This causes atmospheric pressure to force the diaphragm and control rod to the idling setting. With the pedal in any set position, an increase in speed intensifies the venturi depression, which reduces the control-rod opening: a decrease in speed will produce the opposite condition.

As the accelerator pedal is depressed, the butterfly valve is opened and the venturi depression is decreased. This causes the spring to open the control rod and increase the engine speed until a balance is reached between the spring thrust and venturi depression.

A stop screw, acting on the lever controlling the butterfly valve, limits the maximum speed. When the valve reaches its stop, any

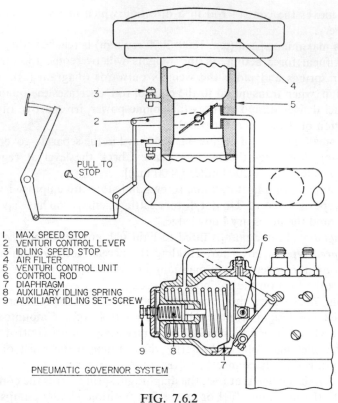

I   MAX. SPEED STOP
2   VENTURI CONTROL LEVER
3   IDLING SPEED STOP
4   AIR FILTER
5   VENTURI CONTROL UNIT
6   CONTROL ROD
7   DIAPHRAGM
8   AUXILIARY IDLING SPRING
9   AUXILIARY IDLING SET-SCREW

PNEUMATIC GOVERNOR SYSTEM

FIG. 7.6.2

tendency for the engine to increase speed will intensify the venturi
depression and reduce the control-rod opening.

A 'stop' control on the dash enables the driver to override the
governor and move the control to the 'no-fuel' position.

*Do not start the engine with any part of the governor system dis-
connected.*

Hydraulic This type is used with in-line pumps where smooth,
slow idling speeds are demanded (e.g. for coaches), but high cost
tends to limit its use. A gear type oil pump, driven from the end of
pump camshaft, supplies oil through various valves to operate
a piston linked to the control rod.

A hydraulic governor is also incorporated in the D.P.A. type
distributor pump. As with the in-line pump application, the governor
is an 'all-speed' type.

Page 275 shows the main governor components—the transfer pump and the metering valve. The driver controls the valve through a spring, so if he depresses the pedal a given amount, the valve will open wide and allow the speed to increase. The build-up in engine speed increases the transfer-pump pressure, which gradually moves the metering valve towards the closed position, until a point is reached where the speed will not increase any more. These events recur throughout the range.

SOME OTHER INJECTION SYSTEMS

The fuel injection systems described in the foregoing chapters include pipes of appreciable length which are subjected to extremely high pressures. In this chapter we describe briefly two injection systems in which these high-pressure pipes are dispensed with.

COMBINED PUMP AND INJECTOR UNIT

A unit of this type is illustrated in Fig. 7.7.1. The pump is basically similar to a single-element pump of the type described in the first part of chapter 7.4 and illustrated in Fig. 7.4.1 (page 271), but the pump is inverted and has the injector nozzle fitted directly to it in the position occupied, in the types previously described, by the delivery valve.

The pump plunger is operated from a cam on the engine camshaft in a similar manner to that used for the valves. The quantity of fuel delivered is regulated by helix-controlled ports, the plunger being rotated within its barrel by a control rack which engages a gear surrounding the plunger: the plunger has one or more flats on it which engage corresponding flats in the bore of the gear, so that while the plunger is free to slide axially through the gear, rotation of the gear by movement of the rack also rotates the plunger in its barrel.

One unit of this type is fitted into the head of each cylinder so that the nozzle projects into the combustion chamber. Each control rack is connected to a control rod which runs the whole length of the cylinder head and is operated by a separate engine-drive governor.

Fuel is supplied to each injection unit at a relatively low pressure by a pump, and in order to assist in keeping the unit cool arrangements are made for fuel to circulate around the space between the outside of the barrel and the inside of the cap nut.

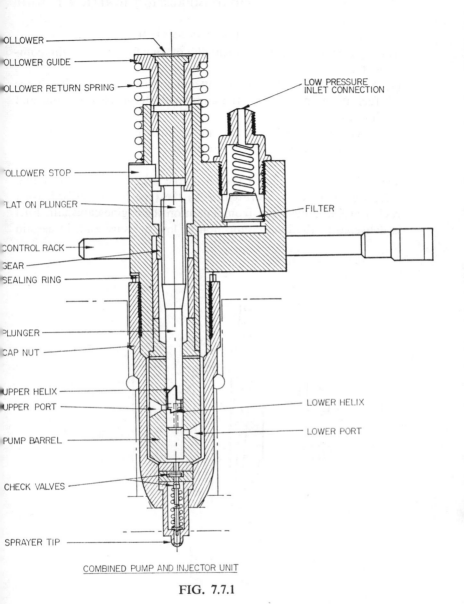

FOLLOWER

FOLLOWER GUIDE

FOLLOWER RETURN SPRING

LOW PRESSURE
INLET CONNECTION

FOLLOWER STOP

FLAT ON PLUNGER

FILTER

CONTROL RACK

GEAR

SEALING RING

PLUNGER

CAP NUT

UPPER HELIX

UPPER PORT

LOWER HELIX

LOWER PORT

PUMP BARREL

CHECK VALVES

SPRAYER TIP

COMBINED PUMP AND INJECTOR UNIT

FIG. 7.7.1

The nozzle shown in Fig. 7.7.1 is an 'open' type having two check
valves to prevent gases entering the pump through the sprayer holes
when the pump is not delivering fuel.

THE CUMMINS SYSTEM

This system consists fundamentally of the following main components:

(1) A combined low-pressure pump and governor unit which delivers fuel at low pressure to the combined high-pressure pump and injector.

(2) A combined high-pressure pump and injector fitted in the centre of each engine cylinder head.

The Injector   A simplified sketch of the injector is shown in Fig. 7.7.2. The plunger is operated, as in the type just described, by a rocker arm and push rod from a cam on the engine camshaft. Fuel is delivered to the inlet connection at low pressure and, in certain

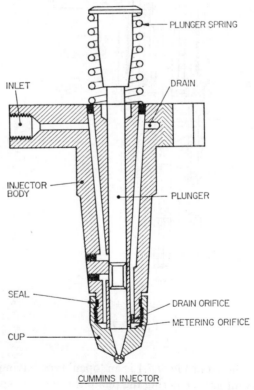

CUMMINS INJECTOR

FIG. 7.7.2

positions of the plunger, circulates through passages in the injector body and returns to the tank, thus assisting in cooling the injector and in pre-heating the fuel as well as purging air from the system.

The operation of the injector is shown in more detail in Fig. 7.7.3.

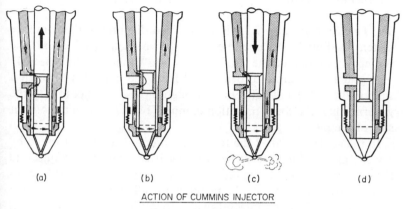

(a) (b) (c) (d)

ACTION OF CUMMINS INJECTOR

FIG. 7.7.3

The four stages illustrated are as follows:

(a) The plunger begins its upward stroke, opening the *fuel supply port* and allowing fuel to circulate through the injector and return to the tank via the *drain orifice*. (About 80% of the fuel supplied to the injector returns to the tank.)

(b) The plunger is at the top of its stroke, the *metering orifice* is open and fuel passes through the metering port into the *cup*. The quantity of fuel which enters the cup depends upon the pressure at which the fuel is supplied to the injector and the length of time during which the metering port is uncovered. The cup is only partly filled with fuel and also contains some heated air which is forced into it through the spray holes during the compression stroke of the engine piston.

(c) The plunger is moving downward and has closed the metering port. The change of fuel and hot air in the cup is being sprayed into the combustion chamber.

(d) The plunger is at the bottom of its stroke and is firmly seated in the bottom of the cup, where it remains until it commences its next upward stroke.

The plunger is timed to close the metering port on its downward stroke when the engine is about 50° before t.d.c. on its compression stroke. The point at which injection commences will be slightly later than this depending upon the quantity of fuel in the cup.

The Fuel System   Fig. 7.7.4 is a simplified diagram of the complete system. Although only one injector is shown, there is, of course, one for each cylinder in the engine: they are connected 'in parallel'.

A gear type pump (15) draws fuel from the tank (17) through a suction filter (16) and delivers it through a pressure filter (13) to the governor barrel (18). A pulsation damper (14) is fitted on the output side of the pump.

In the governor barrel the fuel enters an annular space formed by a waist in the plunger (19) from which it can pass to the injectors through two passages. The idling passage (7) is open only at low engine speeds and maintains the fuel flow for idling. The main passage (8) delivers fuel to the injectors via a throttling valve (5) by which the fuel flow to the injectors can be regulated at part throttle, and the passage is itself closed off by the plunger (19) to limit the maximum speed. A shut-down valve (3) which may be operated either manually or electrically cuts off all fuel to the injectors and is used to stop the engine.

Besides controlling idling and maximum speeds by closing off the passages (7) and (8) at appropriate speeds (depending on the settings of the screw (9) and the spring (10)) the governor also regulates the fuel pressure according to engine speed. Fuel enters a radial hole in the waist of the plunger (19) and passes down an axial hole to the inner end which bears against the pressure control button (11). Fuel forces the button away from the plunger allowing fuel to escape through the return passage (12) to the pump inlet. The pressure required to open this return passage depends upon the force exerted upon the governor plunger (19) by the governor flyweights (21), this force increasing with rise in speed. The torque control spring (20) and the governor assister spring (23) are fitted to modify the engine torque characteristics to suit the engine application.

CUMMINS FUEL SYSTEM

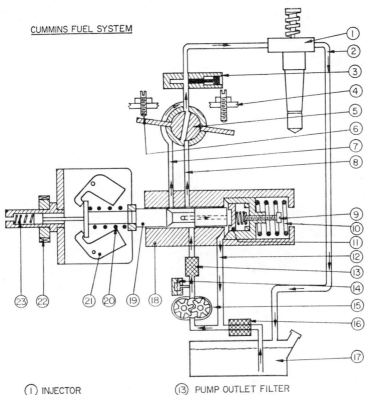

① INJECTOR	⑬ PUMP OUTLET FILTER
② FUEL RETURN TO TANK	⑭ PULSATION DAMPER
③ SHUT DOWN VALVE	⑮ GEAR PUMP
④ MAX. THROTTLE SCREW	⑯ PUMP INLET FILTER
⑤ THROTTLE VALVE	⑰ FUEL TANK
⑥ IDLING STOP SCREW	⑱ GOVERNOR BARREL
⑦ IDLING FUEL PASSAGE	⑲ GOVERNOR PLUNGER
⑧ MAIN FUEL PASSAGE	⑳ TORQUE CONTROL SPRING
⑨ IDLING SPEED SCREW	㉑ GOVERNOR FLYWEIGHT
⑩ GOVERNOR SPRING	㉒ GOVERNOR DRIVING GEAR
⑪ PRESSURE CONTROL BUTTON	㉓ GOVERNOR ASSISTER SPRING
⑫ GOVERNOR RETURN PASSAGE	

FIG. 7.7.4

Supercharging and Superchargers

8.1

PRINCIPLES OF SUPERCHARGING

The power which any internal combustion engine can develop depends fundamentally upon the mass of air which it can consume per minute. The normal method of filling or *charging* the cylinders of a four-stroke engine consists of allowing the pressure of the atmosphere to force air into the engine cylinders to relieve the partial vacuum formed when the pistons move downward on their induction strokes. If the air is forced into the cylinders under a pressure higher than atmospheric a greater mass of air will enter the cylinder and the engine will be *supercharged*. This can be done by using some kind of air pump to deliver air to the engine: such a device is called a *supercharger*.

A two-stroke engine, of course, does not have an *induction stroke* and relies upon air being forced into its cylinders by some kind of pump, but the engine is not supercharged unless the pressure of the air filling the cylinder is above atmospheric pressure. A two-stroke engine is normally *pressure charged,* either by using a separate cylinder as a charging cylinder (as in the Clerk engine—page 47), or by using the underneath of the working piston (as in the Day engine—page 47), or by using some other kind of air pump such as a Roots blower (page 261). Strictly, a two-stroke engine cannot be *supercharged* unless the exhaust ports are arranged to close *before* the inlet ports close.

The first successful application of supercharging to an engine was probably by Chadwick, in America, in 1907, and it was tried experimentally in Europe during 1911–12. During the 1914–18 war some development was done on the supercharging of aircraft engines, and the first application of supercharging to racing cars was by Mercedes in 1921. From about 1923 until about 1952 most racing car engines were supercharged but since that time the international 'formulae' to which racing cars are required to conform have tended to discourage the supercharged engine and it is now no longer used in racing.

A few production cars have been supercharged, but these have been 'special' models: from time time to time 'kits' have been available to convert existing engines to supercharging but they are seldom used.

When first used on petrol engines the supercharger delivered air to the carburetter, but this system was later abandoned in favour of the arrangement in which the supercharger drew mixture from the carburetter and delivered it to the engine.

To give some idea of what can be achieved by supercharging it may be mentioned that the $1\frac{1}{2}$ litre V-16 BRM engine of 1949 was eventually developed to produce almost 500 bhp using a supercharge pressure of about 50 lbf/in² (350 kN/m²). Where high power output from an engine of minimum size is required there is no doubt that supercharging is the most effective method of securing it, but there are normally other considerations, such as fuel consumption, to be taken into account.

So far we have referred to the supercharging of spark-ignition engines, but compression-ignition engines may also be supercharged and may even be more suitable subjects for supercharging than spark-ignition engines. In this connection, that eminent authority on internal combustion engines, Sir Harry Ricards, summed up a lecture on supercharging which he gave in 1950 by saying 'the conclusions I have come to, so far, are that it is not worth while supercharging the spark-ignition engine except in the case of aircraft or racing engines, but that in the case of the four-stroke Diesel engine it pays hands down to do so and would pay most handsomely of all in the road vehicle field if and when a suitable blower can be developed for this service'.

The supercharger may be positively driven by belt, chain or gears from the engine crankshaft, or it may be driven by a turbine which is itself driven by the exhaust gases from the engine. The latter method is particularly suitable for one type of supercharger and has been extensively applied to compression-ignition engines during recent years.

8.2

TYPES OF SUPERCHARGER

THE PISTON TYPE

This consists of a piston moving up and down in a cylinder, very similar to the engine cylinder and piston, having valves to control the air flow. Mechanical considerations would necessitate it being driven at engine speed and it would thus require to have a swept volume somewhat larger than that of the engine cylinder. For a four-stroke engine one supercharger cylinder could supply two working cylinders, but for a two-stroke one charging cylinder is needed for each working cylinder. For the speeds attained by modern engines the valves must be mechanically operated.

Superchargers of this type are bulky and relatively complicated: consequently they have seldom been used.

THE ROOTS BLOWER

This device was patented about 1865 by F. M. and P. H. Roots in America and was used for a number of purposes including (in very large sizes) ventilating mines. Fig. 8.2.1 illustrates the construction generally used for engine supercharging: depending on engine size the width of the casing would be about 6–12 inches (150–300 mm).

It can be regarded as a form of gear pump (see page 235) in which each gear (called a *rotor* in the Roots blower) has only two teeth or *lobes*. (Some Roots blowers have rotors with three or even four lobes.) The rotors have a small clearance inside the casing and are carried on shafts which are geared together outside the casing: one shaft is driven at approximately engine speed and drives the other at the same speed.

The Roots blower is an air *displacer* and not a *compressor*: the air is not compressed within the blower but simply carried round

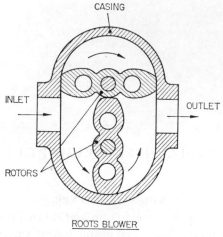

CASING

INLET

OUTLET

ROTORS

ROOTS BLOWER

FIG. 8.2.1

from inlet side to outlet side in the spaces between the lobes and the casing. The pressure at the output side depends upon the relative swept volumes of the blower and the engine and the speed at which the blower is driven.

The rotors operate continuously against the full delivery pressure and thus more power is absorbed in driving this device than would be required if compression took place within the blower: at low pressures this disadvantage is small, but it increases rapidly as pressures rise.

Due to the rotor clearance there will be some 'back leakage' of air: whilst this increases as delivery pressure rises, it decreases as speed increases. Thus this type of supercharger is mostly used for high-speed engines and relatively low supercharge pressures.

THE VANE COMPRESSOR

In its simplest form this consists of a cylindrical casing in which is mounted eccentrically a cylindrical rotor carrying protruding vanes which divide the space between the rotor and the casing into a number of compartments which vary in volume as the rotor turns.

In Fig. 8.2.2(a) the compartment shown shaded is in the position of maximum volume and the vane (1) has just cut off communication between this compartment and the inlet port. In Fig. 8.2.2(b) the rotor has turned to the position where the vane (2) is just about to

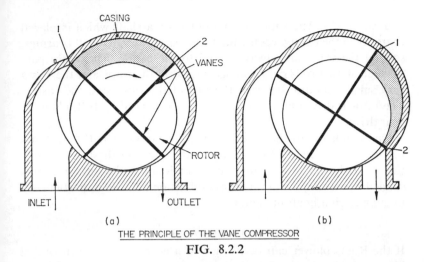

CASING

VANES

ROTOR

INLET

OUTLET

(a)

(b)

THE PRINCIPLE OF THE VANE COMPRESSOR

FIG. 8.2.2

open the compartment to the outlet port, and it can be seen that the volume of the compartment is now smaller than it was in Fig. 8.2.2(a). By altering the position of the leading edge of the outlet port the amount of compression within the compressor can be altered, and this would normally be arranged to correspond with the required delivery pressure.

Fig. 8.2.3 shows one practical form of this compressor which has, at various times, been marketed under the names of Centric, Arnott

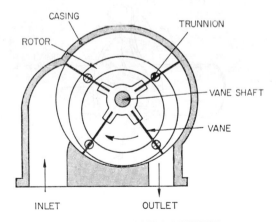

CASING

TRUNNION

ROTOR

VANE SHAFT

VANE

INLET

OUTLET

THE TRUNNION-TYPE RADIAL VANE COMPRESSOR

FIG. 8.2.3

and Shorrocks. The vanes are mounted on a shaft which is placed centrally in the casing, each vane being carried on two ball bearings, so that the vanes are always radial to the casing. The vanes pass through slotted rods or *trunnions* carried in the rotor and there is a very small clearance between the tips of the vanes and the casing. The rotor is driven at approximately engine speed by belt, chain or gear drive.

One minor disadvantage of the vane compressor is the necessity for lubrication due to the sliding of the vanes in the rotor. While this is fairly easy to arrange it is undesirable because oil mist carried into the engine may cause combustion difficulties, particularly in compression-ignition engines.

THE CENTRIFUGAL BLOWER

If the Roots blower can be likened to a gear pump the centrifugal blower can be simply described as a glorified water pump (as used in an engine cooling system—see page 208). The impeller is more carefully designed and made than the corresponding part of the water pump and is driven at considerably higher speed.

Fig. 8.2.4 illustrates the construction. The shaft is driven at some

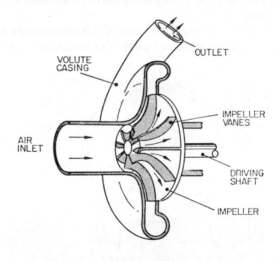

CENTRIFUGAL BLOWER

FIG. 8.2.4

five to six times engine speed: air is drawn in through the intake, carried round between the vanes of the impeller and thrown outwards by centrifugal force into the volute casing from which it passes to the inlet manifold.

The chief merit of this type is that a small size of blower can deliver a considerable quantity of air. It has two main disadvantages for automobile use. The first is the very high speed at which it must be driven (which introduces problems in the drive arrangements during rapid acceleration and deceleration) and the second is that it is efficient over a very narrow speed range only.

THE TURBO-SUPERCHARGER

The problems met with in driving the centrifugal blower at very high speeds can be neatly overcome by driving it by means of a turbine which is itself driven by the exhaust gases from the engine, and the combination of a supercharger driven by an exhaust turbine is called a *turbo-supercharger* or *turbocharger*. Attempts to apply this principle to engines have been made from time to time since the early years of this century, but it is only within recent years that, due to the development of metals capable of operating at very high temperatures and methods of manufacturing components in these metals economically, the method has been applied to motor vehicle engines.

There are two main types of turbine. The *radial flow* type is almost identical to a centrifugal compressor but the gas flow is reversed (Fig. 8.2.5.) The exhaust gas expelled from the engine cylinders is delivered into the casing surrounding the rotor and, either by the formation of the casing or by a ring of guide vanes, is directed tangentially onto the vanes of the turbine rotor. It flows inwards through these vanes to the outlet in the centre, to which the exhaust pipe is connected. The exhaust gases impinging on the turbine vanes rotate the turbine at a speed which depends upon the volume and speed of the gases leaving the engine cylinders.

An alternative to the radial flow turbine is the *axial flow* type (Fig. 8.2.6). In this type the turbine rotor has a large number of blades formed in its rim, and in rushing past these blades the exhaust gases drive the turbine wheel in the same way that wind drives a windmill.

In large sizes the axial flow turbine is more efficient than the radial flow type, but in the small sizes used for motor vehicle engines the

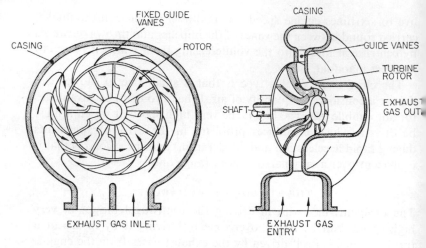

RADIAL FLOW TURBINE

FIG. 8.2.5

radial flow type is not only more efficient but has the additional merit of being easier and less expensive to manufacture.

The exhaust-driven turbine is invariably used in conjunction with a centrifugal type of supercharger, both components being built

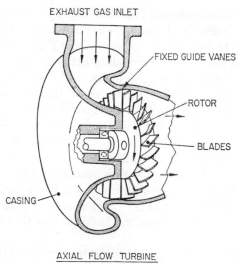

AXIAL FLOW TURBINE

FIG. 8.2.6

into a single unit (Fig. 8.2.7). This unit is mounted on the engine exhaust manifold by means of the flange around the exhaust gas entry. A common shaft has the turbine rotor fitted at one end and the supercharger impeller at the other, and is carried in bearings contained in a bearing housing—usually made of cast iron—with provision for lubricating the bearings from the engine lubrication system. The turbine casing is cast in a nickel or nickel-chromium alloy, iron to withstand the operating temperatures and the supercharger casing is usually an aluminium casting.

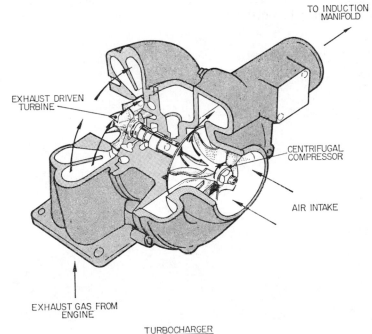

TURBOCHARGER

FIG. 8.2.7

The chief advantages claimed for the turbo-supercharging of compression-ignition engines are:
(1) Greater power from a given size of engine. As an example a 9·6 litre engine which gave 140 bhp (105 kW) when unsupercharged gave 225 bhp (170 kW) when turbocharged. *increase of 37%*
(2) For a given power output a turbo-supercharged engine may be considerably smaller and lighter than an unsupercharged engine.

(3) Fuel consumption is improved by about 10% or more.

(4) Exhaust noise is reduced.

There are greater difficulties in applying this method of super-charging to spark-ignition engines, such as the higher exhaust temperatures and the fact that these engines are, generally, less robustly built than compression-ignition engines. It would be necessary to reduce the compression ratio as the supercharge pressure is raised, resulting in reduced overall efficiency and increased fuel consumption. Nevertheless a useful improvement in performance is obtainable and for certain purposes turbo-supercharging this type of engine may be worth while.

Alternative Types of Engine

9.1

THE GAS TURBINE

'The fundamental idea of all prime movers lies in the direct utilisation of rotatory motion for the performance of work; and of late years there has been a growing tendency to revert from the reciprocatory motion of a piston in its cylinder to a rotatory motion.'

That quotation is from the beginning of a chapter on gas turbines in a book on Gas and Oil Engines written by a German engineer, Alfred Kirschke, an English translation of which was published in 1912. It is equally applicable at the present time to road vehicle engines. Even in 1912 the gas turbine was by no means a new invention. A patent for a gas turbine was granted to John Barber in 1791 but little practical use could be made of it owing to the lack of materials capable of withstanding the working conditions. What is claimed to be the first economically practicable gas turbine was built as a 'stationary' industrial engine in 1909-10 but little further development was done until the 1930s and, particularly for aircraft propulsion, during the 1939–45 war. The gas turbine is now firmly established in aircraft, marine and industrial applications, but is making less rapid progress in the motor vehicle field. The Rover gas turbine car was first shown in 1950, and in 1952 was demonstrated at speeds of over 150 mile/h (240km/h). We have also seen several experimental gas turbine engined racing cars, but as yet no gas turbine engined car is on sale to the public, although there are several gas turbine engined heavy commercial vehicles in the 'advanced prototype' stage. It is proposed, therefore, to describe very briefly the construction and working principles of this type of engine.

Fig. 9.1.1 illustrates a very simple model of a gas turbine. A shaft, mounted axially inside a tube, is supported on bearings and has fixed to it two 'fans', one near each end. Rotation of the shaft will cause one of the fans to blow air along the tube and this moving air

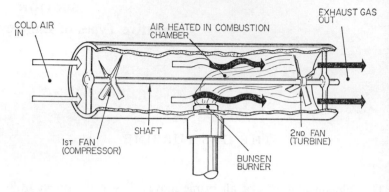

ELEMENTARY GAS TURBINE
FIG. 9.1.1

will tend to rotate the second fan in the manner of a windmill. The power developed by the second fan would only be just enough to drive the first fan if there were no friction, and clearly the device could not be used to drive any outside mechanism. However, by inserting a bunsen burner between the two fans the air passing along the tube can be heated causing it to expand. Thus it will pass the second fan travelling at a higher speed than it passed the first fan, so enabling the second fan to develop more power than is needed to drive the first fan.

The gas turbine can also be considered as a development of the turbo-supercharger (see Section 8) in which the supercharger (or compressor) delivers air to a combustion chamber in which fuel is burned continuously, the hot and expanded gases then being delivered at greatly increased speed to the turbine.

Fig. 9.1.2 shows, in simple diagrammatic form, the arrangement of a turbo-supercharger, and Fig. 9.1.3 shows the engine combustion chamber replaced by a simple combustion chamber in which the gas is merely heated by the continuous combustion of fuel. In the former case the gas does a great deal of work on the engine piston before it is released into the turbine, and consequently only a limited amount of energy is available for driving the turbine. In the gas turbine all the energy put into the gas by the combustion of fuel is available for driving the turbine, and there is usually far more than is required merely to drive the compressor. In the *jet* engine, as used in aircraft, this additional energy is used to provide a *thrust* by dis-

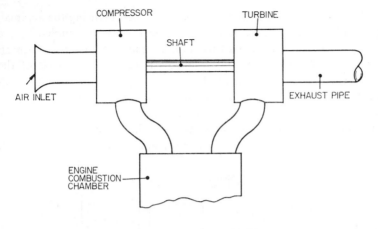

DIAGRAM OF TURBO-SUPERCHARGER

FIG. 9.1.2

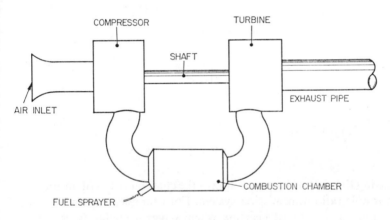

DIAGRAM OF SIMPLE SINGLE-SHAFT GAS TURBINE

FIG. 9.1.3

charging the hot gases through a *jet pipe* after they have passed the turbine. Alternatively the shaft could be connected to some kind of machinery which is required to be driven. In this form the gas turbine would not be very satisfactory for vehicle propulsion: since the torque developed depends upon compressor speed the torque would be low at low speeds, and a mechanism similar to the clutch and gearbox used with a piston engine would be essential.

A considerable improvement can be effected by using the arrangement illustrated in Fig. 9.1.4. Here one turbine is coupled to the compressor while a second turbine is mounted on a separate shaft. The *power turbine* would be coupled to the driving wheels of the vehicle, and this arrangement allows the vehicle to remain stationary with the power turbine stopped but the compressor turbine running. The torque on the output shaft when the power turbine is stationary and the compressor is running at its maximum speed is about 2–3 times greater than when the power turbine is running at full speed,

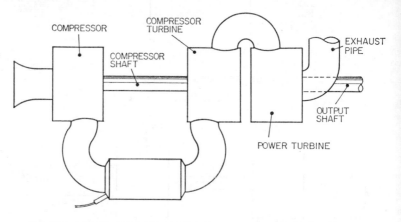

GAS TURBINE WITH SEPARATE COMPRESSOR AND POWER TURBINES (2-SHAFT GAS TURBINE)

FIG. 9.1.4

giving the gas turbine something of the characteristics of an automatic variable ratio transmission system. For example, a car which would require a four-speed gearbox when a petrol engine is used would need only a two-speed gearbox if fitted with a gas turbine. A heavy commercial vehicle needing ten or more speeds when using a compression-ignition engine would need only a four- or five-speed gearbox with a gas turbine.

The early gas turbine engines were less efficient than piston type engines, and had a relatively high fuel consumption. There are several methods which may be adopted to improve this. The first is by the use of a heat exchanger, shown in diagrammatic form in Fig. 9.1.5. The object of this device is to put some of the heat normally carried away by the exhaust gas into the air leaving the compressor,

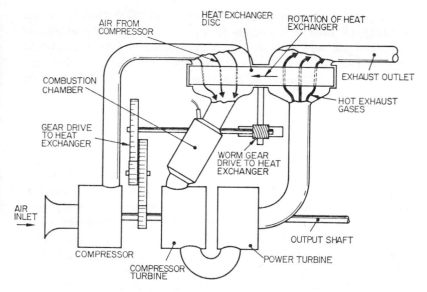

AIR FROM COMPRESSOR

HEAT EXCHANGER DISC

ROTATION OF HEAT EXCHANGER

COMBUSTION CHAMBER

EXHAUST OUTLET

HOT EXHAUST GASES

GEAR DRIVE TO HEAT EXCHANGER

WORM GEAR DRIVE TO HEAT EXCHANGER

AIR INLET

OUTPUT SHAFT

COMPRESSOR

COMPRESSOR TURBINE

POWER TURBINE

TWO-SHAFT GAS TURBINE WITH HEAT EXCHANGER

FIG. 9.1.5

thus reducing the amount of fuel which must be burned to provide a given temperature rise. By this means it has been possible to effect considerable improvements in fuel consumption, and some of the most recent gas turbines are claimed to have a fuel consumption comparable with that of a compression-ignition engine.

Several types of heat exchanger have been tried. The one most recently developed consists of two large discs [about 2 ft (0·6 m) in diameter] of a ceramic material having numerous small transverse passages through them, disposed vertically on each side of the engine and rotated at about 1/2000 of the speed of the compressor shaft. Exhaust gases from the power turbine are led through ducts to one half of each disc and in passing through the small passages in the discs give up some of their heat to the discs before being discharged through the exhaust system. As the discs rotate the heated portions are carried into ducts which direct air from the compressor through the discs before it passes into the combustion chamber, thus heating this air.

A second method by which the efficiency of the gas turbine could be improved is by raising the temperature of the gases entering the turbine. At present this is limited to about 1000–1500°C by the inability of present materials to operate satisfactorily at higher temperatures, and even for these temperatures very special and expensive alloys have had to be developed. However, development is proceeding with ceramic materials which, if successful, should permit the use of higher temperatures.

The maximum gas temperature is limited by restricting the maximum fuel delivery to the combustion chamber to an extent which provides an air/fuel ratio considerably weaker than the chemically correct mixture.

The engine is started by driving the compressor shaft by some external means—usually an electric motor. When it is running fast enough to blow air into the combustion chamber the fuel supply is turned on and fuel is sprayed continuously through a sprayer nozzle into the combustion chamber. Combustion is initiated by a sparking plug and once started will continue as long as fuel continues to be supplied. Power output is regulated by varying the rate of fuel delivery. Compressor speed ranges from about 15 000 rev/min when idling to a maximum of about 40 000–50 000 rev/min. The power turbine speed varies from zero to about 35 000–40 000 rev/min: it is therefore necessary to have a speed-reducing gear giving a ratio of the order of about 10 to 1 between the power turbine shaft and the propeller shaft if a conventional final-drive ratio is to be used.

So far most vehicle-type gas turbines have used a radial flow (centrifugal) compressor, the diameter being about 8 in (0·2 m). The compressor turbine also has been a radial flow type on some engines (e.g. the 1965 Rover-BRM) but most have been axial flow types. The power turbine is invariably an axial flow type, and the two turbines are usually arranged to rotate in opposite directions to eliminate, or at any rate to minimise, the gyroscopic effect.

The chief advantages claimed for the gas turbine are:
(1) High power output from a given weight of engine.
(2) The torque output characteristics permit a notable simplification of the transmission system.
(3) Smooth vibrationless running due to absence of reciprocating parts.
(4) No rubbing parts (such as pistons) so that internal friction and wear is almost eliminated.
(5) Easy starting.

(6) Can use a wide range of fuels and does not require expensive anti-knock additives.

(7) Low lubricating oil consumption.

(8) No water cooling system needed.

(9) Non-poisonous exhaust giving very little trouble with pollution.

(10) Requires little routine maintenance.

THE WANKEL ENGINE

As long ago as 1769 James Watt took out a patent for an engine in which steam pressure drove a rotating vane in a circular housing, and there have since been many attempts to produce an internal combustion engine in which the pressure of gases after combustion acted upon rotating members enclosed in a suitable casing. For a variety of reasons none of these showed any likelihood of challenging the piston engine until, towards the end of 1959 it became known that a German engineer, Felix Wankel, had devised an engine working on the equivalent of the four-stroke-cycle but employing only rotating parts. Development of this engine was taken up by the German firm of NSU and early in 1965 they produced a small car with one of these engines for sale to the public. Two years later they announced the production version of a large car having the equivalent of a 2-litre engine, whilst a month or so earlier the Japanese firm of Toyo Kogyo announced a car of similar size also using this engine. Apart from these, a number of other manufacturers are known to be developing engines of this type.

Each 'element' of this engine consists of three main parts: a housing, a rotor, and a shaft. Fig. 9.2.1 shows a section through one 'element'.

The *housing* contains a shallow bore (4) of a special shape known as *epitrochoidal*. (An *epitrochoid* is the line traced out by a point between the centre and the circumference of a circle as the circle rolls round the outside of another circle twice as large.) Carried on bearings co-axial with the centre of the housing bore is a shaft on which is formed an *eccentric* (9) over which fits a *rotor* (5) shaped like an equilateral triangle but with curved sides or flanks. An internal gear (7) concentric with and fixed to the rotor engages with

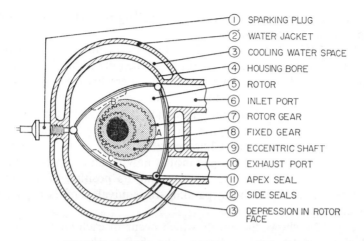

①	SPARKING PLUG
②	WATER JACKET
③	COOLING WATER SPACE
④	HOUSING BORE
⑤	ROTOR
⑥	INLET PORT
⑦	ROTOR GEAR
⑧	FIXED GEAR
⑨	ECCENTRIC SHAFT
⑩	EXHAUST PORT
⑪	APEX SEAL
⑫	SIDE SEALS
⑬	DEPRESSION IN ROTOR FACE

THE MAIN WORKING PARTS OF A WANKEL ENGINE

FIG. 9.2.1

a fixed gear (8) secured centrally in the housing and having a hollow centre through which the shaft passes. This fixed gear has two-thirds the number of teeth in the internal gear (7) in the rotor.

The result of this arrangement is that when the shaft is rotated the rotor is not only carried round eccentrically with it but also rotates in the same direction as the shaft but at one third the speed.

In every position of the rotor its three corners or *apices* (plural of apex) touch the housing bore so that three compartments or *chambers* are formed between the housing bore, the flanks of the rotor and the end plates of the housing. These chambers are made gas-tight by special seals at each apex (11) and the sides (12) of the rotor.

In every *three* revolutions of the shaft the rotor rotates *once*, and during this time the volume of each chamber passes through *two maximum* and *two minimum* values, so that the operations of the four-stroke cycle will be carried out in each of the three chambers. The *difference* between the maximum and minimum volumes represents the *swept* volume of each chamber, and the *ratio* maximum volume divided by minimum volume is the *compression ratio*. The minimum volume is what would be called the *clearance volume* in a piston engine, and the greater part of this is contained in a depression (13) in each rotor flank.

An inlet port (6) and an exhaust port (10) enter the housing at the points indicated in Fig. 9.2.1 and a sparking plug (1) is fitted in the opposite side of the housing.

In Fig. 9.2.1 the flanks of the rotors are identified by the letters *A*, *B* and *C*, and in the description of the operation which follows we use these letters to refer to the chambers between the housing and the appropriate rotor flank. In the position shown chamber *A* is in one of its two minimum volume positions, in this case the equivalent, in a piston engine, to t.d.c. at the end of exhaust and beginning of induction. Chamber *B* has passed its position of maximum volume and the gas in it is now being compressed ready for ignition. Chamber *C* is approaching its position of maximum volume and the gas in it is expanding, the equivalent of the expansion or power stroke.

Fig. 9.2.2 shows the events which occur in each chamber as the shaft completes one revolution. The shaft is shown turning anti-clockwise and Fig. 9.2.2(a) shows the position when the shaft has turned 90° from its position in Fig. 9.2.1.

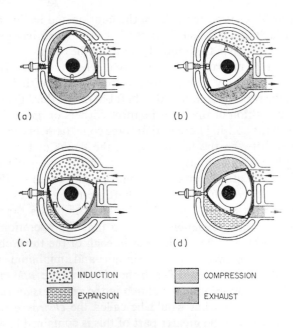

(a)   (b)

(c)   (d)

INDUCTION   COMPRESSION

EXPANSION   EXHAUST

OPERATION OF THE WANKEL ENGINE

FIG. 9.2.2

Fresh mixture is being induced into chamber A which is in communication with the inlet port but cut off from the exhaust port: this is the early part of the induction stroke.

Chamber B is still decreasing in size and is approaching the end of the compression stroke.

Chamber C has just reached its position of maximum volume equivalent to b.d.c. at the beginning of the exhaust stroke, and this chamber is already open to the exhaust port.

In Fig. 9.2.2(b) the shaft has turned a further 90° and chamber A has completed about two-thirds of its induction stroke.

Chamber B is in the position of minimum volume corresponding to t.d.c. at the end of the compression stroke, the mixture has been ignited and combustion is taking place.

Chamber C has completed about a third of its exhaust stroke: its volume is decreasing and the burned gases are being forced out of the exhaust port.

Fig. 9.2.2(c) shows the position after the shaft has turned its third quarter of a revolution. Chamber A has reached its position of maximum volume, corresponding to b.d.c. at the end of the induction stroke and the inlet port is beginning to close.

Chamber B is increasing in volume at the early part of the power stroke.

Chamber C is just starting the last third of its exhaust stroke.

Finally Fig. 9.2.2(d) shows the situation at the end of one complete revolution of the shaft. This is similar to the position shown in Fig. 9.2.1 except that the chambers have all moved round one place. During the next revolution of the shaft chamber A will carry out the same operations as chamber B did on the revolution just described, chamber B will repeat those of chamber C, and chamber C those of chamber A.

During the following revolution of the shaft (the third) chamber A will repeat the operations just described for chamber C, chamber B those of chamber A, and chamber C those of chamber B, and the position will by then have returned to that shown in Fig. 9.2.1.

Thus it is seen that the engine produces one power stroke per, revolution of the shaft, and it is therefore equivalent, in this respect to a single-cylinder two-stroke engine or a two-cylinder four-stroke engine having a cylinder swept volume equal to the swept volume of one chamber.

If two of these 'elements' are used the firing frequency of a four-cylinder four-stroke engine is obtained. Such an engine is called a *two-rotor* or *twin-rotor* engine, and is the type used for the two models at present (1971) in production.

Although basically similar these two engines have a number of small differences. Possibly the most interesting difference is in the inlet port arrangements. The NSU engine has both inlet and exhaust ports arranged as shown in Figs. 9.2.1 and 9.2.2: these are called *peripheral* ports since they are cut in the *periphery* of the housing. The engine used in the Mazda Cosmos car made by the Toyo Kogyo Co. Ltd. has the exhaust ports arranged in this way but the inlet ports enter the *sides* of the housing instead of the periphery. One result of this different port arrangement is that whereas the NSU engine develops its maximum torque at a speed of 4500 rev/min the Mazda engine develops a slightly lower maximum torque at a speed of 3500 rev/min.

Although air-cooled engines of this type have been built, those at present in production have the housing water-cooled. The rotor is cooled by circulating oil from the lubrication system around its hollow interior, and this necessitates the use of an oil cooler.

The main advantages which this type of engine appears to offer are:

(1) Simplicity. Each 'element' has only two moving parts—the rotor and the eccentric shaft—and since communication between chambers and ports is controlled by the rotor, valves and their operating gear are completely eliminated.

(2) The absence of reciprocating parts should allow the engine to operate at higher speeds.

(3) Since all moving parts have simple rotary motion they are easily balanced and vibration can be eliminated.

(4) If peripheral ports are used they are never closed. This leads to improved volumetric efficiency. Values in excess of 100% have been claimed.

(5) For a given swept volume the engine is lighter and less bulky than a piston-type engine. The gain in this direction increases as the number of rotors is increased.

Clutches, Fluid Couplings and Torque Converters

10.1

THE SINGLE-PLATE CLUTCH

REASON FOR A CLUTCH

It has been seen that the internal-combustion engine, unlike the steam engine, does not produce high power at low speeds; therefore the engine must be rotating at a speed at which sufficient power is developed, before the drive to the wheels is established. This condition rules out the use of a dog clutch (Fig. 10.1.1) since the connection of a rotating engine to a stationary transmission shaft would damage the transmission and jolt the vehicle. The clutch used must allow

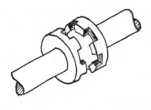

DOG CLUTCH

FIG. 10.1.1

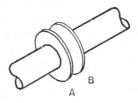

FRICTION CLUTCH

FIG. 10.1.2

the drive to be taken up smoothly so that the vehicle can be gradually moved away from the stationary position.

Once moving, it will be necessary to change gear, and so a disengagement of the engine or transmission is required. This is also part of the clutch's function.

The clutch takes up the drive smoothly; it also disengages the drive. These two duties can be performed by various mechanisms; the friction system is considered to be one of the most effective and efficient. Hydraulic and electric systems are also employed on motor vehicles.

THE FRICTION CLUTCH

The operation of a friction clutch is demonstrated by the two discs shown in Fig. 10.1.2. If discs *A* and *B* are connected to engine and transmission respectively, then when the discs are held apart, no drive will be made. When *A* is moved to contact *B*, the friction between the surfaces will allow a drive to be transmitted. The extent of this drive will be governed by the force which pushes the discs together; therefore if the force is gradually increased, the drive transmitted will increase proportionally. This will allow the vehicle to move smoothly from rest.

When the drive is engaged, both discs must rotate at the same speed, and so the clutch designer must ensure that there is enough pressure and friction to produce this condition. During the life of the clutch, faults may develop which restrict pressure or friction; therefore the clutch will slip and the performance of the vehicle will be affected.

The clutch shown in Fig. 10.1.3 is a construction developed from the previous diagram. Both sides of the friction plate are utilised, and this will mean that double the torque (turning moment) can be transmitted before slip takes place. The friction plate, or *driven plate*, is sandwiched between the engine flywheel and the pressure plate, and the design is known as a *single-plate clutch*.

A *multi-plate clutch* is a unit which employs a number of driven plates. It is described in the next chapter.

SINGLE-PLATE CLUTCH

This is the most common type of clutch in use, and has the advantage of producing a quick disengagement.

Fig. 10.1.3 shows a simple clutch with a driven plate (1) splined to the primary shaft (2) of the gearbox. Riveted to the plate is a pair of linings or facings (3) made of an asbestos-based material, which is bonded with suitable resins to give a satisfactory coefficient of friction, and other useful properties. The pressure plate (4) is located by a number of studs (5), and is forced towards the flywheel (6) by means of springs (7). A withdrawal sleeve (8) allows the clutch pedal (9) to act on the clutch forks (10) and push the pressure plate away from the flywheel. An adjustable link (11) is set to give a small clearance between the clutch fork and the withdrawal sleeve to ensure that the full force of the springs is felt on the driven plate.

This clearance allows the pedal a small amount of free movement which, measured at the pad of the pedal, is normally about 1 in (25 mm). At the centre of the flywheel is fitted a spigot bearing (12), which locates the front end of the gearbox primary shaft and allows for the difference in speed between the two members. This bearing can take the form of a ball race or plain bush; the former is normally sealed with a metal cover to prevent the lubricant being thrown out on to the linings. The plain bearing type is generally manufactured from phosphor-bronze, and made porous so that the bush can be impregnated with graphite to make it self-lubricating.

When the driver depresses the pedal, the clutch forks push the pressure plate away from the flywheel to remove the spring pressure from the driven plate. This allows the plate to run free, and therefore disengages the engine from the transmission.

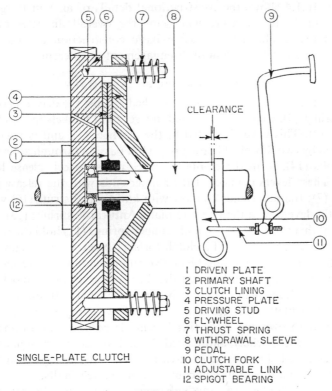

CLEARANCE

SINGLE-PLATE CLUTCH

1 DRIVEN PLATE
2 PRIMARY SHAFT
3 CLUTCH LINING
4 PRESSURE PLATE
5 DRIVING STUD
6 FLYWHEEL
7 THRUST SPRING
8 WITHDRAWAL SLEEVE
9 PEDAL
10 CLUTCH FORK
11 ADJUSTABLE LINK
12 SPIGOT BEARING

FIG. 10.1.3

On releasing the pedal, the spring thrust forces the pressure plate towards the flywheel, and sandwiches the driven plate between the two surfaces. This movement of the pedal must be gradual, or the full force of the springs will be suddenly applied to the driven plate and cause a jolt.

It will be seen that when the pedal is fully released, the drive can take two paths—it can be transferred directly from flywheel face to driven plate, or can be taken via the studs and pressure plate to the rear face of the driven plate.

BORG AND BECK CLUTCHES

The majority of motor manufacturers use a single-plate clutch designed and made by the Borg and Beck Company. This company offers a complete range of clutches from which it is possible to select a clutch which will suit the output of the engine.

Fig. 10.1.4 shows the constructional details of an 8-in Borg and Beck clutch, the measurement being the overall diameter of the driven plate. This has the same basic construction as shown in Fig. 10.1.3, but the system of disengagement is different.

THE PRESSURE PLATE ASSEMBLY

The cast-iron pressure plate (3) is pushed against the driven plate (6) by springs (4), which are mounted in a series of pockets in the clutch cover (2). This cover is bolted to the flywheel (1), and is normally located by two dowels. Floating pins (15), passing through adjustable eyebolts (14), form the pivots for three pressed-steel release levers (12). These levers connect at their inner ends with the release lever plate (7); the outer ends connect with knife-edged struts (16) which link the levers with the pressure plate. Anti-rattle springs (13) exert a slight thrust on the levers, and retainer springs (11) hold the release lever plate in position. The clutch forks (10) carry a steel cup, into which is pressed a graphite block (8), and are adjusted externally to give a small clearance between the faces of the graphite block and the release lever plate. The gearbox primary shaft (9), on to which the driven plate (6) is splined, is located by a spigot bearing. Any lubricant thrown out from this bearing is collected in an annular groove in the flywheel, and passed through holes to the engine side. It is essential that no oil or grease reaches the linings of a 'dry' clutch, since a lubricant will cause various clutch faults.

During manufacture, any unbalance is corrected by removing

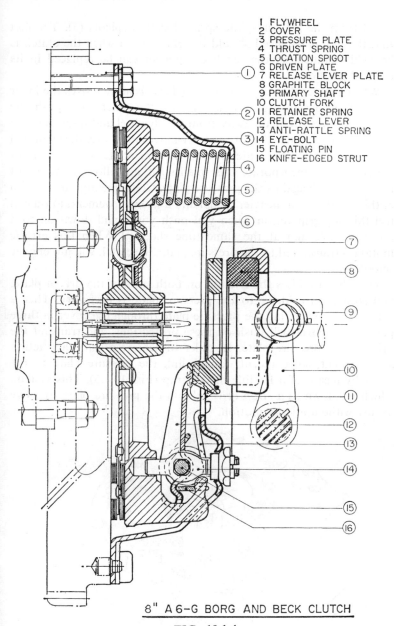

1 FLYWHEEL
2 COVER
3 PRESSURE PLATE
4 THRUST SPRING
5 LOCATION SPIGOT
6 DRIVEN PLATE
7 RELEASE LEVER PLATE
8 GRAPHITE BLOCK
9 PRIMARY SHAFT
10 CLUTCH FORK
11 RETAINER SPRING
12 RELEASE LEVER
13 ANTI-RATTLE SPRING
14 EYE-BOLT
15 FLOATING PIN
16 KNIFE-EDGED STRUT

8" A 6-G BORG AND BECK CLUTCH

FIG. 10.1.4

metal from the pressure-plate spring location spigots (5). The fact
that the unit is balanced should be remembered when the clutch is
being dismantled, so that each component can be replaced in its
original position.

When the pedal is depressed, the release bearing moves the inner
ends of the levers towards the engine; the outer ends push the
struts and pressure plate away from the flywheel and disengage the
drive. Since the outer end of the lever moves in an arc, the strut will
tilt and allow for the difference in movement. Earlier designs of
clutch did not incorporate this small strut, and allowed the end of
the lever to rub against the pressure plate. Consequently, the friction
at this point gave a 'heavier' pedal and a jerky movement. (You can
feel this slip-grip action when you push your hand down on to a
polished table and at the same time slide it.) When this erratic
motion is transferred to the pressure plate, the clutch will not engage
smoothly.

This clutch utilises the friction on both sides of the driven plate,
and so a positive drive to the pressure plate is necessary. This is
achieved by extending the pressure plate through the cover in three
places. The cover will push on these protrusions, and transmit the
drive to the pressure plate. In order to achieve a smoother action
at this point, some recent designs link the pressure plate to the
cover by means of a flexible metal strap (Fig. 10.1.5). This system,
which is known as a *strap drive*, allows the pressure plate to move
axially without a jerky motion.

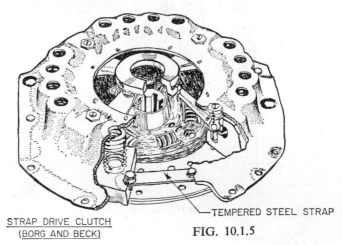

STRAP DRIVE CLUTCH
(BORG AND BECK)

TEMPERED STEEL STRAP

FIG. 10.1.5

The purpose of the release bearing is to link the clutch forks with the release levers so that the pedal thrust may be applied to the pressure plate. Since the levers are rotating at flywheel speed, some form of bearing is necessary. The two main types in general use are *graphite* and *ball*.

The former is used on the majority of private cars, and three advantages are claimed: the bearing is self-lubricating; it is cheap; the wear on the graphite block compensates for lining wear, and so the free pedal movement is maintained approximately constant. In the case of the ball type, the wear on the linings allows the pressure plate to move towards the flywheel, and, if a mechanical linkage is used, the free pedal movement will be reduced or eliminated. When this occurs, slip will be evident; to counter this effect, adjust the pedal periodically. Lubrication of the ball type is arranged by sealing in the lubricant by means of metal end covers.

The facings or linings on the driven plate are secured by brass rivets, the heads being recessed into the lining to prevent scoring of the flywheel and pressure plate faces. As the linings wear down, the inner ends of the release levers move away from the flywheel, and after a predetermined amount of wear has taken place, the levers will touch the cover. Under ideal circumstances, this will happen before the head of the rivet is exposed, and since the full spring thrust is now taken by the cover, slip will be evident, and re-lining will be necessary.

Whenever the pressure plate assembly is dismantled and re-assembled, it is essential to reset the release levers the recommended distance from the flywheel face. This adjustment can only be done when the clutch is bolted in position, or set on a special jig.

THE DRIVEN PLATE

The important features incorporated in the design of a driven plate can best be seen by considering the disadvantages of using a plain steel plate with a lining riveted to each side. These may be listed as:

(1) buckling of the plate due to heat

(2) drag, due to the plate rubbing against the flywheel when the clutch should be disengaged

(3) very small movement of the clutch pedal between the engaged and disengaged positions—the clutch is said to be of the *in* or *out* class, with very little control between these points.

To overcome these troubles, the plate is normally slotted, or set in such a manner as to produce a 'flexing' action. This is generally known as *crimping*, and Fig. 10.1.6 shows one form. Each segment is dished a small amount, so that the linings tend to spring apart when the clutch is disengaged.

If the clutch is in the driving position and the pedal is depressed, the driven plate will tend to jump away from the flywheel to give a 'clean' disengagement. While in this position, the linings will be held apart, and air will be pumped between the linings to take away the heat. During engagement, axial compression of the driven plate spreads the engagement over a greater range of pedal travel and therefore makes it easier to make a smooth engagement.

Fig. 10.1.6 shows a driven plate which is riveted to a splined hub. This arrangement is used occasionally, but in most cases the hub is mounted independently of the main plate, and the drive between the two components made possible by either fitting a series of springs or bonding the hub to the plate by means of rubber. This *flexible*

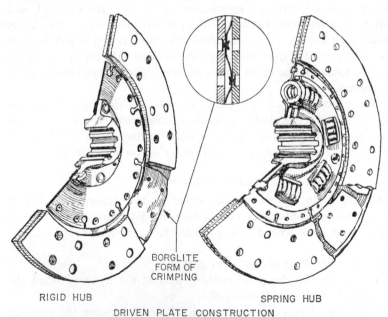

RIGID HUB

BORGLITE
FORM OF
CRIMPING

SPRING HUB

DRIVEN PLATE CONSTRUCTION
(BORG AND BECK)

FIG. 10.1.6

drive absorbs the torsional shocks due to engine vibrations and clutch take-up, which otherwise cause transmission noise or rattle.

COMMERCIAL-VEHICLE CLUTCHES

These clutches are of unit construction similar to the type used on cars, but are made more robust to take the greater engine torque.

A larger number of heavier springs are fitted, and four drop-forged release levers are generally used. The mechanical efficiency of the release mechanism is improved by pivoting the release levers on needle roller bearings.

Large driven plates have a tendency to *spin* (i.e. to continue rotating after the clutch pedal is depressed). To limit this trouble, the plate should be made as light as possible. Some manufacturers use a small *disc brake* (also known as a clutch stop) to bring the driven plate to rest. This brake is mounted on the non-rotating part of the release bearing, and when the pedal is depressed approximately two thirds of its travel, the brake contacts a disc on the primary shaft.

DIAPHRAGM-SPRING CLUTCHES

This very compact design of single-plate clutch eliminates the need for a series of coil springs by using a diaphragm to provide the clamping pressure.

Fig. 10.1.7(a) shows the main details of this type of clutch. It will be seen that the diaphragm spring is a steel disc, pivoted to the cover and connected at the outer edge to the pressure plate. The centre of the disc is slotted to form a number of fingers on to which is mounted a release plate. This plate is contacted with a normal type of release bearing. Protrusions on the pressure plate fit into slots in the driving plate to provide a drive between the two members.

Fig. 10.1.7(b) shows that the diaphragm spring forms a convex or dished shape while in an unloaded state. Clamping the clutch to the flywheel flattens the spring and provides the necessary thrust on the pressure plate and friction facings.

When the pedal is depressed, the release bearing pushes the centre of the spring towards the flywheel and causes the outer edge to move in the opposite direction. This disengages the pressure plate from the friction facings.

The pedal effort needed to disengage this type of clutch is far less than that required on a conventional clutch. This is because the load exerted by the diaphragm spring does not increase proportion-

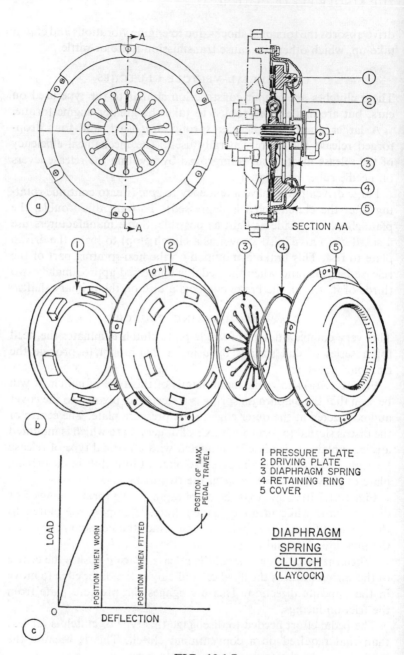

SECTION AA

1 PRESSURE PLATE
2 DRIVING PLATE
3 DIAPHRAGM SPRING
4 RETAINING RING
5 COVER

DIAPHRAGM
SPRING
CLUTCH
(LAYCOCK)

LOAD

DEFLECTION

POSITION OF MAX.
PEDAL TRAVEL

POSITION WHEN WORN

POSITION WHEN FITTED

FIG. 10.1.7

ally to the deflection. Fig. 10.1.7(c) shows a load/deflection curve. Maximum load, or spring thrust, occurs when the spring is flat, but when the spring is deflected past this point, the load decreases. (This effect can be felt when the bottom of a tin can is pressed in —the force increases up to a point where the lid is flat, but from then on, a much smaller force is required.) The curve also shows that the pedal effort required to 'hold-out' the clutch is less than that needed to produce the initial disengagement.

Lining wear on orthodox clutches causes the spring to extend, and this decreases the thrust on the plate. With the diaphragm type, the spring can be set so that no decrease in thrust occurs—in fact the curve shows that a slight increase in thrust is achieved.

The following is a summary of the advantages of diaphragm spring clutches:

(1) lower pedal force required
(2) suitable for extra-high engine speeds—constant spring thrust and accurate balance are maintained
(3) no separate release levers are required, giving improved release efficiency
(4) fewer parts required
(5) spring load remains approximately constant as the facing wears
(6) compactness.

PEDAL LINKAGE

The external linkage between the pedal and clutch may be either *mechanical* or *hydraulic*.

Fig. 10.1.8 shows some systems which may be used. Each arrangement normally includes some form of adjustment to enable the correct free pedal movement to be maintained. If the clearance is non-existent, wear on the release bearing and clutch slip will result. (This effect can also be produced if the driver rests his foot on the pedal.) When the clearance is too great, the pedal will reach the end of its travel before the clutch is disengaged, and this 'drag' will make it difficult to engage gear.

The mechanical systems shown have a pedal mounted on the frame of the vehicle, and a clutch cross-shaft which is mounted on the engine. Rubber-mounted engine bearers allow the engine to move a considerable amount in all directions. If the clutch pedal is partly depressed, any fore-and-aft movement of the engine will adversely affect the smooth operation of the clutch, and 'judder'

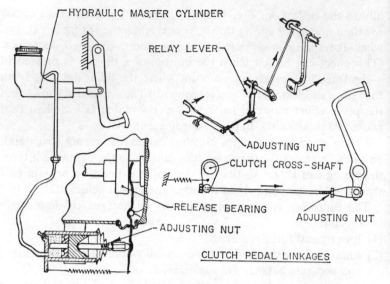

HYDRAULIC MASTER CYLINDER

RELAY LEVER

ADJUSTING NUT

CLUTCH CROSS-SHAFT

RELEASE BEARING

ADJUSTING NUT

ADJUSTING NUT

CLUTCH PEDAL LINKAGES

FIG. 10.1.8

will result. To prevent this, many manufacturers employ some form of tie-rod to limit the engine movement, but these arrangements defeat the object of using flexible engine mountings.

You will see that engine movement has no effect on the hydraulic system, and so judder from this cause is eliminated, and it is unnecessary to restrict engine movement.

THE MULTI-PLATE CLUTCH

The torque transmitted by a plate clutch depends on: (1) number of friction contacts, (2) spring thrust, (3) coefficient of friction, and (4) mean radius.

There are cases, e.g. with motor cycles, when factors 2, 3 and 4 are restricted; consequently the number of plates must be increased to enable the full engine torque to be transmitted. This is the main reason for using a multi-plate clutch.

Although this type of clutch was widely used up to about 1930, the greater advantages of the single-plate type have meant that the multi-plate unit is now rarely used as a main clutch on a motor car. The principle of operation is considered at this stage, however, because the multi-plate construction is used for other important purposes, e.g. to connect various elements in gearboxes of the Wilson and automatic transmission types.

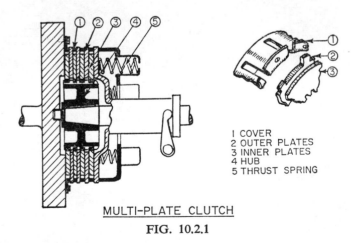

1 COVER
2 OUTER PLATES
3 INNER PLATES
4 HUB
5 THRUST SPRING

MULTI-PLATE CLUTCH

FIG. 10.2.1

Fig. 10.2.1 shows the main constructional details and represents a main clutch of the type used on past motor cars. Bolted to the flywheel is a cover (1) which engages, by means of slots, with a series of lugs on the outer plates (2). These plates, which may be plain steel or fitted with cork or friction material inserts, act on inner plates (3), which are splined to a hub (4). Thrust springs (5) push the plates together to form a drive.

To disengage the clutch, the end plate is withdrawn to compress the springs and release the other plates. It is difficult to ensure that all plates disengage, and to remedy this defect the plates are either dished or fitted with small springs to push the plates apart.

The clutch may be either *wet* or *dry*; the advantage of using the former is that it reduces the fierce engagement by allowing the engine oil to flow into the clutch housing.

The clutch employed in automatic gearboxes is generally of the wet type, and is operated by a piston controlled by hydraulic pressure. Sintered bronze plates, manufactured by partially fusing powdered bronze, are used in many designs. The porous surface obtained traps the oil, to give long life and smooth operation. (This process is also used to produce porous bushes—prior to fitting, the bush is soaked in oil for a number of hours.) A multi-plate clutch used in an automatic gearbox is shown on page 365.

HYDRAULIC TRANSMISSION SYSTEMS

The two main arrangements are known as the *fluid coupling* and the *fluid converter*.

The arrangement was originally intended for marine use, and was invented by Dr. Fottinger in 1905, but it was not until 20 years later that a British engineer (H. Sinclair) introduced the fluid drive on a motor vehicle. With this drive the transmission is connected to the engine by hydraulic means, which provides an effective damper to the torsional vibrations set up by the engine, a smooth take-up to move the vehicle from rest, and, in the case of the converter, a device to amplify the torque.

THE HYDRAULIC COUPLING

This unit is often known as a *fluid flywheel,* since it usually forms a component part of the main engine flywheel, and is generally used in conjunction with a Wilson epicyclic gearbox. In this application, wear on the gearbox is reduced by employing the coupling to move the vehicle from the rest position.

Principle of the Fluid Coupling Flywheel

You will understand the principle of operation if you consider the following steps.

Fig. 10.3.1(a) shows a 'grapefruit' member which is filled with a fluid and rotated. The fluid is thrown tangentially outwards and upwards.

If a plate is held over the member (Fig. 10.3.1(b)), the fluid will strike and tend to rotate the plate in the same direction. The force and torque acting on the plate will depend on the speed of rotation—

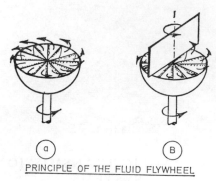

FIG. 10.3.1

the greater the speed, the greater will be the force, since more energy is given to the fluid.

In Fig. 10.3.2(a) the plate is replaced by another 'grapefruit' member which receives the drive and re-diverts the fluid back to the driving member. The fluid 'circuit' can be traced by following the path taken by a particle of fluid. Rotation of A will cause the particle to move outwards from point 1 to 2. This is brought about by the resistance of the fluid to movement in a circular path. (A body will move in a straight line unless acted upon by a force. So that if you consider a plan view of A, you will see that the straight-line path will take the particle to the outside.) The farther from the centre the particle moves, the faster it will have to travel; consequently, energy will be extracted from the engine.

The shape and outward motion will force the particle upwards and cause the tangential flow to strike the vanes of member B, the force of impact being governed by the speed difference of the two members. At position 3, the energy possessed by the particle is less than at 2, since the force of impact causes energy to be given up in the form of heat. This fact means that the energy remaining in the particle is less than that given to it by the engine, and therefore the output speed will be lower than the input.

The fluid following the particle will push it, against its natural tendency, to point 4. During this movement, the linear speed of the particle is decreased, and energy is given up to drive the output shaft. If the speed of both members is the same, the outward force at point 4 will be equal to that at point 1, and no

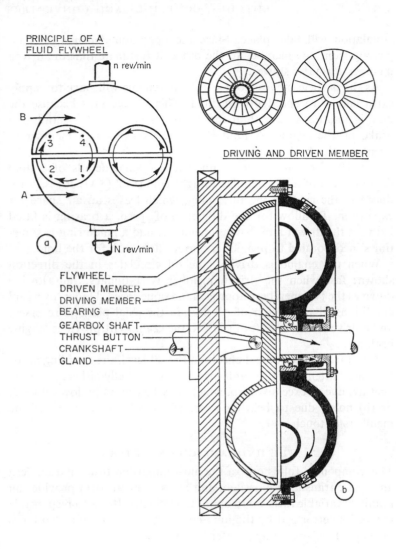

PRINCIPLE OF A
FLUID FLYWHEEL

n rev/min

B

3 4

2 1

A

a

N rev/min

DRIVING AND DRIVEN MEMBER

FLYWHEEL
DRIVEN MEMBER
DRIVING MEMBER
BEARING
GEARBOX SHAFT
THRUST BUTTON
CRANKSHAFT
GLAND

b

THE
FLUID FLYWHEEL

FIG. 10.3.2

circulation will take place. Since the operation depends on fluid passing from one member to the other, it fortunate that the driven member *B* rotates slower.

As the particle moves from 4 to 1, the engine will have to supply extra energy to speed up the fluid. This is necessary because the fluid is rotating slower than the driving member and is acting as a brake on the engine. A fluid converter uses an extra member to overcome this braking effect.

Fig. 10.3.2(b) shows the main constructional details of a fluid coupling. Oil of a type similar to light engine oil (SAE 30) is introduced to the level of the filler plug, which leaves an air space for expansion. To allow for the difference of speed, a bearing is fitted between the driven and driving members, and a guide ring is sometimes incorporated to provide a smooth flow path for the fluid.

When the engine is driving, the oil circulates in the direction shown: fast when the driven member is stationary, but slowing down as the two members approach the same speed. Under 'overrun' conditions, the direction of oil flow in the axial plane is reversed, and a drive from the output shaft to the crankshaft provides 'engine braking'.

Apart from a periodical check on the oil level, the coupling needs very little attention. If a fault arises, it is normally either: (a) overheating, due to excessive slip, which may be caused by low oil level, or (b) noise, due to bearing wear, which allows the faces of the members to touch.

THE HYDRAULIC CONVERTER

This component fulfils one of the most important tasks in a modern automatic transmission system and in its simplest form provides an infinitely variable ratio up to approximately 2:1. It is also responsible for duties performed by the fluid coupling. More complicated types are capable of providing greater torque ratios.

Principle of Operation

Before considering the operation of the converter, an appreciation of the following experiments may be of help.

Anyone who has used a hosepipe will realise that the water leaves the nozzle at a considerable speed. A moving fluid possesses energy and this means that it is capable of doing work. Directing a flow of fluid into a plate causes the fluid direction to change and the extent of this change governs the force which acts on the plate (Fig. 10.3.3).

Varying the speed of the fluid by adjusting the tap also alters the force of impact; a low fluid speed contains very little energy and therefore only exerts a small force on the plate.

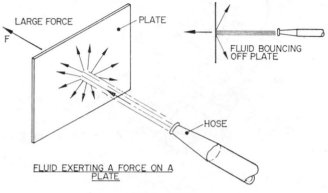

FLUID EXERTING A FORCE ON A PLATE

FIG. 10.3.3

The force of impact can be varied by moving the plate in a manner such that it is tending to travel with the fluid. During this movement the speed of the fluid relative to the plate is slower than in the previous case, so the impact force will be less. If it was possible to move the plate at the same speed as the fluid is moving, then no impact will take place, consequently no force will be produced on the plate.

Fig. 10.3.4 shows a curved plate. In this case the fluid is striking the plate with a velocity of 'v' and the curved surface is redirecting the fluid back at a velocity '$-v$' towards its source. Double the force is obtained with this arrangement, since the plate not only stops the fluid but also has to send it back at the same speed.

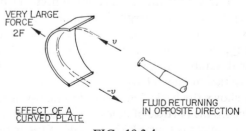

EFFECT OF A CURVED PLATE

FLUID RETURNING IN OPPOSITE DIRECTION

FIG. 10.3.4

Mounting a series of these plates onto a shaft (Fig. 10.3.5) forms a simple turbine. Each plate, which is now called a vane, will extract the energy from the moving fluid to produce a turning action on the shaft.

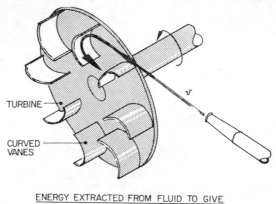

TURBINE

CURVED VANES

ENERGY EXTRACTED FROM FLUID TO GIVE TURNING MOMENT

FIG. 10.3.5

Consideration of the previous experiments will show:
(a) Low velocity of the fluid produces a small turning movement or torque,
(b) high torque occurs when the fluid velocity is high and the shaft speed is low,
(c) gradual decrease in torque occurs as the shaft speed increases.

The term fluid is chosen since the previous experiments can be conducted with air or any liquid, and the arrangements considered could be applied to gas turbines, turbochargers or hydraulic converters since the basic principle is similar.

Having established the basic idea of the turbine, the means of fluid supply will now be examined. From the previous description it will be appreciated that the energy is contained in a particle of fluid by virtue of its velocity, so a compact device is needed to eject fluid at high velocity. In the case of the torque converter this is provided by a centrifugal pump, which in principle is similar to the type used in a cooling system or supercharger.

Fig. 10.3.6 shows the basic features of the pump. Rotation of the member will cause the particle of fluid 'P' to move in the path shown. Initially the movement is towards the outside of the member and the

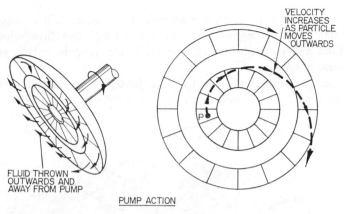

VELOCITY INCREASES AS PARTICLE MOVES OUTWARDS

FLUID THROWN OUTWARDS AND AWAY FROM PUMP

PUMP ACTION

FIG. 10.3.6

greater distance it has to travel in one revolution at this point shows that its velocity has been increased. Work has to be done by the engine to achieve this increase in the energy content of the particle. Shrouding the pump with a container causes the fluid to move away from the pump as shown in Fig. 10.3.7. Observation of the diagram shows the fluid moving around the circumference and it is the velocity in this direction that governs the driving force that is being delivered by the pump. The resemblance between the flow given by the pump and the nozzle shown in Fig. 10.3.5 should now be apparent and the

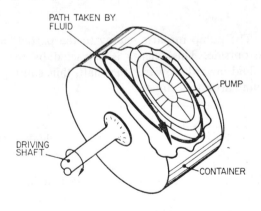

PATH TAKEN BY FLUID

PUMP

DRIVING SHAFT

CONTAINER

CONTAINER FITTED TO PUMP

FIG. 10.3.7

effect of engine speed on the pump's performance will be easy to understand—low engine speed will give a small flow (low velocity) of fluid and consequently each particle will contain only a small amount of energy.

Placing the pump adjacent to the turbine (Fig. 10.3.8) and making the pump act as the container shows how the drive from the engine

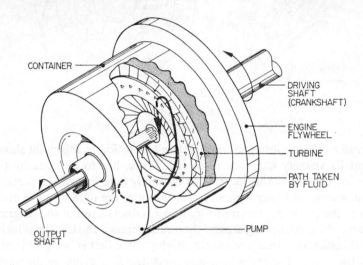

FLUID PATH FROM PUMP TO TURBINE

FIG. 10.3.8

is achieved. The pump imparts energy to the particle as it moves towards the outside. This energy is extracted by the turbine by moving the fluid inwards towards the shaft, thus causing it to slow down. To summarise this stage:

Pump	Turbine
Speeds up particle.	Slows down particle.
Imparts energy.	Extracts energy.

Fig. 10.3.8 is similar to a fluid coupling and in this form the torque output is always less than the torque input.

Applying the earlier analogy of the hosepipe would indicate that when the turbine is turning slower than the pump, the force of impact of the fluid striking the turbine vanes should give a torque increase.

This would be true if the fluid did not have to return to the pump, but since this fluid is having to recirculate then the speed of the fluid compared to the speed of the pump vane must be considered. To give a high impact force on the output member, the pump must be turning at a higher speed than the turbine, so when the fluid is returned to the pump it is travelling slower than the pump vane. In this condition the vane will strike the slower moving fluid particle and this will give a force which is acting against the motion of the pump, i.e. the fluid will tend to act as a brake on the pump. The greater the speed difference between pump and turbine, the greater will be the impact force on the turbine but this will also result in a larger braking action on the pump. To obtain a torque multiplication, this braking action must be eliminated. This is achieved by fitting a separate member called a stator (stationary member) between the turbine and the pump. Mounted on an extension of the gearbox casing, the stator consists of a number of vanes which are shaped in the manner shown in Fig. 10.3.9. Fluid returning to the pump is redirected such that it now enters the pump at a suitable speed and direction. If the path of the oil returning to the pump is considered, the system could be shown diagramatically in the manner shown in Fig. 10.3.10.

Fluid from the pump acts on the turbine T, but if the turbine is turning slower than the oil, then the oil will be deflected in the path

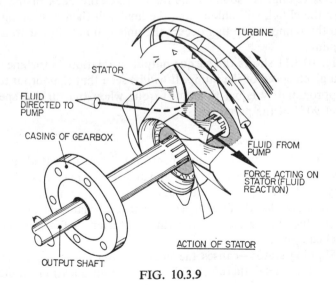

FIG. 10.3.9

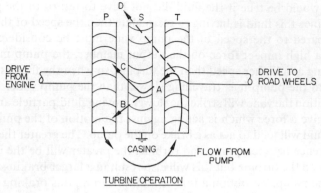

FIG. 10.3.10

marked A; the stator will act as a reaction member and will direct the fluid from path B to path C; a suitable direction for the pump to receive the fluid. As the turbine speed is increased the fluid path A will gradually change until it is taking path D. Fluid attempting to flow in path D will now be obstructed by the stator vanes and the disturbance caused by this obstruction would give a considerable drop in efficiency. To limit this drawback a unidirectional clutch (free-wheel) is fitted between the stator and the extension of the gearbox casing. As soon as the fluid strikes the back of the stator vanes the clutch will unlock and the fluid will then pass along path D to the pump. Once this occurs the unit will act similar to a fluid coupling.

Fig. 10.3.11 shows the torque output in relation to turbine speed for a given speed of the pump. It will be seen that the output torque is approximately equal to input torque when the turbine speed is about 90% of the pump speed.

Three-element Torque Converter

Fig. 10.3.12 shows the arrangement of a three-element single-stage converter. This type is quite common and is used in conjunction with many different types of automatic gearbox. Examination of Fig. 10.3.12 shows that the free-wheel is the only mechanical feature which can produce faulty operation of the converter. A fault in the free-wheel can give:

(a) Slipping stator—causes the fluid to enter the pump at the incorrect angle, therefore full torque multiplication cannot be

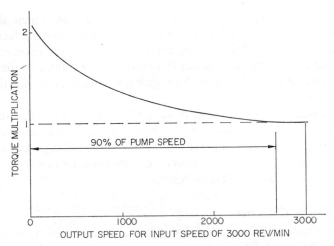

FIG. 10.3.11

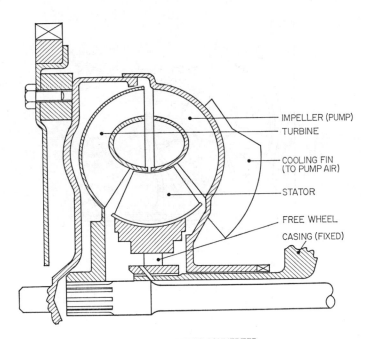

THREE ELEMENT SINGLE STAGE CONVERTER

FIG. 10.3.12

obtained. This fault is detected by a stall test, which should be carried out in the manner recommended by the manufacturer.

(b) Seized stator—fluid striking the back of the stator vanes cannot make the stator free-wheel at the appropriate time so the fluid acts as a severe brake on the engine and produces overheating of the converter.

The fluid for the converter is normally supplied by the automatic gearbox and it is generally a low viscosity mineral oil which contains additives to improve lubrication and resist frothing. Cavitation noise caused by air in the converter is minimised by pressurising the fluid to about 20 lbf/in² (138 kN/m²).

Multi-stage Converter

When greater torque multiplication is required a multi-stage converter is often used. This type uses a series of turbines and stators and Fig. 10.3.13 shows the main features.

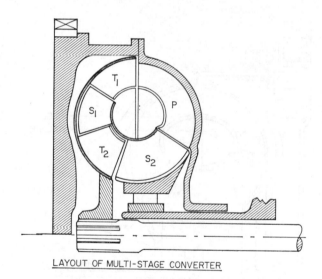

LAYOUT OF MULTI-STAGE CONVERTER

FIG. 10.3.13

Under conditions of low turbine/pump speeds the fluid will follow the path shown in Fig. 10.3.14 and by this means the energy in the fluid is gradually extracted as it pass through each stage.

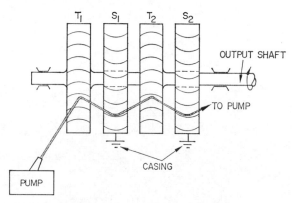

PRINCIPLE OF MULTI-STAGE CONVERTER

FIG. 10.3.14

Gearboxes

11.1

THE GEARBOX

REASON FOR A GEARBOX

The internal-combustion engine used in a modern vehicle will only operate over a limited effective speed range (e.g. 1500–5000 rev/min), and in this range will produce a comparatively low torque (turning effort). When the speed drops below the lower limit, or if the load is too great, the engine will stall and the vehicle will come to rest.

If a vehicle were not fitted with a gearbox, the following disadvantages would soon show up:

(1) *Poor acceleration from rest* The clutch would have to be slipped for a considerable time to avoid stalling the engine. A road speed of approximately 15 mile/h (24 km/h) would have to be reached before full engagement could take place, and during this time the driving force at the wheels (tractive effort) would only be slightly greater than the force opposing the motion of the vehicle (tractive resistance). The rate of acceleration is governed by the difference between the tractive effort and resistance, and since this difference is small, the acceleration will be poor.

(2) *Poor hill-climbing ability* A gradient increases the resistance, and this will mean that as soon as a hill is approached, the engine will slow down and eventually stall. (This could be overcome by employing a large engine with high torque output, but it would be uneconomic (Fig. 11.1.1).)

(3) *Vehicle cannot be driven at low speeds* As the vehicle speed is decreased the engine speed will also be decreased. Slipping of the clutch would be necessary to avoid stalling if the vehicle had to be driven at low speeds.

(4) *No neutral or reverse.*

These items show the importance of fitting a gearbox.

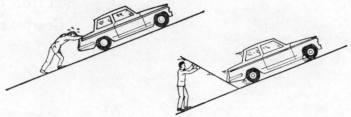

DIAGRAM SHOWS HOW HUMAN EFFORT CAN BE REDUCED BY USING
A LEVER. THE GEARBOX ACTS AS A MECHANICAL LEVER TO
BOOST THE EFFORT OF THE ENGINE

FIG. 11.1.1

GEAR LEVERAGE

Fig. 11.1.2(a) shows a simple lever. A force applied at the end of the lever lifts a load four times as great; this shows that a small force can be amplified by using a lever system.

Fig. 11.1.2(b) shows how two discs may be used to obtain leverage.

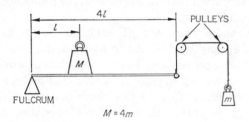

(a) LARGE MASS LIFTED BY A SMALL MASS

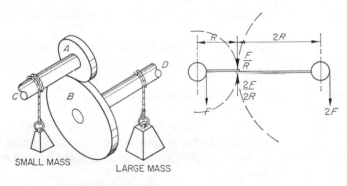

(b) TORQUE MULTIPLICATION

FIG. 11.1.2

In this example a mass acting on shaft C will support a larger mass on shaft D. This arrangement may be considered as a simple gearbox, the engine connected to shaft C, and the road wheels to shaft D. In this example, the output torque is double the engine torque, and if disc B is made three times the diameter of A, the output torque will be trebled. This appears to produce something for nothing, but speed must be taken into account. It will be seen that as the torque increases, the speed decreases proportionally, and therefore the *power remains the same*, assuming the mechanism is 100% efficient. In Fig. 11.1.2(b) the speed ratio (velocity ratio) is also called the gear ratio, and in this case is 2:1, which indicates that two revolutions of the input shaft are required to rotate the output shaft by one revolution.

Belts, pulleys and friction drives were used on early designs of motor car, but when Panhard introduced a sliding gearwheel arrangement, these systems gradually disappeared.

TYPES OF GEARING (Fig. 11.1.3)

Various types of gearing are used on a motor vehicle, but gearboxes employ one or more of the following:

(1) spur—teeth parallel to axis, used on sliding mesh
(2) helical—teeth inclined to axis to form helix ⎫ used on constant-mesh
(3) double helical—two sets of opposing helical teeth ⎬ and synchro-mesh
(4) epicyclic—spur or helical gears rotating about centres which are not stationary.

Gear Material

The gear teeth have to resist severe shock loading and wear, so a case-hardened steel is used to provide a tough core and a hard surface.

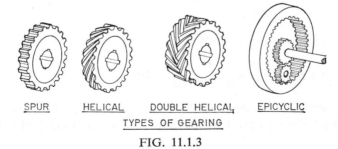

SPUR   HELICAL   DOUBLE HELICAL   EPICYCLIC

TYPES OF GEARING

FIG. 11.1.3

THE SLIDING-MESH GEARBOX—THREE-SPEED

The sliding-mesh gearbox was used on cars up to the early 30s, but today it is rarely used. The construction and operation are most important from a student's point of view, because this type provided the basic layout from which other gearboxes have been developed (Fig. 11.1.4).

The spur gear arrangement is built up on three shafts:
(1) primary shaft (alternative names—clutch or first motion shaft)
(2) layshaft (countershaft)
(3) mainshaft (third motion shaft).

The primary shaft, which is connected to the clutch, is fitted with a pinion to provide a constant drive to the layshaft gear cluster. Gearwheels, splined to the mainshaft, can be individually engaged with corresponding pinions on the layshaft; the movement of the gears is controlled by selector forks which connect with the gear lever.

Neutral All mainshaft gearwheels are positioned so that they do not touch the layshaft gears. A drive will be taken to the layshaft, but the mainshaft will not be turned.

First gear The first-speed gearwheel A on the mainshaft is slid forward to engage with pinion B on the layshaft,, and all other gears are positioned in neutral. In this gear, the reduction in speed which occurs at the constant-mesh gear E and F is further reduced by the first gears A and B.

The gear ratio of any pair of gears is given by:

$$\text{ratio} = \frac{\text{no. of teeth on driven wheel}}{\text{no. of teeth on driving wheel}} \text{ or } \frac{\text{driven}}{\text{driver}}$$

Since two sets of gears are used in this gearbox, then:

$$\text{ratio} = \frac{\text{driven}}{\text{driver}} \times \frac{\text{driven}}{\text{driver}}$$

(N.B. The ratios are *multiplied*)

$$\text{First gear ratio} = \frac{F}{E} \times \frac{A}{B} = \frac{40}{20} \times \frac{40}{20} = 4:1$$

The value 4 indicates that the torque output from the gearbox will be 4 times as great as the input, the speed being $\frac{1}{4}$ of engine speed.

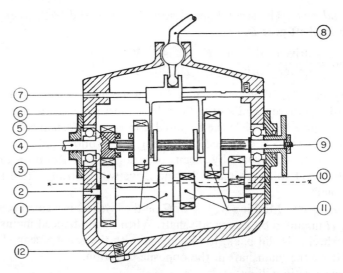

1 2nd SPEED GEARS	5 SPIGOT BEARING	9 MAIN SHAFT
2 LAYSHAFT	6 SELECTOR FORK	10 REVERSE IDLER
3 CONSTANT MESH GRS.	7 SELECTOR ROD	11 1st SPEED GEARS
4 PRIMARY SHAFT	8 GEAR LEVER	12 DRAIN PLUG

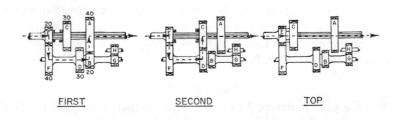

FIRST   SECOND   TOP

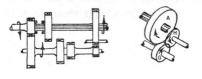

REVERSE

THREE-SPEED GEARBOX

FIG. 11.1.4

Second gear   The second speed gearwheel *C* is slid back to engage with layshaft gear *D*.

$$\text{Ratio} = \frac{\text{driven}}{\text{driver}} \times \frac{\text{driven}}{\text{driver}} = \frac{F}{E} \times \frac{C}{D} = \frac{40}{20} \times \frac{30}{30} = 2{:}1$$

Top gear   For efficiency purposes, the top gearbox ratio is normally 1:1 (direct drive), and so the final drive must provide the necessary ratio to give the vehicle the required 'top gear performance'.

The 1:1 ratio is obtained by locking the second-speed gearwheel *C* to the primary shaft by means of a dog clutch. Rotation of the layshaft will still take place, but no drive will be transmitted from this shaft.

Reverse gear   Meshing with gear *G* on the layshaft is a small reverse gear *H* mounted on a separate shaft. When the first-speed mainshaft gearwheel *A* is slid back, it will engage with the reverse gear *H* and will drive the mainshaft in the opposite direction.

The gear ratio will be:

$$\frac{\text{driven}}{\text{driver}} \times \frac{\text{driven}}{\text{driver}} \times \frac{\text{driven}}{\text{driver}} = \frac{F}{E} \times \frac{\cancel{H}}{G} \times \frac{A}{\cancel{H}} = \frac{F}{E} \times \frac{A}{G}$$

You will see that *H* cancels out in the above expression, which indicates that the ratio will remain the same, irrespective of the size of the reverse gear. This is the reason why it is called an *idler*—it changes the direction, but does not alter the ratio.

GEAR CHANGING

When a gear is moved to engage with another, noise will result if the peripheral (outside) speeds are not the same. To avoid this, the driver performs an operation called *double-declutching*.

On changing up, e.g. from first to second, the layshaft must be slowed down by re-engaging the clutch while the lever is positioned in neutral. The engine slows down quicker than the layshaft assembly, so a 'braking' action on the layshaft is obtained.

The opposite is required when changing down—the layshaft must be speeded up. To achieve this, the engine is reconnected to the gearbox while the lever is in neutral, and the accelerator is depressed. When the layshaft has speeded up the required amount, the accelerator is released, the clutch pedal depressed, and the gear lever moved to the lower gear.

A chamfer on the entry side of each gear tooth allows for easier meshing, but if bad changes are made burrs will be formed and teeth may be broken.

SELECTOR MECHANISM

A selector fork of the type shown in Fig. 11.1.5(a) is used to move the gear along the mainshaft. In the case of a three-speed and reverse gearbox, two selector forks are required, and these are moved by means of a lever of the floor-mounted type or extended by linkage to the steering column; the latter design is used when the front seat is intended for three persons.

Each gearbox must be fitted with a device which (a) locates the selector to resist the gear jumping out of mesh, and (b) prevents two gears engaging at the same time. (The box would be badly damaged if this device was omitted on reassembling the unit.)

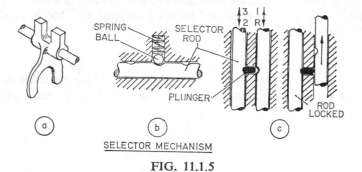

SELECTOR MECHANISM

FIG. 11.1.5

Fig. 11.1.5(b) shows the normal arrangement for holding the gear in position. In this design the selector fork is locked to the rod, into which are ground three indentations representing the two gear positions and neutral. A spring-loaded ball acts on each rod, and therefore a force must be applied to the gear lever to overcome the device and move the rod.

Various safety or interlocking devices are used to ensure that two gears, e.g. first and top, do not engage at the same time. In this type of gearbox, a ball or plunger (Fig. 11.1.5(c)) is generally positioned between the two selector rods. The length of the plunger is greater than the distance between the rods, so it will be impossible to move both rods simultaneously. When one rod is moved to engage a gear, the rod moving to its full diameter will push the plunger into the indentation on the other rod.

The layshaft is rotating whenever the input shaft is turning, so oil introduced to the level xx in Fig. 11.1.4 will lubricate all gears and churn up to supply the other mechanism.

The type of oil used in any gearbox should comply with the manufacturer's instructions, because if the incorrect type is used, wear, corrosive attack or other defects may result. Generally the manufacturer recommends a heavy type of gear oil for sliding-mesh gearboxes.

Sealing arrangements must be provided to prevent the oil escaping.

FAULTS AND THEIR CAUSES

Noise

Gear whine is caused by (a) lack of oil, (b) gear-tooth wear, (c) bearing wear, or (d) shaft misalignment due to bearing wear.
Knocking or *'ticking'* is caused by (a) a chipped gear tooth, or (b) a defective bearing.

Jumping out of gear

This may be due to (a) a defective selector locking device, e.g. a broken spring, (b) misalignment of the shaft due to worn bearings or (c) worn gear teeth.

FOUR-SPEED GEARBOX

Opinion is divided as to whether the advantages of a four-speed gearbox are sufficient to justify the extra cost. The two main advantages are:

(1) It is possible to maintain engine speed between narrower limits, thereby obtaining an improved engine performance.

(2) A gear ratio can be selected to suit the gradient—with a three-speed box, many hills are climbed where second is too low and top is too high.

Up to fairly recent times, a four-speed box was used in most cases, but present-day car designers favour a three-speed box linked with an overdrive.

FOUR-SPEED SLIDING-MESH GEARBOX

The gear layout follows the same basic pattern as that used with the three-speed gearbox. With the addition of one mainshaft gearwheel, it is possible to obtain four speeds and a reverse. Fig. 11.2.1(a) shows a typical design which is set in the neutral position.

First Gear A is moved to engage with B. The drive from the primary shaft is passed by the constant-mesh gears to the layshaft, and then through first-speed gears B and A to the mainshaft.

Second Gear C is moved to engage with D.

Third Gear G is moved to engage with H.

Top The dog clutch locks the mainshaft to the primary shaft to give a direct drive.

Reverse A simple idler gear could be used to engage between the first-speed gears, but Fig. 11.2.1(b) shows a compound reverse gear which provides a reverse ratio lower than first gear, to reduce reversing speed.

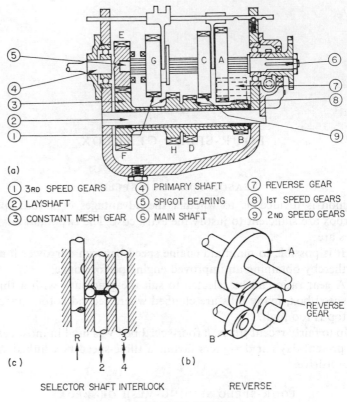

(1)	3RD SPEED GEARS	(4)	PRIMARY SHAFT
(2)	LAYSHAFT	(5)	SPIGOT BEARING
(3)	CONSTANT MESH GEAR	(6)	MAIN SHAFT

(7)	REVERSE GEAR
(8)	1ST SPEED GEARS
(9)	2ND SPEED GEARS

(c)   SELECTOR SHAFT INTERLOCK

(b)   REVERSE

FOUR SPEED GEARBOX

FIG. 11.2.1

Power take-off arrangements

In addition to the mechanism used for driving the commercial vehicle along the road; a power supply is often required for operating the various items of auxiliary equipment. These include the tipping mechanism, pumps for bulk supplies and other systems which are an essential part of the modern specialised commercial vehicle.

Systems dependent upon a hydraulic or electrical supply are normally operated from a pump or generator driven directly from the engine, whereas mechanical arrangements utilise the gearbox layshaft to provide the necessary power.

Fig. 11.2.2 shows a diagram of a power take-off arrangement. which is driven from the gearbox layshaft. Moving the selector lever to the engaged position slides a gear into mesh with the layshaft. The power take-off gear assembly is bolted to the side of the gearbox casing and in cases where the assembly is not required a blanking plate is fitted to seal the opening in the casing.

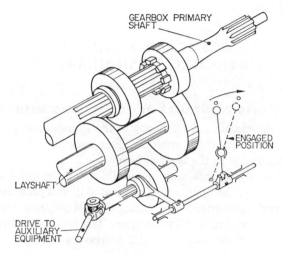

POWER TAKE-OFF ARRANGEMENT

FIG. 11.2.2

CONSTANT-MESH AND
SYNCHRO-MESH GEARBOX

DISADVANTAGES OF THE SLIDING MESH

Although the mechanical efficiency of the sliding-mesh gearbox was high, it suffered from two great disadvantages:

(1) gear noise due to the type of gear

(2) the difficulty of obtaining a smooth, quiet and quick change of gear without the application of great skill and judgement.

Gearbox designs introduced during the last 30 years have endeavoured to overcome these disadvantages. The first step in the development came when the constant-mesh gearbox was used.

CONSTANT-MESH GEARBOX

This was first used on cars in the early 30s, but gave way in a short time to other designs, although it is still used on commercial vehicles and tractors.

The main feature is the use of the stronger helical or double helical gears which leads to a quieter operation. Each pair of gears is in constant mesh, and gear operation is obtained by locking the respective gear to the mainshaft by means of a dog clutch.

The layout of the box follows the sliding-mesh arrangement previously described, and Fig. 11.3.1 shows the main details of the third and top-gear section. The mainshaft gearwheels are mounted on bushes or needle rollers, and are located by thrust washers. When the gear is required, a dog clutch, which is splined to the mainshaft, is slid along by the selector to engage with dog teeth formed on the gear. This has the effect of locking the gearwheel to the shaft. There will still be noise if the dog teeth are not rotating at the same speed when the engagement is made, and so double declutching is neces-

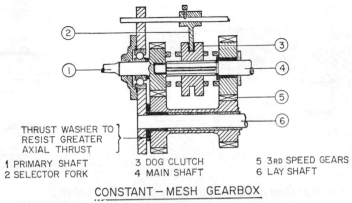

THRUST WASHER TO RESIST GREATER AXIAL THRUST		
1 PRIMARY SHAFT	3 DOG CLUTCH	5 3RD SPEED GEARS
2 SELECTOR FORK	4 MAIN SHAFT	6 LAY SHAFT

CONSTANT – MESH GEARBOX

FIG. 11.3.1

sary, but damage caused by a 'bad' change will be limited to the dog clutch.

SYNCHRO-MESH MECHANISMS

The improvement achieved by fitting a constant-mesh gearbox was great, but a certain amount of skill was still required to produce a quick, quiet change. The difficulty was in double declutching, and the purpose of carrying out this operation was to equalise the speed of the two sets of dog teeth before engaging the gear. It soon became apparent that some device was required to synchronise the speeds mechanically, and when the system was invented it was known as the synchro-mesh gearbox.

CONSTANT LOAD SYNCHRO-MESH UNIT

This was the first type of synchro-mesh used. Fig. 11.3.2 shows the main details of the unit controlling third and top gear. Fundamentally the box is laid out in the same manner as a constant-mesh, with the exception that a cone clutch is fitted between the dog and gear members.

The female cone of this clutch is formed in a hub, which has internal and external splines. A series of spring-loaded balls is carried in radial holes in the hub, and these push outwards into a groove machined in a sleeve. The selector fork controls the position of the sleeve, which has splines of the same pitch as the dog teeth on the gear.

The initial movement of the selector and sleeve carries the hub

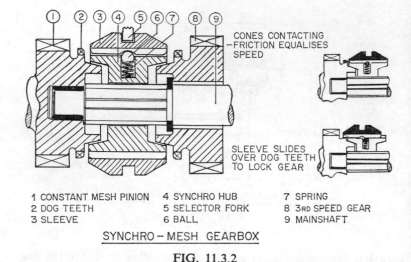

CONES CONTACTING
–FRICTION EQUALISES
SPEED

SLEEVE SLIDES
OVER DOG TEETH
TO LOCK GEAR

1 CONSTANT MESH PINION	4 SYNCHRO HUB	7 SPRING
2 DOG TEETH	5 SELECTOR FORK	8 3RD SPEED GEAR
3 SLEEVE	6 BALL	9 MAINSHAFT

SYNCHRO – MESH GEARBOX

FIG. 11.3.2

towards the gear and allows the cones to contact. At this point, the friction between the cones adjusts the speed of the gearwheel to suit the hub and mainshaft. Extra pressure on the lever will allow the sleeve to override the spring-loaded balls, and positively engage with the dogs on the gear.

If the gear change is rushed, there will not be enough time for synchronisation, and the change will be noisy. The time taken for the speed to be equalised is governed by the frictional force which exists at the cone faces. This force is controlled by: (a) total spring strength, (b) depth of groove in sleeve, (c) angle of cone, and (d) coefficient of friction between cones; therefore, if, because of mechanical defects, any of these factors are reduced, synchronisation will take a longer time, and noise will probably be heard. This time factor has presented problems for the lubrication specialist, since the high-viscosity oil required by the gears takes a considerable time to disperse from the cones. The solution to this problem was to use a lower viscosity oil (similar to medium engine oil—SAE 30) and provide a series of grooves on the cone face to cut through the oil film and disperse the lubricant. Up to recent times it was considered essential to drain and refill the gearbox every 5000 miles (8000 km), in order to remove the particles worn from the cones and gear teeth. With extended service schedules now in operation, this mileage has been increased considerably, and some manufacturers have recommended that after the first change no further changes are necessary.

BAULK RING SYNCHRO-MESH

The *baulk ring system*, which is sometimes called blocker ring or inertia lock, is a later development of the constant load system, and is designed to overcome the main disadvantage of the earlier design —noise or crashing of the gears due to a quick change.

Two main features are incorporated in the baulk ring system:

(a) the cone pressure or load is proportional to the speed of change and

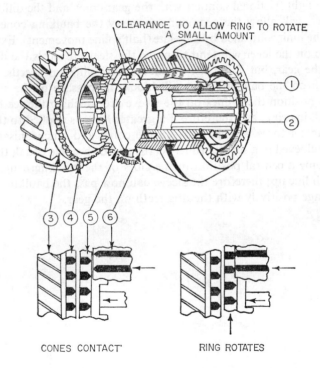

CLEARANCE TO ALLOW RING TO ROTATE A SMALL AMOUNT

CONES CONTACT   RING ROTATES

| 1 SHIFTING PLATE | 3 GEAR | 5 BAULKING CONE AND RING |
| 2 CIRCLIP SPRING | 4 GEAR DOG TEETH | 6 SLEEVE |

BAULK – RING   SYNCROMESH   UNIT

FIG. 11.3.3

(b) an interception device prevents positive gear engagement until the speed of the two members is equal.

Various constructions are used to produce these features, and Fig. 11.3.3 shows one system in common use. Three spring-loaded shifting plates, which push out from the hub into a groove in the sleeve, fit into slots in the baulking cone. Each slot is wider than the plate; the clearance on each side is equal to half the pitch of the splines on the sleeve. The baulking cone, which is made of phosphor-bronze, has specially chamfered teeth on the outside, of a pitch similar to that of the dog teeth on the gear and sleeve.

Movement of the gear lever will move the sleeve and shifting plates towards the gear selected. The plates will push the baulking cone into light frictional contact with the gear cone, and the difference in speed will allow the gear cone to carry the baulking cone around to the limit controlled by the plate (half spline movement). Extra pressure on the lever will tend to move the sleeve towards the dog teeth of the gear, but if the two members have different speeds, the dog teeth on the baulking ring will block the passage of the sleeve. In this position the splines on the sleeve are touching the teeth on the baulking ring, and therefore if a greater force is applied to the lever, a greater force will act between the cones and synchronisation will be achieved in a shorter time. As the speeds become equal, the plates assume a central position in the slots of the baulking ring, and all teeth line up; therefore the sleeve can now pass the baulking cone to engage positively with the dog teeth on the gear.

11.4

EPICYCLIC GEARING
AND AUTOMATIC GEARBOX

With conventional gearboxes, engagement is obtained by either sliding the gear into mesh, or locking the gear with a dog clutch. Both systems produce noise if the speeds are different, which means that time is wasted while the speeds become equal. This disadvantage is overcome with the epicyclic system of gearing. Thus the arrangement is particularly suitable for overdrives and automatic transmission systems.

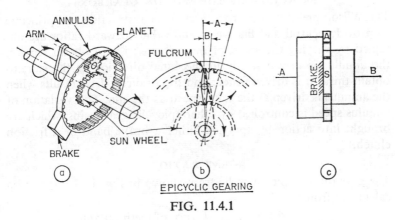

EPICYCLIC GEARING

FIG. 11.4.1

PRINCIPLE OF OPERATION

The principle of operation may be seen from Fig. 11.4.1(a), which shows a gear train or planetary set consisting of:
(1) a sun wheel connected to input shaft
(2) a planet wheel connected to an arm which is attached to the output shaft

(3) an internally toothed ring gear or annulus on to which can contract an external friction band brake (brake shown diagrammatically).

During the period in which the brake is released, the forward-moving sun wheel will drive the annulus round in the opposite direction and no drive will be transmitted (neutral).

When the brake is applied, the annulus will be brought to rest and the sun wheel will now cause the planet gear to be driven round inside the fixed annulus. This motion will rotate the arm and output shaft in the same direction as the input shaft, but at slower speed (first gear).

All gears may be considered as levers; Fig. 11.4.1(b) shows the planet gear as a lever. When the sun is rotated through angle A, the lever will move to the dotted position, which will allow the centre of the lever to push the arm forward through angle B. The ratio between the angles in this example is approximately $3 : 1$. Therefore you will see that the output shaft turns in the same direction as the input shaft, but at a speed approximately one third of the input.

PRINCIPLE OF THE WILSON GEARBOX

The Wilson preselector gearbox uses this construction and principle to provide neutral and first gear, and other forward ratios are obtained by varying the speed of the annulus; i.e. to obtain second, the annulus is driven slowly in the same direction as the sun; to obtain third, it is driven faster; and top or direct drive results when the annulus is driven at the same speed as the sun. This variation of annulus speed is controlled by other epicyclic gear trains, which are brought into action by applying either a brake band or a friction clutch.

GEAR RATIO

The gear ratio of the epicyclic train shown in Fig. 11.4.1(a) can be calculated from:

$$\text{Ratio} = \frac{A+S}{S} \quad \text{where} \quad \begin{array}{l} A = \text{no. of teeth on annulus} \\ S = \text{no. of teeth on sun} \end{array}$$

If $A = 100$ and $S = 20$, then the ratio $= 6 : 1$.

When the gear train is rearranged as in Fig. 11.4.1(c) and the brake applied to the sun wheel, the ratio will be:

$$\frac{A+S}{A}$$

Using the same size gears, this method of connection can give a ratio of 1·2:1 when driving from A to B, and 1:1·2 when driving from B to A. The latter is important because this is the system used in the overdrive unit, which is described in the next chapter.

AUTOMATIC GEARBOX

Although in the past the automatic gearbox was considered a luxury, many drivers now regard this unit as a desirable essential and this has led to the introduction of many different types of box. Two-pedal control relieves the driver of tedious clutch and gear change operations and enables him to concentrate on the other aspects of driving. Many early designs were criticised because they robbed the driver of the job of gearbox control, so modern arrangements generally have provision to enable the driver to override the gearbox if the need arises.

The majority of automatic transmission systems are of American origin and the gearbox made by Borg Warner is one of the most common. In view of this, the principles underlying this type of box will be considered. An understanding of the basic features should provide a foundation on which other systems can be studied successfully.

Driver controls

To provide an effective operation the gearbox requires two items of information from the driver:
(a) the direction he wishes the vehicle to move,
(b) the mood of the driver as regards the rate he wishes the vehicle to accelerate.

Information (a) is given by the selector lever whereas item (b) is communicated to the gearbox by connecting a cable between the engine throttle and gearbox. Depression of the accelerator pedal opens the carburettor throttle and also 'tells' the gearbox to arrange the up and down changes to occur at road speeds which are in accordance with the amount that the pedal is depressed. When full throttle is reached a resistance to the movement of the pedal is felt and if this point is overcome a pedal position called 'kickdown' is obtained. Movement of the pedal from the partly depressed position to 'kickdown' causes an immediate down-change, so enabling the vehicle to accelerate rapidly when the need arises.

The selector lever is marked with the basic positions; L, D, N, R, P.

L. (Lock-up)

A low gear having no free-wheeling action which is suitable for engine braking. No automatic up-changes occur in this position.

D. (Drive)

This is the normal automatic range which provides three gears; first, second and third.

N. (Neutral)

As the name suggests no drive is applied. This is the gear position to use when towing the vehicle, assuming the gearbox is in a suitable state for towing.

R. (Reverse)

Backward movement of the vehicle is achieved when R is selected.

P. (Park)

Most automatic boxes incorporate a device in the form of a parking pawl (mounted on the gearbox casing) which locks into a gear connected to the output shaft. This arrangement gives a positive transmission lock to resist vehicle movement.

An inhibitor switch mounted on the gearbox prevents the starter motor from operating in any position other than *P* and *N*. This is for safety reasons and its purpose should be remembered if ever the engine has to be started with the handle.

GEARBOX CONSTRUCTION

In common with many other automatic transmission systems the Borg Warner unit consists of:

(a) a single stage hydrokinetic torque converter which gives an infinitely variable torque output between 2:1 and 1:1,

(b) a hydraulically operated epicyclic (planetary) gearbox which provides three forward-ratios and one reverse.

Compounding the gearbox with the torque converter enables a smaller and cheaper converter to be used, since forward gearbox ratios generally have to cover the range from about 5:1 to 1:1. Furthermore, the need for a reverse gear, neutral and refinements to allow the driver to vary the gear sequence, show that the mechanical unit is necessary. The converter also performs an essential duty; it bridges the gaps between the mechanical ratios and so allows for a smooth progression from the lowest to highest ratio.

This gradual variation in the driving effort is shown in Fig. 11.4.2.

The driving effort given by a three-speed conventional gearbox occurs at three different levels, hence the name stepped transmission system, whereas the curve for an automatic box approaches the shape of an ideal tractive effort curve. The ideal form could be obtained from a gearbox having an infinitely variable ratio and a constant efficiency.

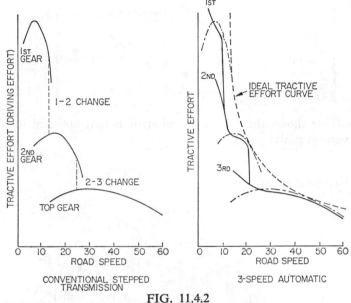

FIG. 11.4.2

Gear Train Layout

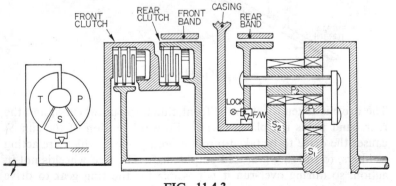

FIG. 11.4.3

The epicyclic gear train (Fig. 11.4.3) consists of two sun gears, two sets of planets, a planet carrier and a ring gear (annulus). Power flow through the train is controlled by two multi-plate clutches, two brake bands and a free-wheel (unidirectional clutch).

Power Flow

	FRONT CLUTCH	REAR CLUTCH	FRONT BRAKE	REAR BRAKE	FREE WHEEL	RATIO
LOCK-UP I	●			●		2·39
DRIVE I	●				●	2·39
LOCK-UP 2 DRIVE 2	●		●			1·45
DRIVE 3	●	●				1·0
REVERSE		●		●		2·09
NEUTRAL AND PARK						

The Table shows the different combinations that are used to give the various power paths.

Lock-up (first gear)

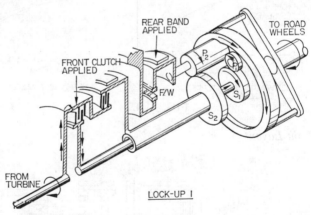

FIG. 11.4.4

The drive is taken through the front clutch to sun wheel S_1 and the rear band holds the planet carrier. Forward motion of the sun S_1 causes the drive to be taken through both planets, which are acting as idlers, to the ring gear and output shaft. The free wheel is not in action, so during over-run it is possible for the ring gear to drive the sun and provide engine braking.

Drive (first gear)

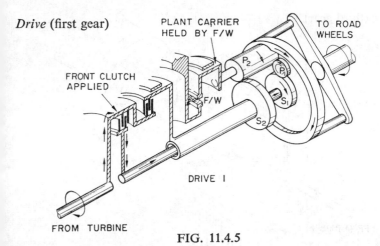

FIG. 11.4.5

This is similar to *Lock-up* (first gear) with the exception that the planet carrier is held by the free wheel instead of the rear band. Under over-run conditions the free wheel unlocks and prevents a drive from ring gear to sun.

Drive (second gear)

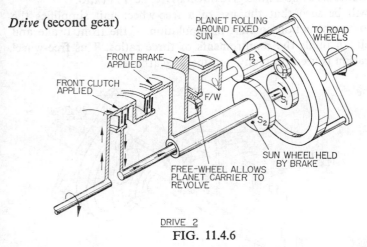

DRIVE 2

FIG. 11.4.6

The front brake is applied and this holds sun S_2. Drive from the front clutch causes sun S_1 to rotate the planet P_1 which in turn revolves P_2 and causes P_2 to roll around the fixed sun S_2. Forward movement of P_2 on its carrier drives the ring gear faster than in first gear since in first the carrier was stationary.

Drive (third gear)

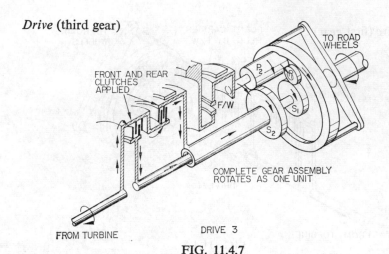

FROM TURBINE

DRIVE 3

FIG. 11.4.7

Application of the rear clutch causes the sun S_2 to rotate at the same speed as S_1 since S_1 is still connected to the applied front clutch. The movement of the sun gears causes both sets of planets and ring gear to rotate as one unit to give direct drive, i.e. 1:1 ratio.

It will be seen that the use of a free-wheel unit simplifies the gearbox construction so that manipulation of the front brake and rear clutch fulfils the requirements of three ratios. This free-wheel application is used on many automatic gearboxes.

Reverse

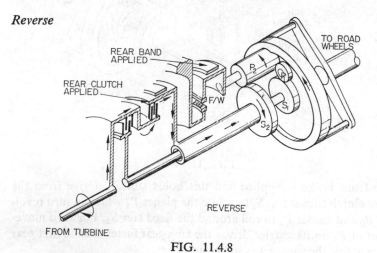

FROM TURBINE

REVERSE

FIG. 11.4.8

The rear clutch is applied and this transmits the drive from the converter to the sun S_2. Application of the rear band holds the planet carrier so, sun S_2, moving in a forward direction, rotates the planet P_2, which is acting as an idler, and causes the ring gear to move in the reverse direction.

Neutral

All clutches and brake bands are released so no drive can be transmitted.

Multi-disc Clutches

Two multi-disc clutches are used and Fig. 11.4.9 shows a rear clutch unit which is typical of the type used in many automatic gearboxes. Steel outer plates, which are slightly dished, are forced against inner plates by a piston. Oil pressure supplied through a drilling in the casing is communicated to the clutch operating cylinder whenever the clutch has to be locked. Leakage between the casing and the rotating member is prevented by square-section cast iron sealing rings and oil escaping past the piston is overcome by using a rubber 'O' ring.

A ball check valve is incorporated in the piston to prevent a build-up of oil pressure when the clutch is inoperative.

If a larger thrust on the clutch plates is needed small levers or toggles can be fitted between the piston and the clutch pressure plate—this arrangement is used in the front clutch.

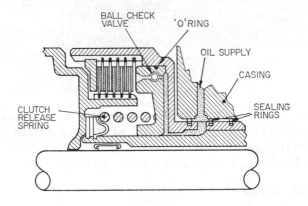

MULTI - DISC CLUTCH

FIG. 11.4.9

Brake Servos

Two external contracting brake bands are each operated by a hydraulic servo. A single acting (oil supplied to one side of the piston only) type is used for the rear servo and this consists of a spring-loaded piston which moves in a cylinder.

Table 1 showed that *Drive 2* is achieved by contracting the front brake and *Drive 3* is obtained by applying the rear clutch. To secure a smooth change, the clutch must be partially applied before the brake has been fully released and this is assisted by employing a double acting servo for the front band (Fig. 11.4.10). When oil

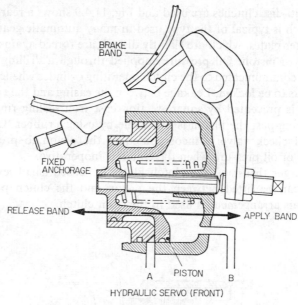

HYDRAULIC SERVO (FRONT)

FIG. 11.4.10

pressure is applied at *A* the servo piston applies the band and the release is obtained by directing oil to *B*. Even though a similar pressure still acts at *A*, the piston will move because the piston area exposed to the oil is greater on side *B*—the release side.

Hydraulic System

This gearbox, like many other automatic transmission units, is controlled by means of a hydraulic system.

Oil pressure is produced by two internal-external gear pumps and these are driven from the input and output shafts. The oil is supplied to various valves and these regulate and direct the fluid to the appropriate clutch or servo.

Valve behaviour Before considering the basic operation of the system it is advisable to study the behaviour of some simple hydraulic valves.

Fig. 11.4.11 shows a spool valve which is typical to that used on

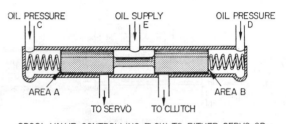

SPOOL VALVE CONTROLLING FLOW TO EITHER SERVO OR CLUTCH

FIG. 11.4.11

automatic gearboxes. If area of face A = area of face B then the valve will:

(a) move to the right when the oil pressure at C is greater than the pressure at D and vice-versa,

(b) remain in a central position when pressure at C=pressure at D.

Any pressure given by the oil supply at E will have no effect on the movement of the valve because the force tending to move the valve to the right will be balanced by the equal and opposite force acting on the other face. In many ways this is similar to the effect of the two springs.

Making the area of one spool larger (Fig. 11.4.12), e.g. area B =2 × area A, will enable the pressure acting on the larger area to

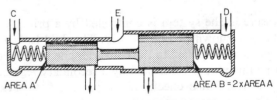

SPOOL VALVE HAVING UNEQUAL AREAS

FIG. 11.4.12

give a greater thrust on the valve than a similar pressure acting at
C, since:

$$Thrust = Pressure \times Area$$

In this case the valve will move to the left if the pressure at D is
greater than half the pressure at C.

Altering the position of the oil supply can produce other effects.
This is shown in Fig. 11.4.13 and the diagram represents a simple

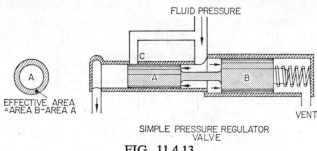

FIG. 11.4.13

regulator valve which has the duty of controlling the pressure delivered by a pump. As the pressure builds up the valve will be forced
to the right because area B is greater than area A (the end elevation
shows this difference in area). Movement of the valve, which must be
vented to avoid trapping the fluid, is resisted by a spring. When the
pressure reaches a given valve, the spool A uncovers a port C and
prevents any further increase in the pressure.

By applying the forementioned principles it is now possible to
build up a simple hydraulic system in simple stages.

Stage 1

Pumps and regulators Fig. 11.4.14 shows the front and rear oil
pumps and the fluid supply to the converter and manual selector
valve.

Line pressure in the system is controlled by a primary regulator
valve of the type shown in Fig. 14.4.13. The fluid leaked from the
primary regulator is supplied to the converter and the lower pressure
demanded by this unit is controlled by a secondary regulator valve.

One-way valves, called check valves, prevent flow-back through
the pump when one pump is producing a lower pressure than the
other pump. As soon as the rear pump is capable of supplying a

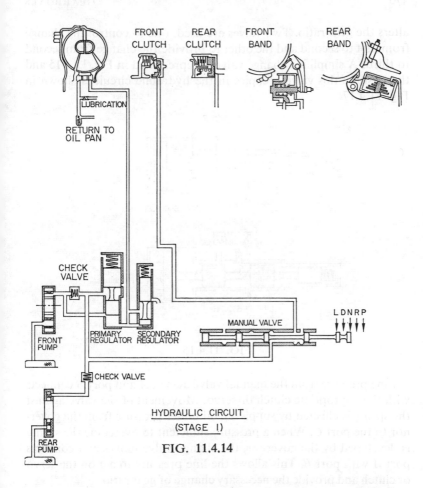

FRONT CLUTCH   REAR CLUTCH   FRONT BAND   REAR BAND

LUBRICATION

RETURN TO OIL PAN

CHECK VALVE

PRIMARY REGULATOR   SECONDARY REGULATOR

FRONT PUMP

CHECK VALVE

MANUAL VALVE

L D N R P

REAR PUMP

HYDRAULIC CIRCUIT
(STAGE I)

FIG. 11.4.14

sufficient quantity, the primary regulator allows the front pump to freely discharge. Consequently, the front check valve closes and the energy that would be lost pumping oil under pressure is saved.

The manual valve which is connected by a mechanical linkage to the driver's selector lever, acts as a distributor for the fluid—it arranges for the fluid to be passed to the items which activate the appropriate clutch or servo.

Stage 2

Change valves and governor   Gear shift is an American term for 'gear change' so the shift valve or change valve is a valve which

alters the gear ratio. Two valves are used, one to control the change
from first to second and the other to provide the change from second
to third. A simplified change valve is represented in Fig. 11.4.15 and
the position this valve occupies in the hydraulic circuit is shown in
Fig. 11.4.17.

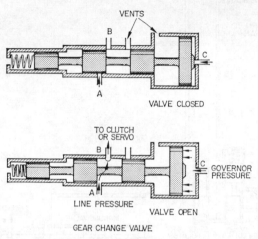

FIG. 11.4.15

Line pressure from the manual valve acts at *A* and port *B* connects
with the appropriate clutch or servo. Movement of the valve against
the spring is effected by supplying oil under pressure from the governor to the port *C*. When a pressure sufficient to overcome the spring
is developed by the governor, the change valve moves and connects
port *A* with port *B*. This allows the line pressure to act on the servo
or clutch and provide the necessary change of gear ratio.

The governor is a sensing device fitted to the output shaft to signal
to the gearbox the speed of the vehicle. Operating in the form of a
regulator valve, the governor supplies fluid to the change valves at a
pressure depending on the speed of the vehicle—as speed increases,
the pressure rises.

The principle of operation of the governor is shown in Fig. 11.4.16.
Fitted in the governor body is a valve and in the centre of this slides
a bob-weight. A spring pushes the valve outwards towards the bob-
weight. This construction gives a two-stage characteristic and as
shown by the graph the high pressure rise in relation to small speed
increase during the first stage ensures that the gear changes between

first and second occur at the most desirable speed, i.e. the speed sensitivity is improved.

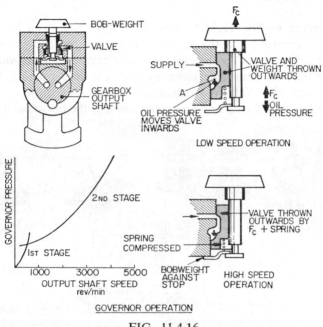

GOVERNOR OPERATION

FIG. 11.4.16

At speeds less than 500 rev/min the first stage applies and this is shown in Fig. 11.4.16. During this stage the bob-weight and valve may be considered as forming one unit. Rotation of the governor throws out the bob-weight and this causes the valve to uncover the supply port. Fluid under pressure flows through the port, and exerts a thrust on the face A. This thrust increases until it is capable of closing the valve against the opposition of the centrifugal force. The action of the valve provides a fluid pressure at the governor outlet which is proportional to the force acting on the bob-weight. An increase in speed causes a repetition of these events but as the speed is greater the pressure required by the fluid to close the valve is also greater.

The second stage operation starts when the bob-weight stop contacts the body. From this point onwards the balance between the opening and closing of the valve is achieved by the centrifugal effect on the valve and the fluid acting on the pressure face of the valve.

Reference to Fig. 11.4.17 shows how three gears can be automatically controlled. In the position shown first gear is engaged. As road speed increases the governor pressure reaches a point which is greater than the resistance given by the light spring acting in the 1–2 change valve. Valve movement allows fluid to be directed to the apply-side of the front band and contraction of the brake band gives

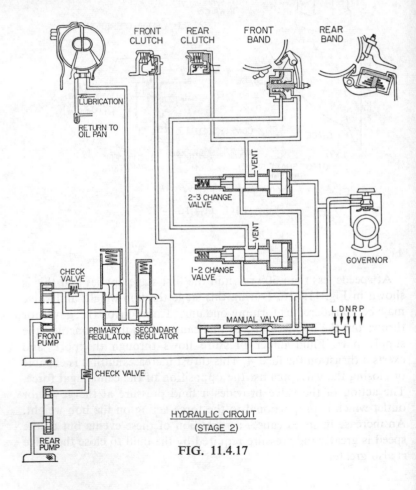

HYDRAULIC CIRCUIT
(STAGE 2)

FIG. 11.4.17

second gear. A further increase in road speed causes the governor output pressure to rise further, and when this pressure overcomes the spring in the 2–3 change valve, the valve allows the fluid to pass to the rear clutch and release side of the front servo to give third gear.

Stage 3

Throttle valve and linkage   In the previous stage the gear changes always occurred at the same road speeds and no account was taken of the 'driver's mood'. To alter these change speeds a throttle valve is introduced and a diagram of a simplified valve arrangement is shown in Fig. 11.4.18.

A cable links the carburettor throttle linkage with a cam controlling the throttle valve. Line pressure acting on the side of the valve is allowed to spill into a separate fluid circuit as the valve is opened. A fluid connection between the 'throttle fluid circuit' and the end of the throttle valve causes the fluid pressure to oppose the action of the cam and allows the valve to close when the pressure reaches a limit governed by the position of the cam.

Depressing the accelerator pedal rotates the cam and compresses the throttle valve spring, and as this action is taking place the fluid pressure in the 'throttle fluid circuit' rises in proportion to the pedal movement. Applying this fluid pressure to the change valves will aid the action of the springs, consequently the road speeds at which the changes will occur will depend on the position of the accelerator pedal—the more the pedal is depressed, the later will the up-changes occur.

Fluid pressure from the throttle valve is also used to increase the main line pressure when the engine is under a heavy load. This pressure increase reduces the risk of slip occurring at the clutch or brake.

The increase is achieved by connecting the 'throttle fluid circuit' to the spring end of the primary regulator valve so the pressure acting in this circuit will assist the regulator spring in its action.

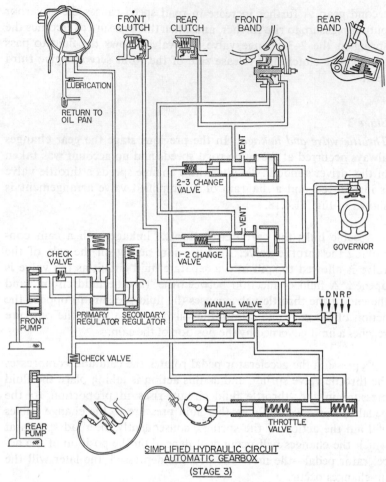

FIG. 11.4.18

Stage 4

Hydraulic system B.W.35 When the previous stages have been understood it is possible to consider the complete hydraulic system of an automatic gearbox.

Reference to Fig. 11.4.19 shows that in the stages already studied all but two of the valves have been covered so the duty of each of these will now be outlined.

Servo orifice control valve is a shuttle valve which controls the

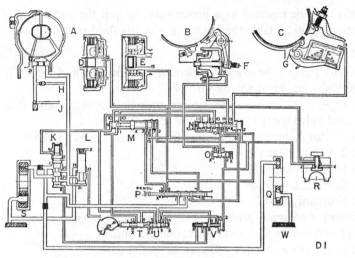

HYDRAULIC CIRCUITS – B.W. MODEL 35.

A Converter	J To oil pan	Q Rear pump
B Front band	K Primary regulator valve	R Governor
C Rear band	L Secondary regulator valve	S Front pump
D Front clutch	M 2-3 shift valve	T Down-shift valve
E Rear clutch	N 1-2 shift valve	U Throttle valve
G Rear servo	O Servo orifice control valve	V Modulator valve
H Lubrication	P Manual valve	W Strainer

FIG. 11.4.19

flow of fluid to and from the front servo release and this governs the speed of change between second and third and vice-versa. At high road speeds the governor pressure closes the valve and in this position the fluid flowing to the servo is restricted by having to pass through a small orifice.

Modulator valve is an arrangement for modulating (making less violent) the throttle pressure, i.e. a valve to reduce the pressure by a given amount. In addition, fluid from this valve is used to reduce the rate-of-increase of the main line pressure and it performs this duty by supplying fluid to the non-spring end of the primary regulator valve.

Operation. In order to help the reader understand the hydraulic circuit Figs. 11.4.19, 20, 21 are presented in an incomplete form. It is recommended that the fluid paths are filled-in by using coloured crayons. The colours show the different circuits and indicate the pressure range.

When the textbook is used in conjunction with a lecture the fluid paths may be inserted as a group exercise and the following information should enable the reader to plot the fluid paths.

D1

(Green) *Pump inlet pressure* Strainers to pumps and return from secondary regulator valve (port 24).

(Orange) *Line pressure* Pumps to primary regulator and then to manual valve (port 1) and throttle valve.

Directed line pressure Supply from manual valve (3,5) to:
(a) 2–3 shift valve (3)
(b) 1–2 shift valve (5)
(c) front clutch (5)
(d) governor (5)

(Brown) *Converter pressure and lubrication pressure* Regulators (21) to converter (21) and lubrication (H and J).

(Blue) *Governor pressure* Governor outlet (2) to:
(a) shift valves (2)
(b) servo orifice control valve (2)
(c) modulator valve (2)

(Yellow) *Throttle pressure* Throttle valve (9) to:
(a) shift valves (9, 10, 10a)
(b) primary regulator (9)
(c) modulator valve (9, 9a)

Modulated throttle pressure from modulator valve (8) to primary regulator (8).

D2

As in D1 with the addition:

Line pressure from 1–2 shift valve (19) to apply-side of front band.
Forced throttle pressure from throttle valve (11) to shift valves (11).

(The diagram shows the cam in the kickdown position. This allows additional fluid pressure to act on the shift valves to either delay the up-changes or provide immediate down-changes if road speed is low.)

D3

As in D1 with the addition:

Line pressure from 1–2 shift valve (19) to 'apply-side' of front band.
Line pressure from 2–3 shift valve (15) to:
(a) rear clutch (15)
(b) 'release-side' of front band (15) via orifice adjacent to servo orifice control valve (15).

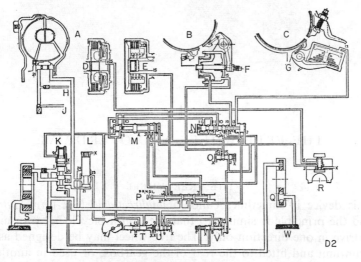

HYDRAULIC CIRCUITS – B.W. MODEL 35

FIG. 11.4.20

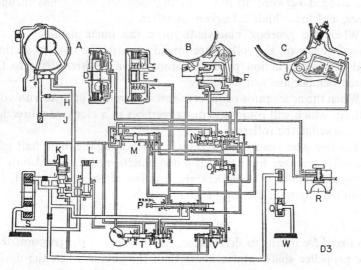

HYDRAULIC CIRCUITS – B.W. MODEL 35

FIG. 11.4.21

THE FREE-WHEEL AND OVERDRIVE

THE FREE WHEEL

This device is sometimes called a *unidirectional* (*one-way*) *clutch*, and the principle is similar to that used on a bicycle—it transmits a drive in one direction only. The free-wheel may be designed as a main unit and fitted to the rear of the gearbox, or used in another unit, e.g. overdrive or automatic gearbox, to fulfil some specific task. In the former case its purpose would be to improve petrol consumption by allowing the vehicle to coast, and to enable 'clutch-less' gear changes to be made once the vehicle is in motion.

One type of free wheel is shown in Fig. 11.5.1. A number of rollers are wedged between an inner driving member, which has inclined faces, and the cylindrical driven member.

When the gearbox mainshaft turns the inner member in the direction shown, the rollers are forced towards the narrow section, and the wedge action produced transmits a positive drive to the outer member and output shaft.

When the accelerator pedal is released, there will be 'over-run' conditions, which will rotate the outer member in a clockwise direction and unwedge the rollers.

The free-wheel can be locked up by connecting the mainshaft with the outer member by means of a dog clutch, which should only be engaged when both members are rotating at the same speed, i.e. when the engine is driving the road wheels.

THE OVERDRIVE

To *overdrive* means to drive faster. In the case of the transmission, the propeller shaft rotates faster than the engine when the device is in use.

Normally mounted at the rear of the gearbox, the unit consists

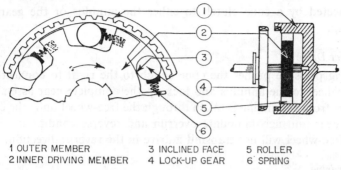

| 1 OUTER MEMBER | 3 INCLINED FACE | 5 ROLLER |
| 2 INNER DRIVING MEMBER | 4 LOCK-UP GEAR | 6 SPRING |

FREE WHEEL UNIT

FIG. 11.5.1

of an epicyclic gear ratio, which provides either direct drive, or a ratio slightly higher than direct drive. This overdrive ratio proves advantageous as regards engine wear and petrol consumption, when the vehicle is cruising on the open road. In applications where an overdrive is fitted to a three-speed gearbox, the unit can often be activated on second gear, and this feature provides a gear ratio which falls between second and top gear to suit the situation where top is too high and second is too low.

Fig. 11.5.2 shows a diagrammatic sketch of one type of overdrive. Mounted on a bearing on the input shaft is a sun wheel, which is

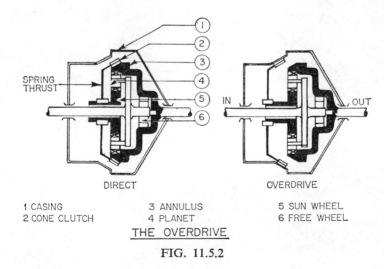

| 1 CASING | 3 ANNULUS | 5 SUN WHEEL |
| 2 CONE CLUTCH | 4 PLANET | 6 FREE WHEEL |

THE OVERDRIVE

FIG. 11.5.2

connected by a cone clutch to either the annulus or the gearbox casing.

Direct Drive

Spring pressure pushes the cone clutch to the right to connect the sun wheel to the annulus and lock up the complete gear assembly. Drive from the engine is taken through the free-wheel unit: the cone and gear unit accommodate overrun and reverse conditions, since the free-wheel will not transmit a drive in the reverse direction.

Overdrive

Oil, under pressure from a pump driven by the input shaft, acts on pistons which force the cone clutch against the casing to prevent the sun wheel from roating. The input shaft will move the planets forward and cause them to rotate around the fixed sun. This motion will drive the annulus slightly faster than the input shaft, to give overdrive.

The overdrive may be engaged without using the main clutch, and thus the operation is quick.

Propeller Shafts and Types of Drive

12.1

UNIVERSAL JOINTS

The purpose of a universal joint is to transmit a drive through a varying angle.

The need for a universal joint will be seen by referring to Fig. 12.1.1(a). In this case the gearbox is mounted on the frame, and the rear axle is bolted to the springs. Road shocks will deflect the springs to the dotted position, which will produce a different propeller shaft angle, and will quickly fracture a shaft rigidly connected to the gearbox and rear axle.

TYPES OF UNIVERSAL JOINT

Flexible Fabric

This type of joint, invented by E. Hardy in 1914, was used on propeller shafts up to the early 30s, but the numerous disadvantages forced designers to use other types. The construction is still used, however, for other applications (e.g. steering) and appears to give satisfactory results.

Fig. 12.1.1(b) shows the main construction. The disc is composed of a series of sheets of rubberised fabric bonded together and connected between two 'spiders'. Flexing of the fabric allows for the variation in angle.

This system has the following advantages:
(1) no lubrication is required
(2) cheapness

Its disadvantages are:
(1) max. angle of drive is very small
(2) size—large diameter required for high torque
(3) failure to maintain shaft alignment, causing vibration.

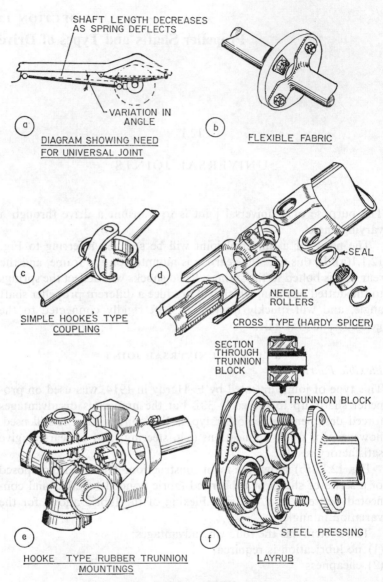

SHAFT LENGTH DECREASES
AS SPRING DEFLECTS

VARIATION IN
ANGLE

(a) DIAGRAM SHOWING NEED
FOR UNIVERSAL JOINT

(b) FLEXIBLE FABRIC

(c) SIMPLE HOOKES TYPE
COUPLING

(d) CROSS TYPE (HARDY SPICER)

SEAL

NEEDLE
ROLLERS

SECTION
THROUGH
TRUNNION
BLOCK

TRUNNION BLOCK

STEEL PRESSING

(e) HOOKE TYPE RUBBER TRUNNION
MOUNTINGS

(f) LAYRUB

UNIVERSAL JOINTS

FIG. 12.1.1

Hooke Type Joint

Credit for the invention of the universal joint is given to Robert Hooke (17th century). Fig. 12.1.1(c) shows the main details of this type of joint.

Two yokes set at 90° to each other are joined by a trunnion block, which is made in the form of either a cross or a ring. Bearing surfaces in the yokes allow for angular deflection.

The modern joint has been developed from this basic type, and details of the construction of a popular type of joint are shown in Fig. 12.1.1(d). A more robust spider or trunnion block rotates on needle roller bearings, which are contained in hardened steel cups, pressed into the yokes and retained by circlips. Accurate positioning of the trunnion and shaft i s arranged by allowing the cups to touch the ends of the trunnion block. To ensure that the needle rollers are lubricated, the trunnion is drilled to connect with a grease nipple at the centre, and the lubricant is retained by fitting cork oil retainers.

The advantages of this system are:

(1) compactness
(2) high mechanical efficiency
(3) ability to drive through a large angle (max. approximately 20°)
(4) accurate positioning of shaft, and hence suitability for high speeds.

This type of joint has a long life if attention is given to lubrication. Neglecting this can cause wear on needle rollers and trunnion faces, and this produces slackness and vibration, which has to be rectified by fitting a new trunnion assembly.

Rubber Trunnion Mountings

One popular small car uses a Hooke type coupling with the trunnion block mounted in specially moulded rubber bushings (Fig. 12.1.1(e)). This type requires no lubrication, and the resilient rubber blocks absorb torsional vibrations.

Layrub Couplings

Fig. 12.1.1(f) shows the main details of this type of coupling, which is suited to vehicles where 'coupling space' is adequate.

A number of moulded rubber blocks, with specially shaped cavities at the ends, which are bonded to a steel sleeve, are retained in position by two steel pressings. Two forks set at 90° to each other connect to alternate rubber blocks.

This coupling has the following advantages:
(1) no lubrication required
(2) capable of driving through a comparatively large angle (max. 15°)
(3) accommodates axial movement, and hence no splining is necessary
(4) torsion flexibility damps shocks and acts as a noise insulator.

Propeller Shafts

A shaft is the most common method of transmitting the drive from the gearbox to the final drive although other arrangements, such as belt, chain, electrical and hydraulic drives, are sometimes used.

When a shaft is employed, it must be strong to resist torsional stresses and prevent sag, since if the latter occurred vibration will be experienced. This is caused by the shaft's centre of gravity not coinciding with the shaft centre line and in this state centrifugal force will 'bow' the shaft to an extent which will depend on the speed of the shaft. The condition is also called 'whip' and the speed at which the vibration occurs is termed the 'whirling speed'.

A lightweight tubular shaft is normally used because of its
(a) high resistance to misalignment
(b) low resistance to any change in the rotational speed which occurs when the drive is taken through an angle by a Hooke type joint
(c) torsional strength—the shaft is only slightly weaker than a solid shaft of similar diameter.

The maximum speed of rotation of the propeller shaft is high, e.g. in top gear, propeller shaft and engine rotate at the same speed and if an overdrive is used, a higher speed is reached. For this reason good balance is essential, so in order to achieve this, small balance 'weights' are attached to the shaft during manufacture.

Any vehicle having a long wheelbase, e.g. the heavy commercial vehicle, needs a long drive-line and in order to avoid 'whirling' or 'whip' a divided type with a centre bearing support is often used.

Fig. 12.1.2 shows two arrangements of a divided drive-line. Although the axle movement only causes angular deflection of the final or rear shaft, the other universal joints are allowing for the slight flexing of the chassis frame. Centre bearings, which sometimes are the self-aligning type, are flexibly mounted to the frame. This allows the bearing a limited freedom of movement and prevents any vibration being transmitted to the frame.

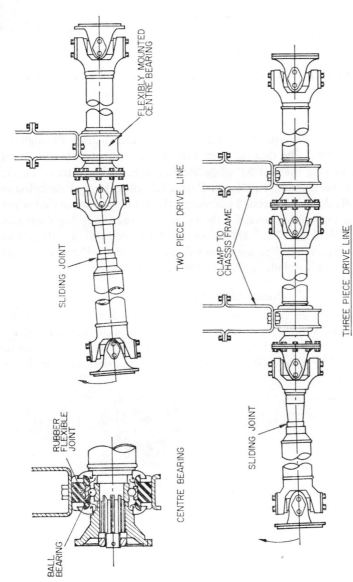

FLEXIBLY MOUNTED
CENTRE BEARING

SLIDING JOINT

TWO PIECE DRIVE LINE

RUBBER
FLEXIBLE
JOINT

BALL
BEARING

CENTRE BEARING

CLAMP TO
CHASSIS FRAME

THREE PIECE DRIVE LINE

SLIDING JOINT

FIG. 12.1.2

CONSTANT VELOCITY UNIVERSAL JOINTS

VARIATION IN SPEED

When a Hooke type joint is used to transmit a drive through an angle, you will find that the output shaft does not rotate at a constant speed. During the first 90° of its motion, the shaft will travel faster, and on the second 90°, slower. Correction of this speed variation is normally done by a second coupling, which must be set so that when the front coupling increases the speed, the rear coupling decreases the speed. Fig. 12.2.1 shows the correct method of fitting two Hooke type couplings, and you will see that the yoke at each end of the propeller shaft is fitted in the same plane.

CONSTANT VELOCITY JOINTS

A single Hooke type coupling fitted at the wheel end of a front-wheel drive vehicle produces considerable vibration due to the speed variation effect, which is aggravated by the large angle. This can be overcome by using a *constant velocity universal joint* of a type shown in Fig. 12.2.2.

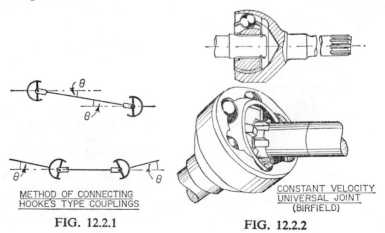

METHOD OF CONNECTING
HOOKE'S TYPE COUPLINGS

FIG. 12.2.1

CONSTANT VELOCITY
UNIVERSAL JOINT
(BIRFIELD)

FIG. 12.2.2

THE HOTCHKISS DRIVE

TORQUE REACTION

'To every action there is an equal and opposite reaction.' This statement means that every component which produces or changes a torque will also exert an equal and opposite torque tending to turn the casing: e.g. when the engine crankshaft exerts a torque in a clockwise direction, the cylinder block will tend to rotate in an anti-clockwise direction. (Some early designs of engine used a fixed crankshaft with rotating cylinders.)

A further example of torque reaction is shown in Fig. 12.3.1, which represents a tractor with its rear driving wheels locked in a ditch. In this situation the driver must be careful, because torque reaction is likely to lift the front of the tractor rather than turn the rear wheels.

TORQUE
REACTION

FIG. 12.3.1

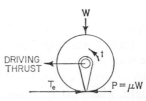

LEVER ACTION OF WHEEL

FIG. 12.3.2

When the law stated above is applied to rear axles, you will see that some arrangement must be provided to prevent the axle casing turning in the opposite direction to the driving wheels.

DRIVING THRUST

A torque (t) applied to the wheel, which may be considered as a lever (Fig. 12.3.2), produces a *tractive effort* (Te) at the road surface, and an equal and opposite forward force at the axle shaft. This driving thrust must be transferred from the axle casing to the frame in order to propel the vehicle The maximum tractive effort is limited by the adhesive force (P) of the tyre on the road; this force depends on the coefficient of friction (μ) and the load on the wheel (W).

Various arrangements are employed to take the torque reaction and driving thrust of the axle casing. The main systems are: (1) the Hotchkiss open type drive, (2) the torque tube drive, and (3) the de-Dion drive.

THE HOTCHKISS DRIVE

This system is the most popular arrangement, and the main details are shown in Fig. 12.3.3.

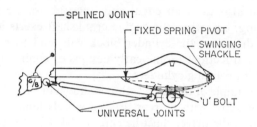

HOTCHKISS OPEN-TYPE DRIVE

FIG. 12.3.3

Two rear leaf springs, longitudinally mounted, are connected to the frame by a 'fixed' pivot at the front, and swinging shackles at the rear. At each end of the exposed or 'open' type propeller shaft is fitted a universal joint, with provision made for alteration in shaft length, which occurs when the springs are deflected.

Torque reaction is resisted by clamping the axle to the springs by means of 'U' bolts. Under heavy driving conditions the springs will deflect up at the front and down at the rear, and vice-versa during braking. This movement will help to damp driving shocks and improve transmission flexibility. Since the axle continually moves first one way and then the other, the need for a rear universal joint is clear.

Driving thrust is transferred from the casing to the spring by the friction between the two surfaces, and then transmitted through the front section of the springs to the vehicle frame. If the 'U' bolts become loose, the spring centre bolt (axle location bolt) will have to take the full driving thrust, and the high shearing force will quickly fracture it.

12.4

THE TORQUE TUBE DRIVE

Whereas the Hotchkiss drive uses stiff springs to resist torque reaction and driving thrust, the torque tube or enclosed drive relieves the springs of all duties other than their intended purpose. This means that a 'softer' ride can be achieved by using either 'softer' springs or another form of spring (e.g. helical).

Fig. 12.4.1 shows a layout using laminated springs, which are connected to the frame by a swinging shackle at each end. Bolted rigidly

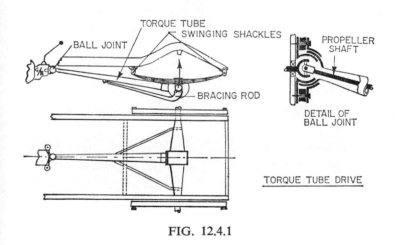

FIG. 12.4.1

to the axle casing is a tubular member, which is located at the front by a ball and socket joint, positioned at the rear of the gearbox or cross-member of the frame. Bracing rods, connected between the axle casing and the torque tube, strengthen the construction. A small-diameter propeller shaft is fitted inside the torque tube and splined to the final-drive pinion. Mounted in the centre of the ball joint is a universal joint to allow for angular deflections of the drive. In this arrangement the torque reaction and driving thrust is taken by the torque tube. When the forward thrust from the ball is taken on the rear housing of the gearbox, means must be provided to transfer this force through the gearbox mountings to the frame.

It was stated in chapter 12.2 that a variation in speed occurred when a Hooke type coupling transmitted the drive through an angle In the Hotchkiss system, this variation was corrected by the rear joint, but since the torque tube drive has only one coupling, a smaller-diameter propeller shaft must be fitted to damp out the vibrations.

Helical or torsion bar springs may be used as alternatives to laminated springs, and in these cases, side movement of the axle must be controlled by fitting some form of transverse stabiliser (e.g. Panhard rod) between the frame and the axle.

12.5

THE DE-DION AXLE

DE-DION DRIVE

The de-Dion axle is often regarded as the halfway stage between the normal axle and independent suspension. Many of the advantages of the latter are achieved in this layout, but since the rear wheels are still linked by an axle tube, the system cannot be classed as independent.

Fig. 12.5.1 shows a basic arrangement: in this design, laminated springs are connected to the frame by a 'fixed' pivot at the front and

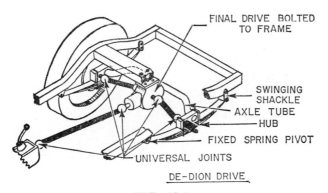

FINAL DRIVE BOLTED TO FRAME

SWINGING SHACKLE

AXLE TUBE

HUB

FIXED SPRING PIVOT

UNIVERSAL JOINTS

DE-DION DRIVE

FIG. 12.5.1

a swinging shackle at the rear. Each spring carries a hub mounting, which is rigidly connected to a tubular axle beam, to support the wheel on a stub axle shaft. Bolted to a cross-member of the frame is the final-drive unit, and from this the drive is taken through two universally jointed shafts to the wheels. The main propeller shaft is fitted with a universal joint at each end to allow for flexing of the frame.

Torque reaction of the final-drive casing is taken by the frame, and the driving thrust is resisted by the springs.

The major advantage of this layout is the reduction in unsprung weight. This ensures that wheel spin is reduced by allowing the light driving wheels to follow the contour of the road surface closely. Wheel spin is caused, too, by the tendency of the normal axle to rotate around the pinion when a high propeller shaft torque is exerted. This lifting effect of the offside wheel is eliminated with the de-Dion system, and weight is equally distributed.

Rear Axles

13.1

FINAL-DRIVE GEARS

PURPOSE

The purposes of a final drive, as applied to a rear axle, are:
(1) to transmit the drive through an angle of 90°
(2) to gear down the engine revolutions so that a 'direct top' gear-box ratio may be employed. In the case of cars this requires a final-drive ratio of approximately 4:1.

These functions can be performed by bevel or worm gears.

BEVEL GEARS

The geometry of a bevel gear layout may be considered by referring to Fig. 13.1.1. This represents two friction cones: *A* forming the crown wheel and *B* the pinion. To avoid slipping and wear, the apex of the pinion must coincide with the centre line of the crown wheel. If the pinion is incorrectly positioned, it will be seen that the peripheral speeds of the crown wheel and pinion will not be equal. Mounting the gear in the correct position will show that the angle of the bevel is governed by the gear ratio.

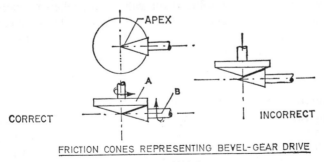

FRICTION CONES REPRESENTING BEVEL-GEAR DRIVE

FIG. 13.1.1

TYPES OF BEVEL GEAR

Straight Bevel

Fig. 13.1.2 illustrates the main features of the bevel type of gear. Tapered teeth, generated from the centre, are machined on the case-hardened steel gears, and then ground together to form a 'mated pair'. The direction of rotation of the axle shaft will be determined by the position of the crown wheel relative to the pinion. (It is possible on some vehicles to fit the crown wheel on the wrong side, and this gives one forward and several reverse ratios.)

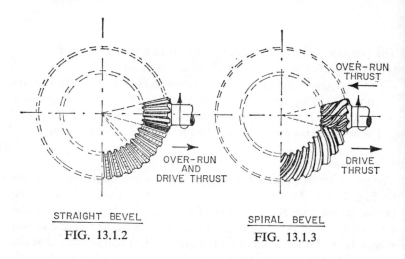

STRAIGHT BEVEL

FIG. 13.1.2

SPIRAL BEVEL

FIG. 13.1.3

Adjusters in the form of distance pieces, shims or screwed rings enable the correct mesh and backlash to be set. When the clearance between the teeth (backlash) is too small, expansion due to heat and wear caused by lack of lubrication will result, whereas excessive clearance produces slackness and noise. Each manufacturer recommends a suitable backlash; this is normally in the region of 0·006 in (0·15 mm) for cars and 0·010 in (0·25 mm) for heavy vehicles.

Spiral Bevel

Although the straight bevel was cheap to produce and mechanically efficient, the meshing of the gears caused an objectionable noise, which was reduced when a *helical* form of tooth was employed. Naturally, it is impossible to generate a helix on a tapered pinion, so the gear is known as a spiral bevel.

The construction of the gear is shown in Fig. 13.1.3. A number of teeth, generated from the centre of the crown wheel, form, in the case of the pinion, a left-handed spiral. This direction causes a large outward thrust on the drive and a smaller inward thrust on the over-run; therefore pinion bearing wear will increase the backlash rather than cause seizure of the gear.

You will see that, since the crown wheel teeth are inclined to the pinion, the tooth pressures are much higher. The *straight* (i.e. no additives) high-viscosity gear oil, which was satisfactory for the straight bevel type, gave poor results when used in spiral bevel units. The oil film broke down under the high loads, and allowed rapid wear and scoring to take place. Special oils to lubricate the surface after rupture of the oil film were developed and these are known as E.P. (extreme pressure) lubricants. They contain various additives such as sulphur, chlorine and phosphorus, which chemically react, at high temperatures, with the metal surface to form a compound of low frictional resistance.

HYPOID

This type of gear, shown in Fig. 13.1.4, is the popular form in use today.

The pinion axis is offset to the centre line of the crown wheel. It can be placed above or below the centre, but in the case of cars is always placed below to give a lower propeller shaft and a reduction in the tunnel height. Pinion offset varies with the application but an offset equal to $\frac{1}{5}$ of the wheel diameter is often used.

It will be seen that, by lowering the axis, the tooth pitch of the

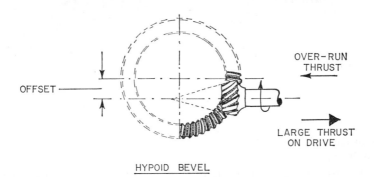

HYPOID BEVEL

FIG. 13.1.4

pinion increases, and so, for a given ratio, the pinion diameter can be larger (30% for normal offset). This gives a stronger gear and is the main reason for its adoption on commercial vehicles.

It is often said that a hypoid is halfway between a normal bevel and a worm drive. In the former case a rolling action takes place, whereas in the latter the motion is all sliding. By increasing the sliding motion in the hypoid gear, meshing noise is reduced, but the high temperature and pressure of the oil film is a strain on the lubricant. To deal with this, a special extreme pressure oil is employed which contains more active agents than those used with the normal spiral bevel. These oils contain expendable E.P. agents to resist scuffing and wear at high temperature, and a fatty acid to improve boundary lubrication at low temperature.

WORM AND WHEEL

This is an expensive form of drive which is currently used on a large number of heavy commercial vehicles. Various arrangements, as shown in Fig. 13.1.5, can be used to give a very quiet and long-

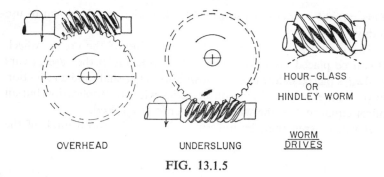

OVERHEAD   UNDERSLUNG   HOUR-GLASS OR HINDLEY WORM

WORM DRIVES

FIG. 13.1.5

lasting gear, but efficiency is not so good as with the bevel (94% against 98%).

The gear ratio of a worm and wheel is given by:

$$\text{ratio} = \frac{\text{no. of teeth on wheel}}{\text{no. of starts on worm}}$$

You can see that this type of gear provides a large reduction in a small space.

The worm may be mounted below (underslung) or above (overhead) the wheel to give either a low propeller shaft or a small drive angle and good ground clearance. When two rear driving axles are used, the overhead layout enables a simple connection to be used.

An hour glass or Hindley worm embraces more teeth than the straight worm but adjustment is more critical.

Friction caused by the sliding action of the worm is reduced by using a worm wheel of phosphor-bronze and a worm of case-hardened steel, but even with this material the unit gets rather hot. A large, well-cooled sump is used to reduce oxidation of the oil. This occurs at high temperature and causes the oil to thicken up. To improve the boundary lubrication, a vegetable-based oil is sometimes used as an alternative to straight gear oil.

BEVEL DRIVE ADJUSTMENTS

Current types of bevel drive operate under severe conditions, but will give satisfactory service provided the gear is adjusted correctly. Every manufacturer gives detailed information of special tools, clearances, etc., and you should refer to this before attempting such an important overhaul.

The following general points should be a guide:

Noise from the final drive is caused by bearing defects or incorrect meshing (the latter may be caused by bearing wear). Generally noise or 'whine' on the drive occurs when the gear is too deep in mesh, and noise on the over-run is caused by insufficient depth of mesh. Whenever a final-drive noise develops, determine the cause as soon as possible. Misaligned gears will 'mate' to the new position, and make it impossible to obtain a quiet operation even when the adjustment is corrected. If repair is delayed, you will probably require a new crown wheel and pinion as well as a bearing.

Pre-loading Most pinions are fitted with adjustable bearings. If the bearings were set so that there was a small clearance, end float and misalignment of the gear would be apparent. This would quickly lead to noise and bearing failure. Even when the clearance is eliminated, the elastic nature of the material will produce similar effects. To overcome these conditions, modern pinion bearings are pre-loaded. This means that the bearings are forced together by the adjusting arrangement to assume the position occupied by the bearings when the unit is under load. The extent of this pre-compression is indicated by the torque required to rotate the pinion in its housing; e.g. a torque of 12 lbf in (1·36 Nm) is required to rotate the pinion with dry bearings and oil seal removed.

Fig. 13.1.6 shows a popular pinion-bearing layout. Pre-load is controlled by tightening the adjusting nut which forces the gearings together. A special collapsible spacer is fitted between the bearings to enable the nut to be pulled up tight and to obtain the recommended pre-load. If, when you check, you find that the pre-load is too high, a new spacer is required.

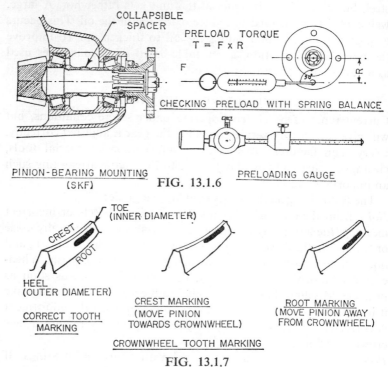

COLLAPSIBLE SPACER

PRELOAD TORQUE
T = F x R

F

CHECKING PRELOAD WITH SPRING BALANCE

PINION-BEARING MOUNTING
(SKF)

FIG. 13.1.6

PRELOADING GAUGE

TOE
(INNER DIAMETER)

CREST
ROOT

HEEL
(OUTER DIAMETER)

CORRECT TOOTH
MARKING

CREST MARKING
(MOVE PINION
TOWARDS CROWNWHEEL)

ROOT MARKING
(MOVE PINION AWAY
FROM CROWNWHEEL)

CROWNWHEEL TOOTH MARKING

FIG. 13.1.7

Pinion Position Special dummy pinion jigs are often used to determine the correct position of the pinion. When these special tools are not available or not recommended, position the pinion initially so that the edge of the crown wheel teeth coincide with the inner edge of the pinion teeth. Obtain the correct backlash by moving the crown wheel, and check by means of a clock gauge. Obtain the final meshing of the gear by applying a smear of marking compound to the driving side of a few crown wheel teeth and turning the pinion in the D.O.R., whilst applying a resistance to the crown wheel. The marking obtained indicates the mesh of the gears (Fig. 13.1.7).

THE DIFFERENTIAL

PURPOSE

If both rear wheels were connected to a common driving shaft, two effects would soon show up: (a) rapid rear tyre wear, and (b) difficulty in steering from the straight-ahead position. Fig. 13.2.1(a) shows that the outer wheel must travel a greater distance when the vehicle is cornering: therefore if the wheels are interconnected, the tyres will have to 'scrub' over the road surface and tend to keep the vehicle moving straight ahead. These effects can be minimised by driving one wheel and allowing the other to run free, but the unbalanced driving thrust and unequal cornering speeds make the arrangement unpopular. The solution to the problem came in 1827 when Péqueur of France invented the differential. This mechanism allows the wheels to rotate at different speeds, but still maintains a drive to both wheels.

PRINCIPLE

Consider the two discs, shown in Fig. 13.2.1(b), to be linked by shafts to the wheels and interconnected with a lever. When a force (F) is applied to C at the centre of the lever, each disc will receive an equal share—i.e. half the force applied. The movement of the discs will depend on the resistances (R) opposing the motion of the shafts. If a larger resistance acts on disc B, the lever will tilt, and push disc A forward a greater amount. This condition is shown in plan view in Fig. 13.2.1(c), and you will see that:

increase in distance moved by A = decrease in distance moved by B

or increase in speed of A = decrease in speed of B

$$\therefore A + B = 2C$$

In Fig. 13.2.1(d) the disc system is replaced by bevel gears, which

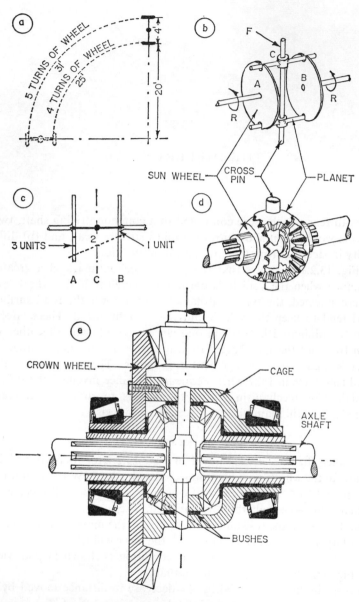

THE DIFFERENTIAL

FIG. 13.2.1

are called sun wheels (discs) and planets (levers). The drive is applied to the cross pin and will push the planet gears forward to exert an equal torque on each sun wheel irrespective of the speed. When the vehicle turns a corner, the inner wheel will slow down and cause the planets to rotate on their own axis to speed up the outer wheel. Straight-ahead motion of the vehicle will allow the whole unit to rotate at the same speed.

The complete differential is shown in Fig. 13.2.1(e). This arrangement shows a crown wheel bolted on to a differential cage. This cage supports the sun wheels on plain bearings and transmits the drive to the cross pin.

Light cars only need two planet gears, but four gears are necessary on heavier vehicles to reduce tooth pressures.

Lubrication is provided by the final-drive oil, which can splash through holes in the differential cage.

Differential Lock

If one driving wheel of a two-wheel drive vehicle loses adhesion, the propelling force is considerably reduced and this results in the vehicle being immobilised. On these occasions the differential action is undesirable so, on vehicles designed to operate over poor surfaces, a differential locking arrangement is often fitted.

Differential action can be prevented by locking together any two individual units of a differential and Fig. 13.2.2 shows one arrangement. Splined to a differential sun wheel is a sliding dog clutch member, which engages with dog teeth formed on the cage of the differential. The clutch is engaged by means of a fork and movement of this can be made by a lever fitted on the outside of the axle.

In the engaged position, the sun wheel, and consequently the rear wheel connected to this sun gear, is made to turn at the same speed as the cage. Locking one sun gear to the cage in this way ensures that the other sun gear also turns at the same speed.

Limited-slip Differential

Although a high mechanical efficiency is desirable for the majority of mechanical components, it is a disadvantage in the case of a differential. In addition to the reduced traction over slippery surfaces, a 'low friction' differential fitted to a highly powered vehicle limits acceleration and causes excessive tyre wear. Observation of such a vehicle during acceleration shows that torque reaction of the

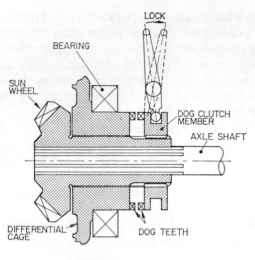

DIFFERENTIAL LOCK

FIG. 13.2.2

engine tends to lift the left-hand driving wheel off the ground and when this is accompanied by an uneven road surface, the presence of excessive wheel spin is apparent. In order to restrict these drawbacks, the differential action is opposed by artificially increasing the friction between the sun wheel and the differential cage. Arrangements having this feature are called limited slip differentials and Fig. 13.2.3 shows the basic layout of one system.

A multi-disc clutch pack fitted behind each sun wheel has the inner and outer plates splined to the sun and cage respectively. Since bevel gears are used, an axial thrust will be developed which will be proportional to the torque applied by the crown wheel to the differential. Under low torque conditions, the differential will function in the normal way, but if the torque is increased, the clutch pack will be loaded and this will resist the sun gear from rotating at a different speed to the cage.

To further increase the load on the clutch pack many designs incorporate:

(a) a Belleville disc-spring washer between the cage and the clutch discs of each pack to provide an initial load on the discs.

(b) angled cam faces between the cage and the cross pins. Driving thrust exerted by the cage on the pin causes the pin to force the planets against the side gear ring. When four planets are used, two separate pins, flexibly linked at the centre and having opposing cam faces, cause two planets to act on one clutch pack and the other two to force in the opposite direction. This layout is shown in Fig. 13.2.3.

The action of this type of differential should be remembered by the mechanic. With only one driving wheel lifted off the ground, a drive transmitted to this wheel from the engine can lead to tragic results.

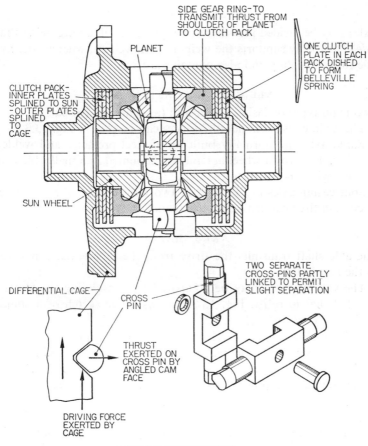

LIMITED SLIP DIFFERENTIAL

FIG. 13.2.3

13.3

AXLE CONSTRUCTION

LIVE AND DEAD AXLES

Axles may be divided into these two types, the difference being that a *dead* axle only supports the weight of the vehicle, whereas the *live* axle fulfils this duty and also contains a drive.

AXLE CASING CONSTRUCTION

Two main types of casing are in use: (a) split, and (b) banjo.

The main constructional differences can be seen in Fig. 13.3.1.

Banjo axles are normally built up of steel pressings and welded together. The crown wheel assembly is mounted in a malleable iron housing which is bolted to the axle.

Split casing axles are formed in two halves and bolted together to contain the final drive and differential.

AXLE SHAFTS

The axle shaft transmits the drive from the differential sun wheel to the rear hub.

The various types may be compared by considering the stresses the shaft has to resist. Fig. 13.3.2 shows a line sketch of a simple shaft which is subjected to:

(1) torsional stress due to driving and braking torque
(2) shear stress due to the weight of the vehicle (Fig. 13.3.3)
(3) bending stress due to the weight of the vehicle (Fig. 13.3.4)
(4) tensile and compressive stress due to cornering forces.

TYPES

Axle shafts are divided into three main groups, depending on the stresses to which the shaft is subjected: (a) semi-floating, (b) three-quarters floating, and (c) fully floating.

FIG. 13.3.1 AXLE CASING CONSTRUCTION

FIG. 13.3.2   FIG. 13.3.3   FIG. 13.3.4

EFFECT OF LOAD ON SIMPLE AXLE SHAFT

Semi-floating

Fig. 13.3.5(a) shows a typical mounting of an axle shaft suitable for light cars. A single bearing at the hub end is fitted between the shaft and the casing, so the shaft will have to resist all the stresses previously mentioned. To reduce the risk of fracture at the hub end (this would allow the wheel to fall off), the shaft diameter is increased. Any increase must be gradual, since a sudden change in cross-sectional area would produce a stress-raiser and increase the

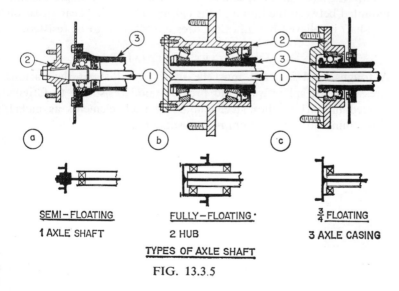

SEMI–FLOATING   FULLY–FLOATING ·   ¾ FLOATING

1 AXLE SHAFT   2 HUB   3 AXLE CASING

TYPES OF AXLE SHAFT

FIG. 13.3.5

risk of failure due to fatigue. (Fatigue may be defined as breakage due to continual alteration of the stress in the material.)

Although the final-drive oil level is considerably lower than the axle shaft, the large amount of 'splash' would cause the lubricant to work along the shaft and enter the brake drum. Sealing arrangements normally consist of an oil retainer fitted at the hub end (the lip of the seal is positioned towards the final drive).

Fully floating

This is generally fitted on commercial vehicles where torque and axle loads are greater.

The construction shown in Fig. 13.3.5(b) consists of an independently mounted hub which rotates on two bearings widely spaced on the axle casing. This arrangement relieves the shaft of all stresses except torsional; so the construction is very strong. Studs connecting the shaft to the hub transmit the drive and when the nuts on these studs are removed, the shaft may be withdrawn without jacking up the vehicle.

Three-quarter floating

Having defined the semi and the fully floating shaft, any alternative between the two may be regarded as a three-quarter floating shaft.

Fig. 13.3.5(c) shows a construction which has a single bearing mounted between the hub and the casing. The main shear stress on the shaft is relieved but all other stresses still have to be resisted.

AXLE SHAFT MATERIAL

A tough, hard material must be used to withstand the various stresses, resist spline wear and provide good resistance to fatigue. A medium carbon alloy steel containing such elements as nickel, chromium and molybdenum is the usual choice.

COMMERCIAL VEHICLE REAR AXLES, MULTI-DRIVE AXLES, FOUR-WHEEL DRIVE

DOUBLE REDUCTION AXLE

The large-diameter wheels of a commercial vehicle require a final-drive ratio lower than the 3–5:1 used with cars. A single-reduction bevel gear may be used with ratios up to about 7:1, but as the crown wheel size is increased, some form of thrust button is required to resist the crown wheel deflection. When 7:1 is exceeded, either a worm-drive or a double reduction axle is necessary.

Double reduction means the ratio is obtained in two steps. If the first step is 4:1 and the second step is 2:1, the final drive overall ratio will be $4 \times 2 = 8:1$.

Various forms of double reduction axle are shown in Fig. 13.4.1:
A 1st stage—spiral bevel gear
2nd stage—double helical gears

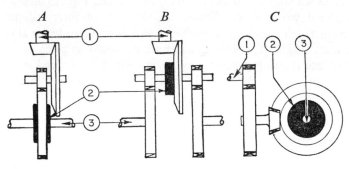

1 DRIVE FROM ENGINE   2 DIFFERENTIAL   3 AXLE SHAFT

DOUBLE REDUCTION UNITS

FIG. 13.4.1

B 1st stage—spiral bevel gear
2nd stage—two sets of spur or helical gears
The differential is placed in the centre of the crown wheel of
the first stage, and so a smaller, lower torque capacity differential may be used, but this advantage is counteracted by having
to use two sets of gears for the second stage.

C 1st stage—spur or helical gears
2nd stage—spiral bevel
This system is convenient when two driving axles have to be
linked together.

MULTI-DRIVE AXLES

Reason for Multi-drive

As the rear axle load is increased, wider tyres or twin wheels become
necessary, and when the load on the rear axle exceeds the legal
maximum, another rear axle must be used. One of these could be a
dead axle, but the reduced proportion of the total weight acting on
the driving wheels would limit the tractive effort which could be
exerted. To obtain maximum propulsion, most heavy commercial
vehicle manufacturers use twin driving axles. This also reduces the
risk of sinking into a soft surface, because the load is spread over
a larger area—a track-laying vehicle is a good example of a distributed
load.

Axle Layout

Fig. 13.4.2 shows two common arrangements. Fig. 13.4.2(a) shows
overhead worm drives linked together by an intermediate shaft
having a universal joint at each end. Provision is made for alteration
in shaft length. The driving axles are mounted as close as possible
to reduce steering problems and tyre wear due to speed difference.

Double reduction drives (Fig. 13.4.2(b)) are linked in a similar
manner to the worm drive.

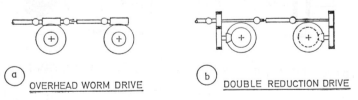

a OVERHEAD WORM DRIVE   b DOUBLE REDUCTION DRIVE

FIG. 13.4.2

FOUR-WHEEL DRIVE

The limitation of a conventional two-wheel drive vehicle is soon appreciated when the vehicle encounters the rough terrain and muddy conditions normally associated with cross-country operations. In these situations the rear wheels often lose their adhesion, consequently the traction available is insufficient to provide a drive. The normal differential adds to these difficulties since if the adhesion of one driving wheel is lost, the drive to the other wheel is generally too low to propel the vehicle. Although a differential locking device reduces the chance of this occurrence, there are still many occasions when both driving wheels are rendered ineffective. It is to overcome this situation that four-wheel drive is provided—when either front or rear axles lose traction the other axle maintains a drive to move the vehicle out of the difficulty.

Fig. 13.4.3 shows a typical layout of a four-wheel drive vehicle. Mounted behind the main gearbox is a transfer gearbox and this unit divides the drive between the axles and normally incorporates

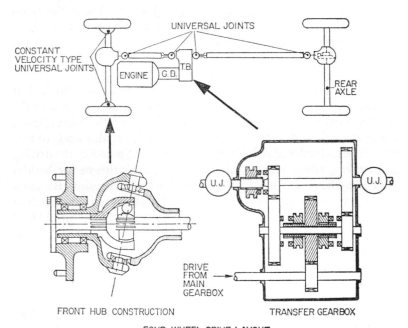

FRONT HUB CONSTRUCTION   TRANSFER GEARBOX

FOUR-WHEEL DRIVE LAYOUT

FIG. 13.4.3

extra gears to provide a very low ratio. The transfer box is generally controlled by two gear levers; one for selecting four-wheel drive and the other to give 'high' or 'low' gear. Drive to the front wheels is transmitted via the final drive, differential and drive shafts. Steering movement of the front wheels is accommodated by fitting extra universal joints at the wheel end of the drive shafts and in order to overcome vibration, the constant velocity type of joint is generally used.

The four-wheel arrangement shown in Fig. 13.4.3 should not be operated on hard surfaced road because of the risk of transmission 'wind-up'. When a vehicle using this arrangement turns a corner the mean speed of the front wheels is higher than that of the rear wheels, so the speed difference causes the propeller shafts to deflect. Drivers disregarding this instruction often cause serious injury to mechanics who are performing a wheel change operation. To overcome the wind-up problem and make the vehicle suitable for four-wheel operation on hard surfaces, a third differential 'between' the driving axles would be needed. This differential is rarely fitted to a vehicle designed for cross-country work, since the differential would defeat the main purpose of four-wheel drive—if one wheel lost adhesion the vehicle would be immobilised.

Four-wheel Drive System (Ferguson formula)

When a vehicle is accelerated or decelerated the effort applied at the road wheel is limited by the friction at the road surface and the weight on the wheel. Once this limit is reached the wheel spins, which not only restricts the change in velocity, but also leads to loss of control and reduced safety for the occupants. Spreading the driving and braking effort over all the wheels improves this factor besides increasing the potential rate of acceleration or deceleration. Backing-up this effort distribution with a device which senses the approach of wheel spin or slip and then adjusts the effort accordingly, would lead to a safer motor vehicle. It is to satisfy all these features that the Ferguson formula is intended.

Fig. 13.4.4 shows a typical layout as applied to a Jensen car. A transfer box, containing the sensing mechanism, is adjacent to a centre (third) differential, and propeller shafts transmit the drive to front and rear axles. A Maxaret unit prevents the possibility of all wheels locking during braking. Driven by the transmission it senses the mean deceleration of front and rear road wheels and just before

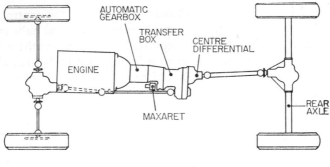

TRANSMISSION LAYOUT
(JENSEN)

FIG. 13.4.4

the wheel locks the hydraulic pressure to the brake is relieved.

The basis of the Ferguson control system consists of a master differential and two one-way multi-disc clutches, the unit divides the torque in the ratio of 37% front and 63% rear, besides allowing for a speed variation between front and rear wheels. The differential is a simple epicyclic gear train which has the input shaft driving the planet carrier; the annulus and sun connected to rear and front wheels respectively. Application of a force to the centre of the planet gives equal forces at the annulus and sun. Since the force at the annulus is acting at a larger radius, the torque is greater, so this member is connected to the rear wheels. As with a normal differential, speed variation can take place. In this arrangement the difference in speed between an output shaft and the planet carrier, causes the planet to rotate around the slower moving gear; a motion which speeds up the other member. The extent of this speed variation is limited by the control unit and in this particular design the front wheels are only permitted to over-run the rears by 16·5%, whereas the rear wheels can only over-run to the extent of 5·5%. Once this limit is reached a multi-disc clutch locks the planet carrier (input shaft) to the sun wheel (front output shaft) i.e. the centre differential is put out of action. This action can occur under traction or braking conditions, and the method of achieving this will now be considered.

The clutch inner plates are splined to the control unit main shaft, which is driven by a gear from the differential sun. Each clutch has the outer discs splined to a casing and this casing is acted upon by three steel balls which are positioned in ramps on the control gear driven by the input shaft. This arrangement of the steel balls means that if the casing is held, the rotation of the gear causes the balls to run up the inclined ramps to exert a force which pushes the clutch discs together. By fitting a ball and ramp mechanism at each end of the double clutch pack assembly, it is possible to arrange the ramps so that one clutch operates in response to an increase in the speed of the gear from the differential sun whereas the other only functions when a speed decrease occurs. Both clutches are also fitted with a chamfered abutment ring and these are forced apart by springs and six radial plungers. A spring-loaded inner sleeve supplies the outward force on the plungers. The size of the control gears is related to the size of the gear from the differential sun; one control gear is slightly smaller, and one is slightly larger than the gear from the differential sun.

Under normal conditions clutch drag will cause both casings to lag behind its control gear and the ball mechanism will be ineffective. As soon as a difference in speed between the input and output shafts occurs, one control gear then approaches the point when it is rotating at the same speed as the clutch casing. As this takes place the balls are moved up their ramps and one set of clutch plates is compressed; this action locks the differential.

When the vehicle is reversing the clutches must be made inoperative. This is achieved by a free-wheel which locks its inner race to the gearbox casing. Due to the inclined surfaces on this race, the inner sleeve is pushed against its spring; an action which allows the plungers to move inwards and unload the clutches.

Steering Systems

14.1

BASIC REQUIREMENTS OF THE ACKERMANN LAYOUT

The fact that vehicles today often travel at high speeds illustrates the need for good steering, but perhaps even more important are efficient maintenance and fault rectification. Steering fault diagnosis can often place great demands on the mechanics' basic knowledge, and so it is essential in the interests of road safety that he has a thorough understanding of this subject.

The steering mechanism must enable the driver to maintain easily the straight-ahead motion of the vehicle, even when bumps are encountered at high speeds, and enable the path of the vehicle to be changed with the minimum amount of driver's effort.

SWINGING BEAM SYSTEM

The geometry of steering may be understood by considering the layout of a vehicle, as shown in Fig. 14.1.1. A swinging axle beam, mounted on a turntable on the frame, turns the wheels and allows the vehicle to move around an imaginary centre Ic. You will see, in the position shown, that all wheels are at right angles to radial lines drawn from Ic, and each wheel forms a tangent to the curved path that the wheel is actually taking. The natural tendency of a wheel is to travel in a straight path, and it is obvious that a curved path will cause greater tyre wear. This wear can be kept to a minimum if misalignment is limited.

ACKERMANN LAYOUT

Many of the disadvantages of the swinging beam system were overcome in 1817 when a Munich carriage builder named Lankensperger first introduced the fixed-beam, double-pivot system. In 1818, his

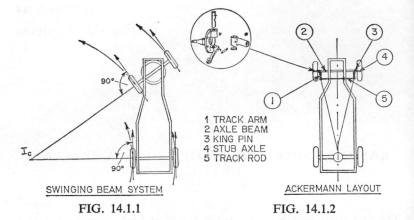

1 TRACK ARM
2 AXLE BEAM
3 KING PIN
4 STUB AXLE
5 TRACK ROD

SWINGING BEAM SYSTEM

FIG. 14.1.1

ACKERMANN LAYOUT

FIG. 14.1.2

agent in England, Rudolph Ackermann, took out a patent on the system which is known as the Ackermann layout and is widely used.

The main details of this layout are shown in Fig. 14.1.2. At each end of the fixed axle beam is fitted a stub axle which pivots on a king pin. Linkage connecting the two stub axles together comprises two short arms, often called track arms, and a track rod. By making the track rod shorter than the distance between the king pins, the inner wheel is forced to turn through a greater angle. Fig. 14.1.3 shows the angular motion of the inner wheel to be greater than the outer for a given movement of the track rod. (You will see this clearly if you draw the layout to scale and measure the angles.) Both wheels must be parallel with each other when the vehicle is travelling straight

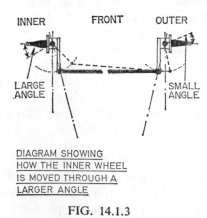

DIAGRAM SHOWING
HOW THE INNER WHEEL
IS MOVED THROUGH A
LARGER ANGLE

FIG. 14.1.3

ahead, but as the wheels are turned, a difference in wheel angle will occur, increasing as the wheels are turned.

The required variation in wheel angle can be seen in Fig. 14.1.4. This shows a condition similar to Fig. 14.1.1, and it was Jeantaud in 1878 who demonstrated that this condition must be fulfilled if tyre wear was to be kept to a minimum. The diagram also shows that the difference in wheel angle is governed by the ratio: $\dfrac{T}{W}$. The Ackermann layout does not completely achieve the conditions laid down by Jeantaud, and is only accurate in three positions—straight-ahead

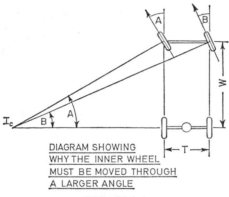

DIAGRAM SHOWING
WHY THE INNER WHEEL
MUST BE MOVED THROUGH
A LARGER ANGLE

FIG. 14.1.4

and one position in each lock; the latter depends on the angle formed between the vehicle centre line and the line taken through the king pin and track rod connection. Since pneumatic tyres are used, any slight inaccuracy can be overcome by the deflection of the tyre.

In order to give engine clearance, some manufacturers mount the track rod in front of the axle beam. Ackermann conditions are obtained by inclining the track arms outwards to enable the track rod connection to fall on the inclined imaginary line taken through the king pin.

OVERSTEER AND UNDERSTEER

Slip Angle

Previous steering geometry has been based on a vehicle using 'hard' tyres. Low-pressure tyres, used on modern vehicles, take a different path when subjected to a side force. Fig. 14.1.5(a) shows a plan view of a wheel travelling in the direction *A*.

If a side force acts on the wheel, tyre deflection will cause the wheel to take the path *B*, although the wheel is still pointing in the original direction. The angle between the path that the wheel is

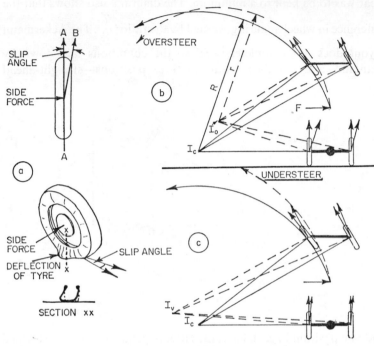

EFFECT OF SIDE FORCE ON A VEHICLE

FIG. 14.1.5

actually taking, and the plane of the wheel (*AA*), is termed the *slip angle*. (This term is misleading since no slip is actually taking place. 'Creep angle' might be a better term, but 'slip angle' is in common use.)

Effect on Vehicle

Tyre slip angles affect the steering characteristics of a vehicle by causing either *oversteer* or *understeer*. A side force, caused by wind, road camber or centrifugal effect, produces a slip angle at each tyre. When the rear angles are greater than the front (Fig. 14.1.5(b)),

the vehicle will turn more sharply than normal—a condition known
as *oversteer*. To correct this, the driver has to straighten up the
steering wheel.

Front slip angles greater than those of the rear (Fig. 14.1.5(c))
make the vehicle take a path of larger radius than normal, and give
the condition termed *understeer*. Weight distribution and relative
tyre pressures can often be altered to modify this.

STEERING MECHANISM

The complete layout of a steering assembly is shown in Fig. 14.1.6,
which represents a system used on a heavy vehicle.

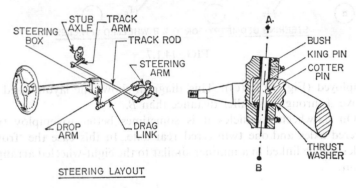

FIG. 14.1.6

A drop arm, splined to the steering box rocker arm, is connected
to the drag link by a ball joint. This link is also ball-jointed to a
steering arm which forms part of the stub axle. Construction of stub
axles takes various forms; the arrangement shown is known as a
reversed Elliot. When an independent suspension system is used, the
king pin is often replaced by ball joints placed at *A* and *B*.

RIGID SIX- AND EIGHT-WHEELED VEHICLES

The six-wheeled vehicle shown in Fig. 14.1.7(a) has one steer axle
and two driving axles. The *instantaneous centre of rotation* falls on
a line extended midway between the driving axles, so there will be
a slight 'scrubbing' action of the driving axle tyres. This action can
be minimised by mounting the axles close together.

Fig. 14.1.7(b) shows the geometry of an eight-wheeled vehicle. A
second 'front' axle is necessary when the load on one axle is too

great, especially since twin wheels cannot be fitted at the front. Each front axle has the normal Ackermann layout, and in order to turn the first axle through a larger angle, a special drag-link system is

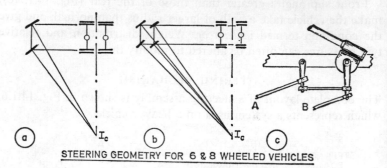

STEERING GEOMETRY FOR 6 & 8 WHEELED VEHICLES

FIG. 14.1.7

employed (Fig. 14.1.7(c)). This diagram shows the layout used to move A through a smaller distance than B.

On six-wheeled vehicles it is sometimes better to employ two steered axles and one twin-tyred rear axle. In this case the 'front' axles will be linked in a manner similar to the eight-wheeled arrangement.

CAMBER, CASTOR AND KING PIN INCLINATION

CENTRE POINT STEERING

Fig. 14.2.1 shows a vertical wheel and king pin arrangement, which has the following disadvantages:

(1) Large splaying-out effect of the wheel—the wheels are pushed along by the force F which is opposed by the resistance R. These two forces produce a couple $(F \times X)$ which becomes very large when the front brakes are applied.

(2) Heavy steering due to the distance between king pin and wheel centre. The wheel has to be moved in an arc around the pin; the radius being x.

(3) Large bending stress on the stub axle and king pin.

To overcome these problems, the wheel and king pin are so arranged that the 'offset' distance x is reduced. When the offset is eliminated, i.e. when the centre line of the wheel meets the centre

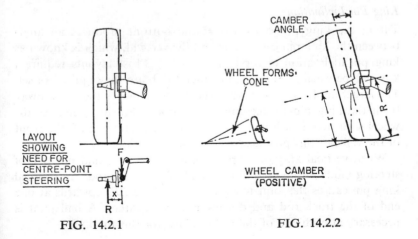

LAYOUT
SHOWING
NEED FOR
CENTRE-POINT
STEERING

CAMBER ANGLE

WHEEL FORMS·
CONE

WHEEL CAMBER
(POSITIVE)

FIG. 14.2.1   FIG. 14.2.2

line of the king pin at the road surface, the condition is termed *centre point steering*. This can be obtained by (a) camber, (b) king pin inclination or (c) dished wheels.

Centre point steering appears to be ideal, but the 'spread' effect of the pneumatic tyre causes the wheel to 'scrub' and give hard steering and tyre wear, so a slight rolling action is induced by arranging the offset x to be 10% to 25% of the tyre tread width.

Camber

The downset of the stub axle tilts the wheel outwards at the top; the angle formed between the vertical and the wheel is termed the *camber angle*.

The bending stress on the stub axle and the 'splaying out' couple are reduced, but the different rolling radii of the tyre produce a cone effect, which causes tyre wear and another splaying out action. Providing both camber angles are equal, this action will be balanced, but if this is not so the vehicle will pull to the side of greater camber. (Unequal tyre pressures can also produce this effect.)

Some independent suspension systems vary the camber angle as the spring deflects: this changes from the positive form shown in Fig. 14.2.2 to the negative form, which is the inner tilt of the wheel.

Since camber is bad from a tyre wear point of view, the angle seldom exceeds 2°. This is sufficient to give a slight outward-thrusting torque and allow for road camber and slight deflections of the beam or suspension members.

King Pin Inclination

Tilting the king pin outwards at the bottom produces an angle between the king pin centre line and the vertical, which is known as king pin inclination or k.p.i. (Fig. 14.2.3). Most layouts require a k.p.i. of between 5° and 10°, in order to obtain the required offset. The larger angles are used when the designer moves the wheel away from the king pin to accommodate brakes, bearings, etc. As the wheel is turned, it will move in the plane AA, and will lift the front of the vehicle: this produces a self-centring action.

When vertical king pins are used, a simple yoke and pin tyre of steering joint can be used at each end of the track rod. An inclined king pin causes the joint to move in the plane BB, upwards at one end of the track rod and downwards at the other. A ball joint is necessary at each end of the rod to allow for this motion.

Dished Wheels

By slightly dishing the wheel (Fig. 14.2.4), the amount of camber and k.p.i. may be reduced. The light pressed-steel wheel must not be excessively dished, or the strength will be diminished.

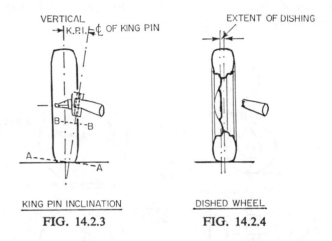

KING PIN INCLINATION

FIG. 14.2.3

DISHED WHEEL

FIG. 14.2.4

CASTOR

Wheel castor is given to enable the driver to 'feel' the straight-ahead position so that he may steer a straight path. When cornering, a torque must be exerted on the steering wheel to overcome the self-centring or castoring action, which tends to keep the wheels pointing straight ahead. From this introduction it will be seen that too much castor produces hard steering, whereas to little causes 'wander'.

The action of this steering feature may be understood by considering the operation of a simple furniture castor (Fig. 14.2.5(a)) fitted to a tea trolley. When a force is exerted on the trolley, it moves in the direction of the force. The effect of this force on the castor is shown in the diagram: the force F acting at the pivot and the resistance acting at the wheel produce a couple which rotates the castor to a position where the wheel is following the line of thrust.

On a motor vehicle the pivot centre line is normally made to strike the road in front of the centre of contact of the wheel. In this case the wheel will follow the path taken by the pivot centre line, which will always be in front of the vehicle.

Castor can be obtained by mounting a vertical king pin in front of the wheel (Fig. 14.2.5(b)) or by inclining the king pin forward at the bottom (Fig. 14.2.5(c)) to give a castor angle. The latter is simpler, and most manufacturers use this arrangement. The angle is generally between 2° and 5°; but once again reference must be made to the manufacturer's recommendation for castor angle and tolerance (normally $\pm\frac{1}{2}°$ for all steering angles).

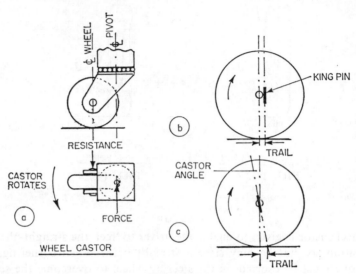

FIG. 14.2.5

The tilting of the king pin can be arranged by using one of the following methods:
(1) upper independent suspension members mounted slightly to the rear of the lower members
(2) tilting the axle beam by:
    (a) fitting wedges between axle and spring
    (b) mounting the axle towards the front of a laminated spring
    (c) inclining the laminated spring.

Fig. 14.2.5 shows the pivot centre line contacting the road in front of the centre line of the wheel. This commonly used arrangement is known as *positive castor*. Occasionally the wheel is made to lead the pivot centre line, and *negative castor* is the term used in this case.

WHEEL ALIGNMENT

Both wheels must be parallel when the vehicle is travelling straight ahead.

To achieve this condition, allowance must be made for clearance in the steering joints which is taken up by the splaying out or in of the wheels. In the case of rear-wheel drive vehicles, the wheels normally move outwards, so a 'toe-in' to the extent of $\frac{1}{16}$–$\frac{1}{8}$ in (1·5–3·0 mm) is given (vice-versa for front-wheel drive vehicles).

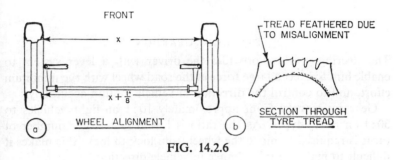

FIG. 14.2.6

Fig. 14.2.6(a) shows the front wheels set to a toe-in of $\frac{1}{8}$ in. This is measured at hub height on the rim of the wheel after taking into account any run-out (buckle) of the wheel. Wheel alignment is varied by altering the length of the track rod. Fig. 14.2.6(b) shows the form of tyre wear produced by misaligned wheels.

STEERING COMPONENTS

STEERING GEARBOX

The steering gearbox provides the driver with a lever system to enable him to exert a large force at the road wheel with the minimum effort, and to control the direction of vehicle motion accurately.

Gear ratios vary from approximately 10:1 on light vehicles to 30:1 on heavy types. As the ratio is lowered, a larger number of turns is required to move the wheel from lock to lock: this makes it difficult to make a rapid change in vehicle direction.

By varying the efficiency, the degree of reversibility (a reversible gear transmits motion from steering wheel to drop arm and vice-versa) can be controlled, to enable the driver to 'feel' the wheels, but yet not subject him to major road shocks.

TYPES OF STEERING GEAR

The main types of steering box in use today are:
(1) worm and sector
(2) screw and nut
(3) recirculating ball
(4) cam and peg
(5) worm and roller
(6) rack and pinion.

Worm and Sector

This type has been developed from a worm and wheel. which was one of the earliest designs of box.

A case-hardened steel worm and sector are located by bearings in a malleable iron or light alloy casing. Fig. 14.3.1 shows the worm connected to the inner column and the sector forming a part of the rocker shaft.

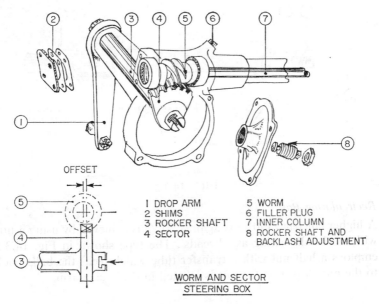

OFFSET

1 DROP ARM	5 WORM
2 SHIMS	6 FILLER PLUG
3 ROCKER SHAFT	7 INNER COLUMN
4 SECTOR	8 ROCKER SHAFT AND BACKLASH ADJUSTMENT

WORM AND SECTOR
STEERING BOX

FIG. 14.3.1

Most steering boxes are provided with the following adjustments:
(1) end float of inner column—generally shim adjustment
(2) end float or rocker shaft—shim or screw adjustment
(3) backlash between gears—gears can be moved closer together.

The greatest wear takes place in the straight-ahead position of the box, so the gear is normally made with a larger backlash in the lock positions. This reduces the risk of seizure at full lock when the box is adjusted to compensate for wear. It is essential to reduce end float and backlash to a minimum, but tight spots must be avoided.

Steering-box lubrication is provided by filling the box to the level of the plug with normal gear oil.

Screw and Nut (Fig. 14.3.2)
A phosphor-bronze or steel nut is screwed on to a multi-start Acme thread formed on the inner column. Rotation of the nut is prevented by a ball fitted in the rocker arm. Axial thrust of the column is taken by a single ball race fitted at the top end, and the nut sliding in the housing supports the lower end. The end float of the inner column is adjusted by the nut at the top end.

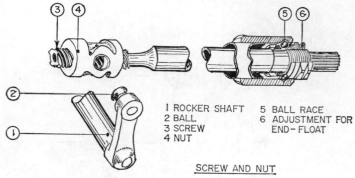

I ROCKER SHAFT	5 BALL RACE
2 BALL	6 ADJUSTMENT FOR
3 SCREW	END-FLOAT
4 NUT	

SCREW AND NUT

FIG. 14.3.2

Recirculating Ball

A higher efficiency (90% as against 50%) is achieved by using a nut with steel balls acting as 'threads'. The type shown in Fig. 14.3.3 employs a half nut with a transfer tube which feeds the balls back to the nut. A peg on the nut is located in the rocker arm.

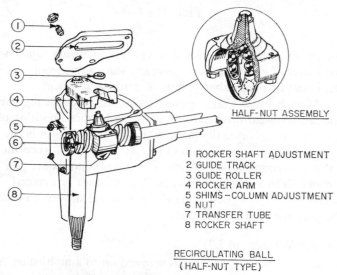

HALF-NUT ASSEMBLY

I ROCKER SHAFT ADJUSTMENT
2 GUIDE TRACK
3 GUIDE ROLLER
4 ROCKER ARM
5 SHIMS – COLUMN ADJUSTMENT
6 NUT
7 TRANSFER TUBE
8 ROCKER SHAFT

RECIRCULATING BALL
(HALF-NUT TYPE)

FIG. 14.3.3

Cam and Peg (Fig. 14.3.4)

A tapered peg in the rocker arm engages with a special cam formed on the inner column. The end float of the column is controlled by shims, and an adjusting screw on the side cover governs the backlash and end float of the rocker shaft.

A modified form known as the *high efficiency cam and peg gear* uses a peg which is allowed to rotate in bearings in the rocker arm.

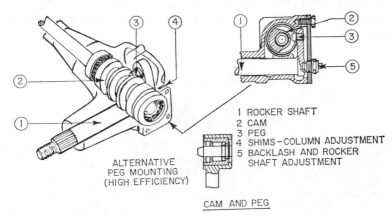

ALTERNATIVE
PEG MOUNTING
(HIGH EFFICIENCY)

1 ROCKER SHAFT
2 CAM
3 PEG
4 SHIMS – COLUMN ADJUSTMENT
5 BACKLASH AND ROCKER
  SHAFT ADJUSTMENT

CAM AND PEG

FIG. 14.3.4

Worm and Roller (Fig. 14.3.5)

A roller follower fitted to the rocker shaft engages with an hourglass worm. The small offset of the roller to the worm enables an adjusting screw to control backlash and end float of the rocker shaft.

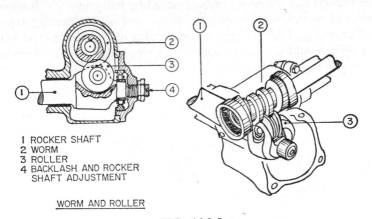

1 ROCKER SHAFT
2 WORM
3 ROLLER
4 BACKLASH AND ROCKER
  SHAFT ADJUSTMENT

WORM AND ROLLER

FIG. 14.3.5

Rack and Pinion (Fig. 14.3.6)

This type is often used with i.f.s. where the rack acts as the centre section of a three-piece track rod. The pinion is normally connected to the column by a universal joint to enable the box to be centrally mounted. Each end of the rack has a ball connection to the track rod, and spring pads acting on the underside of the rack reduce the backlash to a minimum.

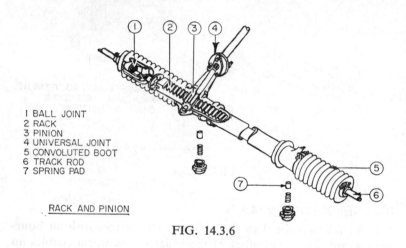

1 BALL JOINT
2 RACK
3 PINION
4 UNIVERSAL JOINT
5 CONVOLUTED BOOT
6 TRACK ROD
7 SPRING PAD

RACK AND PINION

FIG. 14.3.6

STEERING JOINTS

The various steering levers are connected by ball joints which allow universal movement. Many new models use self-lubricating types similar to Fig. 14.3.7. Fitted on either side of the plated steel ball is a split moulded bearing which is compounded with a specially developed metallic lubricant.

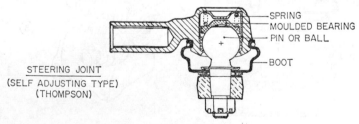

SPRING
MOULDED BEARING
PIN OR BALL

BOOT

STEERING JOINT
(SELF ADJUSTING TYPE)
(THOMPSON)

FIG. 14.3.7

FRONT HUB CONSTRUCTION

Fig. 14.3.8 shows a typical bearing arrangement for a front hub. Two adjustable taper roller bearings, spaced as wide apart as possible, are fitted between the stub axle and the malleable iron or steel

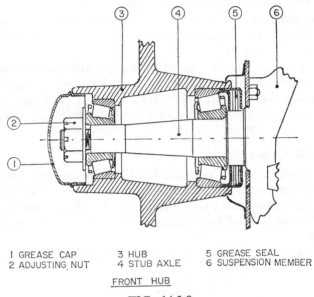

| 1 GREASE CAP | 3 HUB | 5 GREASE SEAL |
| 2 ADJUSTING NUT | 4 STUB AXLE | 6 SUSPENSION MEMBER |

FRONT HUB

FIG. 14.3.8

cast hub. The hub is adjusted by tightening the nut slowly until all clearance is eliminated, and then slackening off one 'flat'.

The bearings are lubricated by packing each bearing and half the cavity between with a lime-soap grease of medium consistency. A seal prevents the grease from entering the brake drum.

POWER-ASSISTED STEERING

With increased loads on steered wheels and wider section tyres the large effort required at the steering wheel makes the driver's job very tiring and difficult. Improvements such as an increase in the mechanical efficiency of the steering system or lower steering box ratios help to reduce drive fatigue, but if the latter is not limited the number of turns made by the steering wheel to move it from lock to lock becomes troublesome. When steering effort exceeds a safe maximum some method must be found and power assistance is the answer.

The power assistance arrangement should obey certain requirements:

(1) It must be 'fail-safe'—if the power system fails the driver must still be able to retain effective control.

(2) The degree of assistance should be proportional to the effort applied by the driver and the driver must be able to retain the 'feel' of the wheels.

Power can be supplied by pneumatic or hydraulic means. Very heavy commercial vehicles already having a compressed-air braking system sometimes utilise this air for steering purposes, whereas designers of other vehicles favour a less bulky hydraulic system.

Hydraulic System

Hydraulically operated power-assisted systems are based on either a constant pressure or constant flow layout—the former employs a hydraulic accumulator to store the pressure, whereas the latter has fluid flowing around the system continuously until assistance is needed.

Fig. 14.3.9 shows the essential components required to operate a

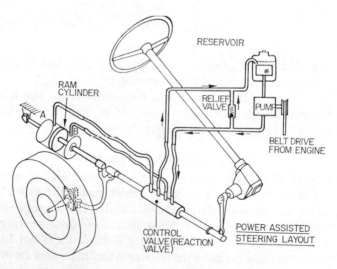

FIG. 14.3.9

constant flow system. In addition to the normal steering components
the system requires a pump, control valve and ram cylinder.

Pump   Generally an eccentric-rotor type (Fig. 5.3.2) driven by a
vee belt from the engine crankshaft. Attached to the pump is a fluid
reservoir and this normally contains a low-viscosity mineral oil
similar to the type used in suspension dampers. A pressure relief
valve limits the maximum pressure (1000 lbf/in² or 7 MN/m²) and
when this is reached the oil passes from the pump outlet back to the
reservoir.

Control Valve (or Reaction Valve)   In Fig. 14.3.9 the valve is
positioned between the two halves of the drag link, but in modern
applications it can be included together with the ram cylinder in the
steering box.

A spool type valve, attached to one half of the drag link, is
held central in the valve body by means of two reaction springs.
Flexible pipes connect the valve to the ram cylinder, pump and
reservoir.

Ram Cylinder   A double acting ram piston connects with the steering
arm to supply the appropriate force to assist the driver. The force
must act in either direction and this is achieved by venting one side
and pressurising the other side of the cylinder. Assistance given by
the ram will depend on the fluid pressure supplied to it by the control
valve.

Operation of the system will depend on the torque that the driver
applies to the steering wheel. Under low torque conditions no assistance is required and this condition is represented by Fig. 14.3.10.

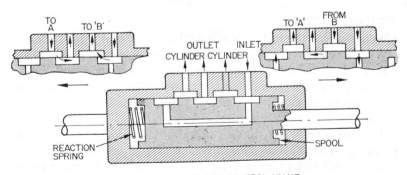

PRINCIPLE OF THE CONTROL VALVE

FIG. 14.3.10

Low torque on the wheel will be insufficient to overcome the reaction springs in the control valve, so fluid will be able to flow back to the reservoir. During this phase the control valve remains in the 'neutral' position and offers no resistance to the oil flow to or from the ram cylinder.

When the torque applied by the driver reached a predetermined value, which is governed by the strength of the reaction springs, the greater force acting in the drag link is capable of moving the valve in relation to its body. This action of the valve connects one side of the ram to the pump and the other side vents to the reservoir. Interruption of the fluid circuit in this way causes the pump pressure to build up quickly. As this occurs the thrust on the ram will also build up until a point is reached where the movement of the ram overcomes the resistance of the road wheel. At this stage the force in the drag link will reduce, the valve will return to the 'neutral 'position and the pressure in the complete system will drop to the original value. Consideration of this sequence shows that steering wheel torque opens the valve and the ram exerts a proportional thrust to close the valve.

Turning the steering wheel the opposite way produces a similar action with the exception that the control valve movement now directs fluid to the other side of the ram piston.

The design of reaction valve and spring takes many different forms. One manufacturer uses a small torsion bar to transmit the drive between the inner column and the gear in the box. When the torque exceeds a given amount the bar twists, moves a valve and activates the ram.

Pneumatic System

Compared with the hydraulic system the air-pressure arrangement is rarely used in this country except for very heavy commercial vehicles. These vehicles already use air-powered brakes, so with slight modification to the size of the reservoir to allow for the heavy air consumption of the steering system, an economic power supply can be obtained.

In many ways the layout and operation of an air-pressure system is similar to the hydraulic arrangement already described.

Air, stored at a pressure in the main reservoir, is delivered to the reaction valve. When the torque applied to the steering wheel exceeds a given value, the valve opens and supplies air to one side of the ram piston; the other half of the cylinder vented to atmosphere. As soon as the resistance to wheel movement is overcome, the valve shuts off the air supply, opens an outlet valve, and allows the ram cylinder to discharge.

The control valve can be sited in the steering box or mounted in any component which reacts to steering movement.

15.1

GENERAL FRAME CONSTRUCTION

THE CHASSIS FRAME

The chassis frame is the structural member to which the main components, such as engine, transmission and body, are attached: i.e. it is the 'skeleton' of the vehicle.

In order to appreciate the various designs, consider the main deflections which the frame has to resist.

Fig. 15.1.1(a) shows the axles mounted by springs on to side members, which are held apart by cross members. This frame would be distorted by the following forces:

(1) the weight of the components and passengers gives a bending action which tends to cause a sagging effect (Fig. 15.1.1(b))

(2) a horizontal force, given by road shocks, will act on the end of the side members to deflect the rectangular frame towards the

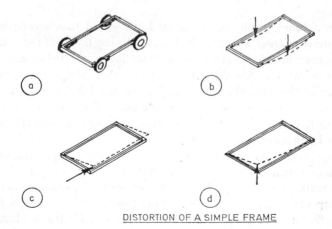

DISTORTION OF A SIMPLE FRAME

FIG. 15.1.1

parallelogram form shown in Fig. 15.1.1(c) (this is often known as *lozenging*)
(3) an upward force on the wheel, caused by road shocks, will twist the frame to give a torsional effect (Fig. 15.1.1(d)).
The design of the frame must be as light as possible, but yet effectively resist these deflections.

FRAME SECTIONS

The ideal frame section has a good resistance to bending and torsional effects. Three main forms are in general use:
(1) *channel* (Fig. 15.1.2(a)), which provides good resistance to bending but is poor as regards torsion
(2) *tubular* (Fig. 15.1.2(b)), which gives good resistance to torsion but poor resistance to bending
(3) *box* (Fig. 15.1.2(c)), which gives comparatively good resistance to bending and torsion.

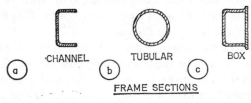

CHANNEL   TUBULAR   BOX

(a)   (b)   (c)

FRAME SECTIONS

FIG. 15.1.2

When a beam bends, the material is subjected to a tensile and a compressive stress. Fig. 15.1.3(a) shows the top layers of the material being compressed, whereas the bottom layers are being extended. The mid layer is not subjected to tension or compression, and is known as the neutral axis. Some idea of the amount of stress can be given by referring to the cross-section of the beam shown in Fig. 15.1.3(b); the length of each horizontal line represents the stress taken by that layer.

From the above it will be seen that a slightly deeper channel or box section can give the same resistance to bending as a much heavier solid rectangular section. In a similar manner, the distance between the top compression member and the lower tension member is the main factor governing the strength of the tubular frame shown in Fig. 15.1.3(c).

Whenever a hole has to be drilled in a chassis member, either to reduce weight or to attach something, it should be positioned in a low-stress region, e.g. the neutral axis.

When a force is applied to the centre of a beam (Fig 15.1.3(d)),

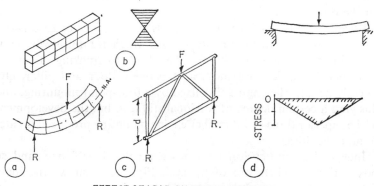

EFFECT OF LOAD ON FRAME MEMBERS

FIG. 15.1.3

there is a tendency for the material to break at the centre: this is because the stress is greatest at this point, as shown in the diagram. In order to resist this stress, either the beam must have the same deep section throughout its length, or a varying section of a depth proportional to the stress: the latter design would be much lighter.

FRAME DESIGN

Fig. 15.1.4 shows a pictorial view of a frame which was in common use until i.f.s. was introduced. The pressed-steel channel-section side members are upswept over the axles, and inswept at the front,

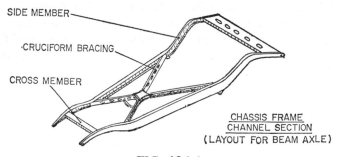

CHASSIS FRAME
CHANNEL SECTION
(LAYOUT FOR BEAM AXLE)

FIG. 15.1.4

to give clearance for 'bump' movement of the axles and steering movement of the front wheels. Bending of the side member is resisted by varying the depth of section to suit the stress.

Lozenging of the frame is prevented by using a cruciform or 'X' type bracing; this is riveted to a plate at the centre to form a tunnel for the propeller shaft.

Because this type of frame has a very poor resistance to torsion, the body shell has to take many stresses which are not always considered in the design calculations. This leads to cracking of certain body panels, rattles and movement between door and pillar, etc. In early designs the engine was fixed by a four-point mounting, and this gave a certain degree of torsional stiffness, but the development of the superior three-point rubber engine mounting produced greater frame difficulties.

Independent suspension demands a much stiffer frame, and so box-section members are often used. Fig. 15.1.5 shows the main details of a frame which is used with i.f.s.

CHASSIS FRAME
BOX SECTION
(USED WITH I.F.S.)
FIG. 15.1.5

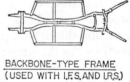

BACKBONE-TYPE FRAME
(USED WITH I.F.S. AND I.R.S.)
FIG. 15.1.6

One popular car using four independently sprung wheels employs a back-bone type of frame (Fig. 15.1.6). Two main longitudinal box-section members are welded close together at the centre, and then diverge to accommodate the engine at the front and the 'fixed' final-drive housing at the rear. The floor is mounted on the laterally extended framework.

COMMERCIAL VEHICLE FRAMES

FRAME MATERIAL

Most frame members are manufactured from low carbon steel (0·15–0·25%) although some highly stressed commercial vehicle frames are made from a steel of slightly higher carbon content (0·15–0·30%) which is responsive to heat treatment.

FRAME DESIGN

Generally the truck frame has a uniform width throughout. Fig. 15.2.1 shows two substantial channel-section side members, onto which

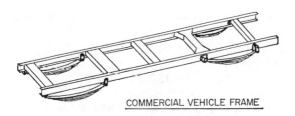

COMMERCIAL VEHICLE FRAME

FIG. 15.2.1

are riveted or welded a number of cross members. These are located at the front end of the frame to support the radiator, at the rear of the engine, half-way along the frame to locate the propeller shaft centre bearing, at the front of the rear spring and at the end of the frame. Rear spring hangers mounted on the outside of the frame support the rear springs. Most arrangements use flexible rubber mountings between the cab and frame to insulate against road shocks and engine vibrations.

FRAME REPAIRS

Whenever the vehicle has been involved in a major collision, it is necessary to check the frame alignment. A visual check generally reveals major misalignment, but if this is not obvious a frame check will be required. This is conducted as follows:

(1) *Wheel base check* (Fig. 15.2.2(a))   Set the front wheels in the straight-ahead position and check the wheel base on each side.

(2) *Alignment* (Fig.15.2.2(b))   After checking to verify that the rear wheels are parallel with each other, hold a cord or straight edge against the rear wheel: then turn the front wheel until it is parallel with the cord, and note the clearance (if any) between the wheel and cord. This should be the same on both sides.

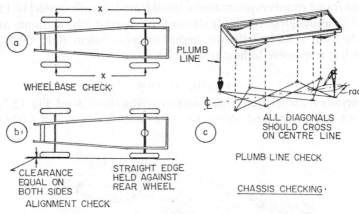

WHEELBASE CHECK

PLUMB LINE

ALL DIAGONALS SHOULD CROSS ON CENTRE LINE

PLUMB LINE CHECK

CLEARANCE EQUAL ON BOTH SIDES

STRAIGHT EDGE HELD AGAINST REAR WHEEL

CHASSIS CHECKING

ALIGNMENT CHECK

15.2.2

(3) *Plumb line check* (Fig. 15.2.2(c))   Drop a plumb line from the outside of each fixed shackle of the spring to give eight chalk marks on the floor. Connect up the points as shown; all diagonals should cross the centre line if the frame is correctly aligned.

The tolerance for each check depends on the size of frame, but $\frac{1}{4}$ in (6 mm) is often laid down as the maximum.

Frame straightening is carried out by using jacks and chains, and is a specialised repair. Unless the frame has been heat treated it is possible to heat the damaged member to ease the straightening operation.

Cracks can be repaired by welding, and when a reinforcement plate is fitted, it is advisable to taper the end to avoid any sudden change in cross-sectional area.

INTEGRAL CONSTRUCTION OF FRAMES

In the earlier work on frames it was said that the body shell resisted torsional movement of a simple frame, but defects in the construction soon showed up because the shell was not designed to withstand these stresses. About 1934, the development of the all-steel body made possible the elimination of a separate frame, the body shell being capable of withstanding the various frame stresses when suitably designed. This *frameless* or *integral* arrangement gives a stiff, light construction, which is particularly suitable for mass-produced vehicles, and since 1945 most light cars have been built with this construction.

Fig. 15.3.1(a) shows a diagrammatic sketch of a body shell which may be considered as a simple frame.

The position of the bending neutral axis indicates that the floor

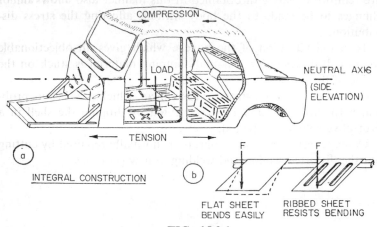

FIG. 15.3.1

is in tension and the roof is in compression. Since these two members are widely spaced, thin sheet metal, ribbed to give increased stiffness (Fig. 15.3.1(b)), can be used. Torsional stiffness of the body can be achieved by forming a scuttle at the front, and by cross ties mounted behind the rear seat squab.

The thickness of the material depends on the stress taken by the panel: structural members such as sills, rails and pillars are often about 0·045 in (1·1 mm) thick, whereas panels such as the roof are 0·035 in (0·9 mm) thick. Component attachment points require reinforcement with thicker material, and in some cases a separate sub-frame is used to mount such items as engine and i.f.s. members. This frame is sometimes connected to the body by rubber insulation mountings.

Since extremely good ductility is essential for the pressing of the panels, a very low (0·1 %) carbon steel is required. The low strength [18 tonf/in² (278 MN/m²)] of this material means that structural members must be stiffened by forming the thin steel sheet into intricate sections, and spot welding into position. Some idea of the number of separate pressings can be gained by the fact that approximately 4000 spot welds are used on a modern car body.

A modified construction is necessary when the roof cannot be used as a 'compression' member. This occurs on drop head coupé models, and in recent instances when thinner pillars are used to improve visibility. To achieve the required stiffness, an 'underbody' frame is incorporated in the main shell, and 'torsional' members are reinforced. Strength obtained in this manner also allows minor changes to be made to the body without affecting the stress distribution.

To avoid vibration of the panels, which gives an objectionable sound called *drumming*, a sound-damping material is stuck on the inside of the panels.

Corrosion of certain structural members, which is a serious problem with this construction, is prevented by dipping the shell in a protective solution to seal all joints.

Damage resulting from a collision is normally repaired by cutting out the distorted section and welding in new pressings.

Suspension Systems

16.1

TYPES AND CHARACTERISTICS OF METAL SPRINGS

PURPOSE OF A SPRING

Mounting the axle directly to the frame of a vehicle would subject the occupants and general components to severe shocks. This can be seen from Fig. 16.1.1(a), which shows the upward movement of the frame when the wheel strikes a bump. In this case the vertical acceleration would cause considerable discomfort: most probably the reluctance of the vehicle frame to move upwards quickly (inertia) would buckle the wheel. (You will have observed this effect when riding a bicycle over a bump.)

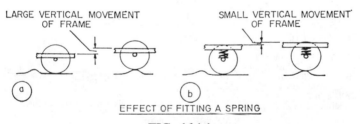

LARGE VERTICAL MOVEMENT OF FRAME

SMALL VERTICAL MOVEMENT OF FRAME

a

b

EFFECT OF FITTING A SPRING

FIG. 16.1.1

A spring fitted between the wheel and the frame allows the wheel to move up and down without causing similar movement of the frame (Fig. 16.1.1(b)). This spring absorbs road shocks, and allows the wheel to follow the irregular contour of the road surface: for this purpose the wheel assembly should be as light as possible.

Road shocks can be further reduced by fitting a 'spring' to the wheel—a pneumatic tyre.

The mechanism introduced between the wheel and the frame is termed the suspension system, the main items being the spring and damper.

TYPES OF SPRING

Various forms of springing can be used. These are:
(1) steel—laminated, helical and torsion bar
(2) rubber
(3) pneumatic.

Laminated or Leaf Springs

Low cost and simple connection to axle make this type very popular for rear suspension.

The main details of a semi-elliptic spring are shown in Fig. 16.1.2(a). A main leaf, rolled at each end to form an eye, has a

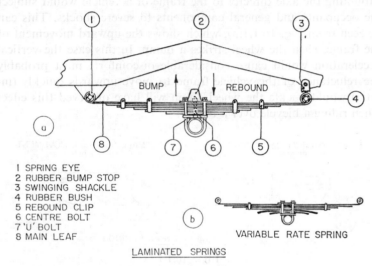

1 SPRING EYE
2 RUBBER BUMP STOP
3 SWINGING SHACKLE
4 RUBBER BUSH
5 REBOUND CLIP
6 CENTRE BOLT
7 'U' BOLT
8 MAIN LEAF

VARIABLE RATE SPRING

LAMINATED SPRINGS

FIG. 16.1.2

number of leaves clamped to it. To ensure a constant stress throughout the spring (see page 437—chassis frames), the leaves are graduated in length. Rebound clips transmit the load to some of the lower leaves during the return motion of the spring, and eliminate the need for fitting a large number of leaves above the main plate. Rubber bushes, fitted in each eye, allow for movement of the spring, and act as noise insulators. Alteration in spring length is accommodated by a swinging shackle.

The stiffness or rate [force required to deflect the spring 1 in (1 m)] of a leaf spring is governed by:
(1) length of spring —shorter spring, higher rate
(2) width of leaf   —wider   „   „   „
(3) thickness of leaf —thicker leaf,   „   „   „
(4) number of leaves—greater number, „   „

To obtain a 'soft' ride, a low-rate spring is required, and this will deflect a larger amount under a given load. Normal springs have a constant rate, and give a deflection which is proportional to the load (Hooke's Law). However, if the lower leaves are set to a reverse camber (Fig. 16.1.2(b)), a stiffening-up of the spring will occur as deflection increases: this is called a progressive or variable rate spring.

As the laminated spring deflects, the plates or leaves slide over each other and cause inter-plate friction. Although this has a beneficial damping effect, the 'hard' ride, noise and wear make it necessary to reduce this friction as much as possible. Old designs of spring had to be sprayed with penetrating oil, but nowadays special features are incorporated to eliminate the need for periodic attention. These are:
(1) synthetic rubber buttons fitted at the ends of the leaves
(2) reducing the number of leaves (as the number is reduced, the width must be increased)
(3) interleaf plates of low friction material.

To gain the full advantage of item (2) many springs in use today have only one leaf. Overstressing at the centre of the spring is avoided by using a tapered leaf; thin at the ends and thick in the centre.

Helical Spring

This spring is normally used in conjunction with independent suspension, although the absence of inter-plate friction has prompted some manufacturers to use it at the rear. Coil and torsion bar springs are superior to the leaf springs as regards energy storage (energy stored in a given weight of spring), but whereas the leaf spring fulfils many duties, the other types require extra members and this adds to the basic weight.

The rate of the spring is governed by the length and diameter of the wire. The wire is wound in the form of a coil, so the length will be controlled by the diameter of the coil and the number of active coils.

Torsion Bar

This is a straight bar of circular or square section anchored to the
frame at one end, and at the other end connected by a lever or wishbone-shaped member to the wheel.

Fig. 16.1.3 shows a torsion bar suspension system used on a car.
At each end of the bar the diameter is increased and serrations
connect the bar with the levers. Adjustment is provided at the frame
end to 'level' the suspension.

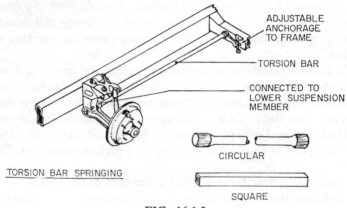

FIG. 16.1.3

Since the coil spring is a form of torsion bar, the rate of both
springs is governed by the same factors—length and diameter. If
the length is increased or the diameter is decreased, the rate will
decrease, i.e. the spring will be softer.

Spring Material

The material used for springs must be capable of withstanding high
stresses and resisting fatigue. Early designs used high-carbon steel,
but nowadays low-percentage alloy steels such as silico-manganese
are used.

AIR SUSPENSION

This form of suspension has been widely used in the U.S.A. and occasionally in this country.

Fig. 16.2.1 shows a diagrammatic layout of an air-suspension system—for clarity, only one air spring is drawn.

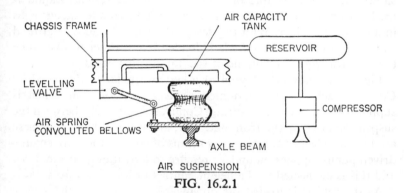

AIR SUSPENSION

FIG. 16.2.1

The reinforced rubber bellows are fitted between the axle and the frame-mounted air capacity tank. Air supply to the spring is regulated by a levelling valve, which can be adjusted to maintain a set distance between frame and ground, irrespective of load: a delay device incorporated in the valve presents instantaneous correction of rebound and roll movements. A compressor supplies the reservoir with air to maintain a pressure of 80–100 lbf/in² (550–700 kN/m²).

When a load is gradually applied to the frame, the spring will be compressed and the levelling valve will be opened to supply air to the spring. This additional air will extend the bellows and raise the frame to the original position, thereby closing the valve.

This type of suspension offers the following advantages:
(1) constant step height in the case of P.S.V.s (Public Service Vehicles)
(2) variable rate—progressive in action (the stiffness of the spring increases as the deflection increases)
(3) constant frequency of vibration—metal springs oscillate more rapidly when the vehicle is unladen.

HYDRO-PNEUMATIC SUSPENSION

This expensive system differs from the normal pneumatic suspension in a number of ways. One main difference is that the suspension unit is supported by a mass of gas which remains constant irrespective of the load carried by the wheel. Gas pressure will increase progressively as the volume is reduced and this desirable feature means that the suspension stiffens as the load on the wheel increases. Fig. 16.2.2 shows the basic principle of a hydro-pneumatic system. Liquid is used to transmit the force from the suspension piston to nitrogen gas in a closed container. With the design shown, a decrease in ground clearance occurs as the vehicle is loaded, so in order to overcome this disadvantage, the volume of the liquid is increased.

Fig. 16.2.3 shows the layout of a system similar to that used by Citroën. Each wheel is mounted on a suspension arm which is supported by a pneumatic spring. Connected traversely, between the suspension arms at the front and rear, are anti-roll bars, and these are linked to height correctors by means of control rods. An engine-driven pump supplies oil under pressure to a hydraulic accumulator and this is connected to the height control or levelling valves.

As the vehicle is loaded the downward movement of the vehicle

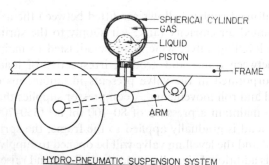

HYDRO-PNEUMATIC SUSPENSION SYSTEM
FIG. 16.2.2

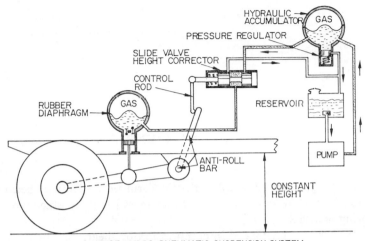

HYDRAULIC
ACCUMULATOR GAS
PRESSURE REGULATOR
SLIDE VALVE
HEIGHT CORRECTOR
CONTROL
ROD
RUBBER
DIAPHRAGM GAS RESERVOIR
ANTI-ROLL
BAR PUMP
CONSTANT
HEIGHT

LAYOUT OF HYDRO-PNEUMATIC SUSPENSION SYSTEM

FIG. 16.2.3

structure causes rotation of the anti-roll bar. This moves the slide valve and uncovers the supply port to allow oil to flow from the accumulator to the suspension cylinders. When the vehicle reaches a predetermined height, which can be varied by a selector inside the car, the anti-roll bar and control rod moves the slide valve back to the 'neutral' position. A decrease on load gives a similar sequence except valve movement causes the oil in the suspension cylinder to be discharged back to the reservoir.

A delay device or dashpot is incorporated in the height corrector valve to prevent rapid oil flow past the valve when the wheel contacts a bump or dip in the road. Without this dashpot, sudden movements of the wheel would mean that the valve is continually working and this would give an unsatisfactory operation.

Damping is provided by partially separating the oil in the spherical chamber from the cylinder in which the piston slides. Small holes, closed by disc type valves, allow the oil to flow to and from cylinder and sphere in a manner similar to other hydraulic dampers.

In the Citroën application the hydraulic pressure is also used for power assistance in steering, braking and gear changing. One model employs a braking system with independent front and rear brake circuits, interconnected with the hydraulic suspension system. This arrangement proportions the effort applied at each brake to the load carried by the wheel.

16.3

RUBBER SUSPENSION

Much weight can be saved with this form of suspension, because rubber can store more energy per unit mass than any other type of spring material.

Rubber springs, loaded in compression or shear, may be used to act as the main suspension spring, or fitted in conjunction with metal springs to modify the suspension characteristics. Many suspension arrangements employ a large rubber 'bump' stop to stiffen the suspension spring at maximum deflection.

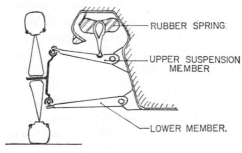

RUBBER SUSPENSION·

FIG. 16.3.1

Fig. 16.3.1 is a simplified drawing of a rubber-suspension system which is similar to the type used on a popular small car. The spring is positioned between the frame and the top link of the suspension system. By connecting the spring to a point near the link pivot, deflection of the spring can be reduced to a minimum, without reducing the total wheel movement.

This design of spring gives a *rising-rate* characteristic, i.e. it is 'soft' for small wheel movements but becomes harder as the spring deflects.

The energy released from the spring after deflection is found to be considerably less than that imparted to it. This internal loss of energy is termed *hysteresis*; it is an advantage, since lower duty dampers may be used.

Some rubber-suspension systems have a tendency to 'settle down' or 'creep' during the initial stages of service, and allowance must be made for this.

HYDROLASTIC SUSPENSION

This system is a development of the previous suspension arrangement and is intended to improve the vehicle's resistance to pitch— the tendency of the body to oscillate in a fore-and-aft direction. This movement is produced if the front springs compress and the rear springs extend simultaneously. The continuous forward and backward pitching motion gives a most uncomfortable ride and this would be serious if the frequency of vibration of front and rear springs was the same.

The Hydrolastic layout on a vehicle consists of rubber displacer units (Fig. 16.3.2) which are interconnected and mounted between the frame and the independent suspension linkage controlling the wheel. The interconnection is made with two pipes; one to link the left-hand-side units together and the other pipe to do a similar job

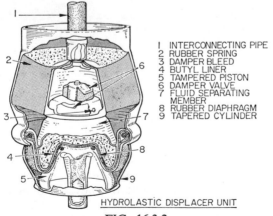

1 INTERCONNECTING PIPE
2 RUBBER SPRING
3 DAMPER BLEED
4 BUTYL LINER
5 TAMPERED PISTON
6 DAMPER VALVE
7 FLUID SEPARATING
   MEMBER
8 RUBBER DIAPHRAGM
9 TAPERED CYLINDER

HYDROLASTIC DISPLACER UNIT

FIG. 16.3.2

on the right-hand side. The system is pressurised with a liquid (water + alcohol + anti-corrosive agent) after the air has been extracted.

Each displacer unit comprises a rubber spring, metal separating member holding two rubber damper valves, rubber diaphragm attached to the suspension linkage holding the wheel, and a metal body which is secured to the frame of the vehicle.

Road irregularities normally tend to cause the vehicle to pitch, roll and bounce, so the operation of the system under these conditions will be considered.

Pitch A sudden upward movement of the front wheel causes the diaphragm to displace the fluid through the damper. This action will in turn force fluid along the pipe to the rear unit where it will move the diaphragm and raise the rear of the car to the level of the front (Fig. 16.3.3). When the front wheel descends, the fluid is

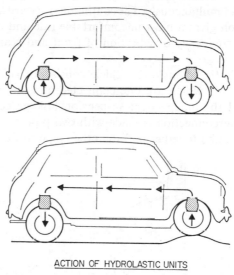

ACTION OF HYDROLASTIC UNITS

FIG. 16.3.3

returned and the vehicle settles back in its normal riding position. During this sequence the fluid has to pass the damper valve in each unit, so restriction to fluid flow at the valves and in the pipeline damps out the pitch oscillation tendency.

Roll When a vehicle is cornering, centrifugal action causes the body of the vehicle to tilt or roll outwards and this action is apparent when 'soft' conventional springs are used. The Hydrolastic system is soft' when a single wheel is moved, but if, as when cornering, the two outside suspension units are loaded, a stiffening of the system occurs. Under this type of loading fluid is not displaced from one unit to the other. Instead the increased fluid pressure deflects the rubber springs and these provide a marked resistance to the roll of the body.

Bounce This condition causes the four wheels to deflect at the same time, so all the Hydrolastic units will perform similar to the action of the outer units when they were reacting to roll.

16.4

THE DAMPER

PURPOSE OF A DAMPER

When the wheel strikes a bump, energy is given to the spring, which is deflected. When the bump is passed, rebound or release of the stored energy will take place, and will carry the spring past the normal position to set up an oscillating motion. This action is similar to the movement of a pendulum—a freely suspended pendulum will oscillate for a considerable time after being struck

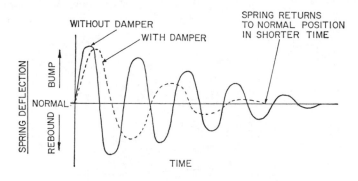

SPRING OSCILLATION CURVES

FIG. 16.4.1

(Fig. 16.4.1). In order to give a comfortable ride, some device must be fitted to absorb the energy stored in the spring and so reduce the number of oscillations occurring between the initial bump and the return of the spring to the rest position. This is the duty performed by the damper (often misleadingly called a shock absorber).

Early designs of damper utilised the friction between two sets of plates, one set attached to the frame and the other set connected to the axle. This type of damper converts the 'spring' energy into heat.

HYDRAULIC DAMPERS

Hydraulic dampers are the main type in use today. They dissipate the energy by pumping oil through small orifices. Resistance of the hydraulic damper increases as the speed of spring deflection increases, whereas the friction damper gives a constant resistance. The resistance to spring movement can apply to the rebound stroke only (single-acting), or to both the bump and rebound strokes (double-acting), or it can offer a differential action by resisting both strokes but exerting a greater action on the rebound.

The two main types of hydraulic damper are: (1) lever and (2) direct acting (telescopic).

Lever Type

Fig. 16.4.2 shows a diagrammatic view of a lever-type damper which is mounted to the frame and connected by a lever and link to the axle. The horizontal cylinder contains two pistons which are fitted with recuperator and pressure valves. A thin, mineral-base, damper oil is introduced to the level of the bottom of the filler plug.

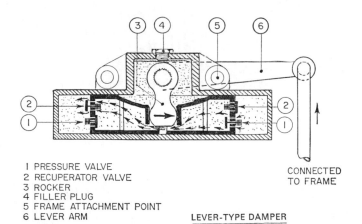

1 PRESSURE VALVE
2 RECUPERATOR VALVE
3 ROCKER
4 FILLER PLUG
5 FRAME ATTACHMENT POINT
6 LEVER ARM

CONNECTED
TO FRAME

LEVER-TYPE DAMPER

FIG. 16.4.2

Bump movement of the axle operates the damper pistons and displaces oil from one chamber to the other. Oil exerts pressure to open the pressure valve, flows through an orifice to provide resistance, and passes through the open recuperator valve to break down the depression created in the other chamber. Rebound of the spring produces a similar action in the opposite direction.

The actual damper differs from Fig. 16.4.2 in various ways—the valve construction and position are different, and in some designs the cylinders are mounted vertically.

Telescopic Direct-acting Type

As the name suggests, this damper is directly connected between the frame and the suspension member or axle.

Fig. 16.4.3 shows a diagrammatic layout which may be considered as two assemblies: top and bottom. The top assembly consists of a dirt excluder, piston rod and piston, which has two valves to seal small orifices. The lower assembly comprises two thin steel tubes which form the cylinder and reservoir. A two-way valve block is

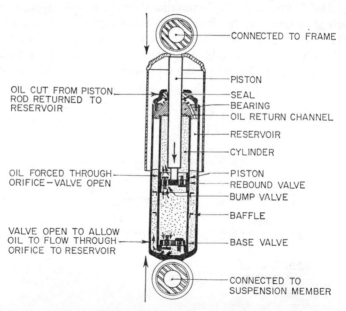

TELESCOPIC DIRECT-ACTING DAMPER

FIG. 16.4.3

fitted at the bottom of the cylinder, and a bearing and seal for the piston rod is at the top end. A thin type of damper oil completely fills the cylinder and nearly fills the reservoir. Rubber bushed eyes, formed at each end of the damper, provide the connection to the frame and axle. A welded, completely sealed unit is used with cars, but an oil filler plug is provided on larger commercial vehicle dampers.

Bump movement of the axle pushes the piston into the cylinder and forces the oil through the appropriate orifice to the upper part of the cylinder. Since the volume above the piston is less than that below the piston, some oil will have to be forced out through the base valve to the reservoir. On rebound, a reverse flow will take place. Resistance to each stroke is governed by valve design and orifice diameter.

The long stroke of the direct-acting damper gives a much lower working pressure than the lever type previously described. Because of these lower stresses, the unit can be made cheaper and more reliable. In certain independent front suspension designs, the damper is mounted diagonally across the suspension to obtain maximum travel, but a more compact arrangement is achieved when it is fitted at the centre of the coil spring. Although best results are obtained by mounting the damper vertically, rear-axle stability may be improved by a diagonally mounted arrangement.

Dampers do not offer any marked resistance to body roll, since this is a slow movement. Roll stiffness is improved by fitting a stabiliser bar to connect both front suspension members. This anti-roll bar is a form of torsion bar, which is normally passed through rubber bushes in the frame.

INDEPENDENT FRONT SUSPENSION (i.f.s)

DISADVANTAGES OF BEAM AXLES

In order to appreciate the advantages of independent suspension, you should consider the disadvantages of the beam axle. These are:
(1) Small maximum spring deflection, therefore 'hard' springing— vertical axle movement is limited by the clearance between the axle and the engine.
(2) Steering geometry is not accurately controlled.

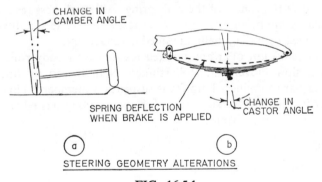

STEERING GEOMETRY ALTERATIONS

FIG. 16.5.1

(a) Fig. 16.5.1(a) shows the alteration to camber angle which occurs when one wheel strikes a bump. Sudden changes in camber angle cause the wheels, which are acting as a form of gyroscope, to 'flap' around the king pin. (This fault is known as *wheel shimmy*.)
(b) Fig. 16.5.1(b) shows the difference in castor angle when the spring is deflected.

(3) High unsprung weight—maximum wheel adhesion is not obtained.

(4) Engine normally has to be situated behind axle to give clearance. If the engine can be moved forward, it may be possible to accommodate all the passengers within the wheelbase—this gives greater comfort.

(5) Poor 'roll stiffness' at the front tends to produce *oversteer*—the front springs have to be mounted close together.

To overcome these disadvantages, independent front suspension (i.f.s.) is employed. This term is used to describe any system for connecting the wheels to the frame in which the movement of one wheel has no effect on the other wheel.

TYPES

Many types of i.f.s. have been used in the past, but nowadays, in this country, most designs fall under the heading of transverse link system.

TRANSVERSE LINK SYSTEM

Wishbone Type

The main details of this system are shown in Fig. 16.5.2. Two links, often parallel in the normal ride position, are made in a wishbone shape to provide fore-and-aft stiffness and resist braking torque. Each wishbone has three bearings, two inner bearings connecting with the frame and an outer one attaching to the stub axle carrier. Rubber or plastic (p.t.f.e.) bushes are fitted at the inner ends of the wishbone, and in many cases a ball joint at the outer end enables the stub axle to swivel. Springing can be provided by using coil springs in the position shown or above the upper wishbone, or a torsion bar at points A or B.

Early designs used wishbones of equal length, but the track variation (Fig. 16.5.2(b)) caused considerable tyre wear. This can be reduced by using wishbones of unequal length, the longer one at the bottom (Fig. 16.5.2(c)), but changes in camber angle will now have to be tolerated.

A constant castor angle is achieved with this design by mounting the top wishbone slightly behind the lower one.

In order to obtain the maximum wishbone length without restricting engine space, the wishbone axis is sometimes inclined towards the rear.

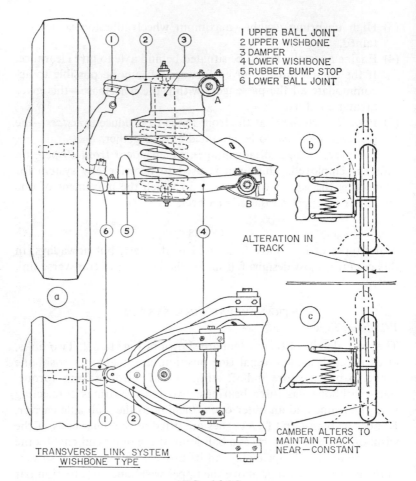

I UPPER BALL JOINT
2 UPPER WISHBONE
3 DAMPER
4 LOWER WISHBONE
5 RUBBER BUMP STOP
6 LOWER BALL JOINT

ALTERATION IN
TRACK

CAMBER ALTERS TO
MAINTAIN TRACK
NEAR—CONSTANT

TRANSVERSE LINK SYSTEM
WISHBONE TYPE

FIG. 16.5.2

Either a piston type damper is mounted to incorporate the inner bearings for the top wishbone, or a telescopic damper is fitted in the centre of the coil spring. In cases where torsion bar springing is used, a large movement of the telescopic damper can be achieved by mounting the damper diagonally: the lower end is connected to the outer end of the lower wishbone, and the upper end to a point on the frame just above the upper wishbone.

Double Link and Radius Rod (Fig. 16.5.3)

Two links, mounted in the normal manner, connect the stub axle carrier to the frame. A semi-trailing radius rod, fitted between the lower link and the frame, resists longitudinal dynamic loads and braking torque. The spring can be positioned above the top link, or a torsion bar can be connected to the inner ends of the lower link.

MacPherson Type

Fig. 16.5.4 shows the main details of this type of suspension. A long telescopic tube, incorporating the damper, is pivoted at the top end and rigidly connected to the stub axle at the lower end. Track control

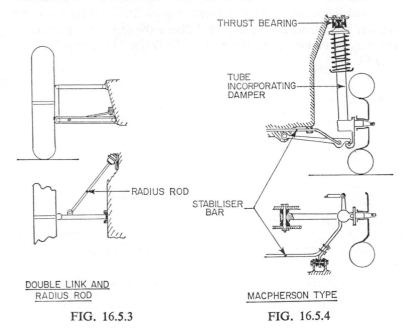

THRUST BEARING

TUBE INCORPORATING DAMPER

RADIUS ROD

STABILISER BAR

DOUBLE LINK AND RADIUS ROD

FIG. 16.5.3

MACPHERSON TYPE

FIG. 16.5.4

is maintained by a single transverse link, attached to the frame by rubber bushes and connected to the stub axle by a ball joint. The coil spring is located between the fixed and floating suspension members. Both front suspension lower links are interconnected by a stabiliser bar, which also provides the required fore-and-aft stiffness.

As in many other suspension systems, castor, camber and king pin inclination are set in production and cannot be altered.

Vertical Guide

The stub axle assembly is allowed to slide on a vertical guide which is rigidly attached to the frame (Fig. 16.5.5). Two springs, main and rebound, are fitted to the guide, which normally incorporates the damper, to form a completely enclosed unit. This system gives constant camber and castor, but it is difficult to connect a track rod in a manner which does not produce wheel misalignment when the wheel is deflected.

Swinging Arm

Two leading or trailing arms of equal length, i.e. longitudinally mounted links, are connected between the frame and the stub axle carrier. The spring can be mounted above the top arm, or a torsion bar may be connected to the arm at the frame location point (Fig. 16.5.6).

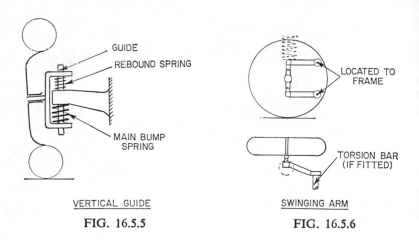

VERTICAL GUIDE

FIG. 16.5.5

SWINGING ARM

FIG. 16.5.6

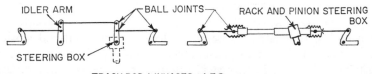

TRACK ROD LINKAGES – I.F.S.

FIG. 16.5.7

Track-rod Linkages

The one-piece track rod used with beam axle layouts is unsuitable for the majority of i.f.s. systems, because wheel alignment would be altered if one wheel was deflected up or down. The stub axle carrier in many i.f.s. systems moves in an arc, so in order to eliminate misalignment, the track rod connection must move in a similar arc. This condition can be met by using a three-piece track rod similar to the types shown in Fig. 16.5.7.

INDEPENDENT REAR SUSPENSION (i.r.s.)

Many of the advantages of i.f.s. apply to i.r.s., but the most important item is the reduction of unsprung weight. The final-drive unit and the brakes are the major weight items, so if 'inboard' brakes are fitted to a frame-mounted final drive, as much as 50% reduction in unsprung weight can be achieved.

The similarity between i.r.s. and the de-Dion drive often makes it difficult to draw a dividing line, but if the definition of independent suspension is remembered, a division can be made.

The following systems are examples of i.r.s.:

Parallel Link System

Two wishbone-shaped links, mounted transversely, connect the wheels to a backbone-type frame (Fig. 16.6.1(a)). Springing is provided by longitudinally mounted torsion bars which connect with the lower wishbone. The drive is transmitted from the final drive through 'wide-angle' universal joints.

Swinging Arm

An alternative method of mounting the wheels is provided by the trailing arm system shown in Fig. 16.6.1(b). A spring, mounted as shown, or a torsion bar, acting at the pivot, may be used. One popular light car uses a rubber spring instead of the normal metal type shown.

Transverse Spring System

An arrangement similar to the one shown in Fig. 16.6.2(a) is used on a Triumph. Springing is provided by a transverse leaf spring, and wheel location is obtained by utilising the drive shaft.

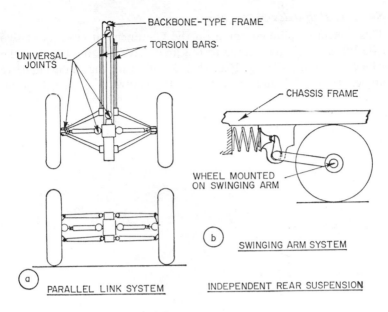

BACKBONE-TYPE FRAME

TORSION BARS.

UNIVERSAL JOINTS

CHASSIS FRAME

WHEEL MOUNTED ON SWINGING ARM

b   SWINGING ARM SYSTEM

a   PARALLEL LINK SYSTEM

INDEPENDENT REAR SUSPENSION

FIG. 16.6.1

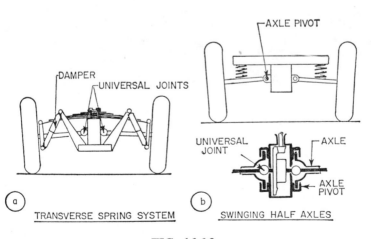

DAMPER

UNIVERSAL JOINTS

AXLE PIVOT

UNIVERSAL JOINT

AXLE

AXLE PIVOT

a   TRANSVERSE SPRING SYSTEM

b   SWINGING HALF AXLES

FIG. 16.6.2

Swinging Half-axles

This system is quite common on the Continent; it consists of two axle tubes which are jointed to the final-drive housing to allow the wheel to rise or fall. (Fig. 16.6.2(b)). To allow for the change in drive angle, universal joints are fitted at the centre of each axle joint.

Wheels and Tyres

17.1

WHEELS

A wheel must be light, to enable the tyre to follow the contour of the road, and strong, to resist the many forces acting on it. It must be cheap to produce, easy to clean, and simple to remove. These conditions are met by the detachable-disc type of pressed-steel wheel: either this is bolted to the hub, or the disc is permanently connected to the hub with a detachable rim: the latter arrangement is often used on Continental cars. In both cases spherically seated nuts ensure a rigid mounting. To reduce the risk of the wheel accidentally coming off, some manufacturers use 'left-hand' threads on the nearside and 'right-hand' threads on the offside; the direction of the thread is generally indicated by an *L* or *R* on the nut.

The wire or spoke type wheel, which was common up to about 1935, is still used on many sports and racing cars. Modern designs use tangential spokes to transmit driving and braking forces; inner and outer sets of spokes are connected to the hub shell as wide apart as possible to provide lateral stiffness of the wheel. A *centre-lock* or *knock-on* mounting is used whereby the drive is taken by serrations and the shell is located between two cones, one formed on the hub and the other on a single large nut screwed on to the hub to retain the wheel. Left-hand threads on the offside hubs and right-hand threads on the nearside hubs are generally used to prevent the nut working loose. This quick-change type of wheel is strong and light, and ensures good circulation of air to the braking system, but is difficult to clean.

TYPES OF RIM

Well-base

Fig. 17.1.1(a) shows the main details of this construction, which is generally used for car tyres. The drop centre or well enables the tyre to be pressed into this recess, so that the opposite side (adjacent to the valve) may be levered over the rim flange. The air pressure in the tyre causes the bead to ride up the slight taper (5°) and 'lock' the tyre to the rim. Rim diameter is stated on the tyre: e.g. a tyre 5·25 × 16 is fitted to a 16-in diameter rim; the 5·25 refers to the nominal sectional width of the tyre.

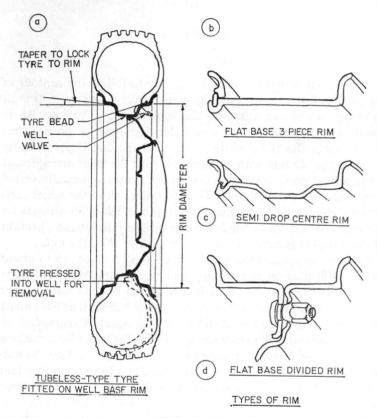

FIG. 17.1.1

Flat-base three-piece rim (Fig. 17.1.1(b))

The stiff, heavy-bead tyres used on heavy vehicles require a detachable-flange type of rim. A split lock ring, like a large circlip, holds the flange in position. When the flange is pushed towards the tyre, the lock ring may be removed.

Semi-drop centre (Fig. 17.1.1(c))
This two-piece rim is a compromise between the well-base and the flat-base rim, and is suitable for light trucks. A split, detachable flange simplifies removal and the slight taper enables the tyre to 'lock' to the rim. The small well must be used when the tyre is being removed.

Flat-base divided type (Fig. 17(1.1(d))
Mainly used on military vehicles, this type of rim is made in two sections and bolted together by a ring of nuts, adjacent to the rim. On no account must you remove these nuts when changing a wheel.

TYRES

The dictionary definition of a tyre is a band of iron, steel, rubber, etc., placed round the rim of a wheel to strengthen it or reduce vibration.

THE PNEUMATIC TYRE

Early tyres certainly strengthened the wheel, but did little to improve the comfort. It was not until R. W. Thomson in 1845 invented the pneumatic tyre that high-frequency vibration could be reduced. This idea was developed by J. B. Dunlop in 1888 for cycle use and was quickly applied to motor vehicles. An air bag or inner tube was contained in a cover so that the vehicle was 'floated' on a cushion of air.

The modern tyre, besides improving comfort, increases the adhesion between road and wheel to give satisfactory grip for braking and steering in various driving conditions.

TYRE CONSTRUCTION

Fig. 17.2.1 shows the constructional details of a tyre.

The *casing* must resist the expansion of the tube, especially when the tube is subjected to road shocks. Fracture of the casing causes the tube to blow out, i.e. burst the tyre; thus the strength of the tyre is governed by the construction of the casing. It is usually made up of four or six layers of fabric; each layer consists of a series of rubberised cords laid side by side to form a sheet. A strong casing is produced by placing a number of sheets or plies together. The number of plies and the relative angle between the cord and the tyre bead governs the tyre characteristics. In the past cotton was the main cord material, but modern tyres use man-made fibres such as rayon

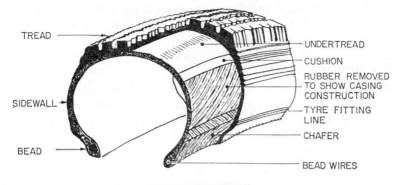

TREAD

SIDEWALL

BEAD

UNDERTREAD

CUSHION

RUBBER REMOVED
TO SHOW CASING
CONSTRUCTION

TYRE FITTING
LINE

CHAFER

BEAD WIRES

TYRE CONSTRUCTION

FIG. 17.2.1

and nylon. These materials are much stronger and also offer greater resistance to the heat built up by the flexing of the tyre. Heavy vehicle tyres require even stronger materials so steel cords are sometimes used.

The *bead* consists of a number of hoops of steel wire which are responsible for retaining the tyre on the rim. The casing is wrapped around the bead wire and moulded into shape.

The *tread* is bonded to the soft rubber which encloses the casing. The material used is natural or synthetic rubber, which is compounded with chemicals such as carbon-black to produce a hard, abrasion-resisting substance. Various tread patterns are used to wipe water and grease off the road, so that the teeth, formed by the zig-zag circumferential grooves, can 'bite' into the surface. An excellent grip, especially on soft surfaces, can be obtained by transversely slotting the tyre to form bold tread bars, but when used on hard roads this type is rather noisy and generally causes the 'heel and toe' form of tread wear.

TUBELESS TYRES

Recent years have seen the introduction of this type of tyre, which is now basic equipment for most new cars. The inside of the casing and outer surface of the bead is lined with a soft rubber, which forms an air-tight seal with the rim and eliminates the need for a separate tube. Two main advantages are claimed:

(1) better air sealing qualities are obtained providing the cover is correctly sealed to the rim, and

(2) the soft inner liner of the cover provides a puncture-sealing arrangement. On fitting or removing this type, be very careful to avoid damaging the bead.

Resistance to a side force

The extent of the side deflection produced when a side force acts on the tyre governs the actual path taken by the wheel (see page 416). This side deflection (Fig. 17.2.2) is increased when the inflation pressure is low but is controlled to a very large extent by the construction of the tyre.

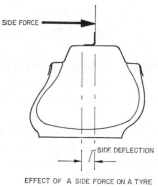

EFFECT OF A SIDE FORCE ON A TYRE

FIG. 17.2.2

Cross-ply Fig. 17.2.3 shows a tyre with the carcass composed of several layers of casing plies. The cords forming one ply run at an angle of about 100° to the cords of the adjoining ply, and each cord of the ply forms an angle of approximately 40° to the bead. This type is called *cross-ply* and has been in use for a long period.

Radial-ply Arranging the cords in a manner such that they form an angle of 90° to the bead (i.e. the cords are radially disposed to the wheel) gives a construction which is called *radial-ply* (Fig. 17.2.4). This type has the great advantage that it offers a large resistance to side deflection and its effect on the vehicle handling is very noticeable. A vehicle fitted with cross-ply tyres often suffers from side drift when it corners and gives the impression to the driver that the tyres are sliding on the road, whereas radial-ply considerably reduce this effect. In a similar manner if the vehicle oversteers badly then this could be reduced by fitting radial-ply to the rear

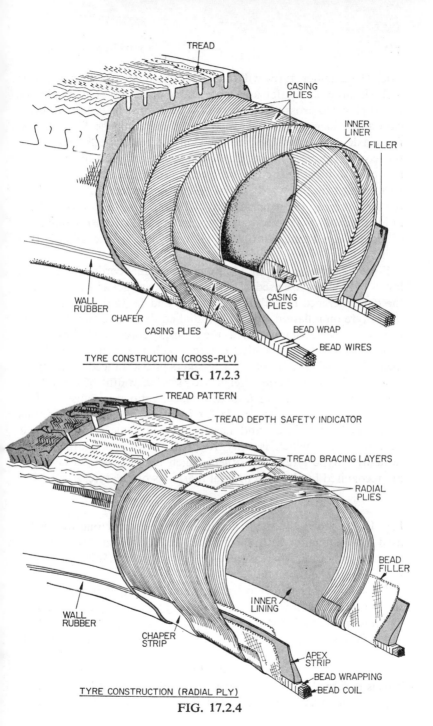

TREAD

CASING PLIES

INNER LINER

FILLER

WALL RUBBER

CHAFER

CASING PLIES

CASING PLIES

BEAD WRAP

BEAD WIRES

TYRE CONSTRUCTION (CROSS-PLY)

FIG. 17.2.3

TREAD PATTERN

TREAD DEPTH SAFETY INDICATOR

TREAD BRACING LAYERS

RADIAL PLIES

BEAD FILLER

WALL RUBBER

CHAPER STRIP

INNER LINING

APEX STRIP

BEAD WRAPPING

BEAD COIL

TYRE CONSTRUCTION (RADIAL PLY)

FIG. 17.2.4

axle. These 'stiffer' tyres will reduce the slip angle of the rear wheels and will produce a safer and more stable condition. This mixing of radial-play and cross-ply tyres on a vehicle must be used with great care and under no circumstances must radial-ply be fitted to the front axle when cross-ply are used on the rear wheels. Mixing in this configuration is illegal, due to the oversteering problem, so care is needed to identify the tyres correctly. Today, radial-ply tyres can be identified by the word 'radial' which is moulded on the wall of the tyre. Prior to the general introduction of this method the means of identification was to note the type letters and refer to the maker's catalogue, e.g. Pirelli Cinturato, Dunlop SP and Michelin X were radial tyres.

Fig. 17.2.4 shows that in addition to the radial cords a number of layers of breakers are used. These bracing layers act as a belt around the circumference to stabilise the tread and resist the enlargement of the tyre on inflation, since the radial cords do not offer the same resistance to tyre enlargement as the cross-ply cords. Textile materials used for these breakers give a tyre which is sometimes called a 'belted' type whereas steel cord breakers give a 'braced' tread type.

Tyre profile The 'section height' to 'section width' of early tyres was approximately equal and this aspect ratio was considered as 100%. As demands were made for increased vehicle stability this ratio has been reduced and has resulted in some tyres having a 'section height' which is only 70% of its 'section width'. These 'wide-oval' type tyres, and others which fall between these limits, are recognised by the dimensional markings on the tyre.

VALVES

Fig. 17.2.5 shows the main details of the Schrader one-way valve used in conjunction with a tubeless tyre. In this case the valve is inserted in the rim, whereas in separate-tube designs it is vulcanised, or bolted, to the tube.

The core is threaded into the stem until the tapered hard rubber section forms a seal with the stem. Spring pressure forces the centre wire and rubber-filled cup onto its seat to prevent an outward flow of air. A dust cap acts as an extra air seal and prevents entry of dirt.

INFLATION PRESSURE

This is governed by the load carried by a given tyre, although manufacturers often vary pressure to modify the steering characteristics.

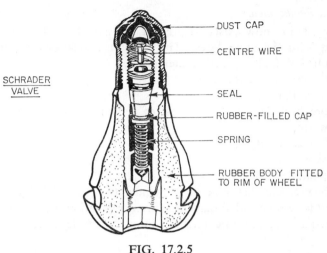

FIG. 17.2.5

Large-section tyres use a lower pressure for a given load, and so greater comfort is achieved, but the resistance to rolling is increased. The pressure recommended by the manufacturer is applicable to a *cold* tyre, i.e. it is the pressure *before* the tyre is used, and takes into account the average pressure rise [4 lbf/in² (28 kN/m²)] which is caused by the temperature increase during use. Recommended pressure is normally suitable for sustained speeds up to 80 mile/h (130 km/h), but a higher pressure is advised if speeds or loads are increased.

Underinflation or overloading leads to rapid wear on each side of the tread and internal damage to the casing, whereas over-inflation wears the centre of the tread.

Interchanging Tyres

At present there are various recommendations regarding the interchanging of tyres so tyre manufacturers' guidance should be followed.

Generally cross-ply tyres should be interchanged at frequent intervals if uniform tyre wear is to be achieved. Longitudinal changes (L/H front to R/H rear, etc.) and diagonal changes (R/H front to L/H rear and spare to R/H rear, etc.) are normally advised.

Some manufacturers of radial-ply tyres recommend that the front tyres are not moved to the rear due to the different wear pattern of front and rear tyres.

Legal Requirements

Legislation now exists to prevent the use of a vehicle which is fitted with defective tyres. The current regulations specify the various tyre faults and these include:

(a) the use of unsuitable tyres,

(b) underinflation,

(c) break in the fabric in excess of 1 inch or 10% of the section width,

(d) lumps or bulges,

(e) exposure of cords,

(f) tread depth less than 1 mm.

The preceding list of faults is intended to outline the requirements and it is recommended that the current regulations be read in order to acquire an accurate understanding of the legal requirements.

WHEEL BALANCING

Independent suspension systems and modern, small-diameter, large-section wheels demand extra care and attention to this point.

Although tyre manufacturers balance tyre and tube, it is often necessary to balance the complete wheel assembly to ensure that the wheel rotates free from vibration.

Out of balance may be caused by: (a) static unbalance, and (b) dynamic unbalance.

Static Unbalance

This is apparent when the wheel is mounted on a horizontal shaft having low-friction bearings (Fig. 17.3.1(a)). The wheel always comes to rest in one position, which indicates the presence of a 'heavy spot' directly below the wheel axis. (A bicycle wheel shows this action clearly.) A wheel used in this condition will tend to cause the unbalanced centrifugal force to lift the wheel off the road periodically (Fig. 17.3.1(b)), and produce conditions known as 'wheel hop', 'shimmy' and uneven tyre wear.

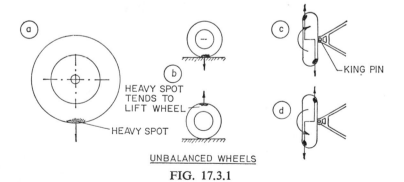

UNBALANCED WHEELS

FIG. 17.3.1

Dynamic Unbalance

Fig. 17.3.1(c) shows a wheel in good static balance, but when this wheel is rotated, the centrifugal forces acting on each 'heavy spot' will not balance, since the forces are not acting through the same line. In Fig. 17.3.1(c) the wheel axis tends to rotate around the king pin in a clockwise direction, whereas the opposite applies to Fig. 17.3.1(d). Serious dynamic unbalance causes the wheel to 'flap' around the king pin, a condition known as *wheel shimmy*.

Wheel Balancing Machines

These enable the operator to determine the position and extent of the correcting mass which must be clipped on to the rim. Simple equipment can be used to detect static unbalance, but since the wheel must be rotated to determine dynamic unbalance, more costly apparatus is necessary.

18.1

SIMPLE BRAKING SYSTEMS

A moving vehicle possesses energy of motion which must be converted into some other form of energy in order to bring the vehicle to rest. The speed of conversion governs the rate of retardation of the vehicle.

The energy of motion is known as *kinetic energy*, and, in the case of a normal brake, this is converted into heat which is given up to the air flowing over the brake.

The modern system has been developed from the simple, single shoe brake used on early vehicles (Fig. 18.1.1(a)). In this case, the friction between wheel and shoe generates heat, this heat is proportional to the force pushing the shoe in to contact. The greater the force applied to the shoe, the quicker the vehicle stops, but a limit is reached when the wheel starts to skid over the road.

In order to control the path of the vehicle and obtain maximum brake efficiency, the wheel should be held on the verge of skidding.

If brakes are fitted to four wheels instead of one, a greater total braking effort can be applied, and the vehicle will stop in a much shorter distance, e.g. approximately a quarter of the original distance, if each wheel supports a quarter of the vehicle mass.

Assuming sufficient effort is available to lock the wheels, it will be seen that the friction between tyre and road is the main factor governing braking. This is clearly illustrated when a vehicle with good brakes attempts to stop on an icy road. The adhesion between tyre and road is affected by: (1) type of road surface, (2) condition of surface, e.g. wet, dry, greasy, etc., and (3) state and design of tyre tread.

Modern braking systems employ either a rotating drum or disc: the necessary friction is obtained by pressing a stationary shoe or pad against the rotating member.

DRUM BRAKES

The internally expanding shoe brake is the most common system in use today, and the main details of a simple system are shown in Fig. 18.1.1(b).

Two tee-section brake shoes are anchored by means of a pin to a back plate, which is bolted to the axle casing. Replaceable asbestos-based friction linings are riveted or bonded to each shoe, and these act against a rotating cast iron drum. Spreading, or expansion, of the shoes can be effected in many ways; the system illustrated employs a cam, which is linked to the driver's pedal by means of levers

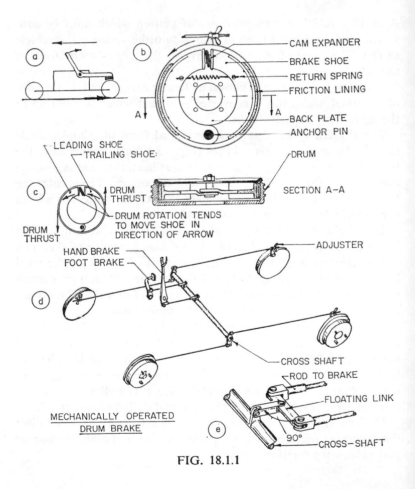

FIG. 18.1.1

and rods. A spring pulls the shoes together to return the mechanism after application of the brakes.

Fig. 18.1.1(c) shows that the friction between shoe and rotating drum will, in one case, push the shoe harder into contact, and, alternatively, tend to return the shoe to the 'off' position. This self-applying or self-energising action is termed the *self-servo effect*, and the shoe which acts in this manner is called the *leading shoe*. It will be seen that this shoe is the first shoe after the expander in the direction of rotation. The other shoe, known as the *trailing shoe*, only contributes a small share (approximately one quarter) to the total braking effort, since the drum rotation is acting against it, and the wear on this shoe is less than on the leading shoe.

OPERATING SYSTEM

The operating system for a brake can be: (1) mechanical, (2) hydraulic, or (3) pneumatic (air).

Fig 18.1.1(d) shows the layout of a simple mechanical system. Four adjustable rods link the cam operating levers to a transversely positioned shaft, which rotates in bearings mounted on the frame. The foot- and hand-brake controls are connected to the cross-shaft by links with elongated holes to allow independent operation of each control.

In this system each brake will receive its share of the applied force only when the mechanism is balanced, i.e. when each shoe contacts the drum at the same time. If one brake has a much smaller shoe-drum clearance than the others, all the applied force will be directed to this brake, and the vehicle will pull violently to this side. Compensating devices may be incorporated in the layout to overcome this problem; a simple arrangement is shown in Fig. 18.1.1(e). Each rear operating rod is attached to a floating link, and the centre of the link is connected to the cross-shaft. If one pair of shoes contacts the drum first, the link will swivel and take up the clearance in the other set before exerting any large force.

To enable a large force to be exerted on the brake shoes, a high leverage must be applied. This gives a 'light' pedal, but it must also be appreciated that a small amount of wear at the shoes will produce a large movement of the pedal; e.g. in the case of a brake leverage of 100:1, the pedal will move a distance of 100 times the amount of shoe wear. It is for this reason that the shoe-drum clearance is set to a minimum, since brake pedal travel increases as lining wear takes place.

Hydraulically Operated System

This highly efficient system is extensively used today, and is suited
to vehicles having independent suspension systems.

Fig. 18.1.2(a) shows the basic features of a leading and trailing
shoe assembly. A wheel cylinder, enclosing two opposed rubber-
sealed pistons, is mounted between the shoes, and a spring returns
the shoes to a limit governed by the setting of a snail cam type of
stop. This is placed so that the lining is just clear of the drum.

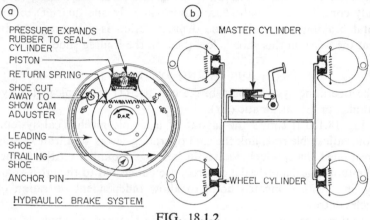

FIG. 18.1.2

The layout of the system (Fig. 18.1.2(b)) shows the foot brake
acting on a master cylinder, which supplies fluid to the various wheel
cylinders. The system is fully compensated: no one brake can apply
until all clearances have been taken up. Depression of the pedal displaces fluid to move each shoe to the drum, and at this point the
pedal feels 'solid'. (For normal practical purposes, the fluid may be
regarded as incompressible.) Extra pedal thrust will now cause the
fluid in the system to be pressurised, and so the force felt at each
shoe will be governed by the piston area; the larger the area, the
greater the thrust. Release of the pedal allows the shoe return springs
to displace the fluid back to the master cylinder.

Means must be provided to remove and prevent the re-entry of
air, since the compressibility of air produces a 'springy' pedal.
Whenever the system is dismantled and reassembled, you should
bleed the air from the special nipples provided at each wheel cylinder.

Brake fluid should have a low freezing point, high boiling point, and low viscosity (thin) characteristics, and must not injure the rubber seals. Always use vegetable-based oil of the type recommended by the manufacturer. You must drain the system completely and replace the rubber seals if mineral oil, e.g. oil used in dampers, is used by mistake.

Legal requirements insist on a mechanically operated brake which can be set to prevent at least two wheels revolving when the vehicle is left unattended. This system uses a rod or cable to connect the hand or parking brake with mechanical expander units fitted between the rear-wheel brake shoes.

DISC BRAKES

A drum type brake cannot easily radiate its generated heat to the moving air flow, so a high temperature is reached, and efficiency is decreased. Disc brakes are fully exposed to the air, and consequently a larger amount of energy can be dissipated. This feature, and other advantages too, have made disc brakes popular today.

Fig. 18.1.3 shows a diagrammatic sketch of this type of brake. Connected to the wheel is a cast iron disc, which is sandwiched between two lined pads. The caliper pad assembly is anchored to the axle casing or suspension member. A piston, acting on each pad, is operated by a normal hydraulic system, which usually includes a vacuum servo unit to boost the driver's effort.

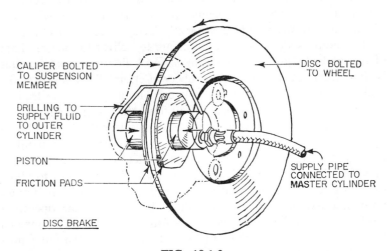

CALIPER BOLTED TO SUSPENSION MEMBER

DISC BOLTED TO WHEEL

DRILLING TO SUPPLY FLUID TO OUTER CYLINDER

PISTON

FRICTION PADS

SUPPLY PIPE CONNECTED TO MASTER CYLINDER

DISC BRAKE

FIG. 18.1.3

18.2

BRAKE ARRANGEMENTS

Brake systems can be divided into two main classes: (1) drum, and (2) disc.

DRUM BRAKE ARRANGEMENTS

Leading and Trailing Shoe Brake—Mechanical (L. & T.)

One of the simplest brake assemblies is the leading and trailing shoe fixed cam brake shown in Fig. 18.2.1.

Although its consistent performance appeals to many commercial vehicle manufacturers, the large cam force and consequential high pedal effort prompt many designers to modify the basic construction. The cause of this problem is the adverse self-servo action of the trailing shoe, and this becomes particularly apparent when the slightly greater wear and subsequently larger shoe-drum clearance of the leading shoe causes the fixed cam to deliver the major share of the applied force to the trailing shoe. A floating expander unit is often fitted to overcome this 'robbery of effort'. This improves the braking power but leads to very uneven lining wear—the leading shoe wear rate may be as much as four times that of the trailing shoe.

Unless specially shaped cams are used, an alternation in the leverage occurs as the cam is rotated. This is overcome in the arrangement shown in Fig. 18.2.2. A cone and roller type expander unit is fitted in a housing which floats on the back plate in order to allow the shoes to centre themselves. The expander has a high step-up ratio (approximately 6·5:1) to reduce the stress in the operating mechanism, and the system is designed to subject most components to a tensile stress rather than a torsional stress, since the latter produces large shaft deflections which lead to excessive pedal movement.

To ensure constant leverage and maximum travel of the expander, a shoe adjuster is fitted. This unit, which also acts as a shoe anchor, consists of a screwed wedge and two links. Flats on the wedge act as a locking device, and also enable the mechanic to 'feel' the correct shoe clearance.

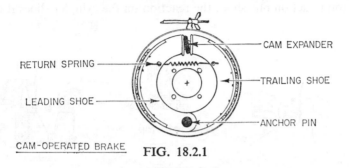

CAM-OPERATED BRAKE   **FIG. 18.2.1**

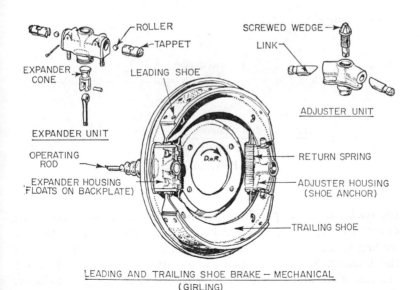

LEADING AND TRAILING SHOE BRAKE — MECHANICAL
(GIRLING)

FIG. 18.2.2

Leading and Trailing Shoe Brake—Hydraulic

The leading and trailing shoe brake shown in Fig. 18.2.3 represents a system often used on the rear wheels. The floating expander can be put into action hydraulically (as in a foot brake) or mechanically (as in a hand brake). Fluid pressure causes the split, rubber-sealed piston to act on one shoe: the reaction on the cylinder slides it over

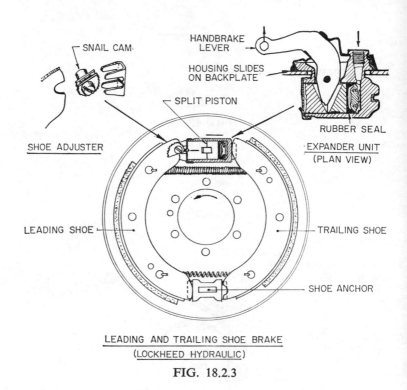

LEADING AND TRAILING SHOE BRAKE
(LOCKHEED HYDRAULIC)

FIG. 18.2.3

the back plate to apply the other shoe. Rod operation moves the cranked lever, and forces the half piston outwards to apply the leading shoe: the trailing shoe is again applied by the reaction of the housing. Specially shaped abutments on the shoes allow for centralisation, and a notched snail cam acts as the shoe adjuster. Each shoe should be set as close to the drum as possible, but binding (rubbing) should not be felt.

Two Leading Shoe Brake (2 L.S.)

Many disadvantages of the earlier arrangements can be overcome if both shoes are expanded in such a way that each shoe tends to apply itself.

The servo action is set less, per shoe, than that acting on the leading shoe on previous designs. But since two effective shoes are utilised, a more powerful, progressive and stable brake is obtained.

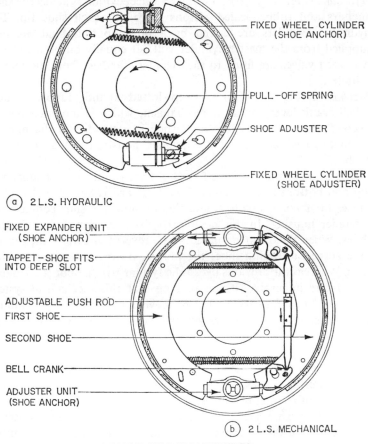

RUBBER SEAL

FIXED WHEEL CYLINDER
(SHOE ANCHOR)

PULL–OFF SPRING

SHOE ADJUSTER

FIXED WHEEL CYLINDER
(SHOE ADJUSTER)

(a) 2 L.S. HYDRAULIC

FIXED EXPANDER UNIT
(SHOE ANCHOR)

TAPPET–SHOE FITS
INTO DEEP SLOT

ADJUSTABLE PUSH ROD
FIRST SHOE

SECOND SHOE

BELL CRANK

ADJUSTER UNIT
(SHOE ANCHOR)

(b) 2 L.S. MECHANICAL

TWO LEADING SHOE ARRANGEMENTS

FIG. 18.2.4

These features make it suitable for front-wheel brakes, the L. & T. shoe brake being retained for the rear wheels. This combination provides effective braking whilst in reverse and allows the front brakes to absorb approximately 60% of the braking energy, the larger proportion being due to the transference of weight which takes place when the brakes are applied.

The system requires two separate shoe anchors and an arrangement for applying force at each shoe tip. Hydraulic or mechanical expanders may be used to apply the brake, and adjusters are provided at each shoe.

Hydraulic (Fig. 18.2.4(a)) Two fixed wheel cylinders act as the shoe anchors and rubber-sealed pistons force out each shoe tip. The hydraulic cylinders are linked by a pipe, so that fluid pressure supplied from the master cylinder will act equally on both pistons. Air bleed valves are fitted to the cylinders farthest from the master cylinder.

Mechanical (Fig. 18.2.4(b)) A deep-slotted expander tappet contacts a bell crank lever and strut mechanism, which is mounted on the 'second' shoe, whereas the 'first' shoe is expanded in the normal manner. Fixed adjuster and expander housings act as the shoe anchors.

Operation of the expander forces out the tip of the first shoe, and top and bottom of the second shoe. Forward rotation of the drum causes the second shoe to rotate slightly until the shoe contacts the expander housing. In this position both shoes now act as leading shoes. When the drum is rotated in the reverse direction, the second shoe acts as a leading shoe; the first shoe now becomes a trailing shoe. Whereas the previous hydraulic system gives a poor two trailing shoe brake in reverse, it will be seen that this mechanical system produces 2 L.S. forward, and L. & T. when in reverse. If you mount a strut system on both shoes you will get 2 L.S. in both directions.

Duo-servo

This system is often called a *self-energising* brake, and is one of the most powerful brakes, but effectiveness falls tremendously if the coefficient of friction decreases.

Fig. 18.2.5 shows a modern, hydraulically operated duo-servo brake. Fluid pressure expands the shoes, and causes the drum to move the shoe assembly in the d.o.r. until the secondary shoe butts against the shoe anchor. In this position the frictional force acting on the primary shoe is transmitted through the floating adjuster unit to apply the secondary shoe.

Some shoe assemblies use a 'lighter' return spring on the primary show to allow this shoe to contact the drum first.

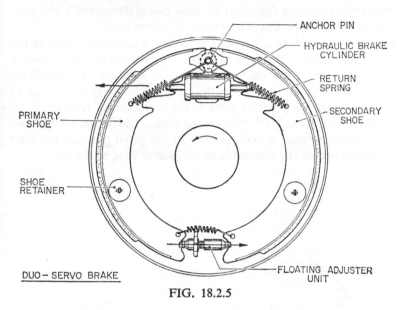

FIG. 18.2.5

Automatic Adjusters

Various methods have been used over the years to provide some form of automatic adjuster to set the brake shoe the correct distance from the drum.

Many early designs of mechanical brake used on heavy vehicles incorporated a rachet system in the main linkage. When the movement of the operating linkage exceeded a specified amount, the pawl jumped a tooth on the rachet and took up the excessive clearance.

Another system relied on a modified arrangement of the shoe return springs. Each leading and trailing shoe brake assembly had only one return spring. This was connected between the shoes in the normal way, but since it was positioned close to the adjuster unit, the pull-off action was only capable of taking the shoe just clear of the drum.

Modern arrangements generally consist of a lever system which 'rachets' over a toothed wheel form of shoe adjuster. When the shoe

movement is excessive the rachet will operate and the clearance will
be decreased.

DISC BRAKE

Disc brakes are now favoured by many manufacturers of high-speed
cars, since this type offers a number of advantages:
(1) The surface on which heat is generated is directly exposed to the
air, whereas in the case of a drum brake this is not so. Easier
dissipation of the heat gives a greater resistance to *fade*. This
is the term used to describe the fall-off in brake efficiency due to
heat. High temperature reduces the coefficient of friction of the
lining, a fact clearly demonstrated when a vehicle fitted with drum
brakes descends a long, steep hill; the pedal pressure required
at the end of the descent is much greater than at the start.

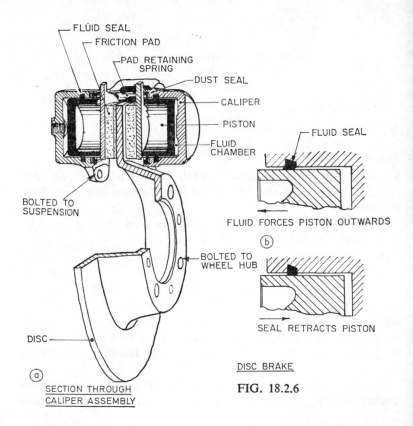

DISC BRAKE

FIG. 18.2.6

(2) Independence of self-servo effect. The non-assisted brake may require more effort but its action is progressive, i.e. the brake gives a braking torque proportional to the applied force.

(3) Brake is not so sensitive to friction changes.

(4) Self-adjusting linings or pads are used which are easily replaced.

(5) Pedal travel does not increase as disc heats up—heating a drum causes expansion which increases pedal travel.

The construction of a light-duty disc brake is shown in Fig. 18.2.6(a). A split caliper assembly, rigidly attached to the stub axle carrier, houses the cylinders and two opposed pistons, which act directly on friction pads mounted one on each side of the disc. Since the pads are visible, the degree of wear may be easily determined, and they are replaced by removing the split pins and pad-retaining springs.

A rubber seal, mounted in a groove in the cylinder, prevents fluid leakage and also retracts the piston and pad after application of the brake (Fig. 18.2.6(b)). This feature compensates for lining wear and keeps each pad close to the disc.

Internal drillings link the two fluid chambers, and a rubber hose supplies the caliper with fluid from the master cylinder. A bleeder screw is fitted to each caliper.

Normally disc brakes are used for front wheels and conventional L. & T. shoe drum brakes are fitted to the rear.

18.3

MECHANICALLY OPERATED SYSTEMS

Rod-operated brake systems are still used on heavy commercial vehicles. The simple rod layout links each brake to a central cross-shaft, but with this non-compensated system, the vehicle will pull to one side if the brakes are incorrectly balanced. Balancing levers, known as compensators, can be introduced into the system to ensure that each brake receives its share of the applied force.

Fig. 18.3.1(a) shows a typical compensator which may be fitted to front or rear brakes. A swivelling tee-shaped lever, linked to the axle, is connected between transverse rods (T.R.) and a longitudinal rod (L.R.). Movement of rod (L.R.) rotates the lever, and pulls the

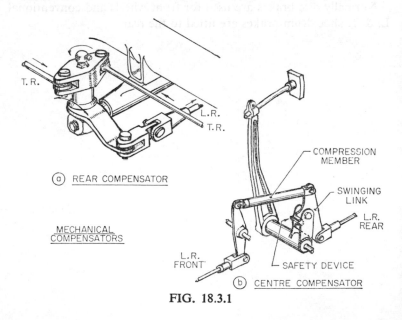

MECHANICAL COMPENSATORS

(a) REAR COMPENSATOR

(b) CENTRE COMPENSATOR

FIG. 18.3.1

rods (T.R.) until all clearances have been taken up. If the 'play' on one side is greater than the other, the unit will move to ensure that the applied force is equally divided.

A fully compensated system requires three compensators: two of the type shown in Fig. 18.3.1(a) to balance front and rear brakes, and a centre unit to compensate between front and rear. Some vehicle manufacturers feel that 'full compensation' is unnecessary, and omit the centre unit.

The centre compensator shown in Fig. 18.3.1(b) is a Girling unit. A swinging link, mounted at the lower end of the pedal, divides the pedal force between front and rear brakes, but the extent of compensation is limited by a safety stop. This stop keeps either front or rear brakes in action if the rod fails.

A spring, fitted inside the anti-rattle compression member, pushes the plunger away from the tubular unit to give a slight load on the complete system when the brakes are off.

Rod adjustment is necessary when the rods become slack. To determine the extent of this slackness, expand the shoes fully in the drums by means of the shoe adjusters, and check the pedal travel. Full shoe expander travel will be maintained if the rods are adjusted while the shoes are kept in this fully expanded position.

N.B. *Rod adjustment must not take the place of shoe adjustment.*

18.4

HYDRAULIC OPERATING SYSTEMS

These popular systems offer the following advantages.
(1) Fully compensated—each brake receives its full share of the pedal effort.
(2) High efficiency—the efficiency of the hydraulic system is higher than the mechanical layout.
(3) Suitable for vehicles having independent suspension.
(4) Easy to alter thrust on shoe—the force exerted on a piston is governed by the piston area: the larger the area, the greater the thrust. For example, if the manufacturer requires a greater thrust on the trailing shoe, a larger piston can be used.

LAYOUT OF SYSTEM

Fig. 18.4.1(a) shows a layout of a typical system operating drum and disc brakes. Each wheel unit is fed from a master cylinder which is controlled from the foot brake. A separate mechanical linkage to the rear brakes connects with the hand or parking brake.

MASTER CYLINDER

Lockheed Type

Fig. 18.4.1(b) shows the construction of an internal reservoir type master cylinder. An alternative is to have a separate reservoir, mounted in an accessible position.

Linked to the pedal by an adjustable push rod is a piston (6), which is sealed by a main rubber cup (8), held in position by a spring, and seated on a thin washer to prevent the rubber entering the feed holes (7). An inlet port (3) allows fluid around the waist of the piston; leakage of this fluid is prevented by a secondary rubber cup (4). Outward travel of the piston is limited by a circlip, and a rubber

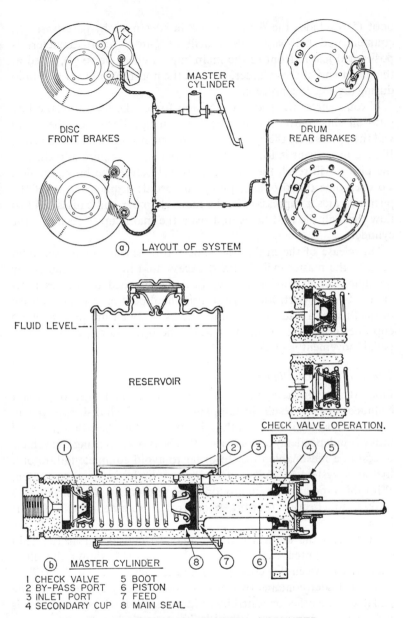

MASTER CYLINDER

DISC FRONT BRAKES

DRUM REAR BRAKES

(a) LAYOUT OF SYSTEM

FLUID LEVEL

RESERVOIR

CHECK VALVE OPERATION.

(b) MASTER CYLINDER

1 CHECK VALVE   5 BOOT
2 BY-PASS PORT   6 PISTON
3 INLET PORT   7 FEED
4 SECONDARY CUP 8 MAIN SEAL

HYDRAULIC BRAKE SYSTEM: LOCKHEED

FIG. 18.4.1

boot (5) excludes the dirt. A 0·028-in (0·7 mm) by-pass port (2), counterbored half-way with a drill of $\frac{1}{8}$-in (3 mm) diameter, is positioned just in front of the main cup. A check valve (1), fitted at the outlet end of the cylinder, ensures the non-return of aerated fluid during the bleeding process.

If you depress the pedal, the piston forces the fluid into the line until all shoe movement has been taken up. Thrust on the pedal will then pressurise the system and force each shoe against the drum. If shoe movement is too great, i.e. if the shoes require adjustment, the piston will reach the end of its travel before the brake applies. To overcome this problem, pump the pedal: a quick return of the piston creates a depression in the main chamber and causes fluid to flow through the feed holes and over the main cup to recharge the cylinder.

On release of the brake, the shoe return springs pump the fluid back to the master cylinder: any excess fluid in the line, caused by 'pumping' or expansion due to heat, is returned to the reservoir via the by-pass port. Blockage of this small port prevents the return of the fluid and leads to 'binding' brakes, so to ensure that the main cup does not obstruct the port when the brake is off, a small free-pedal movement is given.

Tandem Master Cylinder

Pipe fracture in a layout operated by a normal type of master cylinder normally results in complete failure of the foot-brake system. When this occurs it is hoped that the driver remembers that the hand brake is independent, because with this he is able to bring the vehicle to rest in a reasonable time. In order to avoid complete failure of a hydraulic system, a tandem type master cylinder is sometimes fitted. With this type a failure in any one line results in a loss of only two brakes, so effective foot-brake control is retained and safety is improved.

In general the tandem cylinder may be considered as two solo cylinders mounted end to end and Fig. 18.4.2 shows the close similarity between this conception and the actual layout.

The cylinder contains two pistons, one directly connected to the pedal and the other operated by fluid pressure. Each piston, which is fitted with seals to prevent fluid leakage, controls a separate line to either the front or rear brakes. At each of the two outlet points a check valve is fitted. One return spring is positioned between the

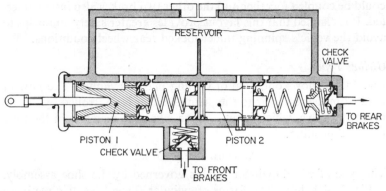

RESERVOIR

CHECK
VALVE

TO REAR
BRAKES

PISTON I

CHECK VALVE

PISTON 2

TO FRONT
BRAKES

TANDEM MASTER CYLINDER

FIG. 18.4.2

pistons and a stronger return spring, acting on the independent piston, ensures that the pistons are forced back to their stops. Fluid is supplied through ports similar to the solo cylinder and the reservoir is divided into two parts to prevent a total fluid loss when one line fails.

Under normal conditions the movement of piston (1) causes an increase in the fluid pressure in the chamber controlled by piston (1). Pressure from this chamber is transmitted to the front brake line and to piston (2) which, being free to move, will pressurise the rear brake line to the same extent as the front line.

Assuming a failure occurs in the front line the movement of piston (1) will discharge fluid at the fracture and will allow the two pistons to contact. Although this stage has taken up some of the pedal travel, the remainder of the movement is available to operate the rear brakes. Repeated applications of the brake will eventually discharge all of the fluid from the portion of the reservoir which supplies the faulty section.

Failure in the rear line causes the initial pressure to move piston (2) to the limit of its travel. Once this point is reached the front brake can be operated successfully. An additional rubber seal fitted to piston (2) prevents fluid from leaking from the serviceable section to the fractured line.

Although this description of the tandem cylinder has referred to the two lines as being front and rear, it must be pointed out that other configurations exist, e.g. front-left brake and rear-right brake could be coupled together and the other two brakes also interconnected. It is claimed that this layout provides greater safety and helps to avoid the vehicle spinning under locked rear wheel conditions.

Girling Type

Fig. 18.4.3 shows one type of Girling master cylinder. The flow of fluid from the reservoir to the main chamber is controlled by a compensating valve, which is set to open when the piston is in the fully returned position.

WHEEL CYLINDERS

The type of wheel cylinder used is governed by the shoe assembly. Fig. 18.4.4 shows two forms of cylinder. Type (a) acts directly on to the brake shoe, whereas type (b) utilises a mechanical expander comprising two sectors and tappets. This arrangement employs a transversely mounted wheel cylinder, positioned behind the back plate. Therefore, a lower operating pressure and fluid temperature is obtained, which makes the unit suitable for heavy commercial vehicles.

PRESSURE REGULATING VALVE

This unit (Fig. 18.4.5) is fitted in the rear brake line, and is designed to reduce the risk of rear wheel skidding by limiting the pressure acting on the rear brakes.

The valve consists of a spring-loaded plunger contained within a body. Low fluid pressure will not overcome the spring, so the full pressure will act on all brakes. When the brake is applied, fluid will initially pass to the rear brakes, but when a predetermined pressure is reached the valve will close and allow any further increase of pressure to be felt only on the front brakes.

BLEEDING THE BRAKES

This is necessary whenever air has entered the system. The main steps in the operation are:
(1) Ensure that the reservoir is full.
(2) Attach one end of rubber tube to bleeder valve and immerse other end in fluid contained in jar.
(3) Open bleeder valve and slowly pump pedal until air bubbles cease to appear. Close bleeder valve as pedal is being depressed.
(4) Repeat at all wheel cylinders.
(5) Top up reservoir.

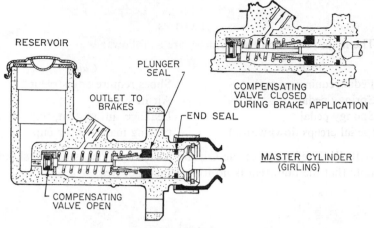

RESERVOIR

PLUNGER
SEAL

OUTLET TO
BRAKES

END SEAL

COMPENSATING
VALVE OPEN

COMPENSATING
VALVE CLOSED
DURING BRAKE APPLICATION

MASTER CYLINDER
(GIRLING)

FIG. 18.4.3

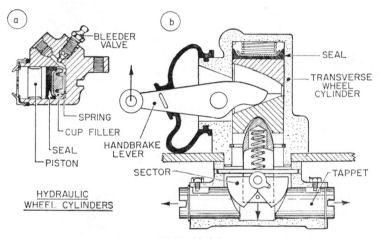

a

b

BLEEDER
VALVE

SEAL

TRANSVERSE
WHEEL
CYLINDER

SPRING

CUP FILLER

SEAL

PISTON

HANDBRAKE
LEVER

SECTOR

TAPPET

HYDRAULIC
WHEEL CYLINDERS

FIG. 18.4.4

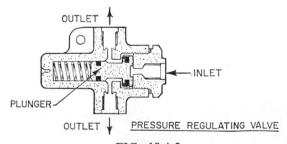

OUTLET

INLET

PLUNGER

OUTLET   PRESSURE REGULATING VALVE

FIG 18.4.5

FAULTS

The main faults and their causes are as follows:

Fault	Cause
Pedal requires pumping	Shoes require adjustment
Springy pedal	Air in system
Spongy pedal	Leakage in system, e.g. fluid
(pedal creeps downwards)	passing main rubber cup

N.B. With reference to the Girling master cylinder, students should note that the fluid seal is no longer incorporated.

18.5

VACUUM SERVO OPERATION

SERVO ASSISTANCE

To provide a large force at the brake shoes, either a large leverage or the assistance of some power device is required. The latter is employed on heavy vehicles since leverage is restricted by pedal travel.

Servo assistance is the term used when energy is utilised to help the driver control the vehicle. Assistance is not only applied to brakes: it can also ease the driver's task when changing gear or steeering a heavy vehicle.

The device can use mechanical, pneumatic or hydraulic means to supply the energy.

A simple mechanical servo consists of two discs, one driven from the gearbox and the other connected to a brake lever. When the discs are pushed together, the friction tends to rotate the disc attached to the lever and energy will be imparted to the brake linkage. The leading shoe of a drum type brake is a form of mechanical servo, since energy is extracted from the rotating drum.

VACUUM ASSISTANCE

This is the most popular form of servo system used on commercial vehicles and cars. Vacuum, or depression to be strictly correct, since the pressure never falls to zero, is obtained by connecting the device to the inlet manifold, or in the case of a C.I. engine, an exhauster driven by the engine. This is an eccentric vane air pump, the 'inlet' side of which produces the depression.

Every servo system must continue to function if the vacuum fails. It must also operate progressively; that is, the assistance given by the servo should be proportional to the force applied by the driver.

Fig. 18.5.1(a) shows a diagrammatic sketch of a Dewandre type of vacuum servo.

The foot-brake rod (1) is linked to a reaction lever (5), which is connected to a piston (6) at the lower end and linked to the distributor valves (2) at the top end. A fixed shaft (4) passes through a hole in the reaction lever: a large clearance between shaft and hole allows the top of the lever to 'float' in order to operate the valves and give a progressive action. The valve linkage is set to open the air-release valve (3) when the brake is 'off'.

Application of the brake initially moves the top of the reaction lever (5) to close the air-release valve (3) and open the vacuum valve (7). Air in the cylinder is evacuated to produce a pressure difference,

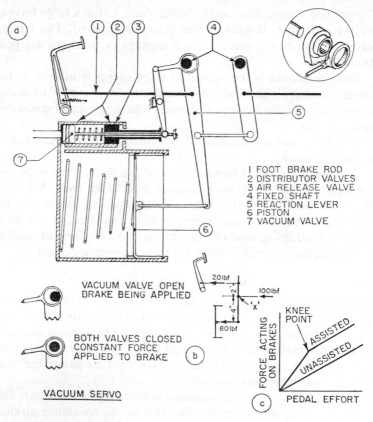

1 FOOT BRAKE ROD
2 DISTRIBUTOR VALVES
3 AIR RELEASE VALVE
4 FIXED SHAFT
5 REACTION LEVER
6 PISTON
7 VACUUM VALVE

VACUUM VALVE OPEN
BRAKE BEING APPLIED

BOTH VALVES CLOSED
CONSTANT FORCE
APPLIED TO BRAKE

VACUUM SERVO

FIG. 18.5.1

which forces the piston into the cylinder. This thrust is transferred to the reaction lever: the movement of the lower end causes the lever to pivot about the foot-pedal connection and close the vacuum valve. In this position, the reaction lever is 'floating', and so the force delivered to the brakes will be the sum of brake pedal and piston forces. In the example shown in Fig. 18.5.1(b), it will be seen that the designer can vary the servo assistance by altering the position of connection x. Normally the output is 4 to 6 times as great as the input.

Fig. 18.5.1(c) shows that extra pedal pressure will cause this cycle to be repeated up to a point (knee point) where the air pressure difference is now incapable of closing the vacuum valve. This point represents the limit of servo assistance.

Release of the pedal opens the air-release valve and enables air to enter the servo cylinder: a spring then returns the piston to the 'off' position.

This type of servo motor can also be applied to a hydraulic brake system, the unit being fitted between pedal and master cylinder.

Servo motors require very little attention apart from occasional lubrication of the piston. By considering the effects of a leaking vacuum or air-release valve, a number of faults can be ascertained.

Suspended-vacuum Servo

Removing the air from a servo cylinder takes time which may be precious when stopping a vehicle in an emergency. To reduce this delay a suspended-vacuum servo is often used. This has a 'vacuum' on each side of the piston when the brake is off. On applying the brake, a valve is opened and air is admitted to one side to produce a thrust on the piston.

Fig. 18.5.2 shows a low-priced construction suitable for a medium-sized car or light van. Fitted in the hydraulic line between master cylinder and wheel cylinder, the unit comprises three main items:
(1) vacuum cylinder containing a spring-loaded diaphragm
(2) slave hydraulic cylinder
(3) control valve actuated by hydraulic pressure.

With the engine running and the brake off, the unit will be as shown in diagram (a). The vacuum valve will be open and equal 'vacuum' pressure will be felt both sides of the piston.

Application of the pedal produces a hydraulic pressure on the brakes and also raises the valve piston in the servo. This movement

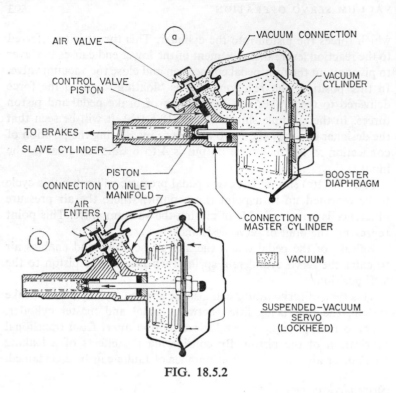

AIR VALVE

CONTROL VALVE PISTON

TO BRAKES

SLAVE CYLINDER

PISTON

CONNECTION TO INLET MANIFOLD

AIR ENTERS

a

VACUUM CONNECTION

VACUUM CYLINDER

BOOSTER DIAPHRAGM

CONNECTION TO MASTER CYLINDER

VACUUM

b

SUSPENDED-VACUUM SERVO (LOCKHEED)

FIG. 18.5.2

closes the vacuum control valve and opens the air valve to allow a break-down of the 'vacuum' in the outer chamber of the vacuum cylinder. Air pressure difference causes the booster diaphragm to apply a thrust on the slave-cylinder piston, which boosts the thrust given by the driver (diagram (b)). 'Proportional' braking is obtained by allowing the difference in air pressure, felt by the booster diaphragm, to act on the control valve diaphragm: as the difference increases, the diaphragm will overcome the hydraulic pressure acting on the valve piston and close the air valve.

Release of the pedal drops the hydraulic pressure to allow the valve piston to return and open the vacuum control valve. Air is quickly evacuated from the outer chamber of the vacuum cylinder and a spring returns the diaphragm.

A hole in the centre of the slave-cylinder piston ensures that the brake can still be operated if the servo fails.

Apart from general inspection of hoses, etc., the only attention the unit requires is the periodic cleaning [every 10 000 miles (16 Mm)] of the air filter.

Vacuum System

Although many servo units operate direct from the induction manifold, an improvement in performance and additional safety is achieved by using a vacuum reservoir. Fig. 18.5.3 shows the layout of a typical system.

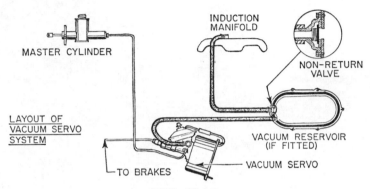

FIG. 18.5.3

Vacuum Exhauster

Since there is no manifold depression in the case of the C.I. engine, an exhauster must be used to produce the necessary depression [20–25 in (0·5–0·6 m) Hg].

Fig. 18.5.4 shows an engine-driven rotary type exhauster. Sliding

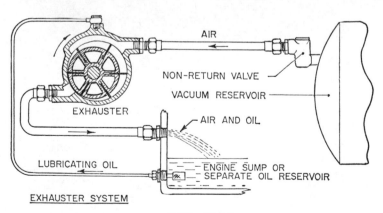

FIG. 18.5.4

vanes, lubricated and sealed with oil, are fitted into slots formed in a hub, which is mounted eccentrically to the bore of the casing. Rotation of the vanes draws in air from the port connected to the reservoir, and delivers it, mixed with oil, through the outlet port to the engine sump or oil reservoir.

COMPRESSED AIR OPERATION

When the maximum speed of lorries was limited to 12 mile/h (19 km/h) and their mass to some 10 tons (10 tonnes) the effectiveness of this braking system was of relatively little importance: indeed it was the custom deliberately to restrict their effectiveness because of the danger of loads shifting if rapid deceleration were attempted. Since that time both speeds and loads have increased, and lorries with an all-up mass of over 30 tons (30 tonnes) may now travel on motorways at speeds of 70 mile/h (110 km/h), so that effective brakes are not only essential for safety on the crowded roads of today but they are also demanded by regulations.

Thus, whilst simple mechanical linkages for operating the brakes of heavy commercial vehicles by the unaided effort of the driver were at one time considered adequate, the improved braking performance required called for much greater retarding forces and it became necessary to provide the driver with some measure of assistance. This first took the form of the vacuum servo system described in the previous chapter and illustrated in Fig. 18.5.1. This system, however, is limited by the best 'vacuum' we can conveniently produce on a vehicle—normally about 13 lbf/in² (89 kN/m²)—and on the heavier vehicles it has been replaced by a system using air at pressures above atmospheric of up to 100 lbf/in² (689 kN/m²) or more.

Fig. 18.6.1 shows a typical layout for a four-wheeled vehicle. The pressure is developed by a *compressor* (4) which is usually belt driven from the engine. It is generally a single-cylinder or two-cylinder reciprocating type, each cylinder having stainless steel disc-type valves, automatically operated, to control the air flow. Clean air is drawn in either from the engine air filter or through a separate small air filter (2) If the vehicle is liable to be used in cold

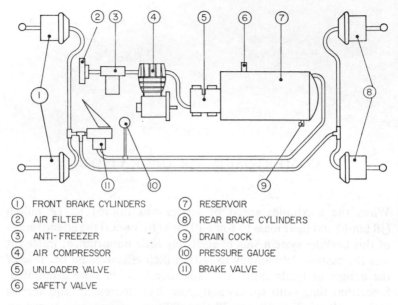

①	FRONT BRAKE CYLINDERS	⑦	RESERVOIR
②	AIR FILTER	⑧	REAR BRAKE CYLINDERS
③	ANTI-FREEZER	⑨	DRAIN COCK
④	AIR COMPRESSOR	⑩	PRESSURE GAUGE
⑤	UNLOADER VALVE	⑪	BRAKE VALVE
⑥	SAFETY VALVE		

SIMPLE COMPRESSED-AIR BRAKING SYSTEM FOR A FOUR-WHEELED VEHICLE

FIG. 18.6.1

weather an *anti-freezer* (3) is also fitted: moisture in the air drawn in will condense in the system and should it freeze it is liable to jam valves. The anti-freezer mixes alcohol vapour with the moisture thus lowering its freezing point. The condensed moisture tends to drain to the lowest point of the system (usually the reservoir) where a *drain valve* (9) is fitted: this should be opened daily and any water drained off.

The compressor delivers the air to the *reservoir* (7), which is a welded steel container for storing a supply of air under pressure. An *unloader valve* (5) may be fitted either on the reservoir or on the compressor, or in the interconnecting pipeline. Its function is to direct air from the compressor to atmosphere when the pressure in the reservoir reaches a predetermined level, thus allowing the compressor to run 'light', consuming less power, until falling pressure in the reservoir necessitates a resumption of delivery. A *pressure gauge* (10) indicates the pressure in the system and a *safety valve* (6) blows off if the pressure becomes excessively high.

Each brake is operated by a *cylinder* (1) and (8) containing either a piston, fitted with leather or rubber seals, or a diaphragm of reinforced rubber. The brake shoes are usually cam operated, the cylinders being linked to levers on the cam spindles. Air is supplied to the cylinders from the reservoir through a *brake valve* (11) which regulates the pressure in the brake cylinders in proportion to the force which the driver exerts on the pedal. Six-wheeled and eight-wheeled vehicles have an appropriate number of additional brake cylinders.

On long-wheelbase vehicles there is likely to be some delay in the operation of the rear brakes due to the time required for the necessary quantity of air to operate the rear brake cylinders to travel from the reservoir via the brake valve, which must necessarily be situated in the driving compartment at the front of the vehicle. This delay may be minimised by operating the rear brakes from a separate reservoir placed towards the rear of the vehicle, supply the rear brakes via a *relay valve* which is itself operated by pressure from the brake valve. Although the relay valve may be just as far from the brake valve as the rear brake cylinders, the quantity of air required to actuate it is very small and the delay in the operation of the rear brakes is practically eliminated.

Many vehicles use compressed air to operate other equipment such as power-assisted steering, gear changing, clutch operation and on 'buses, door operation. In such cases the reservoir either has two compartments or two separate reservoirs are used: a small one which can rapidly be charged after first starting the engine and is used for brake operation, and a larger compartment which is used to operate the remaining equipment. A *charging valve* is used to deliver all the air into the smaller compartment until this is charged to a predetermined pressure after which it diverts air into the larger compartment. This enables the vehicle to be driven off as soon as the small compartment, which operates the brakes, is charged without having to build up pressure in a larger reservoir, thus saving time.

The increased mass of modern vehicles and the requirement that the hand brake must have an efficiency of not less than 25% have led to the use of power assistance for hand brake operation. This is achieved by a separate cylinder connected to the hand brake linkage and supplied with compressed air by a valve actuated by the hand brake lever. Once the brake is applied it is locked on by mechanical means and the pressure can then be released from the cylinder.

Another method of providing power operation of the parking brake is by means of a device called the *lock actuator*, which is fundamentally an arrangement similar in principle to the free-wheel which acts upon the piston rods of the brake cylinders. This allows the piston rods to move freely in the direction to apply the brakes but prevents them from returning to the off position when the pressure is released until the 'free-wheel' is unlocked by a small air-operated piston.

The serious consequences of the failure of the compressed-air braking system on heavy vehicles has led to the development of systems in which the brakes are automatically applied if the air pressure should fail. One such device is the *spring brake*, in which the brake cylinders incorporate powerful springs which apply the brakes. The brakes are normally held in the off position by applying air pressure to a piston or diaphragm which compresses the spring. Normal operation is usually by a separate piston or diaphragm (contained in the same cylinder unit) which applies the brake by air pressure in the usual way.

Trailer Braking

Many heavy commercial vehicles tow trailers whilst others incorporate a 'semi-trailer'; the combination forming an *articulated* vehicle (see Fig. 1.2.10).

The trailer brakes could easily be operated by continuing the pipeline which supplies the rear brake cylinders, through a flexible hose with a *quick-release coupling*, to brake cylinders operating the trailer brakes. This simple *single-line system* is not now used since it suffers from two serious inadequacies. One is the excessive delay in the application of the trailer brake, which is even greater than that in the rear brakes of long-wheelbase vehicles already discussed. The second is that if the trailer should break away from the the tractor it is left brakeless.

Fig. 18.6.2 shows diagrammatically the components of a *two-line* trailer braking system. The parts additional to the simple system shown in Fig. 18.6.1 are:

(5) The *emergency line*, which takes the pressure in the tractor system to the trailer via a flexible hose (11) fitted with a quick-release coupling (9) at the tractor end. (13) The *trailer reservoir* which is charged from the emergency line through a relay *emergency valve* (12) one of whose functions is to close off and prevent the escape of air from the trailer reservoir should the trailer become disconnected

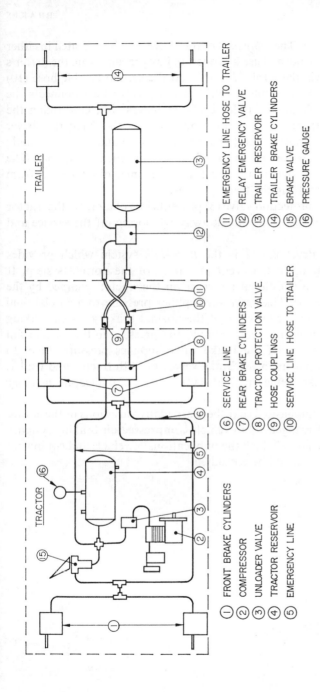

TWO-LINE TRAILER BRAKING SYSTEM

FIG. 18.6.2

TRAILER

TRACTOR

① FRONT BRAKE CYLINDERS
② COMPRESSOR
③ UNLOADER VALVE
④ TRACTOR RESERVOIR
⑤ EMERGENCY LINE

⑥ SERVICE LINE
⑦ REAR BRAKE CYLINDERS
⑧ TRACTOR PROTECTION VALVE
⑨ HOSE COUPLINGS
⑩ SERVICE LINE HOSE TO TRAILER

⑪ EMERGENCY LINE HOSE TO TRAILER
⑫ RELAY EMERGENCY VALVE
⑬ TRAILER RESERVOIR
⑭ TRAILER BRAKE CYLINDERS
⑮ BRAKE VALVE
⑯ PRESSURE GAUGE

from the tractor. The *relay* part of this valve may be operated in either of two ways: in normal use it is operated by pressure from the driver's brake valve via the *service line* (6) and the second flexible hose (10) and quick-release coupling (9). The relay valve then connects the trailer reservoir to the trailer brake cylinders (14), controlling the pressure in these cylinders in proportion to the force the driver applies to his brake pedal. (The two hoses (10) and (11) are usually crossed to allow for the swing of the trailer when cornering.) The relay valve also operates if the trailer becomes disconnected from the tractor, applying the trailer brakes.

The tractor protection valve (8) prevents loss of air from the tractor system should the trailer break away by closing off the service and emergency lines.

A further development is the *three-line* system which provides auxiliary braking in the event of failure of the normal system. It incorporates an additional reservoir on the tractor, charged by the same compressor. This reservoir supplies pressure to a special dual brake valve which controls first the normal braking system, taking air from the main reservoir. Should the pressure in this system fail further depression of the brake valve supplies pressure direct to additional chambers in the brake valves of both tractor and trailer, the trailer brakes being supplied via the third line (called the *auxiliary line*).

It must be emphasised that there are many variations of the equipment and its arrangement in vehicle compressed-air braking systems, for further details of which the publications of vehicle and equipment manufacturers should be consulted.

18.7

HYDRAULIC SERVO OPERATION

In many ways this system is similar to the compressed-air arrangement, the main difference being that liquid is used instead of air. The addition of a hydraulic servo to the normal hydraulic brake system gives the same advantages as the compressed-air system but at a lower cost. Hydraulic pressure can also be used to operate doors and provide assistance in steering, etc.

Fig. 18.7.1(a) shows a diagrammatic sketch of a *continuous-flow* hydraulic servo system.

Mounted behind the conventional master cylinder, the servo valve is supplied with fluid from a multi-cylinder radial pump which is driven from the engine or transmission. The diagram shows the brakes in the 'off' position, and in this state the fluid can easily pass between the master cylinder piston and servo valve to a drilling which leads back to the reservoir.

Depression of the pedal initially closes the conical servo valve and causes the pump to build up a pressure in the region A, which will tend to force piston and valve apart. The piston has a larger area than the valve, and so the thrust exerted on the piston will be greater than that acting on the valve and brake pedal. This *area ratio* governs the assistance given to the driver. As soon as a given pressure, which will depend on the force applied to the pedal, has built up, the servo valve will partially open to maintain the pressure and give assistance. If the pedal force is exceptionally high, a pressure relief valve will open and allow fluid to escape to the reservoir.

Release of the pedal returns and opens the servo valve, releases the brakes, and restores uninterrupted flow of fluid from pump to reservoir.

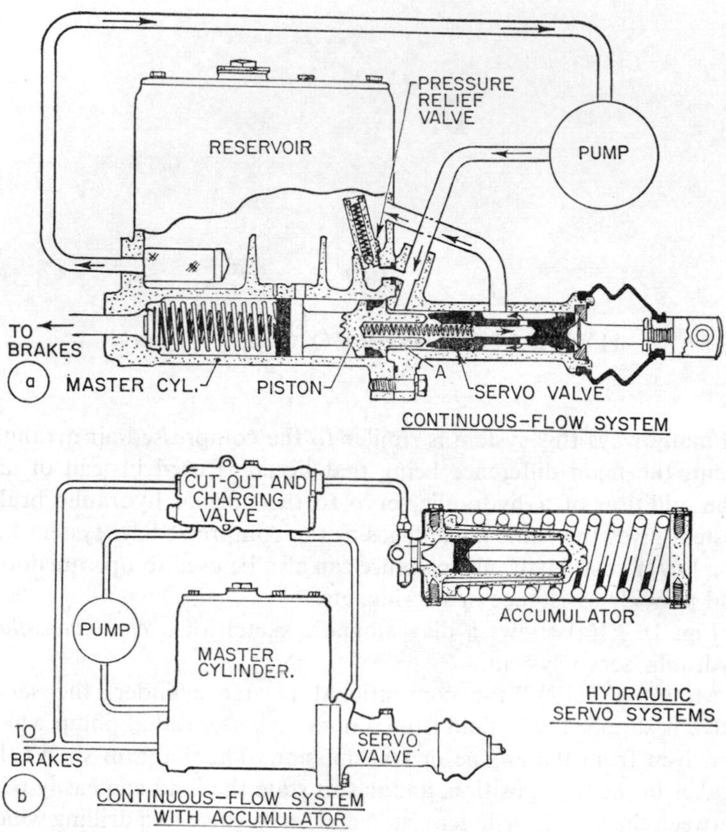

FIG. 18.7.1

CONTINUOUS-FLOW SYSTEM WITH ACCUMULATOR

The assistance given by the continuous-flow system depends on the pump speed, so a 'hard' pedal is felt when the pump is stationary or rotating slowly. To overcome this disadvantage, a hydraulic accumulator is normally incorporated into the system.

Fig. 18.7.1(b) shows the layout of the system, which uses the same pump and master cylinder as the previous system.

The accumulator or pressure storage cylinder contains a spring-loaded piston or air bag, which is acted upon by the fluid: the higher the fluid pressure, the more the bag or spring is compressed. A cut-out valve maintains the accumulator pressure between 800 and

1200 lbf/in² (5·5–8·3 MN/m²), and a charging valve, activated by fluid pressure from the output or brake-line side of the master cylinder, releases fluid from the accumulator to act on the servo valve, should the pump be incapable of supplying the necessary fluid.

Whenever you have to disconnect any part of this system, it is essential that you discharge and drain the accumulator.

18.8

RETARDERS

The term 'fade' has already been mentioned in connection with brakes (see page 490). This can be particularly dangerous, even disastrous, in the case of a heavily loaded commercial vehicle descending a long and steep incline. Descents of this nature are longer and more numerous on the Continent of Europe than in Great Britain, and this led to the development, during the 1930s, of a number of auxiliary braking systems.

These auxiliary brakes may be divided into two classes: those which work on the transmission system on the output side of the gearbox, and those which act on the engine. Both of these types act only on the drive wheels of the vehicle, put whereas the engine brake can be disconnected from the wheels by disengaging the clutch or selecting neutral, the transmission type cannot. Furthermore the effectiveness of the engine brake can be increased by changing to a lower gear.

In both cases the braking effect is only available when the vehicle is moving and cannot therefore be used to bring the vehicle to a complete stop. Neither should they be made so effective as to lock the wheels under any road conditions. Hence their *main* purpose is to limit the speed of the vehicle during long descents, and for this reason they are generally called retarders.

RETARDERS ACTING ON THE TRANSMISSION

A friction type drum brake acting on the transmission was once popular on vehicles, having the claimed advantage that the torque it applied to the propeller shaft was multiplied by the final-drive gearing to produce a very effective brake requiring only light pedal efforts. However, it was capable of applying to the transmission system much greater torque than that developed by the engine necessitating strengthened propeller and axle shafts: and in the event of a broken axle shaft the brake became useless. This led to the abolition of this brake on most vehicles and its use on public service vehicles was prohibited. It has, however, a further attraction compared with drum brakes by the fact that its use did not involve the heating of drums or shoes used in the main braking system, and this has led to a revival of interest in this type of brake. It is not, however, much used for two reasons. One is that it is itself liable to over-heating and loss of efficiency: attempts to overcome this by cooling the brake by interconnecting it with the engine cooling system have increased the complication and done nothing to overcome the second objection, which is the maintenance—periodic adjustment and relining required. The types of retarders in most common use are:

The Electric Retarder This consists of a *stator* fixed to the frame of the vehicle and a *rotor* running on taper roller bearings within the stator (Fig. 18.8.1). The stator is mounted in a frame (4) which is

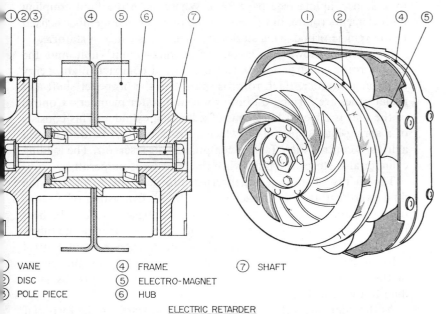

① VANE ④ FRAME ⑦ SHAFT
② DISC ⑤ ELECTRO-MAGNET
③ POLE PIECE ⑥ HUB

ELECTRIC RETARDER

FIG. 18.8.1

itself secured to the vehicle frame. It carries a central hub (6) around which are fixed a number (usually eight) of *electro-magnets* (5). These consist of central iron cores on which copper wire coils are wound and which have a pole piece (3) at each end. The rotor consists of a shaft (7) running on taper roller bearings inside the hub. A steel disc (2) is splined to each end of the shaft so that the discs rotate with a small mechanical clearance past the pole pieces. The electro-magnets are energised by current from the battery, supplied through a relay box and controlled by a switch lever usually mounted under the steering wheel. The switch has five positions, one of which is 'off'. The other four energise respectively 2, 4, 6 and 8 of the electro-magnets. The magnetic field set up by these electro-magnets induces *eddy-currents* in the discs as they revolve, which in turn set up a magnetic drag opposing the rotation of the discs.

These eddy-currents also generate heat in the discs: vanes (1) are therefore formed on the outer faces of the disc to induce sufficient air flow over the discs to prevent over-heating.

The Hydraulic Retarder   Mounted either at the mid-point on the propeller shaft or adjacent to the final drive, this type is comparable to a fluid coupling (see page 327). Where as in the fluid coupling both elements rotate, in the case of the retarder one member is fixed to the vehicle frame. This stationary member is called a stator.

Fig. 18.8.2 shows the layout of a 'mid-mount' unit and the double rotor construction shown provides a compact, high energy absorbing retarder. Each rotor is splined to the propeller shaft and radial vanes are formed on both rotor and stator members. Control of the unit is effected by means of a loading cylinder. This consists of a spring-loaded piston on which air pressure can be directed via a driver's control valve from a compressed-air reservoir. The loading cylinder also stores the fluid when the retarder is inoperative.

The energy of motion is converted into heat and to prevent the fluid over-heating, a heat exchanger is fitted. Consisting of a series of heavily finned tubes in a jacket, the exchanger transfers the heat from the fluid to the engine cooling water flowing through the tubes.

When retardation is required the driver actuates a hand control valve in the cab. Air pressure, to a limit governed by the movement of the valve, is directed on the loading piston and this displaces fluid to the retarder.

As the fluid enters the rotor it is thrown outwards in the torrodial passages which in turn redirects the fluid towards the stator. During

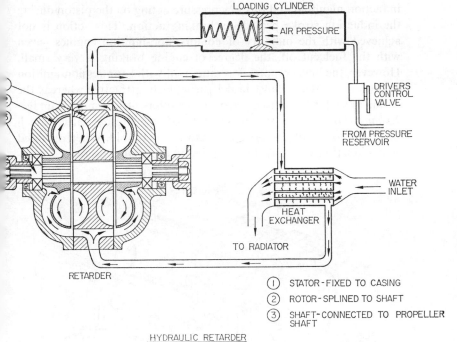

LOADING CYLINDER

AIR PRESSURE

DRIVERS
CONTROL
VALVE

FROM PRESSURE
RESERVOIR

WATER
INLET

HEAT
EXCHANGER

TO RADIATOR

RETARDER

① STATOR - FIXED TO CASING

② ROTOR - SPLINED TO SHAFT

③ SHAFT - CONNECTED TO PROPELLER
SHAFT

HYDRAULIC RETARDER

FIG. 18.8.2

the time the fluid is in the rotor, energy from the rotor is given up to
the fluid so that when the fluid leaves the rotor it is moving around
the shaft axis at rotor speed. Consequently on striking the stator
vanes the fluid attempts to rotate the stator, but as this is impossible
the energy in the fluid is converted into heat. These events show that
the energy stored in the vehicle by virtue of its speed is used to pump
fluid against a stator member. The rate of retardation is controlled
by the quantity of fluid allowed to enter the unit. Since the system
is completely closed, air contained in the retarder during the inoperative period will be compressed into a very small volume during the
working period. After the retarder has been used, the spring in the
loading cylinder, in conjunction with the air in the retarder, evacu-
ates the fluid from the retarder.

Retarders acting on the engine Most drivers appreciate the fact
that the engine acts as a retarder. During over-run conditions,
closing the throttle of a petrol engine increases the depression in the

induction manifold and this low pressure acting on the piston during the induction stroke provides a braking action. This action is not achieved with the majority of compression-ignition engines—even with the fuel cut off, the degree of engine braking is very small. However, the high compression ratio used with compression-ignition engines make the exhaust brake particularly attractive whereas the fitting of such a brake to a petrol engine offers little or no advantage.

Exhaust brake The system consists of a butterfly valve, which limits the escape of gases from the exhaust manifold. When operated in conjunction with a fuel cut-off device the engine becomes a com-

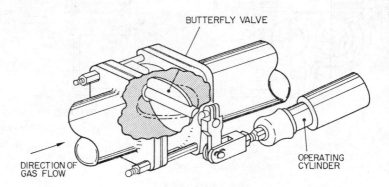

BUTTERFLY VALVE

DIRECTION OF
GAS FLOW

OPERATING
CYLINDER

EXHAUST BRAKE (APPLIED POSITION)

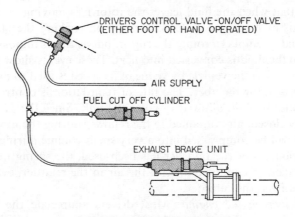

DRIVERS CONTROL VALVE - ON/OFF VALVE
(EITHER FOOT OR HAND OPERATED)

AIR SUPPLY

FUEL CUT OFF CYLINDER

EXHAUST BRAKE UNIT

LAYOUT OF EXHAUST BRAKE SYSTEM

FIG. 18.8.3

pressor driven by the road wheels. The build-up of pressure in the exhaust system acting against the engine piston provides the retarding effect, and in order to achieve a high exhaust pressure the butterfly valve is placed as close as possible to the manifold. When the induction system has no restrictions, i.e. a pneumatic governor is not fitted, the brake is capable of providing a tractive resistance comparable with the full-load tractive effort of the engine.

Fig. 18.8.3 shows the layout of a typical exhaust brake system. Close to the manifold flange, a housing containing a butterfly valve is bolted to a strengthened exhaust pipe. Close attention must be given to flange joints since the gas pressure during brake operation is in the order of 50 lbf/in^2 (350 kN/m^2). Operation of the brake is achieved by electrical or pneumatic control; the arrangement shown utilises compressed air of the main braking system. Movement of the driver's control valve activates the exhaust brake and simultaneously cuts off the fuel supply.

Electrical Equipment

19.1

GENERAL LAYOUT

A modern motor vehicle incorporates a large number of electrical devices, some of which are necessary for essential services such as ignition and lighting, whereas others are installed for the convenience and comfort of the driver and passengers. Electrically operated items in the form of heaters, window washers, etc., were, in the past, regarded as luxuries, but today they are often considered essential. Because of public demand for this type of equipment, the modern motor vehicle electrical system is becoming more complicated.

To simplify the subject and make it possible for the mechanic to diagnose faults quickly, the complete system is divided into the following sections:

Charging—this circuit must supply the necessary electrical energy to operate the various electrical components, and maintain the battery in a fully charged state.

Battery—to supply the energy to operate those components which are needed when the generator is not being driven by the engine, or when the generator output is insufficient.

Ignition—to provide a spark in the appropriate cylinder at the correct time.

Lighting—a vehicle is fitted with sidelamps and rearlamps to indicate its presence, a light to illuminate the rear number plate, and headlamps to enable the driver to see the road ahead. The headlamp system must incorporate some arrangement to prevent the approaching driver being dazzled.

Starting—when current is supplied, an electric motor engages with the flywheel and rotates the crankshaft for starting purposes. This system saves hand cranking.

Auxiliary—incorporates the various accessories such as windscreen wipers and washers, direction indicators, stop lamps, etc.

Each of these systems must be arranged to form complete circuits. For example, in a lighting system, current must flow around the whole circuit, as shown in Fig. 19.1.1(a). Activated by the battery, a continuous flow of current passes through the lamp, and then returns to pass through the battery again.

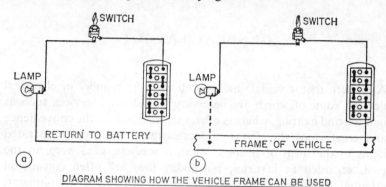

DIAGRAM SHOWING HOW THE VEHICLE FRAME CAN BE USED
TO REDUCE THE NUMBER OF CABLES

FIG. 19.1.1

Earth Return (E.R.)

By using the vehicle frame, it is possible to reduce the amount of cable and simplify the layout. Fig. 19.1.1(b) shows a terminal of the battery and one side of the lamp connected to the frame (generally termed *earth*). A cable connects the other terminals to complete the circuit. This layout is known as *earth return*.

Short Circuit

Since the cables are often clipped to the frame, good insulation and special care must be exercised to prevent the current *shorting to*

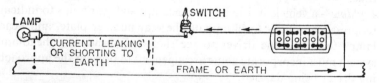

DIAGRAM SHOWING THE SHORTER PATH WHICH EXISTS
WHEN THE CABLE CONTACTS THE FRAME

FIG. 19.1.2

earth or *short circuiting*—taking a short cut back to the battery without passing through the lamp (Fig. 19.1.2). In a bad case, the lamp will not light, and the large current flowing in the cable between the supply and the 'short' will overheat the cable, and perhaps cause a fire.

Some special-purpose vehicles, such as petrol tankers, use a two-wire system or insulated return (I.R.) to reduce the fire risk.

THE BATTERY

LEAD-ACID TYPE

The lead-acid battery is the most popular type used on modern motor vehicles. It is capable of supplying the large electrical current demanded by the starter motor, has a fair life (two years or more), and is relatively cheap. Unfortunately it is rather bulky and heavy although recent designs have greatly reduced these disadvantages.

The battery consists of a container, which houses a number of cells of two volts nominal voltage. The cells are connected in series by lead bars to give the voltage required. Six-volt batteries contain three cells whereas six cells are used in the 12-volt battery (Fig. 19.2.1(a)). Sometimes the connecting bars are sunk below the battery top cover to give a cleaner appearance.

Plates and Separators

The cell is made up of two sets of lead plates, positive and negative, which are placed alternately, and separated by an insulating, porous material such as wood, p.v.c., rubber or glass fibre. Each plate consists of a lattice type grid of lead-antimony alloy, into which is pressed the active material. This is a lead-oxide paste, which is electrically formed into lead peroxide (positive), and spongy lead (negative).

The surface area of the plates governs the discharge current available, so the cell may consist of seven or more thin plates, each set connected in parallel. Connection in this manner does not affect the cell voltage.

Container

Fig. 19.2.1(b) shows the main details of a monobloc type container,

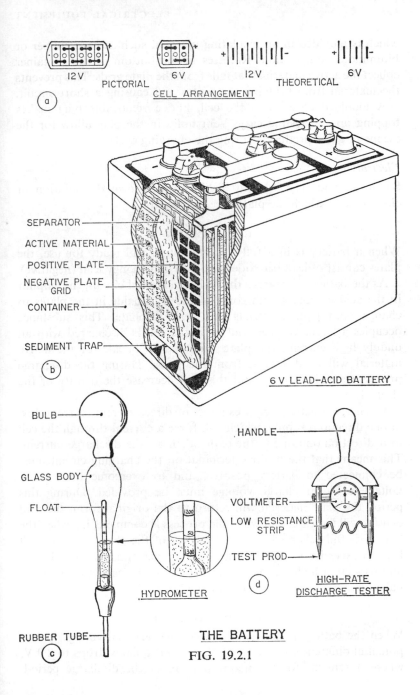

PICTORIAL

12 V   6 V   12 V   6 V

THEORETICAL

CELL ARRANGEMENT

(a)

SEPARATOR

ACTIVE MATERIAL

POSITIVE PLATE

NEGATIVE PLATE GRID

CONTAINER

SEDIMENT TRAP

(b)

6 V LEAD−ACID BATTERY

BULB

HANDLE

GLASS BODY

FLOAT

VOLTMETER

LOW RESISTANCE STRIP

TEST PROD

(d)

HIGH−RATE DISCHARGE TESTER

HYDROMETER

RUBBER TUBE

(c)

THE BATTERY

FIG. 19.2.1

which is moulded in an insulating material such as hard rubber or bituminous composition. Recesses in the bottom of the container collect the active material that falls from the plate grids. This prevents the material from bridging the plates and causing a short circuit.

A moulded cover seals the cell, and a removable plug makes topping up and testing easy. Vent holes in the plug allow for the escape of gases produced during the charging cycle.

Electrolyte

Sulphuric acid (H_2SO_4) and distilled water form the solution or electrolyte in which the plates are immersed.

CELL ACTION

When a battery is in a fully charged state and ready for use, the plates consist of lead peroxide (positive) and spongy lead (negative).

As the battery discharges through an external circuit, the sulphur in the acid combines with some of the lead oxide in the plates to change both plate materials into lead sulphate. This substance occupies a larger volume, and so if the cell is discharged with an unduly high current, the plate will tend to buckle, or the active material will be dislodged from the grids. During the discharge process water is formed, and this will decrease the density of the electrolyte.

To charge a battery requires a d.c. or direct current (current flow in one direction) supply, which will force a current through the cell in a direction opposite to the path taken by the discharge current. This means that the positive terminal on the charging circuit must be connected to battery positive, and to overcome the battery voltage a higher charge voltage must be provided. During this period the plate material will return to the original form, the acid density will increase, and when the process is complete, i.e. when the battery is fully charged, the continuance of the charge current will lead to excessive gassing of the cell. The gas consists of hydrogen and oxygen, a highly explosive mixture, so take care not to have a naked flame or electric spark near the battery.

VOLTAGE VARIATION

When the battery is taken off charge, the terminal voltage, p.d.— potential difference, is about 2·1 V, but this quickly drops to 2·0 V, where it remains for the major portion of the discharge period.

Towards the end of the period, the voltage (p.d.) falls more rapidly until a value of 1·8 V is reached, which is regarded as the fully discharged condition. These readings represent p.d., and so the current must be flowing at the normal discharge rate when the reading is taken.

Terminal voltage during the charging process rises gradually from 2·0 V to 2·5–2·7 V when the cell is fully charged, but soon falls to about 2·1 V when the charge current is stopped.

CAPACITY

The capacity of a battery is expressed in ampere-hours. This represents the current that a battery delivers for a given time. This is based on either a 10-hour or 20-hour period, e.g. a certain battery having a capacity of '40 ampere-hours, based on a 10-hour rate', will supply a steady current of four amperes for a period of 10 hours.

The capacity is governed by the size and number of plates per cell.

BATTERY TESTS

Hydrometer Test

Since electrolyte density varies with the state of charge, this variation can be used to measure the degree of charge in a battery.

The strength of the electrolyte is measured by comparing the mass of a given volume of it with the mass of an equal volume of water. The ratio obtained is termed *specific gravity* (sp. gr.), and is measured by an instrument called a *hydrometer*. Fig. 19.2.1(c) shows the construction of a typical hydrometer.

A sample of the electrolyte is drawn into the instrument, and the sp. gr. is indicated by the point where the liquid level cuts the scale on the float stem. The reading shown in the diagram is 1·250, and this indicates that the electrolyte is $1\frac{1}{4}$ times as heavy as water. For simplicity, the decimal point is often omitted, and in this example the sp. gr. would be stated as 'twelve-fifty'.

Sp. gr. readings vary slightly with the make of battery, but the following table gives a set of typical values:

fully charged	–	1·280
half charged	–	1·200
fully discharged	–	1·150

Temperature will slightly affect the readings. When accuracy is required, a correction factor of 0·004 may be added for every 6°C above an electrolyte temperature of 21°C and subtracted for every 6°C below 21°C.

On many occasions when sp. gr. readings are required, it is found that the electrolyte level in the battery is too low. A false reading will be obtained if the reading is taken immediately after topping up, or if the level is incorrect.

High Rate Discharge Test

Although the battery may pass the hydrometer test, this does not mean that it is capable of supplying the large current required by the starter motor. To test its ability to meet this load, a high rate discharge test is conducted. This instrument (Fig. 19.2.1(d)) allows the cell p.d. to be determined while a current in the order of 150 amperes is conducted through the low-resistance strip. A cell in good order should maintain a reading of 1·5–1·8 V for about ten seconds. This is a severe test and must not be prolonged more than necessary. It should only be applied to a fully charged battery.

CARE AND MAINTENANCE

To maintain a battery in good condition, the following points should be noted:

Electrolyte level This should be maintained at a level ¼ in (6 mm) above the plates by topping up with *clean distilled water only*. Over-filling should be avoided since if the battery top becomes wet it will corrode. Frequent need for topping up indicates that the battery is overcharged.

Security Vibration causes many early failures, so mounting bolts (if fitted) should be periodically checked, but must not be over-tightened.

Terminal corrosion To avoid corrosion, the terminals should be tight and coated with vaseline. A corroded terminal may be cleaned by immersing it in ammoniated warm water or soda dissolved in water.

BATTERY FAULTS

Batteries do not last for ever. In addition to obvious faults such as a cracked container, or a discharged battery due to a faulty charging circuit, the following conditions may occur:

Sulphation A hard, white crystalline substance forms on the plate surface, and acts as a resistance to the passage of charging and discharging currents. It results from:

(a) discharging past the normal limit
(b) topping up with acid instead of distilled water
(c) low electrolyte level.

Mild sulphation can be overcome by prolonged, repeated charging and discharging at low rates, but it is generally more economical to replace the battery.

Buckling of plates or shedding of active material   Since the lead-acid battery has a low internal resistance, take care not to create a short circuit, since a large discharge current can lead to buckling of the plates. Excessive charge rate or sulphation can also cause these faults.

NEW BATTERIES

If a new battery is received in a dry state, it must be filled with acid to the recommended sp. gr. (generally 1·280), allowed to stand for 6–8 hours, topped up with *more acid,* and then charged at the specified rate. The battery is considered fully charged when all cells are gassing and the sp. gr. and cell p.d. readings remain constant for three consecutive hourly readings.

ACID PREPARATION

Acid supplied to garages normally has a sp. gr. of 1·350, and this must be 'broken down', in a glass or earthenware container, to a sp. gr. of 1·280 for use in new batteries. For safety purposes, this must be carried out by *adding the acid to the water.*

Treat acid burns immediately with sodium bicarbonate solution, or failing this, clean water.

Acid splashes on clothes must be treated with an alkali, such as ammonia, if holes are to be avoided.

BATTERY FITTING

Care must be taken to ensure that the correct terminal is earthed. Extensive damage to electrical components may result if this advice is not observed. Most new vehicles have the negative battery terminal earthed to the vehicle frame. If the earth polarity is unknown the workshop manual should be consulted.

NICKEL-CADMIUM-ALKALINE TYPE

The lead-acid battery has a number of shortcomings for motor

vehicle use of which the chief are:
(1) it is heavy
(2) it has a relatively short life
(3) it requires a certain amount of maintenance which, if neglected,
    shortens its already short life and renders it unreliable.

An alternative type of battery which offers advantages in these
respects is the nickel-cadmium-alkaline type. (Note: there is a
somewhat similar type, the nickel-iron-alkaline type, which is less
suitable for motor vehicle use than the nickel-cadmium type. What
follows refers to the nickel-cadmium type only.)

Construction

Fig. 19.2.2 shows a 'cut open' view of one cell. Both positive and

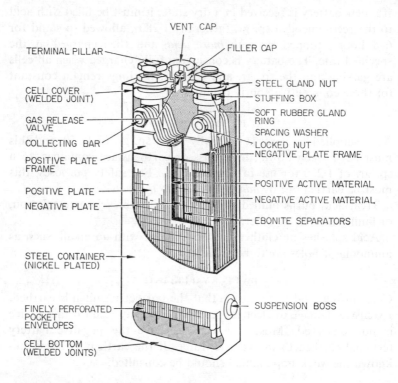

NICKEL - CADIUM - ALKALINE CELL

FIG. 19.2.2

negative plates are made of a nickel-plated steel frame into which are spot welded a number of flat-section perforated tubes, also made of nickel-plated steel. In the positive plates the tubes are filled with powdered nickel hydroxide, and in the negative plates with cadmium oxide.

The plates have lugs by which they are attached to collecting bars to each of which a terminal pillar is also fixed. The plates are assembled into sets in which the negative plates are interleaved between positive plates with ebonite rods between the plates to prevent electrical contact between them.

In what might be called the 'traditional' construction of these batteries each cell is enclosed in a nickel-plated steel container having welded seams. The terminal pillars pass through rubber gland rings in the cell lid and are secured by nuts. Each cell has a combined filler cup and vent cap.

An appropriate number of cells is assembled in a hardwood crate to make up a battery, five cells being used for a 6 V battery, nine for a 12 V and eighteen for a 24 V. Since the steel containers are in electrical contact with the positive plates they must not be allowed to touch one another in the battery crate. Each cell has two suspension bosses welded on opposite sides by which they are located in tough rubber sockets in the wooden crates, gaps being left between adjacent cells.

A recent development is the introduction, for commercial vehicle use, of plastic cell containers. These save space by allowing the cells to be assembled into their crates with the containers touching one another. They also eliminate corrosion problems which were experienced when steel containers in wooden crates were mounted in exposed positions on the vehicle, especially in winter when salt was spread on snow and ice-covered roads. These plastic-cased cells are assembled in metal crates.

Electrolyte The electrolyte is a solution of potassium hydroxide in distilled water. The normal specific gravity is about 1·190—it should be higher than 1·20—and, contrary to that of the lead-acid battery, *it does not change with the state of charge*. The electrolyte deteriorates with time, especially if it is exposed to air (hence the vents must be kept closed except when the electrolyte level is being checked), and this will cause its specific gravity to fall. The electrolyte should therefore be changed every three years or before its specific gravity has fallen to 1·160, whichever is the earlier.

In the British Isles the electrolyte is supplied in liquid form but for use overseas it is supplied in solid form and must be dissolved in pure distilled water. In both solid and liquid form the electrolyte must be handled with extreme care and must not be allowed to come into contact with clothing or the skin. It will cause severe burns on the skin which should be covered immediately with boracic powder or washed with a saturated solution of boracic powder. (A supply of boracic powder should always be available whenever electrolyte is being handled.) Prevention being better than cure it is recommended that goggles and rubber gloves be worn.

The correct electrolyte level is about $1\frac{1}{2}$ in (40 mm) above the top of the plates, depending upon the type of cell. If necessary it should be topped up with pure distilled water and the greatest care must be taken to ensure that no trace of acid is allowed to get into the cells. Nickel-cadmium-alkaline batteries and all equipment used in their maintenance must be kept *completely apart* from lead-acid batteries.

Battery tests   There is no simple test for the state of charge of a nickel-cadmium-alkaline battery. Neither the cell voltage nor the specific gravity of the electrolyte give any useful information. In vehicle applications advantage is taken of the fact that the battery cannot be damaged by overcharging to ensure that the generator charging rate is sufficiently high to provide ample charging. This can be checked by examining the battery from time to time immediately after the vehicle has been running: if the cells are found to be 'gassing' it can be taken as an indication that the state of charge of the battery is being satisfactorily maintained.

A further check is the need for topping up. A reasonable consumption of distilled water is the best indication that the battery is being kept properly charged. Excessive consumption indicates overcharging and a negligible consumption indicates undercharging.

No satisfactory high-rate-discharge tester is available for this type of battery, chiefly due to the difficulty of obtaining an adequate area of contact with the steel cell terminals.

Maintenance   The batteries need very little maintenance, the two most important points being:

(1) Keep the electrolyte topped up to the correct level. In doing this do not keep the vent caps open for any longer than necessary.

(2) Keep the battery clean and dry.

Additional points which may need attention are:

(3) Keep terminals tight and lightly smeared with petroleum jelly.

(4) Plastic cell containers should be protected from fuel oil and hydraulic fluids.

(5) The battery should not be discharged below a cell voltage of 1 volt. (The normal cell voltage is approximately 1·4 V.)

19.3

THE IGNITION SYSTEM

Many early designs of engine used a *hot tube* type of ignition system. This was an externally heated tube attached to the combustion chamber and designed to glow red to ignite the fuel-air mixture. As engines with higher speeds were introduced, the difficulty in varying the timing of the ignition of the charge made designers turn to the *electric spark* system introduced by Lenoir.

To produce a spark across a plug gap of 0·020 in (0·5 mm) at a pressure equal to the atmosphere requires only a few hundred volts, but when the pressure is raised to represent engine cylinder conditions, about 8000 volts are needed.

This high voltage is produced by either a magneto or a coil-ignition system.

Magneto A small self-contained unit which generates pulses of high-tension current and distributes them to the appropriate cylinders at the correct time. Motor cycles often use this system, but it is now rarely used on other forms of motor transport.

Coil-ignition Since a battery must be fitted for purposes such as lighting and starting, then it is economic to utilise it for the supply of low-tension current for the ignition system.

COIL-IGNITION SYSTEM

Fig. 19.3.1 shows the layout of a system suitable for a four-cylinder engine. The main components are:

Coil—produces the high voltage necessary to cause a spark at the sparking plug. Two low-tension terminals connect the coil with the battery and contact breaker, and a centre lead conveys the high-tension current to the distributor and sparking plug.

Contact breaker—a mechanically operated device which breaks the low-tension circuit when a spark is required. A cam, driven by the engine at half engine speed (for a four-stroke engine), acts on a fibre heel and opens the contacts: the closure is effected by a strip type spring. A condenser, which in this case is cylindrically shaped, is mounted adjacent to the contact breaker.

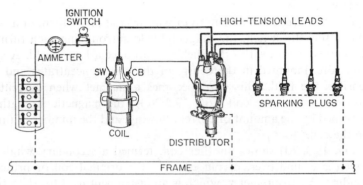

LAYOUT OF A COIL-IGNITION SYSTEM

FIG. 19.3.1

Distributor—required when the system is fitted to a multi-cylinder engine. Mounted above the contact breaker assembly, it acts as a rotary switch. It consists of a rotor arm, which revolves with the cam spindle, and a series of 'segments' in the cap to correspond with the number of engine cylinders. High-tension current from the coil is passed to the rotor, which, in turn, transfers it to the appropriate h.t. lead. The leads connecting coil, distributor and sparking plugs must be highly insulated and kept dry to prevent the current shorting to earth.

Sparking plug—the plug consists of a highly insulated centre electrode, and an earth electrode, which is welded to a metal body. A gap of about 0·020 in (0·5 mm) between the electrodes enables a spark to be produced when a high voltage is delivered to the plug.

MAGNETISM AND INDUCTION

In order to understand the operation of ignition, and other systems, consider the following experiments.

Fig. 19.3.2(a) shows a conductor passing through a piece of paper, on to which are scattered some iron filings. When current flows through the conductor, the iron filings arrange themselves in a series of concentric circles. This indicates the presence of a magnetic field. If the process could be slowed down, you would see that on making the circuit, the field moves outwards from the conductor. When the flow of current is interrupted, a reverse action occurs—the field collapses.

Fig. 19.3.2(b) shows a length of wire wound in the form of a coil. On closing the switch, the magnetic field surrounding each turn of the coil combines with other fields to produce a larger field. A soft iron core, mounted in the centre of the coil, concentrates and intensifies the field. This core becomes a magnet when current is flowing through the coil (Fig. 19.3.2(c)); the magnetic strength is governed by the amount of current flowing, and the number of turns on the coil.

Fig. 19.3.2(d) shows another coil, termed a secondary winding, which is wound over, or placed near, the original coil or primary winding. A galvanometer, which is an instrument used for detecting a small electrical current, is inserted in the secondary circuit, and the switch is operated. On closing and opening the switch, you will find that the galvanometer needle momentarily flicks one way on switching on, and then the other way on switching off. This was first discovered by Faraday (1831), and from his experiments it was concluded that when a magnetic line of force cuts a conductor (or vice-versa), an e.m.f. is induced in that conductor. The magnitude of the e.m.f. depends on: (1) the rate of change of magnetic field, (2) the number of turns on the coil.

In the apparatus shown in Fig. 19.3.2(d), the build-up of the field around the primary causes the lines of force to cut the secondary, and therefore an e.m.f. is induced in the secondary. Since the build-up is slower than the collapse, a much higher e.m.f. is induced when the circuit is broken.

If the secondary contains more turns than the primary (Fig. 19.3.2(e)), it is possible to obtain a higher voltage in the secondary circuit: e.g. if the secondary contains 100 times the number of turns wound on the primary, the e.m.f. will be 100 times greater than the e.m.f. in the primary, assuming the efficiency is 100%. This increase in voltage is balanced by a proportional decrease in the current.

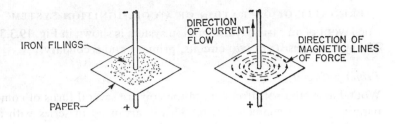

DIAGRAM SHOWS AN EXPERIMENT
TO VERIFY THE PRESENCE OF A
MAGNETIC FIELD

(a)

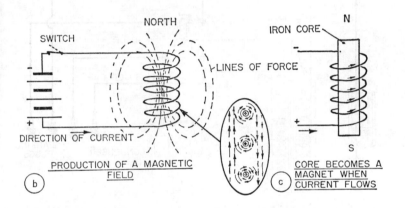

PRODUCTION OF A MAGNETIC
FIELD

(b)

CORE BECOMES A
MAGNET WHEN
CURRENT FLOWS

(c)

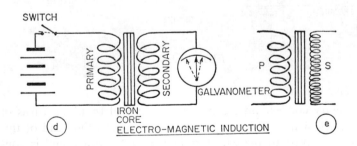

ELECTRO-MAGNETIC INDUCTION

(d)

(e)

MAGNETISM AND INDUCTION

FIG. 19.3.2

PRINCIPLE OF OPERATION OF A COIL-IGNITION SYSTEM

The layout of an earth-return ignition system is shown in Fig. 19.3.3. The system consists of two circuits, primary and secondary.

Primary Circuit

Wound around a soft iron core in the coil are several turns of comparatively heavy enamelled wire. This is arranged in series with a battery, ammeter, switch and contact breaker. A condenser is connected in parallel with the contact breaker.

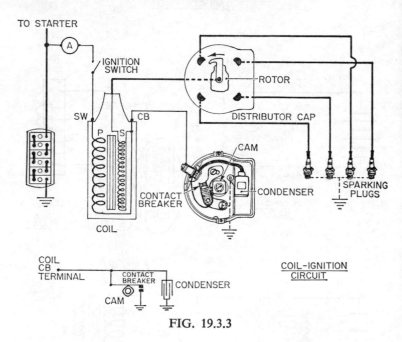

FIG. 19.3.3

Secondary Circuit

A secondary coil winding, consisting of several thousand turns of fine enamelled wire, is wound under the primary. One end of this winding is joined to the c.b. terminal, and the other end is connected in series with the distributor and sparking plugs. A 'return path' from the plug, via earth, passes through the battery and primary winding, and so e.m.f. induced in the primary winding is added to the large e.m.f. produced in the secondary winding. This gives a higher coil efficiency.

When the ignition is switched on and the contacts are closed, the current flowing in the primary winding sets up a magnetic field around the iron core of the coil. Opening the contacts, at a time when the spark is required, interrupts the current flowing in the primary circuit, and causes the magnetic field to collapse, During this collapse, the lines of force cut the secondary winding, and induce an e.m.f. in the secondary: a higher e.m.f. than that acting in the primary is obtained, since the secondary contains more turns. The h.t. current is conveyed from the coil to the rotor arm, which, at this time, should be pointing to the correct distributor segment. This is the segment connected to the plug of the cylinder that requires ignition of the charge.

Condenser (Capacitor)

A condenser is fitted for two reasons: (1) it reduces arcing of the contacts, (2) it ensures a quicker collapse of the magnetic field.

It consists of two sheets of foil or metallised paper, which are separated from each other by at least two sets of insulating material such as waxed paper. These are wound into a cylindrical shape, and inserted in a metal container. One sheet is joined to the earthed container, and the other sheet is connected by a wire or metal strip to the insulated side of the contact breaker.

When a voltage is applied to the terminals, a current can be made to flow into, but not through, the condenser. This voltage charges the condenser to a value equal to the supply voltage, and when this point is reached, the flow of current ceases. If the supply is now disconnected, the charge will be retained for a time, but will gradually 'leak away'. When a charged condenser is connected to a circuit bridging the terminals, the charge produces a current flow in a direction opposite to the original supply current.

In order to understand the function of a condenser, consider the operation of an ignition system which has the condenser disconnected. As the contacts break, the lines of force cut the primary winding as well as the secondary, and therefore an e.m.f. is also induced in the primary winding. This builds up to a pressure sufficient to cause a spark to jump the small contact gap. Arcing maintains current flow in the primary circuit, and thereby prevents the rapid collapse of the magnetic field, as well as causing serious burning of the contacts.

The action is in many ways similar to the hydraulic analogy shown in Fig. 19.3.4. Water flowing along a pipe at great speed will produce a sudden pressure rise if the tap is shut off quickly. This pressure surge could lead to the discharge of a small amount of water through the 'closed' tap, by lifting the tap washer off its seat.

Fitting an air dome to the system allows the water to flow into the dome as the tap is suddenly shut off, but after a short time the air forces the water back into the pipe.

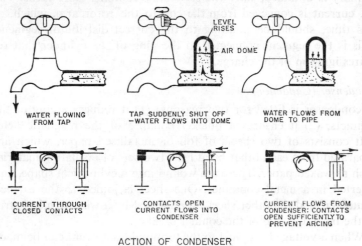

WATER FLOWING FROM TAP   TAP SUDDENLY SHUT OFF —WATER FLOWS INTO DOME   WATER FLOWS FROM DOME TO PIPE

CURRENT THROUGH CLOSED CONTACTS   CONTACTS OPEN CURRENT FLOWS INTO CONDENSER   CURRENT FLOWS FROM CONDENSER: CONTACTS OPEN SUFFICIENTLY TO PREVENT ARCING

ACTION OF CONDENSER

FIG. 19.3.4

The condenser must perform a duty similar to the buffer action of the air dome. When the contacts part, the condenser absorbs the self-induced current, and by the time the condenser is fully charged the contacts have opened sufficiently to prevent a spark occurring at the contact breaker points.

Insulated-return System

A different coil is required when an I.R. system is used on a vehicle. One end of the secondary winding of the coil is connected to a fourth terminal or to the coil case. This terminal (or case) must be earthed to the frame to complete the secondary circuit (Fig. 19.3.5).

An I.R. coil may be used on an E.R. system, but an E.R. coil cannot be employed on an I.R. system. The coil type is generally stamped on the base of the coil.

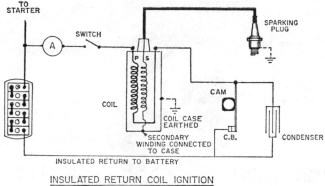

INSULATED RETURN COIL IGNITION
SYSTEM

FIG. 19.3.5

DISTRIBUTOR CONSTRUCTION

Fig. 19.3.6 shows the construction of the complete distributor assembly. This comprises the distributor, contact breaker assembly and automatic advance mechanism.

Distributor A rotor arm, mounted above the cam and driven at half engine speed, is contacted by a spring-loaded carbon brush. This is fed by an h.t. cable from the coil, and housed at the centre of a moulded bakelite distributor cap. Cables from the various sparking plugs connect, in firing order, with brass segments held in the cap. These are positioned so that there is a small gap between the rotor and the segment. Ventilation slots, formed at the spigot joint between cap and main body, permit the escape of gases generated by the sparking.

Contact breaker This consists of two tungsten contacts: a fixed earth contact and a movable insulated contact. This is linked by its return spring to a terminal on the side of the main body. A cam having four lobes (four-cylinder) or six lobes (six-cylinder) operates the contact. Elongated holes, through which the clamping screws pass, allow for adjustment. The contact is set to provide a cam lift or contact gap in the order of 0·014–0·016 in (0·36–0·40 mm).

A capacitor, earthed by a fixing screw to the contact base plate, connects with the insulated screw on the side of the main body.

Automatic advance Maximum cylinder pressure should be developed just after t.d.c. This generally means that the spark must be produced before t.d.c., since time is taken for the gas to build up to

DISTRIBUTOR MODEL 25 D4

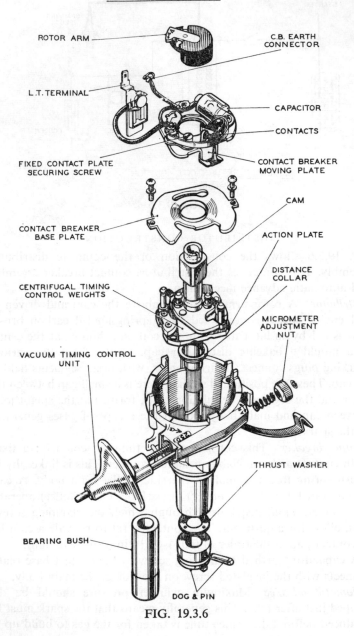

ROTOR ARM

C.B. EARTH
CONNECTOR

L.T. TERMINAL

CAPACITOR

CONTACTS

FIXED CONTACT PLATE
SECURING SCREW

CONTACT BREAKER
MOVING PLATE

CAM

CONTACT BREAKER
BASE PLATE

ACTION PLATE

DISTANCE
COLLAR

CENTRIFUGAL TIMING
CONTROL WEIGHTS

MICROMETER
ADJUSTMENT
NUT

VACUUM TIMING CONTROL
UNIT

THRUST WASHER

BEARING BUSH

DOG & PIN

FIG. 19.3.6

its maximum pressure. The time factor is fairly constant, but the angle moved by the crankshaft during this time varies in proportion to the engine speed. This means that, as the engine speed is increased, the spark must be advanced. This is the duty performed by the automatic advance mechanism illustrated in Fig. 19.3.7(a).

Situated under the contact breaker assembly, it consists of two flyweights, which are pivoted on a driving base plate. These weights are linked to the contact breaker cam by two small toggles. Two springs, each connected between the flyweight pivot and toggle, resist the outward movement of the weights.

As the engine speed is increased, the weights move outwards to a position governed by the speed and spring strength. This action

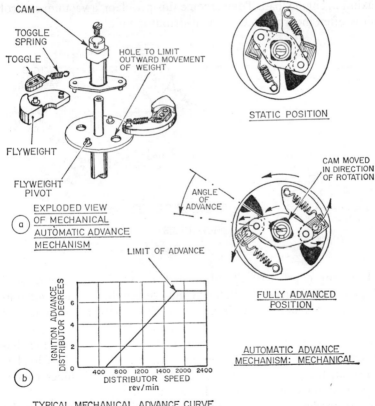

FIG. 19.3.7

partially rotates the toggles, and moves the cam in the direction of rotation, to cause the spark to occur earlier.

Fig. 19.3.7(b) shows a typical advance curve. The advance for a given engine speed can be altered by changing the spring characteristics.

Vacuum Timing Control

The normal centrifugal advance mechanism is sensitive to speed, but cannot 'feel' the degree of load on the engine. This means that maximum advance is restricted to avoid engine 'pinking'. The condition is particularly severe when an economy type carburetter is fitted. Weak mixture and slow burning of the fuel during part-load conditions demand a greater ignition advance than that used for maximum engine load. To overcome this problem, a vacuum control unit is often incorporated in the distributor unit.

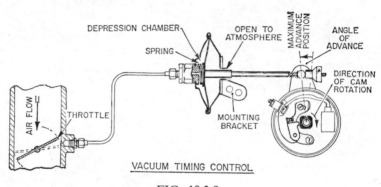

VACUUM TIMING CONTROL

FIG. 19.3.8

The main construction is illustrated in Fig. 19.3.8. 'Depression' felt at a drilling, generally in the vicinity of the throttle, is communicated to a 'vacuum' chamber. This is fitted with a spring-loaded diaphragm, and is linked to the distributor body.

During cruising conditions, a high depression acts on the diaphragm to give maximum ignition advance. When engine load is increased, the pressure alteration in the 'vacuum' chamber rotates the distributor to a position giving less advance.

Most modern units are built into the distributor, so only the contact breaker base plate need be rotated by the vacuum control.

SPARKING PLUGS

Fig. 19.3.9(a) shows the construction of a typical sparking plug. A steel body, screwed in the cylinder head, retains a ceramic insulated centre electrode. This electrode connects with the h.t. lead, and is generally made of a nickel alloy. One or more earth electrodes are welded to the body, and adjusted to produce a spark gap suitable for the engine. Manufacturers' recommendations for the gap vary from 0·018 to 0·040 in (0·45–1·0 mm). Most plugs today have a 14 mm thread diameter, but 10 mm and 18 mm are occasionally used. The length of thread, termed the reach, is governed by the distance through the cylinder head.

To function successfully, the plug must operate at the correct temperature. A low temperature allows oil and carbon to form on the insulator. This *fouling* causes the electrical charge to short to earth and leads to misfiring. When the plug temperature is too high, the plug electrodes get too hot, and pre-ignition occurs.

The heat range of the plug is governed mainly by the distance

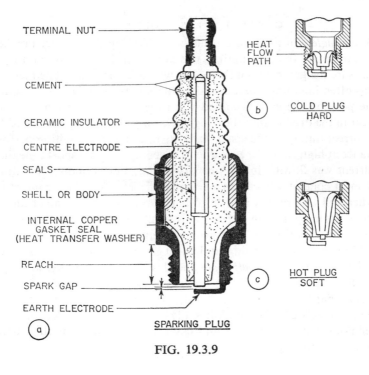

TERMINAL NUT

CEMENT

CERAMIC INSULATOR

CENTRE ELECTRODE

SEALS

SHELL OR BODY

INTERNAL COPPER GASKET SEAL (HEAT TRANSFER WASHER)

REACH

SPARK GAP

EARTH ELECTRODE

HEAT FLOW PATH

COLD PLUG
HARD

HOT PLUG
SOFT

b

c

a

SPARKING PLUG

FIG. 19.3.9

between the electrode tip and the heat transfer washer. Fig. 19.3.9(b) shows a plug which can disperse its heat quickly. This is known as a *cold* or *hard* plug, and is suitable for an engine that has 'hot' cylinder conditions, e.g. high-performance engines. Moving the copper transfer washer away from the electrode (Fig. 19.3.9(c)), raises the plug temperature to give a *hot* or *soft* plug.

Gas leakage is prevented by using a copper asbestos washer between plug and cylinder head.

Whenever an electric spark occurs, waves of electrical energy are radiated. These cause interference with domestic television receivers and car radios. To limit this interference, the law stipulates that some effective form of suppression must be used. The ignition is the main offender, and so special devices are fitted to the h.t. circuit. These generally take the form of resistors of value between 5000 and 25 000 ohms, which can be incorporated in: (1) a special h.t. lead, (2) a special carbon brush fitted between rotor and centre distributor terminal, or (3) a concentrated resistance, which is inserted in the h.t. lead.

CONTACT BREAKER OPERATION

Dwell angle In the past the method of setting the contact breaker was to rotate the cam until it was in the full lift position and then measure the gap between the points with a feeler gauge. The method was often inaccurate because it was impossible to take into account the position the cam occupied when the engine was running. Any wear in the driving shaft bearings gave an incorrect gap which led to incorrect timing of the spark and often caused poor ignition performance at high engine speeds due to the comparatively short time that current was flowing in the primary circuit. Furthermore, operation of most contact sets causes a transfer of metal from one contact to other and this results in a 'pip' building up on one contact and a 'hole' forming in the other. This would defeat the feeler gauge method unless the 'pip' was ground away.

Modern electrical testing equipment generally incorporates a meter which measures the *dwell angle* and this is used as an alternative to the feeler gauge method. As applied to ignition units, *dwell* is the period that the contacts are closed during a cam movement equal to the angle between the cam lobes. (This statement gives the common definition but readers may find cases where the term dwell is used to indicate the 'open' period.)

Fig. 19.3.10 shows a diagram of a cam suitable for a four-cylinder engine. In this case the closed period or 'dwell angle' is 60°. This is typical for a four-lobe cam, whereas a cam used with a six-cylinder engine generally has a dwell angle of 35°; both cases given a tolerance of about ±2°.

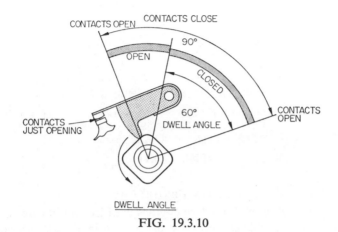

FIG. 19.3.10

Some manufacturers state the setting as percentage dwell. This indicates as a percentage the period that the contacts are closed or:

$$\% \text{ dwell} = \frac{\text{dwell angle (closed)}}{\text{angle between cam lobes}} \times \frac{100}{1}$$

The dwell angle for the cam shown in Fig. 19.3.10 is:

$$\frac{60}{90} \times \frac{100}{1} = 67\%$$

Double contact breakers   Consideration of the dwell angles of units fitted to four and six-cylinder engines show that dwell angle is reduced as the number of cylinders increases. If a single contact breaker was used on an eight-cylinder engine, then the short dwell period would seriously affect the coil's performance at high speeds. To overcome this problem a double contact breaker is often used (Fig. 19.3.11).

Contact set *A* is connected in parallel with set *B* so the circuit is only interrupted when both contacts are open simultaneously. As soon as contact *A* opens to give a spark at the plug, the other contact closes to re-establish the primary circuit.

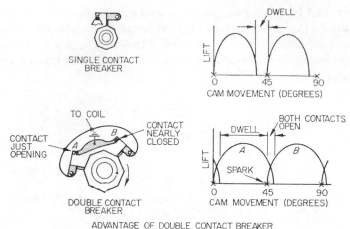

ADVANTAGE OF DOUBLE CONTACT BREAKER

FIG. 19.3.11

STARTING PROBLEMS

Starting difficulties with modern engines are rare and in cases where they arise the trouble can often be blamed on inadequate servicing. Whenever certain models are prone to a particular fault then attention is focussed on possible causes and this generally leads to either a modification or a recommendation of a suitable repair or treatment. Two examples of past trouble are:

(a) Dampness.

(b) Low battery voltage.

(a) *Dampness* may be caused by under-bonnet condensation, climatic conditions or any means which allows water to come into contact with high-tension ignition leads. Moisture on these leads causes the h.t. current to short to earth, consequently this external 'leakage' of electric current prevents a spark occurring at the plug. In the past the manner in which this trouble was avoided was to protect the equipment by preventing moisture coming into contact with the h.t. system. If this precaution was not followed, then it meant that the distributor cap, with leads attached, were removed and taken to a warm place to dry out.

A recent invention has provided a liquid substance which can be applied from an aerosol can to the ignition equipment. Application of this liquid acts as a barrier to the moisture to prevent future trouble, and in cases where the leads are already damp, a spray from the aerosol normally overcomes the problem and allows the engine to start.

(b) *Low battery voltage* is often the cause of an engine failing to start on a cold morning. If the life of the battery is nearing its end, the high starter motor load is sufficient to lower the voltage at the ignition coil to a value less than 9 V. Under these conditions the coil is unable to provide the voltage necessary to produce a spark at the plug even although the starter motor is still operating successfully. This problem is not helped by the driver who operates the starter motor for periods longer than about three seconds at a time, since the longer the motor is operated the lower the battery voltage will become. It is hoped that between each starter operation a period is given for the battery to 'recover'.

Some manufacturers have recognised this problem and have altered the ignition system to a form similar to that shown in Fig. 19.3.12. This diagram shows that the normal 12 V coil has been

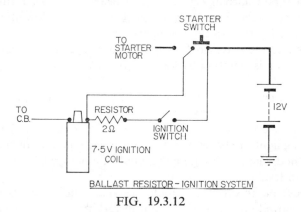

BALLAST RESISTOR – IGNITION SYSTEM
FIG. 19.3.12

replaced by a 7·5 V coil and a ballast resistance inserted in series in the primary circuit. When the engine is running, the resistor drops the voltage from 12 V to 7·5 V. During the starting phase the starter switch shorts out the resistor and applies 'full' battery voltage to the ignition coil.

Fig. 19.3.13 shows how the basic ideas shown in Fig. 19.3.12 can be incorporated into a modern starter system which uses a solenoid. With this circuit the ballast resistor is shorted-out during cranking by means of a relay.

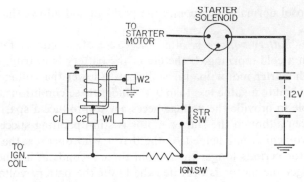

BALLAST RELAY UNIT–IGNITION SYSTEM

FIG. 19.3.13

IGNITION TIMING

Manufacturers normally give detailed instructions for retiming the ignition, but when these are not available, use the following method:

(1) Set no. 1 piston to t.d.c.compression.

(2) Connect the drive so that the contacts are just *opening*, when the rotor is pointing to the distributor segment 'feeding' no. 1 cylinder.

(3) Fit h.t. leads to the distributor in the order of firing.

(4) Start engine and make final adjustment. If an ignition timing mark is provided on the crankshaft fan pulley or flywheel, a timing light can be used. A vacuum gauge serves as an alternative method when a timing light cannot be employed.

(5) Road test.

The use of an offset distributor driving tongue allows the unit to be removed and refitted without disturbing the timing, provided the plate clamped to the distributor has not been moved.

THE LIGHTING SYSTEM

The necessary lighting equipment of a motor vehicle is laid down in various statutory regulations. These Acts specify the number, type and minimum ratings of lamps.

LIGHTING CIRCUIT

Fig. 19.4.1(a) shows a simple E.R. circuit consisting of a battery, switch and lamp. When the switch is closed, the battery e.m.f. produces a current flow through the lamp. This heats the filament to incandescence, and provides illumination.

When more than one lamp is required, the circuit must be arranged so that the full battery voltage is applied to each lamp: i.e. the lamps must be connected in parallel to give maximum brilliance. A circuit incorporating two sidelamps, two rearlamps and a number-plate is shown in Fig. 19.4.1(b). These lamps are all controlled by a single switch.

Headlamps are not always required when the sidelamps are used, so a separate switch, which can be incorporated in the main lighting switch, is fitted. Fig. 19.4.1(c) shows the addition of a headlamp circuit to the original sidelamp and rearlamp system. Current fed to the headlamp circuit first passes to a dipper switch. This determines whether the current is supplied to the main beam or dip beam. Main beam illumination is indicated to the driver by means of a light on the instrument panel.

Fusing of Lamps

If a wire touches the vehicle frame, an excessively high current will flow that can lead to fire damage. This risk can be reduced by inserting a fuse in the circuit. Designed to melt when a specified

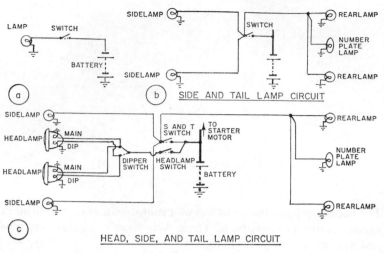

FIG. 19.4.1

current is exceeded, the fuse is connected in series with the circuit it is protecting. Lighting circuits are occasionally fused, and when this is so, a separate fuse is used for each lamp system. This eliminates the danger of all the lamps being extinguished when the fuse melts.

Filament Lamps

The main details of a lamp are shown in Fig. 19.4.2(a). Enclosed in a glass container is a helically wound tungsten filament, which is secured to support wires attached to contacts in a brass cap. Low-wattage bulbs, such as those used in sidelamps, are normally of the vacuum type. The air is removed to reduce heat losses and prevent oxidation of the filament.

Filaments of larger lamps can be made to operate at a higher temperature by filling the lamp to a slight pressure with an inert gas such as argon. Heat loss from the filament due to gas movement is reduced by winding the filament in the form of a tight helix. These gas-filled lamps are often used for headlamps.

Some lamps have two filaments: e.g. headlamps often contain separate filaments for 'main' beam and 'dip' beam (Fig. 19.4.2(b)). One end of each filament is connected to earth by the brass cap, and the other end is attached to one of the double contacts. Means must be provided to prevent incorrect fitting of the bulb.

Lamps are located in their holder by either a *bayonet cap* (B.C.), or a *miniature screw cap* (M.E.S.—Miniature Edison Screw) shown in Fig. 19.4.2(c). The single-pole or earth-return lamp, shown in Fig. 19.4.2(a), is termed a *small single cap* (S.S.C.) type.

All lamps must be marked with their wattage.

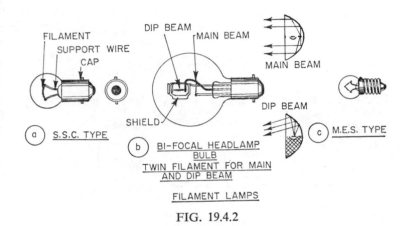

FILAMENT LAMPS

FIG. 19.4.2

Reflector

The function of a reflector is to redirect the light rays, to concentrate them in a given direction.

Modern reflectors are shaped to a parabolic form, highly polished, and coated with a material such as aluminium to give a good reflecting surface.

The lamp filament is placed at the focal point of the reflector, so that the light rays are reflected in a parallel beam (Fig. 19.4.3(a)). Other positions of the bulb put the lamp 'out of focus', which reduces illumination and, in the case of a diverging beam, may cause dazzle. Some older types of lamp incorporated a focussing adjustment, but nowadays *pre-focus* bulbs of the type shown in Fig. 19.4.3(b) are often fitted.

Lens

The modern headlamp is fitted with a glass lens to distribute the light in the required direction. Most designs are based on a block

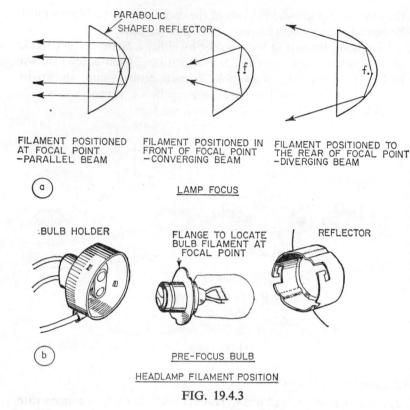

FILAMENT POSITIONED
AT FOCAL POINT
–PARALLEL BEAM

FILAMENT POSITIONED IN
FRONT OF FOCAL POINT
–CONVERGING BEAM

FILAMENT POSITIONED TO
THE REAR OF FOCAL POINT
–DIVERGING BEAM

(a)   LAMP FOCUS

:BULB HOLDER

FLANGE TO LOCATE
BULB FILAMENT AT
FOCAL POINT

REFLECTOR

(b)   PRE-FOCUS BULB

HEADLAMP FILAMENT POSITION

FIG. 19.4.3

pattern. This spreads the light in a horizontal plane, and when the
'dip' beam is used, it deflects the light downwards and to the nearside.

Sealed Beam

Precise location of the filament at the focal point of the reflector, and
elimination of dust, dirt and moisture on the reflector, are advantages
achieved with the unit shown in Fig. 19.4.4.

Fused to the lens is an aluminised glass reflector, into which is
sealed the lamp filament.

Failure of a filament necessitates the renewal of the sealed unit,
i.e., the lamp, reflector and lens.

Dazzle

The amount of light that enters a human eye is regulated by the
iris. When a bright headlamp shines directly into a driver's eye, the

iris contracts, and this makes dark areas of the road appear darker. The effect is known as dazzle.

Various arrangements are employed to prevent this dangerous condition, the most common being the *dip* or downward deflection of the headlamp beam. Tilting of the complete reflector was the old method, but modern vehicles use bifocal bulbs of the type shown in Fig. 19.4.2(b). These bulbs have two filaments: a main filament is set at the focal point, whereas the dip filament is positioned and shielded in a manner that causes the light to be reflected in a downward pattern.

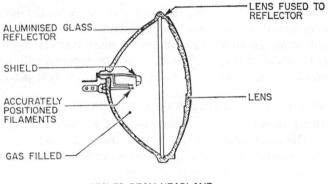

SEALED BEAM HEADLAMP

FIG. 19.4.4

Four-headlamp System

Many vehicles now use four headlamps instead of two. This arrangement gives superior illumination, since each lamp can be set to fulfil a given task. Two lamps provide the long-range illumination, and the other two light the road immediately in front of the vehicle. On dipping the lamps, the long-range beams are extinguished and the foreground illumination is intensified.

Lamp Adjustment

Headlamps must be set so that when the vehicle is loaded normally, the beams are horizontal and parallel with each other.

This setting can be checked by special beam setting equipment, or by positioning the vehicle on level ground, twenty-five feet in front of a blank wall. The light pattern on the wall enables the alignment to be determined.

THE CHARGING SYSTEM

The charging system provides the electrical energy for the operation of the electrical components, and maintains the battery in a fully charged state. To fulfil these duties, it must convert mechanical energy to electrical energy. Batteries must be supplied with a direct current (d.c.) if the correct chemical changes are to take place.

LAYOUT OF SYSTEM (D.C. COMMUTATOR TYPE GENERATOR)
Fig. 19.5.1 shows the main components of a typical d.c. charging system. The main items and their duties are as follows:

(1) The *generator* or *dynamo*, driven by a fan belt, is the unit which produces the electric energy.

(2) The *regulator*, mounted remote from the generator, limits the maximum generator voltage (and sometimes current), to avoid damage to the generator and other electrical equipment. It is set to correspond to the voltage of a fully charged battery. This

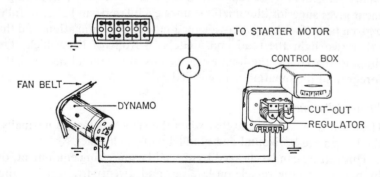

LAYOUT OF CHARGING SYSTEM

FIG. 19.5.1

means that when the battery is discharged, a high charge rate is provided, but this drops to near zero as the battery reaches its fully charged state.

(3) The *cut-out* is an automatic switch that allows the generator to charge the battery, but prevents the battery discharging through the generator. Normally the cut-out is located adjacent to the regulator.

OPERATION OF SYSTEM

The Generator

It has already been stated (page 538) that when a conductor cuts a magnetic line of force, an e.m.f. is induced in that conductor. Fig. 19.5.2(a) shows a conductor moving upwards through a magnetic field. The direction of the current flow can be determined by applying Fleming's Right Hand Rule (Fig. 19.5.2(b)).

By forming the conductor into a loop (Fig. 19.5.2(c)), double the e.m.f. can be obtained, and this can be collected by a simple brush system. In the position shown, the e.m.f. is at a maximum. If the coil is rotated, the e.m.f. will drop to zero at the 90° position, and then build up to a maximum at 180°.

Not only does the magnitude of the e.m.f. vary, but also the direction of current flow. Consequently, a machine of this type generates *alternating current* (a.c.), and this is converted to d.c. by means of a *commutator* (Fig. 19.5.2(d)). This consists of copper 'segments', insulated from each other by mica strips. (Machines having no commutator deliver a.c. These are termed *alternators*, and current destined for the battery must first pass to a *rectifier* to convert the a.c. to d.c.)

Adding more coils reduces the fluctuation of the e.m.f. and increases the output. These coils are wound around a laminated armature made up of soft iron stampings.

Field Magnets

The output from a generator employing permanent magnets is difficult to control, so most generators today use electro-magnets. These are connected in the manner shown in Fig. 19.5.2(e). The diagram shows the field windings connected 'across' the brushes, an arrangement called *shunt wound*.

A small amount of residual magnetism in the pole pieces initially forms the field. As the armature is rotated, a voltage is produced

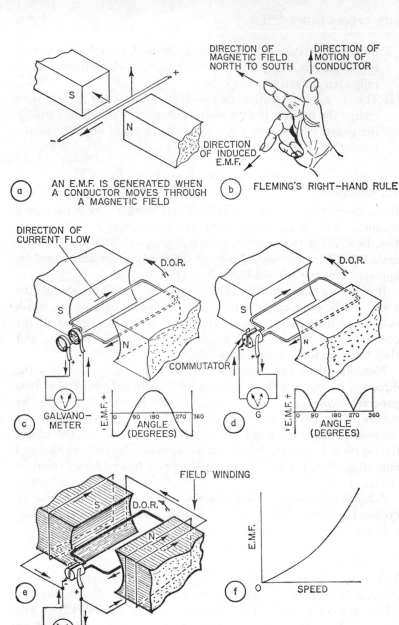

DIRECTION OF
MAGNETIC FIELD
NORTH TO SOUTH

DIRECTION OF
MOTION OF
CONDUCTOR

DIRECTION
OF INDUCED
E.M.F.

(a) AN E.M.F. IS GENERATED WHEN
A CONDUCTOR MOVES THROUGH
A MAGNETIC FIELD

(b) FLEMING'S RIGHT—HAND RULE

DIRECTION OF
CURRENT FLOW

D.O.R.

D.O.R.

COMMUTATOR

(c) GALVANO-
METER

E.M.F. +

0 90 180 270 360
ANGLE
(DEGREES)

(d) G

E.M.F. +

0 90 180 270 360
ANGLE
(DEGREES)

FIELD WINDING

D.O.R.

(e) G

(f) E.M.F.

O   SPEED

THE GENERATOR

FIG. 19.5.2

that is applied to the field circuit. This causes a current to flow through the field; the amount of current is proportional to the voltage applied. Output from a machine of this type is governed by both the speed of rotation and the strength of the field. Since the output can reach a very high value (Fig. 19.5.2(f)), some form of control is necessary.

The Regulator

Nowadays the regulator governs the amount of current fed back to the field. You will see how it functions from the simple layout in Fig. 19.5.3(a). A lead from the field is taken to the regulator, where it connects to the main output lead. This connection takes the form of a pair of contacts and a resistance. When the contacts are closed, the field receives a comparatively large current. Opening the contacts lowers the output, because the only supply for the field is through the resistance. This variation in output causes the contacts to vibrate; the rate of vibration governs the current supplied to the field circuit.

Voltage Regulator

The layout of a simple regulator for limiting voltage is shown in Fig. 19.5.3(b). A shunt coil, consisting of many turns of fine wire, is wound around a soft iron core, and connected 'across' the generator output leads. Two contacts are fitted, one attached to the regulator armature, and the other held by an insulated strip on the L-shaped frame. A spring resists the opening of the contacts.

When the generator is operated, a current flows through the shunt coil, and the core becomes an electro-magnet: the strength of the magnet is governed by the generator e.m.f.

As the output rises, a point is reached where the magnet is of sufficient strength to move the armature and open the contacts. The generator e.m.f. required to open the contacts is controlled by the spring, so by making the spring adjustable, the maximum output can be set to any predetermined figure. This is generally about 16 V for a 12 V system, and is adjusted with the circuit *open*, i.e. with no current flowing to the battery.

Series Winding

A regulator of the type described restricts generator voltage, but does not limit current. This means that the generator can be overloaded if there is a short circuit, or if the battery is in a faulty or discharged

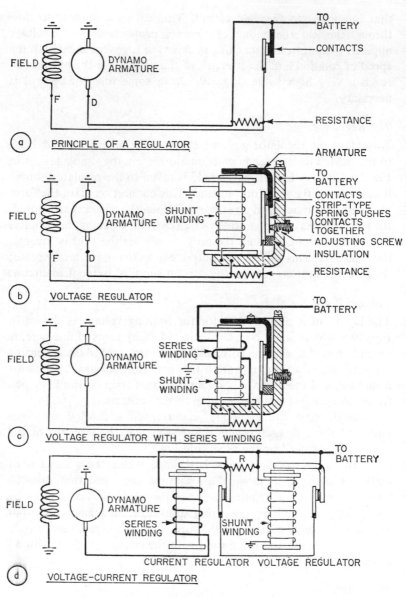

(a) PRINCIPLE OF A REGULATOR

(b) VOLTAGE REGULATOR

(c) VOLTAGE REGULATOR WITH SERIES WINDING

(d) VOLTAGE-CURRENT REGULATOR

THE REGULATOR

FIG. 19.5.3

condition. To reduce this risk, a series winding is often incorporated (Fig. 19.5.3(c)). This consists of a few turns of thick wire wound around the core, connected in series with the generator and battery.

A large current, flowing through the series circuit, opens the field contacts earlier and reduces the output.

Voltage-Current Regulator

Many vehicles now fit this type of regulator. It consists of two regulators mounted side by side, one restricting the voltage, and the other limiting the current.

In the basic circuit shown in Fig. 19.5.3(d), you will see that the voltage regulator uses a shunt coil, whereas the current regulator operates from a series-wound coil. The two sets of contacts are connected in series with the field circuit. If either contact opens, the field current is reduced.

The Cut-out

When the engine is stationary or running slowly, the generator e.m.f. is lower than the battery e.m.f., and so energy will be drained from the battery. A cut-out is fitted to stop this happening (Fig. 19.5.4). It consists of two windings: a fine shunt winding of many turns, and a heavier, shorter series winding. The shunt winding, connected across the generator, is responsive to generator e.m.f., and the series winding is introduced in the generator-to-battery circuit. A pair of contacts is fitted at the generator end of the series winding, and a spring resists closure of the contacts.

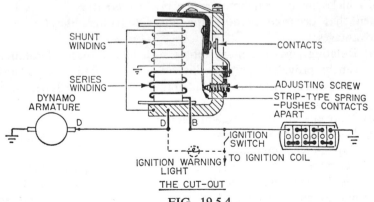

THE CUT-OUT

FIG. 19.5.4

As the generator speed is increased, the current flowing through the shunt winding is also increased, until a point is reached where the contacts close. This allows current to flow through the series winding in a direction that will assist the action of the shunt winding.

When the generator speed decreases, its voltage falls, and when the generator output drops to a voltage less than that of the battery a discharge current will flow through the generator windings. The passage of this 'reverse flow' of current through the cut-out series winding produces a magnetic field of opposite polarity to that created by the shunt winding. The weakening effect of this opposing field enables the spring to open the contacts and terminate the reverse flow of current.

The charging or ignition warning lamp is generally controlled by the cut-out. A lamp, connected 'across' the cut-out contacts, will light when the cut-out is open, since one side of the lamp is connected to earth, via the generator, and the other side is connected to the battery. Raising the generator voltage reduces the difference in voltage acting on the lamp, so as the speed is increased, the light gradually dims. When the cut-out closes, the contacts 'short-circuit' the lamp, and the light goes out.

Since the warning lamp is only required when the ignition is switched on, the lamp is connected from the generator side of the cut-out to the coil side of the ignition switch.

THE ALTERNATOR

Although the previous charging system is still used on a large number of vehicles, many manufacturers now prefer alternators. This development has occurred because the alternator offers the following advantages:

(a) Rotating parts are more robust so a higher speed of rotation can be provided. This produces a high maximum output and also gives a satisfactory output at the low engine speeds necessary to suit traffic conditions.

(b) More efficient for its weight and size.

(c) Less maintenance necessary—output current is not conducted through a commutator and brushes.

In company with the introduction of the alternator has been the increased use of semi-conductors. These have been incorporated into the modern charging circuit in the form of diodes and transistors, so before considering the alternator circuit the behaviour of these devices will be considered.

Semi-conductors Certain materials such as silicon and germanium are neither good electrical conductors nor insulators; instead they come in the borderline category. If crystals of these materials are treated in a special way by adding a trace of a certain impurity then a semi-conductor is obtained. Joining these semi-conductors together in different combinations produces either a diode or a transistor.

A *diode* is a form of electrical one-way valve; it allows current to flow freely in one direction. The symbol ─►├─ represents the normal diode; the direction of the arrow head indicates the direction of the current. (Conventional flow.)

The function of a *transistor* may be compared to a water tap—it responds to very small electrical flow in a circuit just like the flow of water responds to the movement of the handle on a tap. This action makes it suitable for:

(a) amplification (enlargement) of current—an alternative to the thermonic valve,

(b) switching purposes—an alternative to the electro-magnetic relay.

The symbol for a transistor is shown in Fig. 19.5.5. Three connectors called emitter, base and collector are shown and these must be carefully joined to the appropriate circuit. The operation of the unit may be simplified by considering the following experiment.

Fig. 19.5.6 shows a simple layout which uses a transistor to operate

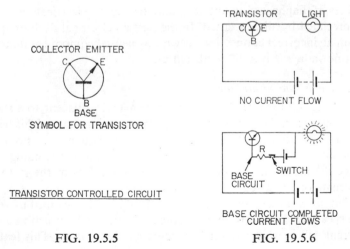

COLLECTOR EMITTER
C   E
B
BASE
SYMBOL FOR TRANSISTOR

TRANSISTOR CONTROLLED CIRCUIT

FIG. 19.5.5

TRANSISTOR   LIGHT
C   E
B
NO CURRENT FLOW

BASE
CIRCUIT   SWITCH

BASE CIRCUIT COMPLETED
CURRENT FLOWS

FIG. 19.5.6

a light. The main circuit, which includes a battery and lamp, connects with the transistor collector and emitter, but in this form no current will flow. To produce a flow in the collector-emitter circuit the 'tap must be turned on'—this is achieved by passing a very small current from the emitter to the base. In the layout shown the base current is produced by a separate base circuit which consists of a switch and low voltage battery; the current flow kept small by the inclusion of a resistor. When the switch is closed the transistor operates and the lamp lights. In this arrangement the transistor functions as a solid state switch and working in this manner a current flow of a few multi-amperes can be made to control a current many times larger.

Amplification of current is obtained in a similar manner. The transistor not only acts as a switch, but it allows the main current to be proportional to the current flowing in the base circuit. This feature is useful in a number of devices, e.g. in the case of a radio, the radio wave may be amplified by this means.

Before leaving this subject a number of precautions against damage to semi-conductor devices should be stated. The unit will be ruined if it is subjected to:

(a) high temperatures,
(b) high voltage surges,
(c) incorrect battery polarity.

Many modern vehicles are fitted with radios, alternators and other semi-conductor controlled devices, therefore it is hoped that the effects of haphazard connecting and testing of electrical units are appreciated by all concerned. In the past an electrical flash or spark from an incorrect connection very rarely caused component damage, but nowadays it is a different matter.

Principle of the Alternator

Fig. 19.5.7 shows a shaft and four-pole magnet adjacent to a stator (stationary member) around which is wound a conductor. This winding is connected to form a simple circuit with a galvanometer. Rotation of the magnet will generate an e.m.f. in the winding, and since the north and south poles present themselves to the stator in alternate order the current produced will be a.c.

Output will increase as the speed of rotation increases, but when the speed reaches a certain point, the rapid change in direction of the current will prevent any further increase in the output. This feature

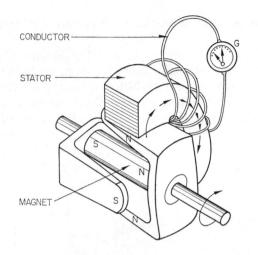

CONDUCTOR

STATOR

MAGNET

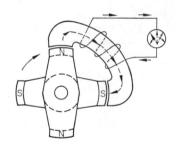

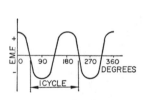

PRINCIPLE OF THE ALTERNATOR

FIG. 19.5.7

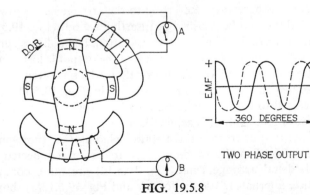

TWO PHASE OUTPUT

FIG. 19.5.8

is advantageous because the machine will protect itself from being overloaded.

Adding another stator winding in the position shown in Fig. 19.5.8 gives two independent outputs as shown by the curves in Fig. 19.5.8. Stator winding *B* gives an output which is 45° out of phase with circuit *A* and this would be called a two-phase output. Similarly if another stator winding is added and all three are spaced out around a multi-pole magnet then a three-phase output is obtained (Fig. 19.5.9). Due to the increase in magnet poles each cycle will be shorter therefore one revolution of the shaft will produce a large number of a.c. cycles.

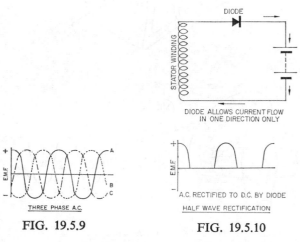

FIG. 19.5.9   FIG. 19.5.10

Alternating current is unsuitable for battery charging so rectification to d.c. is necessary. Reverting to the arrangement shown in Fig. 19.5.7, this could be rectified by inserting a diode (Fig. 19.5.10). This diode only provides half wave rectification, i.e. it allows current flow in one direction only, and since half of the output is lost, a more efficient means has to be found. One method which is often used on mains-operated battery chargers is shown in Fig. 19.5.11. Four diodes are used to form a *bridge circuit* and the two diagrams show how full wave rectification is achieved.

Before the output from a three stator winding (i.e. three-phase) alternator is rectified the windings have to be interconnected and 'star' and 'delta' arrangements (Fig. 19.5.12) are quite common. Most vehicle alternators use the former and Fig. 19.5.13(a) shows a

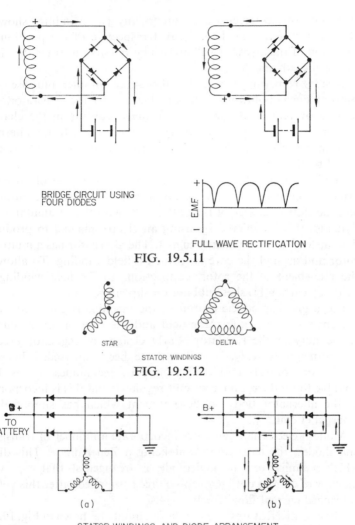

BRIDGE CIRCUIT USING
FOUR DIODES

FULL WAVE RECTIFICATION

FIG. 19.5.11

STAR   DELTA

STATOR WINDINGS

FIG. 19.5.12

B+
TO
BATTERY

B+

(a)   (b)

STATOR WINDINGS AND DIODE ARRANGEMENT

FIG. 19.5.13

typical layout. Connected in this manner the output from all the stator windings is conducted to the diodes and irrespective of the direction of current generated in any winding, the diodes will ensure that the current output is always 'in one direction'. This can be verified by the reader by inserting two arrows to represent the directions-of-the-currents adjacent to any two windings shown in the diagram (e.g. Fig. 19.5.13(b)). Irrespective of the position and direction of the arrow, it will always be possible to trace the circuit between earth and $B+$.

Besides rectifying, the diodes also serve another purpose—they prevent current flowing from the battery to the generator. This feature overcomes the need for fitting a cut-out in the charging circuit. With the engine stationary the connection to the alternator ($B+$ in the case of negative earth) is 'live' and this should be remembered by the mechanic.

Having covered the main points about generation of an e.m.f., attention must be given in finding a way to control the output to suit the state of charge of the battery. As with the commutator-type dynamo, this is achieved by using an electro-magnet to produce a field instead of a permanent magnet. The alternator has a multi-pole rotor and around the core is formed a field winding. To allow for the movement of the rotor, connections to the field winding are made by carbon brushes rubbing on slip rings.

For a given speed the output of the machine is governed by the current supplied to the rotor field and the control of this current is the duty of the regulator. Early designs of regulator used an electro-magnetic relay, but these have been superseded by semi-conductor control units. With modern techniques it has been possible to produce a microcircuit regulator and this is incorporated in the alternator body—a development which has simplified the external circuit.

Modern electronic regulators incorporate a number of transistors and diodes, the most important being a Zener diode. This diode, which is similar to a normal diode, is arranged so that it prevents the flow of current until a given voltage is supplied; after this voltage is reached current flows freely.

The essential features of a regulator circuit are shown in Fig. 19.5.14 and the basic principle is as follows:

When the alternator output voltage is low, current will flow from $B+$ through resistor R_1 to base of transistor T_2 and then to earth. Current through the base circuit of T_2 will 'switch' the transistor and cause the field F to be linked with earth. During this phase a strong magnetic field is obtained, since the field coil is connected to terminals $B+$ and earth, i.e. 'across' the battery.

As the output voltage increases, a proportion of the voltage is

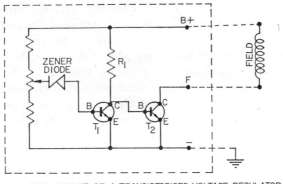

SIMPLIFIED CIRCUIT OF A TRANSISTORISED VOLTAGE REGULATOR

FIG. 19.5.14

applied to the Zener diode. When the voltage reaches a given value (approx. 14·2 V), the diode conducts the current through the base of transistor T_1. This switches T_1 and allows current to flow freely through T_1 from R_1, consequently the base current in T_2 is reduced, which will decrease proportionally the T_2 collector-emitter current and so result in a weakening of the field.

By varying the ratio between the period of time that the current flows through T_1 in relation to the time that current flows through T_2, the alternator's maximum output voltage can be controlled.

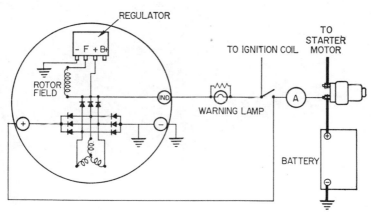

CIRCUIT DIAGRAM FOR ALTERNATOR CHARGING SYSTEM HAVING INTERNAL REGULATOR

FIG. 19.5.15

In addition to the items shown in Fig. 19.5.14, various other refinements are included in the regulator to improve its performance. The construction and circuit for a modern alternator are shown in Figs. 19.5.15 and 16 (see page 573). This model has a built-in transistorised regulator and also contains three 'field' diodes which isolate the rotor field from the battery when the machine is stationary. These diodes allow the machine to self-excite the rotor field and also act as a device to operate the charge indicator light.

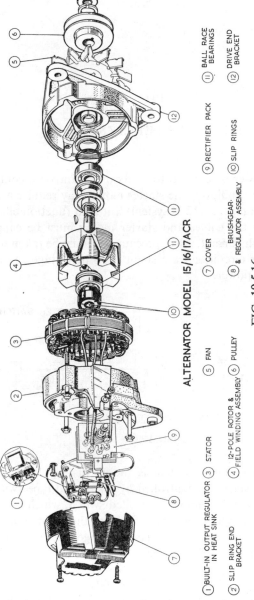

ALTERNATOR MODEL 15/16/17ACR

① BUILT-IN OUTPUT REGULATOR IN HEAT SINK
② SLIP RING END BRACKET
③ STATOR
④ 12-POLE ROTOR & FIELD WINDING ASSEMBLY
⑤ FAN
⑥ PULLEY
⑦ COVER
⑧ BRUSHGEAR- & REGULATOR ASSEMBLY
⑨ RECTIFIER PACK
⑩ SLIP RINGS
⑪ BALL RACE BEARINGS
⑫ DRIVE END BRACKET

FIG. 19.5.16

19.6

THE STARTER SYSTEM

Considerable power is required to crank an engine on a cold morning. Under these conditions the starter motor may require a current higher than 200 amperes (12 V system) if it is to function efficiently. This means that the cables and starter motor must be capable of handling this high current. Also, precautions must be taken to avoid resistances in the circuit, since a slight drop in voltage causes considerable loss of power.

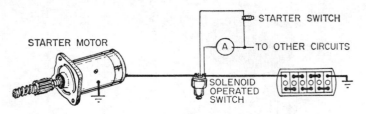

LAYOUT OF A STARTER SYSTEM

FIG. 19.6.1

The layout of a starter system is shown in Fig. 19.6.1. In this arrangement the starter is controlled by a solenoid type switch. An alternative to this is the remote-controlled switch, which is operated by a cable or rod. Whatever system is used, the main supply cable must be kept as short as possible, since the longer the cable, the lower s the voltage applied to the starter.

THE STARTER MOTOR

'Like poles repel.' This is normally demonstrated by bringing the 'like' poles of two permanent magnets together (Fig. 19.6.2(a)). In

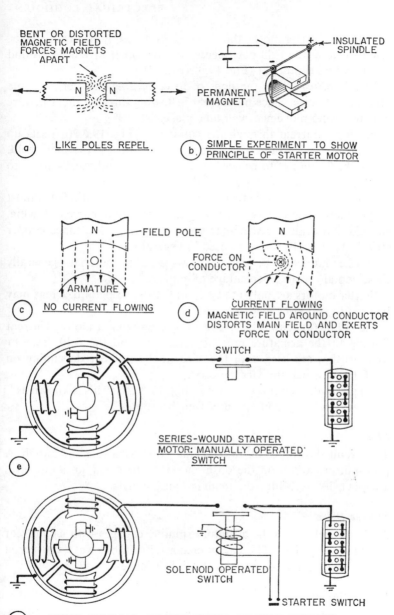

a) LIKE POLES REPEL.

b) SIMPLE EXPERIMENT TO SHOW PRINCIPLE OF STARTER MOTOR

c) NO CURRENT FLOWING

d) CURRENT FLOWING MAGNETIC FIELD AROUND CONDUCTOR DISTORTS MAIN FIELD AND EXERTS FORCE ON CONDUCTOR

e) SERIES-WOUND STARTER MOTOR: MANUALLY OPERATED SWITCH

f) SERIES-PARALLEL STARTER MOTOR: SOLENOID OPERATED SWITCH

THE STARTER MOTOR

FIG. 19.6.2

the case of a starter motor, the action is produced by electro-magnets, one formed at the field pole pieces, and the other produced around the armature conductor (Fig. 19.6.2(b)).

Fig. 19.6.2(c) shows the lines of force passing between the pole and the armature. Since no current is flowing through the armature conductor, no movement will take place.

Passing a current through the conductor (Fig. 19.6.2(d)) sets up a magnetic field around the conductor and 'bends' the main field. These 'bent' lines of force act like elastic bands and exert a force to produce motion.

In order to get a large turning force, strong magnetic fields must be produced. These are governed by the quantity of current flowing, so field and armature windings are made of low-resistance copper strip instead of the fine wire used in generators.

Brushes must also be made of low-resistance material—generally these contain a large percentage of copper.

Starter motors are only used intermittently, so plain bearings may be used to support the armature.

Fig. 19.6.2(e) shows the circuit of a series-wound motor. Current flowing to the armature must first pass around the field. Two or four brushes are used with this circuit, the number depending on the form of armature winding used.

An alternative circuit is shown in Fig. 19.6.2(f). This is known as a *series-parallel* system and uses four brushes.

Starter Solenoid

The circuit shown in Fig. 19.6.2(f) incorporates a solenoid switch. A push-button switch on the dash energises the solenoid, and causes a copper disc to bridge the main circuit contacts.

Starter Drive

A pinion, splined to the armature spindle, engages with a ring gear fitted to the flywheel. This can be engaged in various ways, the inertia system being the most popular for light vehicles.

Inertia System

The main details of this arrangement are shown in Fig. 19.6.3. Splined to the armature spindle is a hardened steel sleeve, which has helical splines machined on the outer surface. A pinion, with internal helical splines, fits loosely on the sleeve, and is lightly held in the disengaged position by a light spring. Axial movement of the sleeve in the drive direction is resisted by a strong compression spring.

When the starter switch is depressed, the armature is accelerated. This rapid movement rotates the sleeve, but owing to the inertia effect, the pinion does not revolve. At this stage the rotation of the sleeve causes the pinion to move axially and engage with the flywheel ring gear. Once the pinion has reached the limit of its travel, it begins to rotate and the flywheel revolves. The sudden shock of engagement is absorbed by the reaction of the sleeve against the main spring.

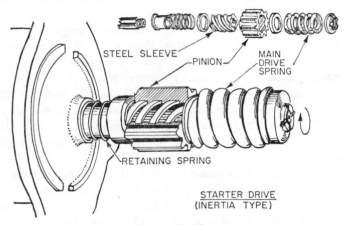

FIG. 19.6.3

When the engine fires, the increase in flywheel speed moves the pinion faster than the armature, and causes the pinion to be thrown away from the flywheel. The shock of the pinion hitting the end of the helical spline is taken by the main spring.

Two main faults can arise with this system. They are: (1) *The pinion fails to engage.* Assuming the speed of rotation is sufficient, the most frequent cause is dirt on the helical sleeve. Generally, this fault can be attributed to oil in the sleeve, which leads to the accumulation of dust. (2) *Jammed pinion.* After initial engagement has taken place, the starter will not operate and the engine will not rotate. This is caused by a worn starter ring on the flywheel. The four-cylinder engine generally comes to rest in one of two positions (six cylinders—three positions), causing greater wear in these regions.

The pinion can usually be disengaged from the burred ring gear by applying a spanner to the square formed on the end of the armature spindle. Turn the spanner in a direction opposite to normal starter rotation. When this fault persists, a new ring gear must be fitted, and the armature spindle must be checked for alignment.

The Pre-engaged Starter Drive

The inertia type of starter drive just described has the great merit of being almost completely foolproof and it is successfully used on petrol engines of up to about 4 litres swept volume. For larger petrol engines and for compression-ignition engines, however, it has serious limitations:

(a) The larger petrol engines and compression-ignition engines require a greater torque to start them and this demands the use of a larger starter motor. The momentum built up by the heavier armature during engagement imposes a considerable shock on the pinion and flywheel teeth and is liable to result in damage.

(b) Whilst a petrol engine will usually start when turned at about 50–75 rev/min, a compression-ignition engine needs to be driven at a somewhat higher speed—about 100 rev/min—in order to start it.

(c) Because the compression-ignition engine always draws in a full charge of air and has a very high compression ratio the maximum torque required to drive the pistons over compression is greater than in the case of the petrol engine, and once over t.d.c. the high pressure on the piston will accelerate it downwards rapidly enough to throw an inertia-engaged pinion out of mesh.

For the larger sizes of petrol engines and the smaller sizes of compression-ignition engines a type of starter drive is used in which the pinion is splined to the shaft and is slid along the shaft into engagement with the flywheel ring gear *before* the starter motor is switched on. A criticism of this arrangement is the mechanical damage that would be done to the starter if the pinion were held in engagement after the engine had started, resulting in the armature being driven at an excessive speed. This is overcome by including an overrunning clutch—or free wheel—in the drive to the pinion. Fig. 19.6.4 illustrates the arrangement.

The pinion is mounted by a free wheel on a sleeve splined to the starter shaft. A grooved collar is positioned on the sleeve between a circlip and a light spring: engaging with the collar are two pegs

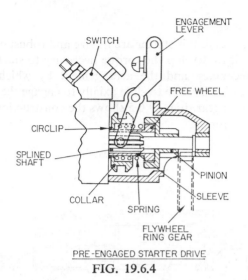

PRE-ENGAGED STARTER DRIVE

FIG. 19.6.4

carried in a forked lever which is pivoted to the starter casing, the outer end of the lever being connected by a rod or a cable to a control knob or lever in the driving compartment.

When the engagement lever is operated the sleeve is moved along the shaft pushing the pinion into engagement with the flywheel gear. When the pinion is almost fully engaged the engagement lever operates the starter switch. Should the pinion teeth meet the ends of the flywheel teeth so that engagement is not possible the engagement lever is allowed to complete its travel against the pressure of the spring: as soon as the switch contacts close and the starter begins to revolve the pinion will be moved into a position where engagement can take place under the pressure of the spring.

The engagement lever is spring loaded so that when it is released it allows the switch to open and withdraws the pinion from engagement with the flywheel gear. If the lever is not released immediately the engine starts, the free wheel prevents the engine from driving the starter at an excessive speed.

Two additional refinements are sometimes incorporated. One is a small multi-plate friction clutch between the sleeve and the pinion which is arranged to slip if an excessive torque is applied as, for example, would occur if the engine backfired due to faulty timing. The other is a solenoid to operate the engagement lever, thus simplifying the installation of the starter.

The Axial Starter

The main features of this starter are its size and robust construction, which enable it to develop the torque necessary to start large high-compression engines, and the arrangement by which the whole armature assembly is made to slide axially to engage the pinion with the flywheel ring gear. Fig. 19.6.5 shows the construction in a somewhat simplified form.

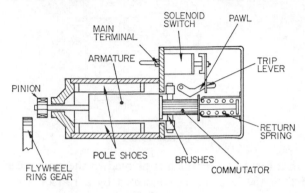

CONSTRUCTION OF AXIAL STARTER

FIG. 19.6.5

The starter is shown in the rest position, where the armature is held by a spring displaced axially from the centre of the pole shoes. When the field coils are switched on, the armature is thus pulled to the left, causing the pinion to engage with the flywheel.

Fig. 19.6.6 shows the electrical circuit, from which it is seen that the machine has three field windings. The main winding is the usual thick-section low-resistance winding and is connected in series with the armature in the usual way. The auxiliary winding is wound with thinner wire and has a relatively high resistance: it is also connected in series with the armature but in parallel with the main winding. The holding winding is also a high resistance winding but is connectected in parallel with the armature as well as with the other windings.

The starter is operated through a solenoid switch, mounted on the starter, which has two pairs of contacts. The solenoid is energised through a push-switch located in the driving compartment and the first pair of contacts close as soon as this switch is pressed, the second

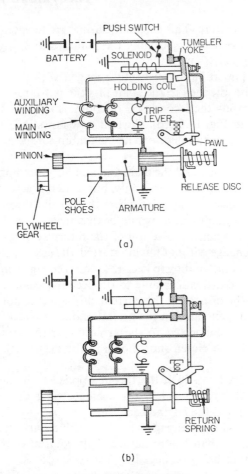

PUSH SWITCH

BATTERY

SOLENOID

TUMBLER
YOKE

HOLDING COIL

AUXILIARY
WINDING

MAIN
WINDING

TRIP
LEVER

PINION

PAWL

RELEASE DISC

POLE
SHOES

ARMATURE

FLYWHEEL
GEAR

(a)

RETURN
SPRING

(b)

ACTION OF AXIAL STARTER

FIG. 19.6.6

pair being prevented from closing by a pawl engaging a slot in the trip lever which is attached to the tumbler yoke until the pinion is almost fully engaged with the flywheel gear.

Fig. 19.6.6 shows the electrical circuit of the starter, and diagram (a) illustrates the first stage of its operation. The push-switch has been pressed, energising the solenoid, and the first pair of contacts (the upper pair in the diagram) have closed, the lower (second) pair remaining open. The auxiliary winding and the holding winding are energised so that a small current passes through these windings and through the armature. This causes the armature to rotate slowly and to slide towards the left, bringing the pinion into engagement with the flywheel gear.

When the pinion has almost fully engaged with the flywheel gear the release disc attached to the shaft lifts the pawl, releasing the trip lever and allowing the second pair of contacts to close, this position being shown in Fig. 19.6.6(b). Current now flows through the main winding and the starter develops its maximum torque and drives the engine. As the engine speed (and starter speed) increases, the current through the armature and the main and auxiliary windings decreases, and if the engine fires spasmodically, but does not actually start, the speed may increase to the point where the current through the main and auxiliary windings alone would be insufficient to hold the pinion in engagement against the action of the return spring, allowing the starter to disengage without having started the engine. It is the purpose of the holding winding to keep the pinion engaged until the push-switch is released: this it is able to do because, being connected in parallel with the armature, the current through it is not reduced by the back e.m.f. generated in the armature due to its rotation.

The pinion is connected to the armature shaft through a small multi-plate friction clutch (not shown in the diagrams). This serves two functions:

(1) It is arranged to slip if the torque applied to it exceeds a pre-determined limiting value, thus safeguarding the starter from damage should the engine backfire.
(2) It is arranged to disengage when the engine starts and drives the pinion faster than the armature shaft rotates, thus preventing the armature being damaged by excessive speeds.

This type of starter is used on the larger sizes of compression-ignition engine. It has been used on a few of the larger motor car engines, particularly those where a high degree of refinement is desired: it is quieter in operation than the inertia-engaged type. It is available for operation from either 12 V or 24 V batteries.

The Co-Axial Starter

This type is suitable for the starting of high-compression engines — both petrol and compression-ignition types—up to about 6 litres swept volume and is available for either 12 V or 24 V operation.

In its action it resembles the axial type in that the pinion is moved into engagement with the flywheel gear under reduced power, and

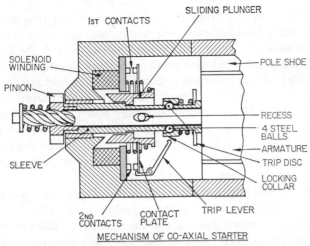

MECHANISM OF CO-AXIAL STARTER

FIG. 19.6.7

full power is applied only when the pinion is fully engaged: but it differs from it in the manner in which this is achieved.

Instead of the whole armature assembly sliding, the pinion is made to slide along helical splines on the shaft by a sleeve which is itself made to slide along the shaft by a solenoid mounted in the housing co-axially with the shaft. Fig. 19.6.7 shows the mechanical arrangement and Fig. 19.6.8 the electrical circuit.

The main terminal is connected directly to the battery and the terminal marked 'SOL' is connected to the battery through a push-

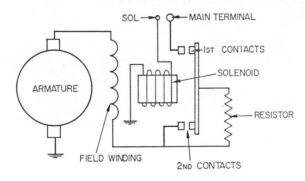

ELECTRICAL CIRCUIT OF CO-AXIAL STARTER

FIG. 19.6.8

switch placed in the driving compartment. When this switch is operated the solenoid is energised and its magnetic field draws the plunger forward moving the sleeve and pinion towards the flywheel gear. As the pinion begins to mesh with the flywheel gear the first contacts close allowing current to flow through the field and armature windings via the resistor. (The second contacts are prevented from closing by the trip lever holding back the contact plate.) The resistor limits the current to a value which causes the armature to rotate slowly, and the pinion, now prevented from turning by the flywheel gear, is moved fully into engagement with that gear by the action of the helix and the slowly rotating armature.

Just before full engagement is reached the trip disc operates the trip lever, freeing the contact plate and allowing the second contacts to close. These contacts short-circuit the resistor and allow maximum current to flow through the field windings and armature: the starter now develops its maximum torque and drives the engine.

Premature disengagement of the starter if the engine should fire spasmodically without actually starting is prevented by a locking device consisting of four steel balls located in holes in the sleeve. As the pinion and sleeve move forward the balls drop into recesses in the shaft and are locked into position by the locking collar which is pushed forward by a spring.

When the engine starts the push-switch must be released (failure to do this may result in serious damage to the starter motor by overspeeding). On releasing the switch the solenoid circuit is opened and its magnetic pull disappears, allowing the pinion, sleeve and plunger to return to their original positions.

ELECTRICAL ACCESSORIES

The modern vehicle contains many electrical devices in addition to the basic systems already described. Two of the most important, from a legal point of view, are the horn and the windscreen wiper, although these can be operated by means other than electricity.

Directional indicators and stop lamps, although not compulsory like horns and wipers, must conform to certain regulations. For instance, direction indicator lamps must be fitted with a bulb of

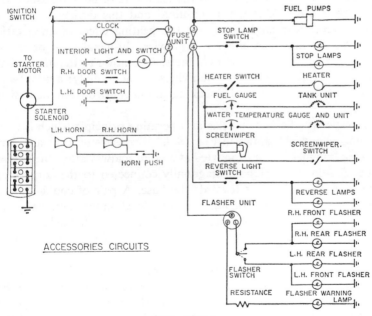

ACCESSORIES CIRCUITS

FIG. 19.7.1

between 15 and 16 watts, and the rate of flashing (if a flasher type is fitted) must be between 60 and 120 flashes per minute.

A wiring diagram showing the various accessories is shown in Fig. 19.7.1.

It will be seen that supply for a particular system is taken from one of four terminals. British vehicles mark these terminals A_1, A_2, A_3 and A_4.

A_1—generally supplied from the battery side of the starter solenoid —this terminal is always 'live'

A_2—fed from A_1 and fused

A_3—connected to the switch side of the ignition coil—this terminal will only be 'live' when the ignition is 'on'

A_4—linked to A_3 with a fuse—this is the main auxiliary supply terminal.

Directional Signalling System

Semaphore type indicators used in the past have now been superseded by flashing light systems. This change has been brought about by the greater reliability of the latter.

In order to flash the lamps at the legal rate of 60–120 flashes per min, some form of switch is required and this device is called a flasher unit. Normally relying on the heating effect of an electric current, the unit uses either a 'hot wire', bi-metal strip or metal ribbon to activate the switch contacts. Indication to the driver that the system is functioning is given visually and audibly; a pilot warning lamp on the facia and a clicking sound emitted from the flasher unit.

A vane type flasher unit has an operating principle which is easy to understand. As shown in Fig. 19.7.2 it consists of a rectangular, snap action metal vane supported at a point midway along the longer side. A thin metal ribbon, diagonally connected to the corners of the vane, pulls the vane towards the base. A pair of contacts; one on the centre of the ribbon and the other fixed on the base, make the electrical circuit. The flasher unit is fitted in series with the lamps and current to supply these lamps is taken through the metal ribbon, vane and contacts.

Operation of the directional indicator switch instantly illuminates the signal lamp bulbs. Due to the heating effect of the current on the metal ribbon, the extension in length of the ribbon allows the vane to 'click' upwards. This produces an 'oil-can' action which flicks

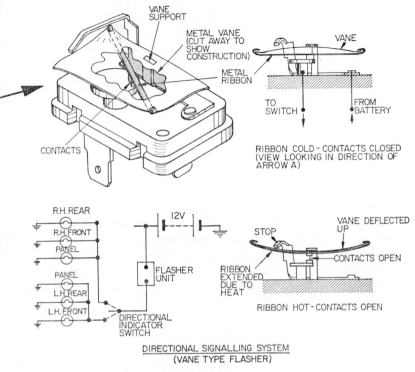

VANE SUPPORT

METAL VANE (CUT AWAY TO SHOW CONSTRUCTION)

METAL RIBBON

VANE

A

CONTACTS

TO SWITCH

FROM BATTERY

RIBBON COLD – CONTACTS CLOSED
(VIEW LOOKING IN DIRECTION OF ARROW A)

R.H. REAR
R.H. FRONT
PANEL
PANEL
L.H. REAR
L.H. FRONT

12V

FLASHER UNIT

DIRECTIONAL INDICATOR SWITCH

VANE DEFLECTED UP

STOP

CONTACTS OPEN

RIBBON EXTENDED DUE TO HEAT

RIBBON HOT – CONTACTS OPEN

DIRECTIONAL SIGNALLING SYSTEM
(VANE TYPE FLASHER)

FIG. 19.7.2

open the contacts, breaks the circuit and extinguishes the signal lamps. After the ribbon has cooled and contracted, the cycle is repeated.

Since the heating effect is controlled by current, the frequency of flashing will be governed by the lamp load.

TESTING AND MAINTENANCE

CIRCUIT TESTING

Knowledge of the circuit is essential for quick and accurate fault diagnosis. Circuit faults fall under the three main headings of short circuit, resistance in circuit and open circuit.

(1) *Short circuit*—when all, or part, of the current takes an alternative path back to the battery. This means that more current will flow from the battery, but only a fraction of this current will flow around the main circuit.

Test for short circuit An ammeter inserted in *series* with the circuit shows a higher reading than normal when a short exists. N.B. The instrument will be damaged if it receives full battery voltage.

(2) *Resistance in circuit*—a resistance drops the voltage and prevents the full flow of current.

Test for resistance in circuit The quickest way to detect this fault is to apply a voltmeter test similar to that shown in Fig. 19.8.1(a). You will note that during this test, current must be flowing in the circuit. No current flowing gives readings of battery e.m.f. at all positions, but when current is forced to flow through a resistance, a drop in voltage occurs. The voltage readings taken at the various positions while current is flowing are termed *potential difference* (p.d.).

With the switch closed, readings are taken at positions 1 to 6. If the circuit is serviceable, all readings will be similar. A circuit, with a fault as shown, will give similar readings at position 1 to 4, but a lower reading will be indicated at position 5.

The difference in the readings is termed *voltage drop*, and by knowing this the value of the resistance may be calculated from:

$$R = \frac{\text{voltage drop}}{\text{current flowing}}$$

By mounting the voltmeter in parallel with the resistance (Fig. 19.8.1(b)), the meter actually indicates the voltage drop. (This is a quick method for checking contacts—with contacts closed and current flowing in the circuit, a reading greater than 0·2 V indicates that cleaning is necessary.)

(3) *Open circuit*—an incomplete circuit will not allow any current to flow.

Test for open circuit A voltmeter, used in the manner shown in Fig. 19.8.1(a), or a test lamp, may be used to find a break in the circuit.

With all faults, it is advisable to start at the source—the battery—and then proceed through the circuit.

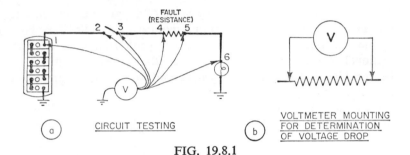

FIG. 19.8.1

FUSES

A fuse melts when the circuit is overloaded. The driver first knows what is happening when all the units protected by the blown fuse fail. Having observed the burnt paper inside the glass tube of the fuse, he may be tempted to fit a new fuse straight away. Normally this will not help, since the trouble is most likely to be caused by a short circuit, and will blow the new fuse immediately.

Generally, many accessories are supplied from the same fuse, and so to locate the faulty circuit the method shown in Fig. 19.8.2 is recommended.

Assuming the short is in one of the accessories supplied from A_4, disconnect all cables from the A_4 terminal, and fit a new fuse of the correct rating. Connect one lead of a test lamp to the A_4 terminal, and the other lead to each of the cables in turn. The test lamp lights when the defective cable is contacted. Then investigate the circuit to find the trouble.

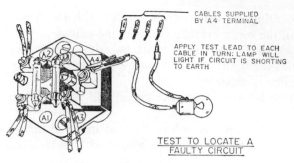

CABLES SUPPLIED
BY A4 TERMINAL

APPLY TEST LEAD TO EACH
CABLE IN TURN: LAMP WILL
LIGHT IF CIRCUIT IS SHORTING
TO EARTH

TEST TO LOCATE A
FAULTY CIRCUIT

FIG. 19.8.2

CABLES

Motor vehicle cables are generally made of copper, and in order to give flexibility they are made up of a number of strands.

The resistance of the cable is inversely proportional to its cross-sectional area, and proportional to its length. These two factors must be considered if serious overheating and voltage drop are to be avoided.

Cable sizes are given as the number of strands and the diameter of each strand: e.g. 44/·012 means 44 strands of ·012 in diameter wire.

The main sizes of cable used for 12 V equipment are:

starter circuits	37/·036
mzin battery feeds	44/·012
other main feeds	28/·012
lightly loaded circuits	14/·012

When a defective cable has to be renewed, it should be replaced by a cable of similar size. If a new circuit is to be installed, the maximum current load should be estimated in order to determine the cable size. Assuming the length is not exceptional, a maximum current of $\frac{1}{2}$ ampere/·012 strand of cable is allowed.

Cables are insulated with p.v.c. and cotton. To avoid chafing, the cables are often bound together with cotton braiding and formed into a harness. For identification purposes, the cables are colour coded. Various codes are used. This is one of the most common:

black —earth circuits

blue —headlamps

brown—circuits directly coupled to the battery

red   —sidelamps
purple—fused circuit from battery (A_2)
green —fused circuit from ignition switch (A_4)
white —circuit directly coupled to ignition switch (A_3)
yellow—overdrive circuits

This system is subdivided further by using a coloured tracer with the main colour to enable a lead in a particular circuit to be identified.

MAINTENANCE

Vehicle manufacturers issue precise instructions regarding maintenance of electrical equipment. The main recommendations, excluding the battery, are:

First 500 *miles* (800 *km*)

Distributor C.B. adjustment—this is set to the recommended gap [generally 0·014–0·016 in (0·36–0·40 mm)]. With the contacts fully open, check the gap with a feeler gauge of the appropriate thickness. Alternatively you can use a tach-dwell meter. This is an electronic instrument that measures *dwell* or *cam-angle* (the angle moved by the cam whilst the contacts are closed).

Fan belt—check and adjust if necessary.

Every 3000 *miles* (5 *Mm*)

Distributor (1) Cam—a smear of grease or engine oil on the cam face.

(2) Cam bearing—remove rotor, and add a few drops of thin machine oil to the screw locating the cam to the spindle.

(3) Automatic timing control—a few drops of thin machine oil are introduced through the aperture in the contact base plate.

(4) C.B. pivot—a spot of grease or oil to the pivot.

Fan belt—adjust tension.

Every 6000 *miles* (10 *Mm*)

Distributor (1) Cap—clean the internal and external surfaces of the cap with a soft, dry cloth, and check carbon brush.

(2) C.B.—examine and clean if necessary with a fine carborundum stone or very fine emery cloth. To do this efficiently, the contact breaker should be removed. After cleaning, the gap must be reset.

Sparking plugs—clean, adjust and test.

Every 12,000 *miles* (20 *Mm*)

Dynamo (1) Lubrication—a few drops of medium engine oil should be applied to the rear bearing.

(2) Brushes—check brushes for freedom of movement and wear.

(3) Commutator—check for cleanliness—if dirty, clean with cloth moistened with petrol.

Starter motor—examine brushes and commutator as in dynamo above.

INDEX